BLACK'S NEW TESTAMENT COMMENTARIES
GENERAL EDITOR: HENRY CHADWICK, D.D.

THE BIRTH OF THE NEW TESTAMENT

THE BIRTH OF
THE NEW TESTAMENT

C. F. D. MOULE

Emeritus Lady Margaret's Professor of Divinity
in the University of Cambridge

Third edition
Revised and rewritten

ADAM & CHARLES BLACK
LONDON

REPRINTED 1990
THIRD EDITION, REVISED AND REWRITTEN, 1981
FIRST PUBLISHED 1962
SECOND EDITION, WITH MINOR REVISIONS, 1966
A. & C. BLACK (PUBLISHERS) LIMITED
35 BEDFORD ROW, LONDON WC1R 4JH

© 1981, 1962, 1966 Charles Francis Digby Moule
ISBN 0 7136 2133 8

Moule, Charles Francis Digby
    The birth of the New Testament. – 3rd ed. –
(Black's New Testament commentaries).
    1. Bible. New Testament – Criticism,
interpretation, etc.
    I. Title
    225   BS2395

    ISBN 0–7136–2133–8 Pbk

Printed in Great Britain by BPCC Wheatons Ltd, Exeter

CONTENTS

ACKNOWLEDGEMENTS
for the First Edition

Of all to whom I am consciously indebted (and this is a very large number) I must specially express my gratitude to Dr Henry Chadwick, who first suggested that I should write a book to go in his series, and whose frequent readings of drafts and patient help have rescued me from many mistakes and considerably enriched the material. All the errors that still remain, both of commission and omission, are in spite of his labours. Gratitude is due, further, to Mr G. M. Styler for kindly contributing an excursus. I must also thank very warmly the two typists who did the bulk of the transcription (often from very difficult manuscripts), Mrs A. N. Thompson and Mrs A. de Q. Robin; Mrs Milne, who brought order and clarity to several heavily corrected and altered sheets of notes; and the publisher and printer who have shown much courtesy and skill.

for the Third Edition

Those who have contributed, consciously or unconsciously, to the re-written edition of this book by helping to educate me further are innumerable, and to all I owe thanks— particularly to reviewers. But I must thank certain persons by name: Professor Henry Chadwick, now back in Cambridge to the pleasure of his friends there and to the great benefit of the Divinity Faculty, who patiently read the revised version and offered valuable comments; Mr G. M. Styler, because he has generously devoted time to re-writing his celebrated excursus on the priority of Mark; Miss Helen Bowers, for her miraculously skilful and patient work in turning a pathless wilderness of untidy copy into a typescript exceptionally near to perfection, and Mrs Barbara Shannon, for doing the same with the rough cards of the bibliographical index; the Publisher, for courtesy and care; and Mr P. C. Harris, who prepared the typescript for press with meticulous accuracy.

Thanks are due also to Penguin Books Ltd for extracts from pages 102, 110, 233 and 237 of *The Dead Sea Scrolls in English* by G. Vermes (Pelican Books, Second edition 1975 Copyright © G. Vermes 1962, 1965, 1968, 1975. Reprinted by permission of Penguin Books Ltd.) and to the Society for Promoting Christian Knowledge for extracts from *The New Testament Background* by C. K. Barrett.

Most of the Biblical quotations are from *The New English Bible* by permission of the copyright holders, the Oxford and Cambridge University Presses.

C.F.D.M.

March 1980

PREFACE TO THE THIRD EDITION

Each time the previous edition of this book was reprinted, the publishers courteously asked whether I wanted anything altered. In latter years I found myself, with increasing emphasis, wanting to reply, 'Yes—everything!'—so fast does the debate move, so enormous is the output of literature, so quickly do books in this area become out of date. But now that at last I have been driven to attempt total revision, I am acutely aware that it has had to be done under pressure and that, ideally, a much longer time should have been spent on mastering the new material. I can only say that I have tried to re-think each of the positions I had occupied, modifying some and reinforcing others; that I have eliminated at least some mistakes and filled some lacunae; and that the bibliographies have been greatly enlarged, though I realize that there must still be innumerable gaps and oversights—for which I apologize to the authors. The eyes of Argus and the years of Methuselah would be needed to do the job properly. Anyone who had nothing better to do—but this is a fate I would not wish even for my worst enemy—might try source and redaction criticism on the new edition, asking why I omitted this or added that or where I got my more peculiar ideas from. He would find very little in the *Urschrift* unchanged.

About two areas not included in the explanatory discussions of the introductory chapter a few words of explanation are called for here. First, the study of gnosticism has advanced greatly since the original edition of this book, but confusion still reigns over its terminology. A great deal of dust is thrown in the eyes of students by loose and imprecise uses of the words 'gnosis', 'gnostic', and 'gnosticism'. The conference on gnosticism at Messina in 1966 proposed confining 'gnosis' to the description of certain general tendencies ('knowledge of the divine mysteries reserved for an élite'), and using 'Gnosticism' only for a certain group of developed *systems* such as those of Basileides and Valentinus;[1] but the proposal has not been uniformly followed. It is still the practice of many scholars to describe as 'gnostic' certain attitudes attacked by Paul, especially in I Corinthians (if not on occasion certain tendencies discernible in Paul himself), and this opens the door to the assumption that certain New Testament situations may be explained in terms of the later gnostic systems. But this is an unfounded assumption, and can be misleading.[2] It would make for clarity and precision if the less ambiguous 'dualism' were used when it is a matter simply of the disparaging of matter in favour of spirit.[3] Such an attitude is of course visible in parts of the New Testament, certainly in opponents who are attacked, but sometimes also—though only in a minor degree and certainly not consistently—in the writers themselves. For that matter, it will be found here and there in almost any religious literature, even centuries earlier—certainly in the Qumran documents. But to call this by terms which suggest or imply the developed systems of such second-century heresiarchs as Basileides and Valentinus is doubly misleading: it gives unjustified colour to what is indicated in the New Testament; and it prejudges an open question, namely, whether gnostic systems were not Christian heresies, dependent on Christianity and with no pre-Christian history of their own.[4]

Secondly, structuralism is a technique which had scarcely begun to be heard of in New Testament studies fifteen years ago, but is now much in vogue.[5] No attempt, however, is

[1] See Bianchi, pub., 1967, xxvi, and 1978; R. McL. Wilson 1967; B. Aland, ed., 1978.

[2] See Nock 1964; Yamauchi 1973; Smalley 1978, 54.

[3] Or, when it is clear that a philosophical judgment is not intended, 'dualism' might be used for the moral dualism of light and darkness, truth and the lie, etc., as in the Johannine writings.

[4] See Dunn 1977, 288 ff.; Smalley 1978, 49 ff.; and Nock and Yamauchi as above.

[5] A sympathetic though not uncritical account of it is given by Thiselton (1977 and 1977–78); see also Funk, ed., 1974, Crossan 1977–78 (with bibliography), and A. M. Johnson, ed., 1979.

made in this new version of the book to discuss it. This is partly because its methods are not entirely lucid, and partly because I am not fully convinced of its importance, since much that is claimed for it belongs properly to other disciplines and not to structuralism; but most of all because it scarcely concerns the processes by which the New Testament came to birth, and it is these that are the main concern of this book. It is clear, at any rate, that in so far as structuralism plays into the hands of treating the New Testament documents on a purely literary level, without regard to historical questions, it tends to eliminate a vital factor in the study of Christian origins.

Most of the other noteworthy new or newly prominent features in New Testament studies, so far as they are germane to the purpose of this book, are, I hope, at least touched on in what follows.

So far as I am aware of them, I have quoted or referred to English translations of foreign books without specifying the originals, believing that those who wish to consult the original will not have difficulty in tracing it *via* the English version. Accordingly, the great Kittel-Friedrich *Theologisches Wörterbuch zum Neuen Testament*, which appears throughout the original version of this book as *T.W.N.T.*, having now been not only triumphantly completed by G. Friedrich, but translated in its entirety by the Herculaean labours of G.W. Bromiley, appears as *T.D.N.T.* Citing English translations involves often giving misleading dates (what novice would guess that the English of Wrede's *Messiasgeheimnis*, dated 1971, represents a German original of which the first edition appeared seventy years earlier?); but that cannot be helped, once it is decided to omit the details of the original. In the same way, I have cited American books by the English edition, when I am aware of one; and this, too, usually involves a certain time-lag, but a gain, one hopes, in accessibility. In the first edition, indications of editions were given with some of the patristic citations; but these were not consistently or exhaustively included, and I think it best now to omit them almost entirely. The best editions can better be discovered through introductions and reference books.

To
the Senatus Academicus
of the
University of St Andrews
as a token of gratitude for
their greatly honouring me
with the degree of
Doctor of Divinity

ABBREVIATIONS

Note: abbreviations of the titles of works by ancient writers may be identified through the index of references. What follows is mainly for use with the bibliographical index in the case of terms which occur there frequently enough and are long enough to make abbreviation useful.

Ang. Theol. Rev.	*Anglican Theological Review* (Evanston, Illinois).
Austr. Bibl. Rev.	*Australian Biblical Review* (Melbourne).
B.J.R.L.	*Bulletin of the John Rylands Library* (Manchester)
C.B.Q.	*Catholic Biblical Quarterly* (Washington, D.C.).
D., L. and T.	Darton, Longman and Todd.
E.T.	*Expository Times* (Edinburgh).
H. and S.	Hodder and Stoughton.
H.T.R.	*Harvard Theological Review* (Cambridge, Mass.).
J.B.L.	*Journal of Biblical Literature* (Philadelphia).
J.T.S.	*Journal of Theological Studies* (Oxford).
LXX	The Septuagint.
M.T.	Massoretic Text.
N.E.B.	*New English Bible.*
n.F.	neue Folge.
n.s.	new series.
N.T.S.	*New Testament Studies* (Cambridge).
Nov. T.	*Novum Testamentum* (Leiden)
R.B.	*Revue Biblique* (Jerusalem).
R.G.G.	*Die Religion in Geschichte und Gegenwart* (Tübingen 1957–65).
R.S.V.	*Revised Standard Version.*
S.-B.	Strack und Billerbeck 1922–28.
S.C.M.	Student Christian Movement Press.
S.J.T.	*Scottish Journal of Theology* (Edinburgh).
S.P.C.K.	The Society for the Promotion of Christian Knowledge.
T.D.N.T	*Theological Dictionary of the New Testament*, ed. G. W. Bromiley (Eng. trans., Grand Rapids: Eerdmans 1965–74).
T. und U.	*Texte und Untersuchungen zur Geschichte der altchristlichen Literatur* (Berlin).
Th. Lz.	*Theologische Literaturzeitung* (Leipzig).
Th. Z.	*Theologische Zeitschrift* (Basel).
U.P.	University Press.
V. und R.	Vandenhoeck und Ruprecht.
Z.N.T.W.	*Zeitschrift für die neutestamentliche Wissenschaft* (Berlin).
Z.Th.K.	*Zeitschrift für Theologie und Kirche* (Freiburg 1891–97, Tübingen 1900–; n.F. 1920–).

CHAPTER I

INTRODUCTORY

THE character and purpose of this book need explanation. It does not set out to be an introduction to the New Testament in the ordinarily accepted sense of the word, for it attempts no systematic investigation of the authorship, date, and composition of each writing. Already there are sufficient works on these lines.[1] Yet neither is it primarily a theology of the New Testament, although in fact a number of theological issues will come up for discussion. What it tries to do is to investigate the circumstances which led to the making of the New Testament. It is concerned with the birth of Christian scripture—or, still more, with its antenatal period.

The steady pressure of biblical research has fortunately brought about an atmosphere in which it is much easier than it used to be to remember the living community, and there is less danger now of imagining a study-table procedure and mere 'scissors-and-paste' methods behind those vivid and practical documents.[2] Indeed, there are now many books

[1] Since 1962, several new titles have appeared, in addition to successive editions of W. G. Kümmel's *Einleitung* ([18]1973). The following are some that have come to my notice: R. M. Grant 1963; Guthrie 1964, 1965; Marxsen 1963; Schelkle 1963; Wikenhauser 1963; Cools 1965; Fuller 1966; Klijn 1967; Cullmann 1968; Spivey and Smith 1969; Selby 1971; Tyson 1973; Perrin 1974; Vielhauer 1975; George et Grelot 1976, 1977; R. P. Martin 1975, 1978. Beck 1977 is an admirable introduction to the critical study of the New Testament. For a recent introduction to the New Testament in its cultural setting, see Köster 1979.

[2] To speak of 'study-tables' literally in the New Testament period, and, indeed, until as late as perhaps the eighth century, would, incidentally, be an anachronism even in connexion with scholarly study. B. M. Metzger inquired further into the curious fact (already noted by others before him) that writing at a table seems to have been a comparatively late development. The scribes of antiquity either stood (for relatively brief notes), or sat on a stool or bench, or even on the ground, and rested their material on

dealing with the life and worship of the early Christian communities in which the New Testament took shape.[1]

Of one in particular, special mention must be made. Dr J. D. G. Dunn did me the honour of dedicating to me his important book, *Unity and Diversity in the New Testament* (1977). On p. xii of the Preface, he is kind enough to call the original version of my present book something of a pioneer in a type of introduction to the New Testament of which, he says, more are still desiderated—the kind of introduction, namely, which, without dealing in detail with the usual introductory questions of authorship, place, date, and the rest, 'provides an overview of areas and issues that go beyond the usual run of introductory questions, and introduces the advanced student to particular problems without requiring him at once to entangle himself in a maze of detailed discussion, and which stimulates him to feel after the reality of Christian origins for himself at a deeper level'. Dr Dunn's book was written to supply precisely this need. Its title, *Unity and Diversity in the New Testament*, is similar to the title of Chapter IX of my own book, and supplies incomparably more than that short chapter. Indeed, his is the most important treatment of that theme since W. Bauer's *Orthodoxy and Heresy in Earliest Christianity* (Eng. trans., 1971, but from an original decades earlier—1934)), from which, in part, Dr Dunn's book took its origin (see pp. 3 ff.); and Dunn concerns himself primarily with the first century, which Bauer did not. Thus, it might be argued that his book supersedes mine, as it certainly surpasses it in bulk and in its range of learning. *Unity and Diversity* is indispensable—as, for that matter, are Dr Dunn's earlier *Jesus and the Spirit* (1975), which constitutes, among other things, an investigation into conditions prevailing in the early Church, and his most recent work, *Christology in the Making* (1980). But I think that there is reason to believe that, brought up to date, my book still has a modest

their knees. See Metzger 1959, 509–515; and 1960, 355 ff.; and, cited there, such earlier authorities as Birt 1907; Sanday, ed. 1911, 16 ff.; Dain 1949, 22; Černý 1952, 13 f.; Skeat 1956, 138.

[1] In addition to the literature on 'form criticism', see p. 3 n. 2, the books on worship in New Testament times are relevant; see p. 19 n. 1.

place and a use, alongside his, as concentrating, within reasonable compass,[1] on the processes by which the New Testament came into existence, and providing a more general initiation into these.

This book, then, looks at the New Testament in the light thrown on the earliest days of the Christian Church by such techniques as that of 'form criticism'[2] (although by no means all the standard assumptions of form criticism are here accepted); and it attempts to place in their setting in life and thought the processes which led up to the writing of early Christian books and the beginnings of the process of the selection from among them of what we call the scriptures of the New Testament. This will take us into many fields of language, history, and theology where many mistakes are sure to be made, many factors overlooked, many false guesses offered. But it will have been worth while if it leads readers back again to the New Testament with an imagination more alive to the questions that need to be asked—and especially the questions that actually were asked in those early days and from which the New Testament took its genesis.

'Form criticism' is essentially the study of the function of each unit of tradition under consideration. It will ask, for instance, what controversies in the early Church are intended to be met by the Matthean and Lucan forms respectively of the parable of the great feast (Matt. xxii.1 ff.,

---

[1] Albertz 1947–57 is magnificent but bulky; moreover, there are many, including myself, who do not share its doctrinal presuppositions in their entirety.

[2] This is the term generally used in English for the German *die formgeschichtliche Methode*, the method (of critical investigation) which proceeds by reconstructing the history of the forms assumed by each unit of tradition as it passes from mouth to mouth and place to place, and by asking about the use to which each unit was put. Among introductions to the method and discussion of its scope and limitations see Easton 1928; V. Taylor 1933; Dibelius 1934, 1936; R. H. Lightfoot 1935, 1950, 98 ff.; Moule 1958; Cullmann 1960; Gerhardsson 1961; Bultmann 1963; Riesenfeld 'Gospel Tradition' (1970); Ellis 1975. It is interesting that Harrisville 1976, 99 f., can claim that, long before form criticism came to the fore, B. W. Bacon was well aware of its basic concerns, and his own pupil, S. J. Case, might be called America's pioneer in the method.

Lk. xiv. 16 ff.), and, in a subsequent period, by the version of the same parable in *The Gospel of Thomas* (Saying 64). It will ask what concerns are implied by the application of the parable of the lost sheep in Matt. xviii. 12 ff., as contrasted with its setting in Lk. xv. 3 ff. This kind of question and many others in similar vein are basic to this book. But the original edition of it was criticized by some reviewers for not giving sufficient weight to the implications of such questions and for still holding on, in a conservative way, to the belief that, despite the early Church's free adaptation (or even creation) of the material, a substantially reliable reconstruction could be made of the teaching and work of Jesus himself. If there is no change of heart in this respect in the new edition, it is not (I hope) because I am deaf to criticism, or because, originally or subsequently, I have held any doctrine of the inerrancy or special, divinely authenticated authority of the Gospels. It is mainly for two reasons. First, that it does not seem to me that the evidence makes plausible the theory of 'midrashic' creation out of nothing. And, secondly, that I still believe that the Synoptic Gospels (not St John) were written not primarily to convey the Christian message independently and self containedly, but to supplement the preaching of it with historical explanations. They are to answer such historical questions as, Why did Jesus fall foul of the religious leaders? Why do you Christians claim that he was the very coping-stone of the edifice of God's dealings with his people? Certainly the Synoptic Evangelists do not always succeed in writing without anachronism or exaggeration: the Easter joy does break in and give a special glow to the scene; enthusiasm and adoration do colour the narrative; adaptations to new circumstances have left their mark. But if the evangelists' main purpose was explanation rather than 'preaching', it gives a different perspective to one's estimate of the liberties taken with traditions.

One's use of the Synoptic Gospels is, of course, considerably conditioned also by one's interpretation of the Synoptic problem. It is since the publication of the original edition of this book in 1962 that Professor W. R. Farmer formally threw down the gauntlet to Marcan priority, in his book, *The*

Synoptic Problem (1964). Already there had been rumblings, and a footnote had appeared in my book, alluding to Farmer's article 'A "Skeleton in the Closet" of Gospel Research' (1961). But the Excursus on the priority of Mark which Mr G. M. Styler was good enough to supply for my book was mainly concerned to reply to Bishop (then Dom) B. C. Butler's *The Originality of St Matthew* (1951), and Farmer only came in for the footnote already mentioned. I am still not persuaded that Mark is not the earliest extant Gospel, in spite of the momentum lent to Professor Farmer's cause by subsequent publications both by himself and by others.[1] But I do not believe that such serious scholars may be ignored. I am grateful, therefore, that Mr Styler has agreed to write a new Excursus, in which readers may acquaint themselves with developments in this field. It is a question, incidentally, whether adequate attention has yet been given to Dr J. C. O'Neill's proposals (1974–5) to explain some of the phenomena by postulating a Semitic *Urschrift*, the order of linked units in which was followed by Mark, Matthew, and Luke.[2]

Not without its repercussions on the Synoptic problem, as on most other branches of New Testament inquiry, is Dr J. A. T. Robinson's *Redating the New Testament* (1976). I had already called attention in the original version of *The Birth* (121 ff.) to the surprising paucity of traces left on the New Testament by the disaster of the Jewish war and its culmination in A.D. 70, and had suggested that one reason for this might be simply that there is extremely little in the New Testament later than A.D. 70. I was thus already in sympathy with Dr Robinson when he asked why any documents of the New Testament must be dated later than the fall of Jerusalem, even if I have my doubts when it comes to St John's Gospel (in its final recension), II Peter, and Jude. Certainly, scholarship owes it to itself and to him not to dismiss the question out of hand.

But another matter of importance for the present under-

[1] See, e.g., Stoldt 1977; Orchard and Longstaff 1978.
[2] See Excursus IV, § VI.

taking is the extent to which the Acts may be used by the historian of New Testament times. The original edition of *The Birth* was criticized for reposing too much faith in it. Of course it is all but demonstrable that Luke-Acts contains mistakes. The census-passage in Lk. ii seems to have gone wrong.[1] Luke may have got his chronology muddled in Acts v. 36 f. The account of Paul's earliest days as a Christian is notoriously difficult to reconcile with Galatians. Another 'crux' is the so-called Jerusalem council of Acts xv,[2] though the problems here are less formidable if one assumes an early date for Galatians. Furthermore, there is no denying that Acts simplifies and selects. One would not guess, for instance, what anguish of spirit and what complicated travellings to and fro are concealed in Acts xix. 21 f. (as they must be, if the Corinthian Epistles are any guide).

But all this added together is not enough to justify the conclusion that Luke is writing nothing more than edifying legend. Even to regard him as highly tendentious evidence is not fair.[3] On the whole, the Acts narrative solves more problems than it raises. If Paul is consistently represented as vindicated by the Roman authorities, that is not to be written off as mere propaganda: Rom. xiii is well in line with it. And if there is in Acts little understanding of the profounder levels of Pauline thought,[4] this does not, in itself, prove that the writer never knew him. We do not know that Paul exposed those levels in his initial evangelism—for we only have epistles addressed to those who had already become Christians. Besides, must Boswell understand Johnson's mind perfectly before he can produce a valuable account of him? The fashion of making only the most grudging concessions to Acts needs to be carefully examined

---

[1] Despite Hoehner 1978, 13 ff., where πρώτη is taken to mean 'before'. See the discussion in I. H. Marshall 1978, *in loc.*

[2] Catchpole 1976–77.

[3] See Moule 1984.

[4] Barrett 1977 shows that even admittedly Pauline ideas in the speech to the Ephesian elders in Acts xx are given slightly un-Pauline twists. There is a formidable criticism of the portrait of Paul in Acts by Bornkamm, 'Das missionarisch Verhaltung' (1971); cf. *Paul* (1971).

before falling in with it. Even in the matter of the speeches, it is a mistake to assume that ancient writers always invented their speeches, and therefore that Luke must have done the same.[1] Thucydides, who is always quoted in this connexion, in fact says clearly that he aimed at getting as near to the actual words as he could; and, in any case, Thucydides is not the only ancient historian.[2] Nothing in my book depends, in fact, on the assumption that we can trust the speeches as a true record of what was actually said on the occasion; but to assume that they are pure fiction seems unjustified.

Another thorny question is how much development of thought and outlook may be postulated before Paul, our earliest datable Christian source, and after him. It is one thing to apply the technique of form criticism to each unit. It is another matter to assume definable stages—early Palestinian Christianity, pre-Pauline Gentile Christianity, Paul, deutero-Pauline writings. This has great dangers. Obviously, the earliest Christians were Palestinians and mostly spoke Aramaic, and there may be echoes from their communities in the phrase *maranatha* (I Cor. xvi. 22) and in Semitic words and ideas elsewhere in the traditions. Obviously, too, Paul was not the first to evangelize Gentiles, though he must have been among the earliest. Certainly there are passages in the Pauline Epistles that may, with more or less plausibility, be detected as pre-Pauline. Certainly, form criticism can help us to speculate about the way traditions were shaped. But there is simply not enough evidence to speak confidently about the stages of development prior to Paul. R. N. Longenecker (1970) has contributed usefully to the study of early Palestinian Christianity, as before him did F. J. A. Hort and A. Schlatter and others. We have to be content to grope,

---

[1] I cannot offer anything approaching a full bibliography. The following (in addition to the works already referred to in this discussion) is a selection of relevant work since 1962: Wilcox 1965; Keck and Martyn, edd., 1966; Gasque and Martin, edd., 1970; I. H. Marshall 1970; O'Neill 1970; Smalley 'Christology' (1973) (see 79, n. 3, for a fine bibliography); Bruce 'Speeches' (1974); Gasque 1975; Hemer 1977; Hengel 1979.

[2] Cf. Glasson 1964–65; Mosley 1965–66.

with them, behind our existing documents. I have not the confidence to offer any separate treatment of the subject.[1]

But I do confess to believing, still, that there is little evidence within the New Testament period for a wholesale Hellenizing of the Gospel. Followers of Bultmann will regard the paucity of allusions in this book to the world of Hellenic thought and religion as a distortion and a perversion. But I find myself among those who detect the minimum of such influence in the New Testament, as far as basic themes are concerned; and, where it leaves its mark, it seems to me to be more often by way of recoil from it than acceptance of it. This is not to deny that there are numerous borrowings of words and phrases and even ideas from the Hellenic world, but these are on a level shallower than that of the basic themes.[2] The substance is usually Hebraic, even when the terms are Hellenic[3]—except when (as is often the case) something quite original to Christianity is presented, which can be traced neither to Jew nor Greek, as such, but simply to Christ.

If readers are surprised that not more weight is given in this book to Greek influences, equally it may seem strange that the evangelistic activities of Christians are not assigned a whole chapter as a major factor in generating writing that would ultimately become part of the New Testament. But although evangelism is, of course, absolutely inseparable from the life of the Church; although the Church lives by evangelism as fire by burning, and a non-evangelizing Church is dead or dying; and although of course there are in the Acts plenty of allusions to preaching and summaries of sermons, evangelism as such does not seem to have directly yielded a distinctive class of written material—except in so

[1] For a survey, see Riegel 1977–78, 410 ff.

For a new attempt to identify a pre-Pauline element in Gal. i. 4, see Bovon 'Paganisme' (1978).

For warnings against light assumptions: I. H. Marshall 1972–73, and Hengel 1972, 43 ff.

[2] In any case, J. Barr 1961 constitutes an important warning against sweeping classifications of concepts as 'Greek' or 'Hebrew'.

[3] Cf. Hill 1967.

far as the synoptic Gospels represent material ancillary to the apostolic proclamation. In those days, before books could be readily produced in quantity, literature was less prominent as a medium of propaganda than it is today (though now it is coming to take second place to broadcasting). The initial 'kerygma' or proclamation was spoken; and when it came to be supplemented by a written 'Gospel', there is reason to believe that this Gospel-book was intended as explanatory rather than as primary evangelism. No doubt the pattern of evangelistic preaching is discernible behind a great deal of the New Testament.[1] But that is not to say that it gave rise to any one, distinctive type of writing. St Luke's Gospel, with the Acts, was possibly meant as an apologia for the Christian movement and message, an evangelistic tract for non-Christian readers rather than something to be read and listened to within the Christian community; and it is arguable that St John's Gospel is directed to non-Christians. But direct evangelistic preaching has left no distinctive class of writing behind: there are no collections of sermons as such.

By way of starting to consider how Christian literature did arise, a couple of typical phenomena may now be considered—the Gospels of the New Testament and the Pauline type of Epistle. It would not be true to say without qualification that the four Gospels represent a totally new type of literature—something totally distinctive generated by the Christian movement. Their message is distinctive, but their genre less clearly so. Long ago C. W. Votaw made a case for recognizing them as falling in certain respects into an already known type of ancient biography;[2] and more recently C. H. Talbert (1977, cf. 1974) has returned to the same theme. His thesis is that Bultmann[3] and others were not justified in claiming novelty for the Gospels on three grounds

---

[1] See Dodd 1936. For further reflexion and comment on the apostolic proclamation, see: Evans 1956; Baird 1957; Reumann 1964; Sweet 1964–65; J. M. Robinson 1965; Reumann 1968, 18 ff; E. M. B. Green 1970.

[2] C. W. Votaw 1970 (with Reumann's bibliography there).

[3] E.g. 1971.

(as they did), namely, (i) that they present Jesus as an 'immortal' (i.e. a man who has become divine), or as an 'eternal' (i.e. a divine being who became a man), (ii) that they belong in a 'cultic' setting, and (iii) that their world-view is a pessimistic, world-denying one. With regard to the first two points, Talbert is able to cite non-Christian parallels, though the sense of 'cultic' requires a certain amount of stretching. With regard to the third, he argues that the alleged world-denial of the Christian documents has been exaggerated and that they are not separated from antecedent types of literature in this respect. If the Gospels could be described in terms as simple as these, the case against the Gospels' being a novelty would be strong (even if not equally strong at all three points). But actually the matter is more complex. In the first place, it is an unfounded assumption that the Gospels are controlled by the determination to present Jesus as (to use these terms) an 'immortal' or an 'eternal'. The Synoptic Gospels are often assumed to be full-scale, self-contained Christian confessions, so that, for example, a Marcan Christology may be contrasted with a Pauline Christology. But if the Synoptic Gospels are meant to be only ancillary to the preaching (and probability leans in this direction), rather than a self-contained, complete proclamation of the gospel, then this is a false step. Moreover, the ancillary function of the Synoptic Gospels is in the case of Luke more than a matter only of probability. If Acts is by the same hand as the Gospel of Luke (as is generally agreed) then the fact that the Christology of Lk. xxiv (post-resurrection) and Acts is different from that of Lk. i-xxiii proves that the writer was deliberately refraining, in the body of the Gospel, from the full proclamation that he himself entertained (see further below, pp. 123 f.).[1] If it is true, then, that the Synoptic Gospels (not, admittedly, St John) were intended not primarily to present what may be called an 'Easter' interpretation of Jesus—a fully Christian gospel or proclamation of him as Lord—but rather to explain and support the full Christian gospel of the resurrection by

[1] See Moule 1959, 'Christology' (1966).

recounting how Jesus came to collide with the authorities and how he appeared to his own contemporaries, then Talbert's parallels at this point are not so clear. More relevant would be those non-Christian biographies mentioned by Talbert which are aimed at defending the hero against a false interpretation. But even here there are conspicuous differences, notably the fact that in the Synoptic Gospels there is very little explicit argument or discussion: they simply narrate the traditions and let them speak. This is not to deny that the Evangelists' own standpoints are often discernible through their selection and placing and modification of their materials; but it is to affirm that their apologetic intentions are not explicit or conspicuous as in the case of the alleged parallels. Secondly, how clear is the allegedly cultic setting of the Synoptic Gospels? Undoubtedly they were written within communities in which Jesus was confessed as Lord; and they may have been used in gatherings for worship (but see below, p. 40). But if their primary purpose is to supply material ancillary to the proclamation of the gospel, one must think twice before comparing them to 'aretalogies' or cultic presentations of a deified hero. Here, again, the parallels cannot be drawn in a simple or straightforward way. As for the eschatological question, Talbert is surely right to deny that the Christian documents are distinctively world-denying. In the main, Jewish and Christian thought is, because of its theistic faith, essentially world-affirming. And it would certainly be far from truthful to call the Gospels, in particular, world-denying. If there are passages where the present age is disparaged, this is because of its transitoriness and its false outlook, not because of a belief that matter is inherently evil. In the New Testament there is no thoroughgoing dualism in that sense. But if in this respect Bultmann was not justified in claiming a distinctiveness for the New Testament documents, there is, nevertheless, a new factor distinguishing New Testament eschatology, namely, the conviction that in Jesus Christ the 'End' of history has already been attained within history. The realization of the ultimate, in history, under Pontius Pilate, in Palestine—this preposterous 'scandal of particularity'—

does give to the New Testament gospel a novelty unparalleled in Judaism or beyond it.

Thus, even if in literary form the Synoptic Gospel is not in all respects a novelty, the reader is presented by its contents with a new and surprising phenomenon. It is true that there are other types of literature, subsequent to the New Testament, which, styling themselves Gospels, do not present this distinctive feature. One thinks of the self-styled *Gospel of Thomas*, which is virtually only a sayings-collection—and of a more or less gnostic sort; or some of the narrative Gospels outside the canon, which are more like collections of 'divine man' stories. But if *euangelion* is applied to these, it must not obscure the fact that the canonical *euangelia* are distinctive and were new in a decisive way.

The Fourth Gospel, while sharing many of the features of a Gospel-book as we know these from the Synoptic Gospels, is unlike them in that it represents Jesus as recognized by some of his contemporaries from the start as Messiah and as proclaiming himself a messenger from heaven. Early and authentic as much of its material may well be, it makes no attempt to avoid anachronism in respect of his claims. Also, unlike the Synoptists, it answers the question 'What must I do to be saved?' in a 'post-Easter' manner. Unlike the Synoptists, it presents a self-contained Christian gospel. Thus, evangelizing lies behind all the Gospels, but the Synoptists do not, by themselves, present the complete evangelistic message. In summary, that message might have run as follows:

A certain Jew named Jesus had, during his lifetime, been marked out as God's special representative by supreme goodness, and by exceptional deeds of power, such as the healing and the rescue of those who were in the grip of evil, and by his exceptionally powerful words. He had been cruelly put to death by Gentiles at the instigation of his fellow-Jews. But God had brought him through to total, permanent life. All this was in fact

[1] For a well documented discussion of the Gospel genre, see Hengel 1979, Ch. 1; and for discussion of the meaning of 'gospel' see Schneemelcher 'Gospel' (1963); and for examples of apocryphal Gospels, Hennecke-Schneemelcher 1963, 1965. See also Nock's critique, 1960; and Bornkamm, Barth and Held 1963.

in line with God's plan for his People as it may be traced in the Jewish Scriptures. Thus it is clear that Jesus is God's supreme Agent for the rescue of his People from evil and for the fulfilment of his purpose in the world. And this constitutes a challenge to you who hear to trust him and give him your allegiance, and be baptized into membership in him.

This is at once less and much more than mere narrative: it is a declaration of conviction about the significance of a few events. And St Mark's Gospel is supplementary to this brief framework of declaration, filling out its first part with some circumstantial detail: it is the story of God's fulfilling and bringing to a climax in Jesus the age-long destiny of his People. Thus a special sort of writing seems to have sprung from the explanatory elaboration and expansion of a very early, very spontaneous, spoken proclamation. Substantially, it is neither biography nor moral exhortation, it is neither history nor ethics. It ministers to Christian witness: it is the supplementation of a herald's announcement. So beautiful an early Christian writing as *The Epistle to Diognetus* (to be found among 'The Apostolic Fathers') serves, by way of contrast, to throw into relief this strangely different type of book. *The Epistle to Diognetus* is a gracious little statement about God's generous love to man and about Christian qualities. It is not a Gospel.

But although in certain respects new and unprecedented, the Christian proclamation is nothing if not rooted in the antecedent life of Judaism. It is true that it constituted a direct indictment of the Jews for sentencing their King to death. For although the charge of 'deicide' levelled by Christians of subsequent generations at the Jews was outrageous and led to atrocities inexcusable and too terrible for words, the fact remains that the evidence does seem to point, despite all efforts to prove the contrary, to the complicity of the Jews in the death of Jesus.[1] Yet, if so—the early Christians went on to say—it was, paradoxically, good news for them. For the Jews' share in the death of Jesus had—so it declared—unwittingly led to the placing of the coping-stone on the structure of God's salvation-plan for Israel. The stone

[1] See Bammel and Moule 1984.

13

rejected by the expert masons turned out to have come into its own, through that very process of rejection, as the most vital member of the building. And Israel's salvation lay in admitting the crime, and entering, through repentance and baptism, into union with this Jesus, who was the divinely anointed King of Israel, the Lord of Glory. However, St Mark's Gospel stops short of that last step. It represents an elaboration only of the Christian proclamation—the statement of fact and conviction which precedes and leads up to that final appeal to repent and be baptized.

There is no convincing evidence that any complete Gospel existed before St Mark's,[1] but before he set to work there were probably sheets of papyrus already circulating on which were written, in Aramaic (and possibly Hebrew) or in Greek, anecdotes or sayings such as eventually went into his composition. Several phenomena point in this direction. There are traces in Mark of the use of various sources —perhaps one which called the apostles 'the Twelve',[2] perhaps another identical with a sayings-collection or group of collections drawn upon also by Matthew and Luke;[3] there are traces, even earlier, in some of the epistles, of traditions (whether written or oral) of the sayings of Jesus and possibly of some incidents from his life;[4] and the arguments already framed in Rom. ix-xi can be paralleled from the subsequently written Gospels.[5] At all events traditions containing what we know as evangelic material can be certainly discerned in the background, before ever our extant Gospels took shape. But not an entire Gospel: Mark's seems to be the first example of that. After Mark, however, a large number of others came to be written, as well as collections of sayings of Jesus. Many of these other writings have been lost, and we know of them, if at all, only by name or through brief quotations in other writers. Of others,

[1] Assuming (see p. 253) that Mark's is the earliest. See Excursus IV.
[2] E. Meyer, i (1923), 133 ff.
[3] For 'Q' in Mark, see (e.g.) Streeter 1911; Bacon 1925, 11, n. 7. But the existence of Q is questioned; see p. 127 and Excursus IV.
[4] See pp. 118 ff.
[5] Munck 1967, 14 ff.

besides the other canonical Gospels, we have fragments or even almost complete copies. The most recent additions are from the library of Coptic books discovered near Nag Hammadi in the 'forties.[1]

But the only ones besides Mark which were ultimately retained by the general consensus of Christians throughout the world were Matthew, Luke, and John. For some years the traditions of Jesus seem to have flowed in many more or less parallel channels; but in the end these four Gospels emerged above the welter—or possibly were in fact the only complete Gospels ever to take shape. Their mutual relations, as is well known, are the subject of close study and controversy. It is remarkable that only two of the four bear apostolic names, while the other two bear the names of individuals who were believed to be apostles' assistants. All these attributions are traditional: none of the Gospels explicitly carries an author's name within it (though Jn xxi. 24, a note indicating the author, is now part of the Gospel).

Meanwhile, before the first Gospel had been written, and at the stage when the good news was presumably being proclaimed almost entirely by word of mouth, the evangelist Paul of Tarsus was writing letters of advice and exhortation to the communities that had sprung up as a result of his work. These constitute our second typical phenomenon, in the story of how the Christian movement created new types of literature. No Christian letter has so far been dated earlier than the earliest datable Pauline letter, and it is possible that it was Paul who brought this other novelty of Christian literature into existence. A novelty it is. There is nothing much like it in the Old Testament or Apocrypha.[2] A partial parallel, it may be, is provided by some of the letters of the

[1] See, e.g., J. Doresse 1960.
[2] Pardee 1978–79 examines the letters in these. See II Sam. xi. 15; I Kings xxi. 9 f.; II Kings v. 6; Ezra iv. 11-16, 17-22; v. 7-17; vi. 6-12; vii. 12-26; Neh. vi. 6 f.; Jer. xxix. 4-28; Additions to Esther xiii. 1-6; xvi. 1-24; Letter of Jeremiah (= Baruch vi); I Macc. v. 10-13; xi. 30 f.; xii. 6-18, 20-23; xiv. 20-23, 27-45; xv. 2-9, 16-21; II Macc. ix. 19-27; xi. 22-26, 27-33, 34-37.

Greek philosophers—those, for instance, of Epicurus.[1] In these, personal and philosophical ingredients mingle in a way comparable to the blend of theology, ethics, and personal messages in the Pauline letters. But the Pauline letter is new in such features as the Christian transformation of the secular style of greeting and farewell, the space devoted to thanksgiving for God's work in Jesus Christ, the application of Christian convictions in detail to the outlook and ideas prevailing in the communities addressed, and the ethical deductions from these presuppositions; and all this, still in a genuine letter addressed very personally to actual groups and congregations. The result is something that is a real letter, not a treatise or a disquisition dressed up in epistolary form, and yet something much longer and more weighty than the average personal letter of antiquity, and something with a recognizable pattern.

The Pauline letters, whether or not absolutely the pioneers of their type, were certainly followed by others, and even by homilies artificially cast in epistolary form. Some of Paul's, and some by other writers, were evidently treasured by the recipient communities, and eventually came to be collected—how, is an obscure and fascinating question (see below, pp. 258 ff.)—and ranked alongside the Gospels as recognized Christian literature: 'the Gospel' and 'the Apostle' stood side by side, somewhat as 'the Law' and 'the Prophets' of the Hebrew scriptures. The New Testament letters reflect an interesting variety of situations, in face of which one is compelled to ask Why?—Why did this problem or that present itself, and why did St Paul and the communities he represented give this anwer and not that? Why did the early Church break out from the conservatism of Jewish ritual requirements? What controlled the decisions reached regarding the relations of Christians with pagans?

In addition to the Gospels and Epistles, there are the Acts and the Apocalypse; and behind much of the New Testament there lie, no doubt, earlier and more fragmentary documents—component pieces, absorbed and transformed so as to be usually beyond assured reconstruction. The

[1] I owe this observation to C. H. Roberts 1963.

circumstances in which such a medley of writings of a new type was created and then sifted and established in authority alongside, even above, the scriptures of the Old Testament— this is our story. One of the morals of it is that the only hope of reconstructing and understanding the genesis of the Christian scriptures is in asking Why? at every turn: Why this and not that? Why such and such an omission? Why this decision and not that? This book sets out chiefly to ask 'Why?' and only by this route, if at all, to arrive at any answers to the question 'How?'

One positive conclusion, however, is the degree of unity that was achieved through all the differences and varieties. If it is asked how this came about, the only answer is that the common factor holding all together is devotion to the person of Jesus Christ—the historical Jesus acknowledged as continuous with the one now acknowledged as the transcendent Lord. In the chapter on variety and uniformity in the early Church (Chapter IX), an attempt is made to do justice to the very wide range of diversity in emphasis as between different individuals and different traditions. But the rainbow spectrum thus presented is undeniably thrown by one luminary alone. Common to every writing of the New Testament, without even the exception of the Epistle of James, is devotion to Jesus Christ. Whether he is viewed as the Davidic Messiah or as the pre-existent Word of God, it is to Jesus that each writer acknowledges allegiance. All of them, in one way or another, acknowledge his sovereignty.

If there is anything equally conspicuous that the New Testament documents possess in common besides this distinctively Christian allegiance—this common confession of Jesus as both historical and transcendent—it might be that, with few exceptions, they are Jewish writings, or, without any exception, monotheistic. This only makes it the more remarkable that, strictly maintaining their monotheism and without the slightest concession in this respect to pagan thought, they all evince this reverence for Jesus—indeed, a linking of him, in a unique way, with God. Christological formulations vary, but monotheism is never far from the consciousness of the writers, and in some cases it is possible to detect the influence of polemical or apologetic purposes in their variations. The danger either of scandalizing a Jewish monotheist or of appearing to make concessions to a Gentile polytheist may lie behind such a formula as: '. . . that at the name of Jesus every knee should bow—in heaven, on earth, and in the depths—and every tongue confess, "Jesus Christ is Lord", *to the glory of God the Father*' (Phil. ii. 10 f.).[1]

Some discussion will be devoted in Chapter X to the process of selection which ultimately segregated the books of the New Testament from other Christian writings, and it will be seen that an important factor was this 'Christ-centredness'—this test of devotion to the historical Jesus as also the transcendent Lord. Any Christology that attempted to resolve this tension—for tension there is in any confession of the incarnation—tended to be rejected, however reverent might be its form, and even if an apostolic name were attached to it.

[1] I owe this observation to P A. Glendinning. Cf. Rowland 1980, 8,11.

CHAPTER II

THE CHURCH AT WORSHIP[1]

NOBODY reading the New Testament with a grain of imaginative insight could fail to recognize that considerable blocks of its material glow with the fervour of worship. But in comparatively recent years the glow has (seemingly, at least) been blown into a flame by reason of a special concern with worship which has pervaded all departments of Christian practice and research. In England in the first half of the twentieth century, the Anglican Church experienced a kind of liturgical revival, typified by the movement called 'Parish and People'.[2] More recently, the radical revision of prayer books in various denominations has been taking place. Over roughly the same period came a liturgical awareness in academic research. There were new interpretations of the Psalms in the light of their original liturgical purpose and setting, along lines already pioneered in Scandinavia by such scholars as Sigmund Mowinckel[3] and elsewhere by others.

This interest in liturgy brought a great deal of fresh understanding and threw a vivid awareness of corporate life and movement and poetry into passages which had been treated in a far too static and prosaic and individualistic way: the words began to sing themselves, the mind's eye to see the rhythm of processions and the swing of censers. If anything, the fashion overreached itself a trifle, and scholars sometimes cried 'worship, worship' where there was no

[1] For this subject generally, see: Hopwood 1936; Reicke 1951; Cullmann 1953; Reicke 1957; Schweizer 1961; Delling 1962; R P. Martin 1963; Jeremias 1966; Hahn 1973; Dunn 1975, 1977, Ch. 7; Moule 1977, 78.

[2] See the Journal *Parish and People* as a mirror of this movement.

[3] E.g. 1922. Another famous figure in this connexion is H. Gunkel (e.g. 1913). For more recent work, see Anderson 1972, with bibliography there.

worship. The liturgical clue is a suggestive guide but must not be a tyrant. A distinguished Dutch scholar, the late Professor W. C. van Unnik, rightly complained of a certain 'panliturgism' invading New Testament scholarship.[1]

But that is a caveat only against abuse of the new awareness: it remains perfectly true that many of the component parts of the New Testament were forged in the flame of corporate worship, and that this has left its stamp on its whole vocabulary. So it is to the Christians at worship that we now turn, as an important part of our study of the birth and growth of the New Testament. Or rather, we must start with the Jewish Church at worship.

Christian worship,[2] like Christian literature, was continuous with its Jewish origins, and yet showed certain marked contrasts as compared with them. Like the Christian scriptures, it grew out of words borrowed, out of traditions remembered, and out of inspired utterances; and, as with the scriptures, so in worship, the Jesus who was remembered was found to be the same Jesus who was experienced and who was present wherever two or three were assembled in his name. Christian worship was continuous with Jewish worship and yet, even from the first, distinctive.

As is well known, the Temple at Jerusalem continued, at least until A.D. 70, if indeed it was completely destroyed even then,[3] to be the focus of Jewish worship. The Jewish synagogue (an institution of obscure origin, but perhaps dating virtually from the time of the exile) was in essence simply a 'gathering together' (which is what the Greek, *synagoge*, means) of a local group to hear the scriptures read aloud, to praise God and pray to him together, and to be instructed. In theory at any rate, the synagogue system was not an alternative to the Temple cultus. Religion on the level of its national consciousness and in its official form still found

---

[1] Van Unnik 1959, 272.

[2] The next 9 pages, with slight modifications, are borrowed (by kind permission of the Lutterworth Press and Grove Books) from my 1977–78.

[3] See p. 173 n. 2, and p. 175 n. 4.

expression in the sacrificial cults at the single Temple, the one centre of world Judaism.[1]

Indeed, even when a worshipper was not himself offering a sacrifice, his prayers seem often to have been offered actually in the Temple, or at least linked with the hours at which sacrifice was offered. In Lk. i. 10 the whole congregation pray in the court while Zecharias offers the incense in the Holy Place[2] (cf. Rev. viii. 3 f.); in Acts iii. 1 Peter and John go up to the Temple at the hour of prayer which was also the hour of the evening sacrifice (see Exod. xxix. 39, etc.); and in Acts x. 30 a God-fearing Gentile prays at the same evening hour.[3] So in the Old Testament, in I Kings xviii. 36 Elijah's prayer and offering on Mount Carmel are at the time of the offering of the oblation (cf. Ezra ix. 5, Dan. ix. 21, Judith ix. 1); and in Dan. vi. 10 Daniel prays towards Jerusalem three times a day[4] (cf. Ps. lv. 17, and, for Christian usage, *Did.* viii. 3). (Incidentally one may ask whether it is significant for the provenance of the traditions behind Matthew and Luke respectively that in Matt. vi. 2 ostentatious prayer is in the synagogue, but in Lk. xviii. 10 in the Temple. In Matt. v. 23 f., however, there is no doubt about the Temple's being in view.)

'In theory', then, one might be inclined to say, the synagogue was secondary to the Temple. But in whose theory? For it is probably a mistake to imagine that there was any one Jewish 'orthodoxy' in the New Testament period. Rather, we have to imagine various types of thought and practice existing side by side.[5] No doubt the priestly aristocracy, mainly Sadducean, maintained that the Temple cult was essential, and alone essential. But equally, we have some idea, through the accounts of the Essenes in Philo and Josephus, and, more recently, through the Qumran writings, of how differently a sectarian, but still priestly, group might

---

[1] For certain parallels between Temple and synagogue, and for the derivative nature of the synagogue's status, see *T.D.N.T.*, *s.v. συναγωγή*.
[2] For references to Jewish literature, see I. H. Marshall 1978, 54.
[3] Peter's prayer at noon is deemed by S.-B., ii. 699, to be irregular.
[4] See S.-B., ii. 696 ff.
[5] Cf. Goodenough 1953, and Nock's review 1955.

be behaving at the same time.[1] Evidently the Qumran sect maintained a priesthood and a ritual organization, but one which was independent and sharply critical of the Temple hierarchy. Although not in principle opposed to animal sacrifice as such, they seem to have regarded the Jerusalem hierarchy as so corrupt that they must for the time being dissociate themselves from the system; and in the meantime, making a virtue of necessity, they were able to console themselves with the reflection that praise and prayer, 'the offering of the lips', was equal in value to the traditional sacrifice.[2] In addition to groups which held such an attitude, it is just possible that there were extreme movements within Judaism which were opposed to the Temple cultus on principle, and were content with a synagogue type of worship alone—a kind of 'Quaker' Judaism. (Isa. lxvi. 1-4 may represent something of the sort in the Old Testament.) Dr Marcel Simon has published interesting speculations about this in connexion with the Christian martyr Stephen and the so-called 'Hellenists' of Acts;[3] and it is possibly relevant to note that no lamb is mentioned in the accounts of the Last Supper itself (as distinct from its preparation, Mk xiv. 12 and parallels). It is possible that this is only because the accounts of the Last Supper are influenced by later Eucharistic practice; or it might be because the meal was no Passover; or, again, it might be (as Ethelbert Stauffer suggested)[4] because Jesus had already been banned as a

[1] Philo, *Prob.* 75; Josephus, *Ant.* XVIII. 18. The most important of the Qumran documents for this purpose is the so-called *Manual of Discipline* (designated 1QS in current notation), which may be conveniently read in Lohse 1964, and, in English trans., in Vermes 1962.

[2] See Baumgarten 1953; Carmignac 1956; Black 1961, 39 ff.; Mowry 1962, 219 ff.

[3] Simon 1958, and earlier studies there cited. (I find myself unable to agree with all his conclusions.)

[4] E.g. in 1960, 94 (but the evidence is slender). Gärtner 1959 suggests that Jesus might the more easily have held a lambless but Passover-like meal on the day before the Passover if Jews of the dispersion were familiar with such celebrations when they could not come up to Jerusalem. Evidence that this was the case is scanty, but he cites Josephus, *Ant.* XIV. 214 for Jews in Delos, and Mishnaic evidence for the usage in Palestine

false teacher by the officials of Judaism, and a heretic was not permitted a lamb. But might it, alternatively, be that Jesus was a non-sacrificing Jew? Or may it even be that Jesus, prescient in his anticipation of the fall of Jerusalem and the de-judaizing of the Gospel, deliberately attached his teaching not to the lamb (whether there was lamb on the table or not) but to those elements of the food and drink which would always be available?

But that was a digression about varieties of attitude within Judaism. The important point for the present purpose is that the Christian Church was born within a context of Temple and synagogue; indeed, it has always been tempting to find already there the two components of Christian worship—the Sacraments, corresponding to the Temple, and 'the Word', corresponding to the non-sacrificial, non-sacramental synagogue, with its strong element of reading and instruction. Accordingly, there have been times when, for example, what has been represented in the Anglican tradition by Matins and Evensong and by the 'Ministry of the Word' in the Eucharist has been traced to the synagogue service, while 'the Liturgy', the Holy Communion or Eucharist proper, has been treated as a kind of counterpart to the sacrificial and the cultic in Judaism. But in fact neither Judaism nor Christianity is so simple as to be fairly stylized in this manner; and it is better simply to note the Jewish setting and to see what picture of Christian worship emerges from such evidence as we possess, before we try to make rash generalizations or formulate principles.

It is impossible to doubt that Jesus worshipped in the Temple. All four Gospels preserve allusions to this. According to Luke, he is found in the Temple as an infant when his parents bring him to be presented as their first male child, in accordance with the Law; and again when he goes up to Jerusalem as a boy for his first Passover. According to the unanimous witness of all four Gospels, it was when he had come to Jerusalem for the Passover that he was arrested and

outside Jerusalem. So Black 1959, 32 refers to 'the [Passover] celebrations in the synagogue, especially in the Diaspora, without a paschal lamb'.

put to death. The Fourth Gospel expressly mentions his presence in the Temple also for the 'feast of tabernacles' (Jn vii. 2 f.) and for the winter festival of *Ḥanukkah* or Dedication (Jn x. 22).

What is not expressly evidenced is that Jesus himself ever offered an animal sacrifice. The nearest that the Gospels come to it is in sayings which might suggest approval of the sacrificial system (Mk i. 44 and parallels and Matt. v. 23 f.). But such sayings can hardly be pressed to mean positive approval of sacrifice. The meaning of Matt. v. 23 f., 'First go and make your peace with your brother, and only then come back and offer your gift', is not far off from Hosea vi. 6 (quoted in Matt. ix. 13, xii. 7), 'I desire mercy and not sacrifice'. Whether this phrase was actually quoted by Jesus or not,[1] and whether it originally meant a rejection of sacrifice,[2] or (in Hebrew idiom) an assertion merely of the superior importance of 'mercy' over sacrifice, does not matter for the present purpose. In either case, its attribution to Jesus is evidence of a tradition that, like the Hebrew prophets before him, he was critical of the cultus. The question whether he actually sacrificed or not is still open.

However, that Jesus cared about the Temple worship, whether or not he actually joined in sacrifice, is evident enough, if only from the story of the expulsion of the dealers from its outer court. Whether this was an attack upon mercenary mindedness or a gesture towards the Gentiles, in either case it betokens a reckless zeal for the reform of the Temple. It is difficult to see it as an attack upon the Temple system as such.

Equally clearly, however, Jesus also saw that the Temple was doomed. The charge that he had said 'I will destroy this Temple . . .' was, according to Mk xiv. 57-59, not substantiated. But that he had indeed said something that might have been so interpreted, emerges from the taunts levelled at him in Mk xv. 29 (parallel to Matt. xxvii. 40). And in the introduction to the apocalyptic discourse (Mk xiii. 2 and parallels) he foretells the destruction of the Temple; while Jn

[1] See Hummel 1963, 97–99; Hill 1977–78.
[2] Heaton 1968, 302.

ii. 19 has the saying 'Destroy this temple and in three days I will raise it'; and Matt. xii. 6, 'something greater than the Temple is here'. There is enough in these traditions to explain the attitude of Stephen (Acts vi. 14) who is accused of saying that Jesus is going to destroy 'this place'. Whatever his immediate practice, Jesus stood for a completely radical principle. Ultimately, it became clear to his circle of follow-ers that he himself was the supreme meeting-place of God and men,[1] and it is characteristically 'through Jesus Christ' that Christian worship is offered. In this sense, Jesus himself replaces temple and sanctuary (cf. Jn ii. 21, Rev. xxi. 22). This does not mean that places of worship are no longer necessary. And, even if sacrifice is superseded,[2] the sacra-mental use of material things remains indispensable, while time and space remain. But one's attitude to the places and things of worship is revolutionized by the supreme revelation of God in a Person.[3]

If there is no doubt that, whatever his reservations, Jesus worshipped in the Temple, it is equally clear that he regularly went to synagogue on the Sabbath (cf. Acts xvii. 2, of Paul). In Lk. iv. 16 it is expressly described as his custom to do so; and even if we were to discount this as evidence, there is, all over the Gospels, a sufficient number of refer-ences to Jesus' teaching and healing in synagogues to leave us in no doubt on this score.

It is sometimes alleged that in synagogue Jesus would necessarily have recited the entire Psalter in the course of public worship. Of this there is no clear evidence. That the Psalter was at some period divided into sections correspond-ing with the lectionary cycles for other parts of the scriptures[4] neither proves that this held good for the time of Christ nor that, even if it did, all the Psalms in the sections were publicly used.[5] That Jesus was steeped in the scrip-

---

[1] See W. D. Davies 1974; Bowker 1978.
[2] As I still believe it was, *pace* Young 1975 and Daly 1978. See my essay 'Sacrifice' (1962).
[3] W. D. Davies 1974.
[4] See *T. B. Megillah*, and (e.g.) *The Jewish Encyclopaedia*, vi. 136.
[5] This is worth mentioning, in contrast to the indiscriminate use in

tures, including the Psalter, is suggested by the sayings attributed to him in the Gospels. But the same evidence seems to suggest also a very considerable freedom in selection.

In sum, then, it may be said that, while Jesus used at least some of the Jewish institutions of worship, and apparently did so with great devotion, he refused to shut his eyes to the nemesis which was to overtake a Temple which had been made mercenary and exclusive; he saw in his ministry and in his own self the focal point of the 'new Temple'; and he was satisfied with nothing but the absolute sincerity and spirituality of which the Temple was meant, but too often failed, to be the medium: 'the time is coming when you will worship the Father neither on this mountain [in Samaria], nor in Jerusalem ... those who are real worshippers will worship the Father in spirit and in truth' (Jn iv. 21, 23).

Coming now to the Acts, we find at once that the apostles in Jerusalem seem, as a matter of course, to have gone to prayer, at first, at any rate, in the Temple (Acts iii. 1; cf. Lk. xxiv. 53, Acts ii. 46, and see Lk. xviii. 10); and there are references to Paul as not only worshipping in the Temple (Acts xxii. 17) but being ready to pay the expenses of sacrifice for a group of men, presumably poor men, as an act of Jewish piety (Acts xxi. 23–26). In the same way, contact is scrupulously maintained with the synagogue by such as Stephen (Acts vi. 9) and Paul (Acts *passim* and cf. II Cor. xi. 24), both in Jerusalem and outside Judaea in the dispersion, until they are expelled from it. Expulsion from the synagogue inevitably took place sooner or later (as Jn xvi. 2, cf. ix. 22, implies, and Acts xviii. 6 f. bears witness);[1] and it is likely that the final recognition that Christianity was incompatible with non-Christian Judaism had far-reaching influence on the shaping of Christian ways of worship.

But that was not immediately; and in the meantime not only were the Jewish places of worship frequented by the Christian Jews but doubtless also the Jewish religious calen-

certain traditions of Christian worship of the entire Psalter, including the fiercely nationalist and bloodthirsty songs.

[1] Though see p. 135 n. 4.

dar was observed. Many, at least, of the early Christians are to be assumed to have gone on observing the Sabbath (Saturday) even if the next day of the week (Sunday) eventually came to occupy a dominant position as the day of the resurrection (Ignatius, *Magn.* ix. 1; *Barnabas* xv. 9; etc.; cf. Rev. i. 10 and the vision which follows). In any case, the Sabbath (Saturday) remained in Jewish societies the only day free for worship (in Gentile societies there was no *weekly* free day, only the pagan festivals at irregular intervals); and it is likely enough, as H. Riesenfeld (1959) suggests,[1] that the Christians began simply by prolonging the Sabbath during the night of Saturday-Sunday, by way of observing the accomplishment in Christ of the Jewish Sabbath. The rationalization of an *eighth* day—the day after the seventh—as marking the beginning of a new creation seems to be an idea brought in from Jewish apocalyptic (see *Barnabas* xv. 8 f.).[2] Rom. xiv. 5 f. bears witness to the existence, within the Christian community, of a diversity of views on the observance of holy days. Of the great festivals, the Jewish Passover probably continued to be kept by Christians long after they had found an existence of their own, especially as it lent itself so naturally to a Christian connotation and was bound up with the traditions of the death of Christ (cf. Acts xx. 6, I Cor. v. 7). Other Jewish festivals too must have persisted.[3] In Acts xx. 6 it is implied that Paul observed the Passover (so far as that was possible outside Jerusalem) before leaving Philippi; then, in Acts xx. 16, we find him hurrying so as to reach Jerusalem by Pentecost. Is this in order to celebrate with fellow Christians the Birthday of the Christian Church? Even if it was, it would of necessity have meant also celebrating the festival publicly with the non-Christian Jews: how could that be avoided if one was actually in Jerusalem?

---

[1] Cf. Dugmore 1948, 28, 30.

[2] Note also the possible implications of the Matthean genealogy (Matt. i. 17)—a new creation in Christ? See Farrer 1955, 87. But see, now, the exhaustive study by Brown 1977.

[3] See Daube 1958–59, 174 *fin.*; Lohse in *T.D.N.T.* vi. 50, and n. 35, discussing the Passover of I Cor. v. 6–8; and the possibility of Christian Pentecosts outside Jerusalem. See also Kretschmar 1954–55.

There must have been a great deal of overlapping of Jewish feasts and Christian connotations, the one merging into and tending to colour the other. Passover and Pentecost, in their Christian forms as Easter and Whitsunday, were destined to form the basis of the 'Christian Year'.[1] Only when the observance of a certain calendar became bound up with views incompatible with the freedom of the Christian Gospel and the Christian estimate of Christ do we find Paul protesting against it, as in Gal. iv. 10 f., Col. ii. 16.

The same is true of circumcision. The practice of it alongside of Christian baptism by a judaizing party within the Church only becomes a matter of contention when it encroaches upon the essential Gospel and challenges the uniqueness and finality of Christ (Acts xv, etc.). Paul is prepared to circumcise Timothy so that he may be acceptable to the Jews (Acts xvi. 3); but he will not yield for an instant to those who want to treat circumcision as a necessary condition of membership in 'God's Israel', over and above incorporation in Christ (Gal. ii. 5, vi. 11-16, cf. Col. ii, 11).

Thus, whatever distinctive forms of Christian worship there were, sprang up side by side with Jewish worship or even within it. Take an instance. The cry 'Blessed [is or be] the Lord!' is at the heart of Jewish adoration. J.-P. Audet (1958, 378 ff.) observed that there is something deeper here than even thanksgiving. Thanking God for specific mercies is only a special (and to some extent a man-regarding) expression of that deeper and even more extrovert adoration of God for his own sake, expressed by the Hebrew '*baruch Adonai*', 'blessed [is or be] the Lord!'; and the Old Testament furnishes plenty of stately examples of liturgies of adoration based upon this phrase—not, of course, confining themselves to this unspecified adoration, still less to this single word, but shot through with this attitude of adoration of God for his own sake, for his being, for his creation, and for his mighty works, as well as, in particular, for his work of rescuing his People. J.-P. Audet cites, as a good instance of this attitude (although here the actual phrase 'Blessed . . .' is reserved to

[1] A. A. McArthur 1953.

the end), the great liturgy of I Chron. xvi. 8-36, which comprises parts of the Psalter:

> O give thanks to the LORD,
> call on his name,
> make known his deeds among the peoples!
> Sing to him, sing praises to him,
> tell of all his wonderful works!
> Glory in his holy name;
> let the hearts of those who seek the LORD rejoice!
> Seek the LORD and his strength,
> seek his presence continually!
> Remember the wonderful works that he has done,
> the wonders he wrought, the judgments he uttered,
> O offspring of Abraham his servant,
> sons of Jacob, his chosen ones!

*   *   *

> Blessed be the LORD, the God of Israel, from
> everlasting to everlasting!
> Then all the people said 'Amen!' and praised the LORD.

This attitude of 'benediction' is at the heart, then, of Jewish worship; and the devout Jewish exclamation, 'blessed [be or is] he!', still finds its way, here and there, into the phrases of Paul the converted Pharisee: Rom. i. 25, ix. 5, II Cor. xi. 31. But what is distinctively new about Christian expressions of worship is, of course, the reference to Jesus. This is well illustrated by the 'benedictions' in Eph. i. 3 ff., I Pet. i. 3 ff.[1]

There were certain Jewish benedictions and prayers which made allusion to David the Servant of Yahweh. For instance, the prayer of a Passover *haggadah* (exposition) contains the phrase 'David the son of Jesse thy servant, thine anointed'.[2] A Christianizing of this is strikingly illustrated in the *Didache* (ix) where next to thanks for 'the holy vine of *David thy Servant*', comes 'which thou madest known to us through *Jesus thy Servant*'. Here the replacement of 'thy Servant ($\pi\alpha\hat{\iota}\varsigma$) David', by 'thy Servant ($\pi\alpha\hat{\iota}\varsigma$) Jesus' can be seen actually in process of taking place: the non-Christian thanksgiving for

---

[1] See Milling 1972.
[2] See *T.D.N.T.* v. 681, n. 184.

King David, the Servant of the Lord, and for all the blessings promised for his messianic line, becomes, on Christian lips, a thanksgiving for the fulfilment of that messianic promise in David's greater Son. Whatever the chronological position of the *Didache*, this represents a logically primitive stage in the Christian consciousness. In the New Testament itself παῖς is applied to Jesus only in two chapters, Acts iii and iv, and it seems probable that at any rate in Acts iv. 27, 30 it is intended in just the same sense as when it was applied to David, and means not so much the suffering as the royal Servant of God. Acts iv. 24 ff. is undoubtedly liturgical. True, it is anything but formal. Quite apart from the fact that the Greek is chaotic and possibly corrupt, the occasion is represented as one of exultant spontaneity—an outburst of praise in the group of Jerusalem Christians, after the clash with the hierarchy in which the inflexible confidence and boldness of the apostles have been signally vindicated. But the interesting thing is that—whether (as seems quite possible) the writer has this from early oral tradition, or whether he is simply writing the kind of prayer that might have been used—the phrases fall into typically Jewish form:

Address to God as Creator, and as the inspirer of prophecy:

>   Sovereign Lord, maker of heaven and earth and
>   sea and of everything in them,
>   who by the Holy Spirit, through the mouth of David
>   thy servant, didst say,

Quotation from Psalm ii about God's vindication of the Messiah:

>   Why did the Gentiles rage and the peoples lay
>   their plots in vain?
>   The kings of the earth took their stand and the
>   rulers made common cause
>   Against the Lord and against his Messiah.

Allusion to God's dedicated Servant Jesus as the anointed King, and as vindicated against his enemies:

>   They did indeed make common cause in this very city against
>   thy holy servant Jesus whom thou didst anoint as Messiah.

Herod and Pontius Pilate conspired with the Gentiles and peoples of Israel to do all the things which, under thy hand and by thy decree, were foreordained.

Prayer for continued help and championing, through the Name of God's Servant Jesus:

And now, O Lord, mark their threats, and enable thy servants to speak thy word with all boldness.

Stretch out thy hand to heal and cause signs and wonders to be done through the name of thy holy servant Jesus.

Here are praise and prayer according to a familiar pattern, only with the difference that the centre of God's championing is identified—identified in Jesus, who is hailed as the anointed King, and as the medium of God's continued triumph.

Thus we are watching here, as we did in the words of the *Didache*, the bending of Jewish liturgy to the distinctively Christian standpoint. Where παῖς is used of Jesus in the preceding chapter (iii. 13) it is in explanation rather than in worship; and it seems, on the whole, more probable that there the reference is to the suffering Servant of Isa. liii. It is in the liturgical context of chapter iv that the royal note is dominant.[1]

Other examples in the New Testament of what purport to be spontaneous extemporizations of praise and worship are the Lucan canticles—the Benedictus, the Magnificat, and the Nunc Dimittis; but all these purport to be, in the strict sense, pre-Christian, and it is by no means demonstrable that they are really Christian compositions read back into the pre-Christian period.[2] In the Benedictus, indeed, it is difficult to resist the impression that John the Baptist is being hailed as *the* forerunner, *par excellence*, not of Jesus but

[1] For a discussion of the distinction in Christological vocabulary between worship and explanation, see Moule 1959.

[2] Among much that has been written about the Lucan canticles as genuinely Semitic compositions, see Aytoun 1916–17; and Winter 1954, 1956. These studies, taking different sides in the Aramaic versus Hebrew controversy, should be read against the background of the studies referred to on p. 243 n. 3.

of the Lord God—as the Elijah who was to precede the dawning of the final day, or (though this is not the term here used) as himself the Messiah.[1] At any rate, here again we have the allusion to David the Servant ($\pi\alpha\hat{\iota}\varsigma$) of God (Lk. i. 69), to the blessing of God, to God's work in actual history (the birth of the child), and to the aspiration and hope of a good time coming. Christians were able to assimilate this by interpreting $\varkappa\acute{\upsilon}\varrho\iota\varsigma$ of the Lord Jesus instead of God; and, since John preceded Jesus, if John is Elijah, then the coming of Jesus stands in the position of the final Day itself. Thus what was perhaps extempore pre-Christian liturgy is taken up and given a Christian direction, exactly as happened also to so many of the Psalms. Since the Magnificat is not a strictly messianic Psalm, but is mainly praise of God for his mighty deed in transposing the fortunes of low and high, Christians could use this, too, unaltered. Like the other fragments just examined, the Magnificat contains its allusion to God's $\pi\alpha\hat{\iota}\varsigma$, but this time it is his Servant Israel (Lk. i. 54).

The next most Psalm-like pieces among the New Testament exclamations of worship are the songs of the Apocalypse. It is a familiar fact that students of the Psalter recognize certain 'enthronement Psalms'—Psalms such as xlvii, xciii, xcvi, xcvii, xcviii, xcix, which may have been used at an annual festival of the enthronement of Yahweh as divine King. There is no need here to debate the pros and cons of this theory,[2] but the Apocalypse certainly presents some splendid Christian enthronement Psalms:

> The sovereignty of the world has passed to our Lord and his Christ, and he shall reign for ever and ever! (Rev. xi. 15.)
> Alleluia! The Lord our God, sovereign over all, has entered on his reign! Exult and shout for joy and do him homage, for the wedding-day of the Lamb has come! His bride has made herself ready, and for her dress she has been given fine linen, clean and shining. (Rev. xix. 6-8.)

[1] See J. A. T. Robinson, 'Elijah, John and Jesus' (1962).
[2] For discussions see, e.g., Weiser 1950, 17, 35 ff.; A. R. Johnson 1935; Kraus 1960, xlii, lv; Anderson 1972.

Even if these, and the other Christian Psalms and exclamations in this extraordinary work, were composed by the seer expressly for the occasion or given him in ecstasy, it is hard to doubt that they represent the kind of poetry which Christians actually used in corporate worship. Again, therefore, it is to liturgy that we are able to trace the genesis of such parts of the New Testament—and to liturgy deeply influenced by Jewish forms.

Considerably further, in language and form, from any known Jewish antecedents are the little snatches of distinctively Christian hymnody (for such they are most naturally accounted) in Eph. v. 14 and I Tim. iii. 16. They therefore seem to take us one step further inside purely Christian worship: these, it would appear, are not mere adaptations of Jewish formulae but fresh creations of the Christian genius of worship. I Tim. iii. 16 provides, in this respect, an interesting parallel and contrast to the more Jewish enthronement-psalms of Revelation:

> He who was manifested in the body,
> vindicated in the spirit,
> seen by angels;
> who was proclaimed among the nations,
> believed in throughout the world,
> glorified in high heaven.

J. Jeremias (1953, *in loc.*) proposed to interpret it as reflecting an ancient oriental enthronement ceremonial (e.g. in Egypt), comprising elevation, presentation, and finally the actual enthronement. A similar three-fold pattern has been proposed for Phil. ii. 9-11; and Matt. xxviii. 18-20 and Heb. i. 5-14 are invoked in the interests of the same theory. But it is difficult to sustain the parallel convincingly for I Tim. iii. 16; and R. H. Gundry (1970) has shown how subtle are the parallels, and contrasts within the structure of the hymn itself, and how complicated is the task of interpretation. He suggests that it may have sprung from the early Jewish Christians who, according to Acts, migrated from Palestine to Syrian Antioch because of the persecution over Stephen. Whatever speculations may be offered about detail, however, it remains likely that I Tim. iii. 16 is, at any rate, a hymn, and from an early period: the very fact that, in the Greek, it starts abruptly with a relative pronoun unattached (apparently) to any antecedent suggests a quotation from something that the reader already knew and would recognize; the succession of aorist indicative passives makes a monotonous rhyme; and, like many of the greatest Christian hymns, it is essentially credal—a great adorative confession, like the *Te Deum* after it.

As for Eph v. 14, this is, if possible, even more elusive. A narrative springs to mind which has a strikingly similar outline. In Acts xii, in the dramatic story of Peter's rescue from prison by an angel, we read (*v.* 6) that Peter was *sleeping*, in chains, between two soldiers, when suddenly an angel of the Lord was there, and a light *shone* in the building; and striking Peter's side the angel aroused him saying '*Get up* quickly!' And here is Eph. v. 14:

> Awake *sleeper*,
> Rise from the dead,
>   And Christ will *shine* upon
> you.

The vocabulary of the Acts story is not identical with this: 'sleeping' and 'shining' are represented respectively by different verbs. But the command to get up or arise is, in both passages, given in the *koine* form ἀνάστα, which is not common in the New Testament: it occurs only in these two places and, in ms. B, at Acts ix. 11.[1] One is tempted to associate narrative and hymn together,[2] and to link both of them with the paschal baptism season of the early Church. (The story of Peter's release is placed at Passover-time, Acts xii. 3.) But that is sheer speculation. That the Ephesians passage is baptismal is, however, likely enough; and that it is a quotation is shown by the introductory words, 'it says' (λέγει); and that it is a hymn is suggested by its rhythm and imaginative quality. Clement of Alexandria quotes it, but

[1] See Blass–Debrunner–Funk 1961, § 95(3), p. 48.
[2] For this association (over which one reviewer declared he did not know whether to laugh or cry), cf. Strobel 1957–58.

runs on in less rhythmic and more prosaic style. After 'Christ the Lord [so his version] will shine upon you', he adds: 'the sun of the resurrection, who is begotten before the morning star, who by his own beams bestowed life'.[1] At any rate, we may say with tolerable certainty that in I Tim. iii. 16 and Eph. v. 14 we are overhearing something of what early Christians sang.

Many other passages have been claimed as hymns: Phil. ii. 6-11, Col. i. 15-20, I Pet. i. 3 ff., to mention only a few.[2] But in actual fact the criteria are inconclusive. These passages may or may not be strophic—i.e. symmetrical and balanced in their lines or their rhythms: nobody has conclusively demonstrated that they are quite consistently such. Even if they are not, as a matter of fact, they might still have been sung, just as Psalms and other irregular or metre-less pieces in English can be sung. But who is to prove that they were hymns?[3] Prose and poetry, adoration and statement, quotations from recognized liturgical forms and free, original composition, mingle and follow one another so easily in the mind of a Christian thinker that, without some external criterion, one can never be certain how much or how little of 'common prayer' one is overhearing. But we can be sure that parts of what a Paul or a Peter wrote or dictated for a letter he might equally well utter in public worship; and the stately eulogies, beginning with the word εὐλογητός, 'blessed', in Eph. i. 3 and I Pet. i. 3 are undoubtedly liturgical in *type*, whether or not either is, in fact, a fresh composition not previously used.

---

[1] *Prot.* ix. 70. See further Stone and Strugnell 1979, 75 ff.

[2] See literature in Moule 1977, 1978, 69, n. 4; R. P. Martin 1967; Dunn 1977, 134 ff. It has even been proposed to derive certain elements in the New Testament from pre-Christian lyrics, such as hymns to Wisdom (see J. T. Sanders 1971). But, if one distinguishes between semi-poetical laudations of Wisdom (of which, of course, there are examples as early as Prov. viii) and hymns in a stricter sense, as used in some kind of cult, it is difficult to establish the existence of the latter.

[3] For a light-hearted but telling critique of the mania for hymn-detection in the New Testament, see Lash forthcoming; and, for a questioning of the hymnic character of the prologue to St John's Gospel, see Barrett 1971.

Besides such snatches of actual hymns as can be recovered with more or less certainty, there are several allusions, in the New Testament, to the singing of psalms and hymns by Christians. There seems to be very little practical distinction, at this period or in this literature, between hymn ὕμνος (ὑμνεῖν), psalm ψαλμός (ψάλλειν), and song ᾠδή (ᾄδειν). So far as it is possible to test, the Old Testament Psalms are never described in the New Testament by any other noun than ψαλμός (though in the LXX there are plenty of other words[1]); but the verb ὑμνεῖν is certainly used of singing the *hallel* Psalms at the Last Supper (Matt. xxvi. 30, Mk xiv. 26), and it certainly does not follow that ψαλμός and ψάλλειν never refer to Christian compositions or, conversely, that ὕμνος necessarily means a Christian hymn. In I Cor. xiv. 26, Paul says that when the Christians come together for a meeting, each one has a psalm or a teaching or a revelation or a 'tongue' or an interpretation; and, although ψαλμός here might mean a Psalm from the Jewish Psalter which the worshipper comes ready to sing or recite, side by side with items produced *ad hoc*, it is more likely to be a Christian extemporization. Conversely, it is conceivable that Jewish Psalms are intended in Acts xvi. 25 where Paul and Silas προσευχόμενοι ὕμνουν τὸν θεόν—'prayed and sang [in praise of] God'. The only passages where anything like a clear distinction might be presumed are those in which all three words come together, in Eph. v. 19, Col. iii. 16; Christians are to sing (ᾄδοντες) with psalms and hymns and odes. But both passages are enthusiastic and effusive in style and it would be prosaic to insist that a conscious distinction is intended between (say) Jewish Psalms, Christian hymns, and perhaps more formal poems of praise. In any case, in both these passages the singing and psalming is to be done τῇ καρδίᾳ or ἐν ταῖς καρδίαις—that is, perhaps, silently and in the secret of the heart. The direct reference is thus conceivably not to audible, corporate worship at all, but to the constant secret recollection of corporate praise which the Christians are to cherish—all unknown to their heathen

[1] See article ὕμνος etc. in *T.D.N.T.*

masters or companions—as they go about their work (cf. especially Col. iii. 17).[1]

At any rate, there is no doubt that the more jubilant moments of primitive Christian worship were marked by outbursts of song—generally, one assumes, unaccompanied,[2] though one never knows whether a harper, or zither-player, κιθαριστής, might not sometimes smuggle in his instrument to the secret place of assembly. Incidentally, it is interesting that a vision of heavenly worship in the Revelation is accompanied (xiv. 2) by the sound of κιθαρῳδοί, which should strictly mean not mere instrumentalists (κιθαρισταί) who play the zither, but bards like the Homeric rhapsodists who also use their voices, and sing to their own accompaniment. Was the ᾠδή or song, perhaps, a solo performance of this sort?

But are there fragments of Christian liturgy in the New Testament besides the songs and psalms? Many scholars answer with a confident yes. 'The grace' in II Cor. xiii. 13 may well be from liturgical usage. Certainly the explicit threefold baptismal formula in Matt. xxviii. 19 looks like a liturgical formulation; and it has even been maintained that I Peter is virtually a Baptism Service (minus the 'rubrics', so to speak), complete with its exhortations and homilies, its hymns and prayers. This latter theory does not actually come out very well from scrutiny. The evidence, examined point by point, is rickety and must rely upon cumulative effect for whatever weight it carries; and—still more significant—it is not really easy to imagine a situation in which the substance of a baptism rite would naturally be dressed up in letter-form and sent to remote non-participants. It is far simpler to think of I Peter as a noble recall to former baptismal vows and promises, addressed to Christians who, facing the threat of persecution or actually undergoing it, needed just this bracing comfort. It is full of baptismal

[1] W. S. Smith 1962, 165 f. discusses this, but decides (172 f.) in favour of 'heartily'. See also Quasten 1930, 79; R. P. Martin 1967; 12.

[2] Cf. W. S. Smith, *op. cit.*, 53.

allusion, but need not be other than genuinely epistolary.[1] In any case, the language of Christian preaching and exhortation is virtually indistinguishable from what may be assumed to have been used at the administration of the sacraments; so that what we may describe as baptismal or eucharistic language is not necessarily to be associated with the moment of liturgical performance. The sacraments are evangelic and the gospel is sacramental: word and sacrament are in that sense one. Even the very word βαπτίζειν can be metaphorical. Not every passage containing the word is a reference to the actual rite with water. Baptism with Holy Spirit is clearly a metaphorical use (Matt. iii. 11, etc.), as are the sayings 'Can you be baptized with my baptism?' (Mk x. 38, etc.) and 'I have a baptism to be baptized with' (Lk. xii. 50). It is therefore legitimate to ask whether, e.g., being baptized into Christ, in Rom. vi. 3, may not, at any rate primarily, mean accepting Christ's death into oneself—being, as it were, 'swamped' by it—rather than carrying a primary reference to the rite of baptism.[2] More often than not, the likelihood is that a reference to actual water is intended; but such liturgical conclusions should be drawn with care and caution. Similarly with unclothing and reclothing (Col. iii. 9 f., Eph. iv. 22, 24): although baptismal procedures may well have suggested these metaphors, it is not necessarily so.

However, when, in I Cor. xi. 23 ff., Paul alludes to the words spoken by Jesus at the Last Supper, there is no reason to doubt that he is quoting from traditions which were actually repeated at the eucharist; or, indeed, that the synoptic accounts of the Institution had themselves been transmitted through repetition at the eucharist, long before they came to be written into the Gospels. Indeed, it is a familiar observation that the institution narratives in Mk xiv. 22-25 and Matt. xxvi. 26-29 shows signs of accommodation to liturgical use. For, quite apart from details, there is a clear difference between the Pauline account and those

[1] See Moule 1956–57, with literature there cited. For criticism and discussion, see Beare 1958; Thornton 1961; Kelly 1969; Best 1971.
[2] Cf. Dunn *Baptism* (1970).

others. In I Cor. xi. 25 Paul explicitly separates the cup from the bread by the phrase 'after supper'; and he presents the words over the cup in a form which is not parallel to those over the bread: over the bread 'This is my body . . .'; but over the cup, not 'This is my blood . . .', but 'This cup is the new convenant in [?i.e. sealed by] my blood'. In contrast to this, both Mark and Matthew indicate no interval between bread and cup, and both use the parallel phrases, 'this is my body . . .', 'this is my blood . . .'. It is hard to resist the conclusion that—to this extent at least—Paul's version is the more historical, while the other two represent a modification arising from the sacramental use of the two sayings from the Last Supper in close juxtaposition. In all probability, the facts are not really so simple as that. A microscopic examination of the language and structure of the relevant passages by H. Schürmann[1] has led to the conclusion that in certain respects the Synoptists may be in closer touch than even Paul with original or very early forms of the tradition; and in any case, the Lucan institution narrative presents peculiar problems of its own.[2] But it is enough here simply to illustrate the influence of liturgy on the formation of the New Testament by the undoubted signs of this process in the various forms of the words of institution, however delicate and complex a full statement might need to be.

A plausible case can be made, similarly, for detecting the echoes of the liturgy (perhaps in the Roman congregations) behind both Hebrews and I Clement, whose writers show certain significant traits in common.[3] Again, the guess has been hazarded that the 'farewell discourses' of Jn xiii-xvii owe their phrasing and form in considerable measure to the president's prayer at the Eucharist in the Ephesian tradition.[4]

Thus, much that we know about the words, and even

[1] Schürmann 1955. See also Jeremias 1966; Schürmann 1968, 39 ff.; Dunn 1977, 161 ff.
[2] In addition to literature already mentioned, see Chadwick 1957; S. K. Williams 1975, 204 ff.
[3] See Nairne 1922, xxxiv; van Unnik 1951.
[4] See Macpherson 1940.

deeds, of Jesus must owe its preservation to assemblies for worship. Even if only a scrap here and a scrap there can be recovered of the actual formulae of worship, this does not alter the fact that very much of what now constitutes the New Testament owes its existence to the requirements of worship. It is argued in this book, that the Gospels were not primarily intended for use in worship, so much as for instruction and explanation and (in some cases) even for apologetic; but that is not to deny that the words and deeds of Jesus must have been recalled at worship, and that worship was a very important factor in the preservation and transmission of the traditions. D. Daube (1958–9) has suggested, indeed, that the Gospel-form may have grown out of the Christian Passover, as an extension and development of the Jewish practice of the Paschal *haggadah*—the recitation of the story of salvation. But on the whole, although we later have Justin's evidence for the reading of apostolic reminiscences (i.e., no doubt, Gospels) at worship (see p. 257), and although no Christian worship could have substance without some knowledge of the facts behind the faith, yet the written Gospels, from Mark onwards, seem to fit more naturally into the setting of instruction, explanation, and defence. Baptism and the Eucharist no doubt invited the recitation of certain words and deeds. Baptism is the most natural setting for early Christian creeds whether the briefest of confessions, 'Jesus is Lord' (see I Cor. xii. 3, Phil. ii. 11), or the slightly extended one, 'I believe that Jesus Christ is the Son of God' (Acts viii. 37, 'Western' text); and the Eucharist was the setting in which the institution words and narrative lived on. But creeds, as we have just seen, are really hymns of praise; and it is for adoration, praise, and petition that one more reasonably looks to worship, rather than for narrative.[1]

It is possible, however, that worship early provided a matrix for the formation of Christian exhortation and ethical direction in the shape of the homily or sermon. Not that the primary *kerygma* need have been repeated in Christian sermons any less often than today; only, the assumption

---

[1] See Moule 'Intention' (1967); and pp. 123 f.

being that the congregation, by definition, knew and had accepted the *kerygma*, the speaker is more likely to have devoted himself to drawing out its ethical consequences. The *kerygma* is the right basis for praise and the ground of prayer; the homily would most naturally follow the line of exhortation to the congregation to *become* what, thanks to the Gospel-proclamation, they essentially *were*. It has been guessed that the Epistle of James may represent substantially some kind of Christian (or at least Christianized) synagogue sermon;[1] the homiletic quality of parts of I Peter has been observed;[2] and the rules for domestic and family life which the Germans, at least since Luther's day, have called 'household codes' (*Haustafeln*)[3] in Colossians and Ephesians and (to some extent) in Romans and in other epistles, may owe much to sermons as well as to the more private instruction of catechumens.

The fact that apostolic letters were certainly designed to be read to an assembled house-church leads naturally to the suggestion that they might, on such occasions, fulfil the function of a homily; and the closing words of I Cor. xvi. 20b-24:

> Greet one another with the kiss of peace.
> This greeting is in my own hand
> —PAUL.

[1] See Thyen 1955, 14–17; but see criticisms of his view on p. 219 n. 2. Dr J. Adamson, whose commentary is now available, 1976, kindly informed me in a letter (11 December 1960) that the idea that the epistle of James may have been originally a sermon seems to have been first suggested by Luther (Erlangen edition 63, 156 ff., Weimar edition, *Deutsche Bibel* 7, 384 ff.), and taken up also by Jülicher (a penitential sermon), and Harnack (homiletic patchwork by an anonymous teacher), as well as by Moffatt, Goodspeed, Kennedy, J. Weiss, and H. F. D. Sparks. He calls attention to the short note by J. S. Stevenson 1923–4, imagining James the Lord's brother sending scraps from his addresses in Jewish and Christian synagogues to Jewish Christians in the dispersion. He also notes Paul Feine's valuable little book (1893), where Feine argues for its origin in a synagogue homily by James himself (see, e.g., p. 95). (On p. 96 Feine cites, besides Luther, also Palmer, Weizsäcker, and Holtzmann for this view. But Luther does not really make a point of the sermon-form: he merely says that the Epistle may have been written by someone else, from James' preaching.)

[2] See commentaries, and Streeter 1929, 123 ff.

[3] See Weidinger 1928; Lillie 1974–5; Schweizer 1977.

If anyone does not love the Lord, let him
  be outcast.
Marana tha—Come, O Lord!
The grace of the Lord Jesus Christ be with
you.
My love to you all in Christ Jesus. Amen

have ingeniously been linked with the Eucharist, and the
conclusion has been drawn that Paul had actually designed
this letter to lead into that act of worship, with its ban upon
the excommunicate (*anathema*), its invocation (*maranatha*), its
kiss of peace, and its salutation. But this latter refinement is
less convincing, on closer examination, than at first sight,
and is certainly not firmly established. The *maranatha* may
reinforce the ban rather than open the Eucharist. There is
remarkably little trace of anything clearly eucharistic at the
end of any other New Testament epistles.[1]

This *anathema-maranatha* is, on any showing, however, a
reminder of the remarkable legacy of Aramaic words and
phrases which worship, in particular, rendered current
among Greek-speaking Christians. Besides the (apparent)
invocation *maranatha* ('Our Lord, come!'), there is the frequent *amen*, evidently used in worship in preference to such
Greek alternatives as ναί, ἀληθῶς, γένοιτο, which sometimes
occur outside worship; there is *alleluia, hosanna* (though in the
New Testament this latter is not clearly used in Christian
worship as it is in *Did.* x. 6[2]), and *Abba* (which seems to be
the opening word of the Lord's Prayer as still recalled even in
Greek communities, Rom. viii. 15, Gal. iv. 6).[3]

Whether worship has in other directions greatly influenced the choice of words in the New Testament is more
questionable. But the striking way in which what we might
describe as 'secular' words such as λειτουργεῖν (to render
civic service) are applied also to 'divine service' provides a
very salutary reminder that worship, for a truly religious

[1] For discussions of this point, see Moule 1959–60, and the literature
there cited.
[2] *Contra* Köster 1957, 196 f.
[3] Jeremias 1971, 63 ff., 197.

person, is the be all and end all of work; and that if worship and work are distinguished, that is only because of the frailty of human nature which cannot do more than one thing at a time. The necessary alternation between lifting up holy hands in prayer and swinging an axe in strong, dedicated hands for the glory of God is the human makeshift for that single, simultaneous, divine life in which work is worship and worship is the highest possible activity. And the single word 'liturgy' in the New Testament, like *'abodah*, 'work' or 'service', in the Old Testament, covers both.[1]

The Christian community at worship, then, must always stand in the very front of our search for the settings in which the component parts of the New Testament came into existence. Only, together with an enthusiastic recognition of this illuminating fact, it is important to bear in mind that there was necessarily an alternation between times of conscious worship and other activities; and it is even possible, in keeping with this distinction, that certain terms which were applied to Jesus in early Christian thought belong rather exclusively to these other contexts. The apparent location of the suffering servant idea in the context of explanation rather than of worship (hinted at in passing on p. 30 above) is an instance of this.[2] We turn next, therefore, from adoration and worship to examine the more consciously rational activity of explanation.

[1] See Moule 1977, 78, 75.
[2] See Moule 1959.

CHAPTER III

THE CHURCH EXPLAINS ITSELF:
1 Stages of Self-awareness

IT would be a mistake to attempt too precise a distinction, within the general term 'explanation', between the explanations offered by the Church to outsiders and the teaching and instruction offered to its own members or to definite enquirers. Or again, it is a faint line, in the last analysis, that divides explanations given to outsiders on the Church's own initiative, in the course of evangelism, and those given in reply to inquiry, criticism, or attack—explanations, that is, which constitute Christian apologetic. These various categories merge insensibly into one another. For the sake of clarity, however, the subject of 'catechesis'—the instruction of enquirers ('catechumens') or the newly baptized—and of 'edification' thereafter will be raised again in a later chapter; and for the present we turn our attention more generally to the Church's understanding of itself in the face of problems and pressures, whether from within or from without, so as to see the stages by which an awareness of its distinctive calling dawned.

It must be remembered at the outset that the Church in the first century, unlike the Church today, did not need to spend much time defending the existence of God. True, there were the Epicureans, whose system relegated God to such a distance from the physical world as to constitute virtual atheism, and there were the Stoics whose pantheism made the divine only the most rarefied component of a material universe.[1] But for the most part everybody took some doctrine of deity and the supernatural as an axiom. Indeed, it was the Christians who seemed like atheists, because they had no visible altar, shrine, or priest. In *The Martydrom of*

[1] For details, see Pohlenz 1948, 93 ff.

Polycarp, written shortly after the martyrdom, which probably happened in A.D. 155 or 156, the crowd in the arena cry, 'Away with the atheists!' (iii). At about the same period, Justin Martyr also says (I *Apol.* vi) that Christians are described as atheists; and in Lucian's *Alexander* (also second century) Christians and Epicureans are lumped together as atheists.[1] Christians, therefore, did not have to begin by persuading their opponents of the existence of God, least of all when they were confronted by Jewish monotheism. They might have a radically new conception of God; but his existence was taken for granted.

Chronologically, indeed, one of the earliest questions to be faced was what might at first seem far more pedestrian and less doctrinal—the question of the relation of the followers of Jesus to the rest of Judaism. This was forced upon the Church from within, as well as being pushed at it from outside; and, as we shall see eventually, it is really a major doctrinal issue. Even during the ministry of Jesus, onlookers had exclaimed in amazement, 'What is this?' and, in the same breath, had answered, 'New teaching!' (Mk i. 21 ff.). It was not long before the Christian community had to face a similar question: What was this that they were caught up in? What were they? Were they in fact something new and revolutionary or were they only an improved and expurgated version of the old? Were they a new race, a *tertium genus*, an addition to the familiar twofold classification into Jew and Gentile, or were they simply Israel, a sect perhaps but a sect that represented true Israel—a purified, inner nucleus of the one ancient People of God?

Unfortunately for the cause of simplicity and clarity, it proved to be unrealistic to come down exclusively on one side or the other, for there were senses in which both were true. God, by his purging of the old, had made a new creation. The message was at once both old and new (as I Jn ii. 7 f. says, though with a rather different connotation). Consequently, the New Testament contains evidence of both standpoints, and it is obvious enough that the emphasis is

---

[1] *Alexander* xxv. This was pointed out to me by C. H. Roberts 1963.

determined by the varying requirements of the circumstances and the tone in which the questions were asked.

On the side of the continuity of Christianity with Israel, a vigorous stream of thought issues out (like Ezekiel's stream from the Temple), and forks in two directions. As against anti-Christian Judaism, it stresses that the only Jews who acknowledge the logic of events are those who confess Jesus as Messiah: 'So far from not being Jews', Christians said in effect, 'we are the only Jews who fulfil the Jewish destiny'. As against an anti-Semitic, or, more correctly, anti-Judaic,[1] tendency in Gentile Christianity, it stresses that to be a Christian is necessarily to be growing, whether naturally or by grafting, on the stock of Israel: so far from not being Jews, Christians cannot be Christians unless they are Jews. The disputed point, however, was, How may a Gentile be grafted into this 'Christian Israel'? Is circumcision a necessary step? Or is Christian baptism sufficient, and more than sufficient, by itself? There is little room for doubt that Jesus himself began by appealing to Israel—and, so far as his earthly ministry goes, virtually ended with Israel also. He addressed his message to Israel, and saw his own mission and vocation in terms of the fulfilment of Israel's destiny. Even if one sets aside the question whether or not he accepted the title of Messiah, the anointed King of Israel, his use of the term 'the Son of Man' was related at the very least to God's plan for Israel through him—probably to his very self as the epitome and representative of loyal Israel. That he chose a body of twelve men to be his messengers and intimates (unmistakably suggesting the twelve patriarchs representing the twelve tribes, cf. Matt. xix. 28, Lk. xxii. 30), and that he virtually restricted his ministry to Israelite territory, are themselves significantly Israelite gestures. If Jesus had himself given explicit instructions to go out to fetch in the Gentiles, there could hardly have been so much debate and uncertainty about the Gentile mission in the early Church as is reflected in Galatians and Acts.

In the Acts, not only are the earliest Palestinian Nazarenes represented (as we have seen) as going on worshipping in the

[1] See W. D. Davies 1977–78, 18.

Temple and practising Judaism, but scrupulous care is taken to show even Paul both as making a regular practice of going first to the Jewish community whenever he was beginning to preach the Gospel in a new area (Acts xiii. 5 and *passim*; cf. Rom. i. 16), and also as claiming himself to be still a good, Pharisaic Israelite (Acts xxiii. 6, xxiv. 12-15, xxvi. 5-7). And it is well known that the Acts represents Christianity as acceptable to the Roman government, which it would not have been (so the implied argument seems to run) had it been a totally new religion. Acts is often regarded as highly tendentious,[1] especially when Paul is presented as acceptable to the Jerusalem leaders; but there is, in fact, nothing implausible in this particular respect about its picture of Paul. (See his own admissions, Rom. xiv. 14—xv. 6, I Cor. ix. 19 ff.) It appears from Gal. v. 11 that there were even some (possibly the most radical anti-Judaic Christians[2]) who complained that, in effect, Paul (of all people!) was 'still' proclaiming the need for circumcision (contrast Acts xxi. 21!). What he did proclaim, in Rom. xi. 13 ff. especially, was that *salus extra Israel non est* (to adapt the Cyprianic phrase, *Epp.* lxxiii. 21). If the Gentiles are to be given wholeness, salvation, they must be grafted into the original stock, they must become Jews by adoption. Similarly, Eph ii. 11—iii. 7 speaks of the salvation of the Gentiles in terms of fellow-citizenship with Israel. *A fortiori*, those who are already Jews by birthright will—even if temporarily excluded because of obstinacy—be brought back in the end into the community to which they belong by birth. As J. Munck remarks, Paul never turned his back on Jerusalem; or, at least, as H. Chadwick points out, he moved in an ellipse, with Jersualem as one of the foci. He did not think of a *tertium genus*, but rather of the Covenant renewed by God with the children of Abraham.[3]

[1] See pp. 6f., 159.

[2] Or possibly the Judaizers, arguing that the *logic* of Paul's position, whatever his *practice*, was that he still maintained that circumcision had much value in all directions (Rom. iii. 1 f.). See further D. W. B. Robinson 1964; Drane 1975.

[3] Munck 1959, especially ch. 10 (see p. 277); Chadwick *Circle* (1959), esp. 13 ff.; van Unnik, 'Conception' (1960), 122 f.; P. Richardson 1969; D.

This attitude set up tensions and caused complications. Paul, in particular, was evidently torn between, on the one hand, his instinctive love of Judaism and loyalty to his own people, and, on the other hand, the new freedom and universalism he had found in his relation to Jesus Christ. It would be easy, but an over-simplification, to say that, after becoming a Christian, Paul abandoned all distinctions of race or tradition, recognizing as true Israel only those baptized 'into Christ', whether Jewish or Gentile Christians, whether circumcised or uncircumcised.[1] To identify as true 'Israel' all who were true Christians, and only these, would be a clear, consistent, and radical position for a radically converted Jew. It would mean that what Paul calls 'dying with Christ' would include and transcend anything that mere circumcision could bring. And it is true that there are passages in the Pauline epistles which, by themselves, could be so construed. Col. ii. 10-12, for instance, seems to substitute union with Christ's death for the requirement of circumcision. So, too, Phil. iii. 3 claims that:

> We are the circumcised, we whose worship is spiritual, whose pride is in Christ Jesus, and who put no confidence in anything external.

Similarly, Gal. ii. 14 ff. seems to argue that a Jew as such has no advantage over a Gentile, and that all are equal in the community. In Gal. i. 6-9 Paul pronounces a ban—virtually a sentence of excommunication—on those who preached 'another gospel', which appears to mean those who demanded circumcision as a *sine qua non* for Christian membership. And in I Thess. ii. 14-16 there are harsh words about the doom of those Jews who opposed the gospel (though it is arguable that not all Israel is meant):

> You have fared like the congregations in Judaea, God's people in Christ Jesus. You have been treated by your countrymen as they are treated by the Jews, who killed the Lord Jesus and the

W. B. Robinson 1959, 1964, 1965, 'circumcision' (1967), 1974; W. D. Davies 1977-78.
[1] E. P. Sanders holds that Paul did abandon belief in the Sinai Covenant as ensuring 'election': see 1978, 124; and, very fully, 1977.

prophets and drove us out, the Jews who are heedless of God's will and enemies of their fellow-men, hindering us from speaking to the Gentiles to lead them to salvation. All this time they have been making up the full measure of their guilt, and now retribution has overtaken them for good and all.

Yet, illogically perhaps, Paul seems in fact to hold on to the distinctiveness and priority of 'Israel', even while he welcomes Gentiles into the Christian community. In Rom. iii. 1 f. he declares that Jews have special advantages—though he does not make explicit, then and there, what these are. In Rom. xi. 13 ff., as has already been said, he says, emphatically, that, if the Gentiles are spiritually nourished and fruitful, it is only by virtue of being grafted into the olive tree of Israel. And Gal. vi. 15 f. is possibly another instance of Paul's recognizing the independent status of Israel as such:

> Circumcision is nothing; uncircumcision is nothing; the only thing that counts is new creation! Whoever they are who take this principle for their guide, peace and mercy be upon them, and upon the whole Israel of God!

Here, commentators are divided in their interpretation of the phrase 'and upon the whole Israel of God' ('whole' is, as a matter of fact, not in the Greek). Is it explanatory of what precedes, identifying as 'God's Israel' all who live by the principle enunciated in verse 15? Or is it additional, asking for blessings not only on these but *also* on 'God's Israel'? And, if so, is 'God's Israel' all Israel without distinction, or is it only those in Israel who respond to God?[1] In Gal. iii. 16, 26–29, 'the seed of Abraham' is identified as Christ; and

---

[1] J. B. Lightfoot 1884, *in loc.*, takes it as explanatory; so Lietzmann 1932, *in loc.*, and Bonnard 1952, *in loc.* Lagrange 1918, *in loc.*, takes the clause as additional rather than explanatory, but thinks that 'God's Israel' means the whole Christian Church, as contrasted with the Galatians who followed the Pauline principle. P. Richardson, however, 1969, 82 ff., argues for the clause as additional and for 'God's Israel' as meaning the faithful in Israel (perhaps potentially all Israel, once they become responsive to God's approach?). There is a fine discussion of these questions in W. D. Davies 1977–78, 9 f. For the phrase 'God's Israel', Gutbrod in *T.D.N.T.* iii. 391, n. 135, compares 'Thy People Israel' in the Eighteen Benedictions.

therefore the Gentiles who are 'in Christ' are participants in
the promise of blessing 'in Abraham':

> Now the promises were pronounced to Abraham and to his
> 'issue'. It does not say 'issues' in the plural, but in the singular,
> 'and to your issue'; and the 'issue' intended is Christ . . .
> For through faith you are all sons of God in union with Christ
> Jesus. Baptized into union with him, you have all put on Christ
> as a garment. There is no such thing as Jew and Greek, slave
> and freeman, male and female; for you are all one person in
> Christ Jesus. But if you belong to Christ, you are the 'issue' of
> Abraham, and so heirs by promise.

But participation in the promises made to Abraham is not
necessarily identical with becoming 'Israel'.

Thus, for all his zeal as the apostle of the Gentiles, Paul by
no means unequivocally replaces 'Israel' by the Christian
Church; and despite the fierce antagonism from the con-
servatives, both in Judaism and Christianity, which ultimately hounded him to his death, he seems never to have
given up the hope of Israel's recognizing in Jesus Christ the
completion and crown of God's design for their own fulfilment. Thus, curiously enough, if Paul was inconsistent, it
seems to have been in his loyalty to Israel rather than in his
concessions to Gentiles. It is by no means clear[1] that Paul's
tolerance in I Cor. viii-x and Rom. xiv is out of line with his
stringency in Gal. ii. In the latter case, what was at stake was
the sufficiency of Christ; in the former, this is not the issue at
all. Where Paul seems most radically to have broken with
Judaism is in abandoning (as E. P. Sanders, 1977, plausibly
argues that he did) the Jewish conviction that 'election' was
ensured for all Jews by the Sinai Covenant, and that they
only had to respond with acceptance of the Mosaic Law to
remain in this state of election. By contrast, Paul as a
Christian regards all—Jews and Gentiles alike—as needing
to be saved afresh in Jesus Christ. In this he seems to have
been perfectly consistent.

It is harder to be sure what expectations Jesus himself

---

[1] *Pace* Dunn 1977, 254.

entertained for Israel and the Gentiles.[1] There is no reason to doubt the substantial authenticity of the harsh saying in Matt. viii. 11 f. and Lk. xiii. 28 f., which speaks of at least certain unresponsive Jews being thrown out of the Kingdom of God in favour of responsive Gentiles. But that would not, in itself, suggest that the Gentiles were to come in without circumcision, or that a new body of Jews and Gentiles was to replace Israel as a whole. The very hesitancy attending the beginnings of the Gentile mission suggests that the disciples of Jesus found little or no direct instruction on the matter among their traditions of the Master's teaching. It was not until after the New Testament period that the Christian Church came to be recognized explicitly as a 'third race', neither Jewish nor Gentile but Christian.[2] Yet, the seeds of this development are already there. They are there in the implications of Paul's gospel, despite his own conservatism or inconsistency about Israel. They are visible in the Epistle to the Hebrews, with its argument that Christians, so far from being deprived and 'unchurched' from Israel, are the only ones to whom belong, in an absolute degree, the priesthood, the sacrifices, the altar, and the sanctuary. They are visible when I Pet. ii. 9 f. hails Christians as the real, worshipping People of God:

> But you are a chosen race, a royal priesthood, a dedicated nation, and a people claimed by God for his own, to proclaim the triumphs of him who has called you out of darkness into his marvellous light. You are now the people of God, who once were not his people; outside his mercy once, you have now received his mercy;

and similarly in Rev. i. 5b, 6 it is they who are the royal and priestly people:

[1] See Bowker 1978, 161: 'Jesus was claiming that relatedness to God depends on the condition of faith, not on the conditions in the covenant'. Cf. p. 57.

[2] See, again, P. Richardson 1969. Hengel 1976, 113 n. 50, says that the 'third race' idea first appears in early Christian tradition in the *Kerygma Petrou* (Eng. trans. in Hennecke-Schneemelcher 1965, 100) = Clem. Alex., *Strom.* VI. v. 41; cf. *Ep. to Diognetus* i. But Hengel observes that in pre-Christian times, the threefold division 'Jew, Greek, barbarian' already obtained.

To him who loves us and freed us from our sins with his life's blood, who made of us a royal house, to serve as the priests of his God and Father—to him be glory and dominion for ever and ever! Amen.

Yet, with all these pointers towards an eventual recognition of the Church as Israel, there dawned very soon, if not simultaneously, a realization of how different, how new, the Church was, in contrast to Israel. There is a sense in which Christianity became Hellenized as it went out into the Gentile world. But perhaps it is even more important that it eventually became aware of being neither Jewish in a normal sense nor yet at home in other religions. This distinctiveness was not sought, still less fought for by argument: all the instincts of the Christians were on the other side—that of claiming continuity and antiquity. The earliest Christians may have thought of themselves as a sect; but if so it was as Jewish a sect as, for instance, the Qumran sectarians were. There was no desire (unless it was in a radical type of thought—possibly that of the martyr Stephen[1]) to break away or to start a new religion. It was only that the character of Christian experience and the centre of gravity in Christian teaching were so different that, sooner or later, they had to be acknowledged.[2] And the seeds of this revolutionary differentiation were sown by Jesus, even if his explicit teaching did not formulate it. His ministry was marked by an attitude to those religious authorities with whom he came into collision, and a manifestation of his own personal authority, which were entirely unacceptable to them. They evidently sought authority in tradition or written documents rather than in the personal encounter, the dialogue, between the living God and man.[3] For guidance, they looked to the

[1] See Simon 1958; Cullmann 1976.

[2] See Dix 1953, 109; Bornkamm, 'Wandlungen' (1971) 117 f.; Lindeskog 1978. But Lindeskog also shows the elasticity of *non* 'normative' Judaism. Stauffer 1959 (Ch. 3 with n. 45) took the extreme position that Jesus' own 'de-judaizing' of religion was almost immediately 're-judaized'—even by Paul!

[3] C. H. Roberts 1963 called my attention to the contrast in Plato's *Phaedrus* between dead books and the living word (λόγος ἔμψυχος). See, e.g, *Phaedrus* 276A. (One is reminded of Papias' celebrated saying, reported by

precedents of past authority, or to recognized techniques of scriptural exposition, rather than to the divine encounter within the worshipping community. In a word, those with whom Jesus collided were 'authoritarian', not 'prophetic'. Jesus himself, by contrast, reached out a hand—so far as he reached backwards at all and was not altogether forward-looking, new, and different—not to the authoritarian scribes' religion of the post-prophetic period but to the mighty prophets of Israel. His ministry, heralded by the prophetic ministry of the Baptist—the only great prophetic voice since the ancient prophets fell silent—went on, and went still deeper, into the ancient prophetic tradition. Unlike the authoritarians, he went straight behind legislation and casuistry to the great controlling principles and motives—to the creation of man and wife by God (Mk x. 6); to God's call to love, to love of God and of neighbour (Mk xii. 28 ff.); to the supreme dignity of man within creation, and his accountability before the living God (Mk ii. 27).[1] It was in the framework of these fundamental, personal categories that Jesus found his own direct contact, in prayer and converse, with his Father, and in this living, personal contact that he found and followed his Father's will and purpose. The outward manifestation of this absolute harmony of will between Jesus and the Father was the creative power that showed itself with unprecedented majesty in deeds of healing. When he spoke, it was with the Creator's words of power.

All this is only another way of saying that the ministry of Jesus pointed to such a new covenant as is described in Jer. xxxi—a relation between God and man not of propositional statement such as may be written and engraven on tablets of stone, but of personal obedience in the realm of heart and conscience: a relation properly belonging to the new age of which those same deeds of power were harbingers (see Paul's

---

Eusebius *H.E.* III. xxxix. 4: '. . . I did not suppose that information from books would help me so much as the word of a living and surviving voice'—Loeb translation. Perhaps one should compare also Ignatius, *Philad.* viii. 2.)

[1] For a recent assessment, see Lindars 1978, 63.

exposition of this theme in II Cor. iii). And one more way of expressing this is to say that the community which Jesus formed round himself was the community of the new age: it was Israel, indeed, but it was the Israel of the latter days; and in committing their loyalty to Jesus, the Twelve and others with them constituted in that sense a new community.[1]

Thus, if the very number twelve bears witness to the Israel-consciousness of Jesus, and if (as we have seen) he scarcely began to extend his ministry beyond the confines of Israelite territory, yet his teaching and his attitude no less clearly bear witness to the radical, the 'eschatological', newness of this Israel: here are contained the germs of its universal expansion. True, it is a well-known (though often forgotten) fact that the New Testament nowhere countenances the term 'New Israel'—indeed, the very term 'New Testament' (i.e., New Covenant) implies continuity with the recipients of the earlier covenants; yet the fact remains that *God's* Israel, *true* Israel, was so radically different from what counted as Israel in the contemporary world, that there is an undeniable sense in which it is 'new'.[2]

We have seen how even the radical sayings of such epistles as Galatians and Romans fit into the 'continuity' side of the argument, and we have observed that discontinuity (or at least startling newness) was not argued for and defended, so much as (almost reluctantly) accepted and recognized. But those radical passages in Paul's letters do argue clearly enough, if not directly, for this newness also. To be in Christ is, as he acknowledges, to be part of a new creation: and though this new world is indeed that to which the most profound prophecy and apocalyptic of Israel looked forward, it is strikingly different from the Judaism of those days.

Another way of putting the same point is to look back once more at the traditions of the ministry of Jesus. Here there is evidence that, long before the climax, he had begun to fall

---

[1] See Goppelt 1970, 25 ff.; van Unnik 'Conception' (1960) *passim*.

[2] It is interesting, as E. Schweizer, *s.v. σάρξ*, *T.D.N.T.* vii. 127, points out, that 'Israel according to the spirit' is not found, as a contrast to 'Israel according to the flesh', in I Cor. x. 18.

foul of the religious leaders, who regarded him as a dangerous false teacher, and that he was warning his disciples to
expect the same sort of opposition, leading to excommunication (Mk iii. 6, vii. 1 ff., viii. 15, x. 29 ff.; cf. Matt. x. 17, 25,
Jn xvi. 2, etc.). It is true, there is no evidence that Jesus ever
positively set up his own authority against the books of
Moses or any other scriptures regarded at that time as
authoritative.[1] But his way of using the scriptures and of
selecting from them, and the conclusions he drew, were so
subversive to the scribal scheme of life that it is not
surprising if he was regarded as a breaker of the law. It was
of small avail if, in breaking the Sabbath law as the tradition
had defined it, he appealed behind the tradition to scripture.
It is true that this may not have greatly disturbed the
Sadducees; indeed, it is noteworthy[2] that only once before
his trial is Jesus recorded to have had any clash with them
(Mk xii. 18 ff. and parallels), while, if the story of the temple
tax in Matt. xvii. 24 ff. is any reflection from the actual
period of his ministry,[3] it shows Jesus scrupulously avoiding
offence to the Temple hierarchy. It was not until the end of
the ministry that the political interests of the Sadducees
came into conflict with Jesus: thereafter, they were going to
play a prominent part, in the very early days of the Church,
in attacking the Christians as upsetters of the peace (e.g.
Acts iv. 5 ff., and contrast the comparative friendliness of the
Pharisees in Acts xxiii. 9). But all through the ministry, the
genuinely religious leaders of Judaism—those Pharisees, and
especially those scribes and teachers, with whom he came
into conflict—did recognize the threat to their system presented by this revolutionary and subversive teacher. Luke, it
is true, alludes to some degree of friendliness from Pharisees
(vii. 36 ff., xiii. 31 ff., xiv. 1 ff.). Jesus has even been claimed
by some (but without justification) as a kind of Pharisee
himself. But, for the most part, it seems to have been from
among them—or rather, perhaps, from the scribes—that the

[1] Jeremias 1971, 205–7, is hardly a contradiction of this. Cf. Dunn 1977,
98.
[2] Cf. G. Stählin, *T.D.N.T. s.v. σκάνδαλον.*
[3] See Horbury 1982.

55

real antagonism came.[1] Jesus' way of authority simply did not square with theirs. For instance, when he pronounced love of God to be the first commandment, it is arguable that he did not mean that from it could be deduced all the current regulations, but that it must take priority over, and, if necessary, nullify any others.[2] And Jesus not only saw the implications of this attitude for himself, but, as we have seen, seems to have warned his followers of impending excommunication and persecution for them. If E. Stauffer and E. Bammel are right, there was even systematic spying and collecting of incriminating evidence against Jesus by the scribal authorities long before he was actually indicted, and when he came to Jerusalem for the final Passover he was already a marked heretic, already, perhaps, excluded from normal participation in the festival.[3]

Thus, when the Christians claimed (Acts iv. 11, etc.) that Jesus was the foundation-stone or the corner-stone of God's Israel, they were inevitably proclaiming the radical newness, the essential *differentia* of their faith. For this was the very stone which the accredited builders in Israel had decisively rejected. The experts of Israel were confronted with a dilemma: either they must confess to a vast mistake, or else declare the Christian edifice to be something utterly alien; you either fell foul of that stone and found it a *skandalon*, or you discovered in it the one foundation of the whole building.[4]

[1] See Klijn 1959; *T.D.N.T.*, art. φαρισαῖος; Bowker 1973; Vermes 1973, esp. 35 f.; Cook 1978; Lindars 1978; and, more radically, Merkel 1977–78.

[2] Stauffer 1959, ch. 5, argues that the Marcan form (Mk xii. 31) alone preserves this radical and revolutionary sense: the other versions reduce it to precisely the rabbinic 'deduction' form. I cannot go with him in all his further strictures on other New Testaments writers (including Paul!); but here he has put his finger on a striking fact. *Contra* Barth in Bornkamm, Barth and Held 1960, 70 ff. See below, p. 128 n. 2.

[3] Stauffer 1960, 94; Bammel 1970.

[4] See also Swaeles 1959–60, arguing that (a) Matt. xxi. 44 is genuine; (b) both *vv.* 43, 44 are reminiscent of Dan. ii and vii (θ); (c) Matthew's use of ἔθνος (LXX) rather than θ's λαός is due to Matthew's own deliberate choice: he wants to oppose the new ἔθνος to the λαός from whom the Kingdom is taken. This last step is not very convincing; but it may be important for the development of the 'third race' concept.

But this newness did not become immediately evident, and the evolution of the Christian writings may, in part, be traced in terms of the gradual dawning of this very consciousness. About the time of Christ, there were already Jewish sectarians who, eager to separate themselves from the corruption of Judaism, had styled themselves 'the community of the New Covenant'.[1] And no doubt the early Christians too believed themselves to be no less Israelite than a reforming group of this kind—a kind of religious confraternity (a *haburah*[2]) within Israel. As we have seen, their very habits of worship bore witness to their assumption that they were truly Israelite. Yet their one distinctiveness was so fundamental that their extrusion from Judaism could only be a matter of time. It turned on the vital question of the seat of authority. For Judaism, granted the divine election belonging initially to all who were within the Sinai Covenant, what mattered was to keep within the Covenant by faithfulness to the Law;[3] and comparably, the extreme Judaistic wing of Christianity may, for its duration, not have been far from such a position. Jesus may, for them, have been only one stone in their building, side by side with circumcision and keeping within the Law. But for Christians such as Paul and John, Jesus was the supreme and unique test: he was the keystone of the building, the only door into the sheepfold; and the one decisive test was loyalty to him and trust in him. He was of necessity either foundation-stone (Isa. xxviii. 16) or *skandalon* (Isa. viii. 14). Decision was inescapable. And inevitably, therefore, the cleft occurred. The Christians

---

[1] See Jeremias *Jerusalem* (1969), 246 ff., appealing to the Damascus 'Community of the New Covenant' (see CD vi. 19, viii. 21, etc.), and to evidence in the Talmud which he interprets as pointing to the existence in Jerusalem in the first century A.D. of a Pharisaic purist group calling themselves 'the holy community of Jerusalem'. Cf. Goppelt 1954, 72 n. 7, on the use of *haeresis* (αἵρεσις) for Jewish groups.

[2] For *haburah* see Jeremias *Jerusalem* (1969), 247.

[3] See E. P. Sanders 1977. See also II Esdras ix. 7, cf. xiii. 23 (Law and faith side by side); and the interpretation of Hab. ii. 4 in 1Qp Hab. viii.1-3, for which, see Jeremias 1965, 68. See also Dodd, 'Johannine Dialogue' (1968), 46, discussing Gal. ii. 15 f.

found themselves squeezed out by the logic of their position, even when they were themselves reluctant to go.

A factor which must have accelerated the process of segregation was the implication of blame in the Christian declaration that the rebel condemned and handed over to execution by the Jews was in fact Israel's divinely-chosen King—that the expert builders had made the great mistake of all time. On top of the conservative Sadducean fear that the Nazarenes might upset the political equilibrium, on top of the scorn of the Zealots, at the opposite wing, for revolutionaries who refused to revolt,[1] on top of the Pharisaic belief that they were purveyors of dangerous heresy, this implication of blame (coupled with sheer jealousy at the Christians' success with the common people) must have helped to awaken a fierce resentment and antagonism.

But in this there seem to have been differing degrees of intensity, corresponding to differing degrees of provocation. If the picture in the Acts is any indication, there is no sign that the apostles in the early days in Jerusalem took the line that all but a small 'remnant' or nucleus within Israel had always gone wrong. That was Stephen's argument. It is Stephen (and cf. Matt. xxiii. 31) who calls the Jews sons of the murderers of the prophets (Acts vii. 52); Peter calls them sons of the prophets (iii. 25 f.).[2] It seems to have been Stephen's argument which precipitated the first serious persecution. Thereafter there followed two consequences. One was that even the Jerusalem apostles began to be suspect as disloyal to the heart of Judaism, so that Herod Agrippa I (A.D. 41-44) was able to execute the apostle James, and, finding this acceptable to the Jews, to make an attempt on the life of Peter (Acts xii. 1 ff.). The other was that among those actually scattered by the Stephen persecution were some bold enough to preach about Jesus to non-Jews (Acts xi. 20).

Boldness it needed; for the ministry of Jesus had virtually confined itself, with resolute concentration, to the People of Israel, while, if the teaching of Jesus did contemplate the

[1] See Goppelt 1954, 98.
[2] Goppelt 1954, 78.

exclusion of some Israelites and their replacement in the Kingdom of God by aliens from afar (Matt. viii. 11 f., Lk. xiii. 28 f.), this seems at first to have either been simply forgotten, or else construed as applying to the Jewish diaspora and not to Gentiles (perhaps cf. Jn vii. 35). It was a courageous application of Stephen's arguments, then, coupled with sheer eagerness to share the good news, which led to the beginnings of the Gentile mission. And once begun, it had to be reckoned with. The Jerusalem leaders, according to Acts xi. 22 ff., sent Barnabas to investigate. He approved, and fetched Paul to help to consolidate the gains. So the greatest mind of the early Church was lent to the advance of the Gospel beyond the limits of Judaism, and thus prepared the way for a step which, however, Paul, as we have seen, did not himself take, the definition of the Church as a *tertium genus* over against Jew and Gentile.[1]

And then the breach was no doubt clinched by political circumstance. In the disastrous war of A.D. 66-70, the 'Nazarenes' (a term by then applied to the Jewish Christians) refused to participate in the Jewish resistance movement, the Zealot insurrection (see pp. 58, 72 n. 2). If the crisis of A.D. 40—Caligula's threat to the sanctity of the Temple— might have closed the ranks of world monotheism, the crisis of A.D. 66 decisively separated Jew from Christian. The Epistle to the Hebrews is plausibly placed at this point[2] (though an even earlier crisis is conceivable—see p. 161 n. 1 below), when intense political and psychological pressures must have been exerted on Jewish Christians to show their loyalty to their ancestral religion and their nation by sinking differences and helping to present a united front in the bitter struggle for existence. But it is exactly such a situation that forces the distinctiveness of Christianity painfully into view. And the heroic and the percipient, like the writer to the

---

[1] Eph. iii. 5 ff. can claim that the inclusion of the Gentiles is a divine revelation to God's dedicated apostles and prophets—that is, apparently, the early Church's media of authority: see commentators *in loc.*, and a discussion in Grudem 1978.

[2] See especially Nairne 1913 and 1922; though his is not the first exposition of this view. Cf. J. A. T. Robinson 1976, 200 ff.

Hebrews, then see it their duty to say: Now is the crisis: to go back into Judaism (even Judaism of a liberal, Philonian type) is to desert the Crucified and to join the ranks of the crucifiers.[1] The only way to life is the way forward, not back: we must go outside the camp, bearing Christ's reproach. And, he adds, do not be deflected from your purpose by the ignorant taunts of Jews and pagans, who, both alike, say that Christians are atheists because they have cut themselves adrift from priesthood, altar, sacrifice, and shrine: all these we *have*, and have them on the heavenly level of the absolute (Heb. viii. 1, x. 19 ff., xiii. 10 ff.). We alone are citizens of that true Jerusalem, the city which, as the Psalmist puts it, has the foundations:

> ... he was looking forward to the city with [the] firm foundations, whose architect and builder is God (Heb. xi. 10);

apparently a reminiscence of:

> His foundations [plural] are on the holy hills ... (Ps. lxxxvi. 1, LXX);

cf. Gal. iv. 26,[2] Phil. iii. 20.

Thus there emerges, in succession to the primitive, unexamined assumption, 'of course we Christians are Jews', a polemical and carefully reasoned apologetic for the Church of Christ as alone the real Church of Israel. Ultimately, this logically involves also the paradoxical conclusion that the scriptures of Israel not merely belong, but belong exclusively, to Christians.[3] But long before this ever became explicit,

[1] Dodd, 'Johannine Dialogue' (1968), 46 f.

[2] Gore 1926, 770, pointed out that in this verse Paul appears to be quoting Ps. lxxxvi. 5 LXX, Μήτηρ Σιων, ἐρεῖ ἄνθρωπος.

[3] G. Schrenk, *s.v.* γράφω etc., *T.D.N.T.* i. 759, cites Rom. iv. 23 ('those words were written, not for Abraham's sake alone, but for our sake too'), I Cor. ix. 10 ('Do you suppose God's concern is with oxen? Or is the reference clearly to ourselves? Of course it refers to us ...'), x. 11 ('these things ... were recorded for our benefit as a warning'), as pointing to the conclusion (in the mind of Paul) that the Old Testament scriptures were written for the Christian community. But this, of course, is not the same thing as to claim that they belong *exclusively* to Christians (as Tertullian, *De Praescr. Haeret.* xix, argues that [Christian] scripture belongs only to the orthodox). *The Epistle of Barnabas* (iv etc.) is a fairly early example of this claim.

and before the Jewish war had precipitated the split on a large scale, the tools of thought had already been sharpened by Paul[1] in his personal conflicts; and there begins to appear a tendency to distinguish between Jews in general —Jews by birth—and a 'true'[2] or 'spiritual' Israel. As has already been said, Paul does not himself reach the simple equation, 'true Israel = Christians (whether Jews or Gentiles)'; neither does he use such terms as 'Jews', 'Hebrews', 'Israel', 'seed of Abraham' in such a way as to constitute an entirely consistent distinction between the merely racial and the religious.[3] But the tendencies are already discernible. W. D. Davies (1977–8) observes that: 'Where he seeks to emphasize the specifically ethnic and religious dimensions of "the Jews" he speaks of the Hebrews and the Israelites and again of the "seed of Abraham" . . .'[4]

If this is a tendency in Paul, in the Fourth Gospel it is even clearer. John only twice uses 'Israel' (i. 31, iii. 10, cf. i. 47); but the term 'the Jews' is used often, and in a remarkable way, always as though by a non-Jew or an outside observer,

---

[1] Cf. Meyer 1924, 584, cited by Brandon 1957, 12 (but my translation): 'It is a widely held opinion that the destruction of Jerusalem in the year A.D. 70 was of decisive importance for the development of Christianity, and that it was this which first definitely emancipated Christianity from Judaism and decided the victory of Gentile Christianity. But the facts do not correspond to this view; rather, the break away from the Jerusalem moorings had already been achieved by Paul. The further events which took place there naturally aroused the interest of Christians, and the destruction of city and temple appeared to them like the fulfilment of prophecy and the condign punishment for a stiff-necked people; it was the establishment of the position that the Jews had in fact wholly misunderstood revelation and scripture, that the Christians were alone true Israel, the chosen people and the bearers of the divine promise. But, actually, this brought no further significance to the claims of Christianity; these had been established long before by Paul.' Cf. Chadwick, *Circle* (1959). Yet see p. 173 below.

[2] This is first made absolutely explicit in Justin, *Dial.* cxxiii. 9, cxxxv. 3, etc. See P. Richardson 1969, 1, 10 ff.

[3] See D. W. B. Robinson, 'Salvation' (1967).

[4] For the use of these terms he refers to Schmidt 1947; Georgi 1964, 51–63. C. H. Roberts 1963 observes that Ἰσραηλ is commonly treated as a *nomen sacrum* in early Christian mss., but 'Ἰουδαῖος never. Cf. *id.* 1979.

for the benefit of non-Jews or outside observers. Of course one cannot tell how far this belongs to the essence of the Gospel, because one does not know how many different redactors have been at work on the Gospel as we have it now. But as the Gospel stands now, it contains elementary explanations such as that Passover and the Feast of Tabernacles are festivals of 'the Jews' (vi. 4, vii. 2, xi. 55), and elementary comments on Jewish customs (ii. 6, xix. 31, 40, 42); and in it, with few exceptions, 'the Jews' are identified as hostile to Jesus. Some of them, it is true, are expressly distinguished as those who had come to believe in him (viii. 31, xi. 45, xii. 11). Again, in iv. 9, Jesus himself is described as a Jew, but only by the Samaritan woman who is distinguishing his race from her own; and the same applies at xviii. 35, where Pilate says indignantly, 'What! am I a Jew? ... Your own nation and their chief priests have brought you before me ...' Further, it is in the dialogue with the Samaritan woman that Jesus says that it is from the Jews that salvation comes (iv. 22). But mainly, as J. A. T. Robinson says,[1] 'The term "the Jews" is found overwhelmingly in polemical contexts: they are the representatives of darkness and opposition throughout the Gospel'. The significance of this for the milieu of the Fourth Gospel is a matter which must be discussed elsewhere (see pp. 133 ff., 266 f. below); but meanwhile, the usage well illustrates the terminology of separation. One other example of the same tendency worth mentioning here is Matt. xxviii. 15, where the false story of the theft of the Lord's body is described as current among the Jews. This is the only occurrence of this usage in Matthew, though in iv. 23, vii. 29, ix. 35, x. 17, xi. 1, xiii. 54 the narrator refers to the Jews as 'they', as though he himself were not one of them.

But if such writings bear witness to the sharpening of the consciousness of the gulf, how did the Christians explain and rationalize it? Was such a situation anticipated in scripture?

---

[1] 'Destination ... of St John's Gospel' (1962), 118. Relevant here, in addition to W. D. Davies 1977–78, are discussions such as Dodd, 'Johannine Dialogue' (1968), Goppelt 1954, 101 f., Riesenfeld 1965, Kossen 1970, Barrett 1975.

Could it be fitted into the purposes of God? There were sufficient scriptures about the Gentiles coming into Israel and bringing their wealth and glory into the Temple (Isa. lx, etc.). But did not that mean as *proselytes?* And ought not converts from the Gentiles therefore to be circumcised and made true Jews? The logic of the questions is obvious enough. To secure membership in 'God's Israel', true Israel, what was to be the minimum requirement? Surely circumcision, and all else that went to the full instatement of a proselyte, in addition to the distinctively Christian confession of Jesus. If the Christians were true Jews, distinguished from others only in that they identified Jesus as Messiah or called him Lord, or associated him closely with God, surely this was the logic of the situation.

The Church as a whole answered, No, and therein enunciated far-reaching Christological decisions. Even within non-Christian Judaism, there was a liberal wing—at least towards the end of the first century A.D.—which was prepared to discuss whether a Gentile had already become a Jew by the time he was baptized and even before his circumcision.[1] But the Christian debate did not turn simply on the issue 'liberalism *versus* rigorism', nor did it rely upon an inward and spiritual interpretation of circumcision (though Paul does allude to this in Rom. ii. 28 f.): it was (implicitly) a Christological controversy. And Paul is the fullest and most explicit spokesman of—not liberalism but high Christology. It was probably his influence, also, in the Christian world generally which turned the scale. His argument, as we have seen, was that Christian baptism included and obviated circumcision; and to demand circumcision in addition would have been to pronounce this baptism insufficient. Once incorporate in the Messiah, how could one go further inside Israel? To add to baptism would therefore have been to pronounce upon the non-inclusiveness of Christ (cf. Gal. ii. 5, v. 4). If Jesus had been only an individual and his death only a noble martyrdom, things might have been different.

---

[1] See *T.B. Yebamoth* 46a, adduced by Klausner 1946, 39, 339, 367, and Daube 1956, 109; and a discussion in Rowley 1940, 317 ff.

The vehement Pauline refusal to require circumcision in addition to baptism implies an estimate of Christ's person and work which sees them as all-inclusive and as absolute.[1]

This line of argument involved Paul's viewing Abraham rather than Moses as the true symbol of Israel. The great Pauline manifesto on it is the Epistle to the Romans, gathering up and ordering the results, no doubt, of prolonged and widespread controversy. That the Sabbath controversy (which of course has left very clear marks in the Gospels—the Beza *logion*, Lk. vi. 5 (D), in particular looking like a polemic 'reply' to Nu. xv. 32 ff.[2]) does not figure in Acts xv, nor even at all prominently in the Pauline epistles, must presumably be due to the fact that, whereas circumcision would have been practicable for Gentile converts, Sabbath observance simply was not. Unless they came inside the Jewish ghetto, where there was an ordered life adjusted to the cessation of work on the Sabbath, they could not earn their living or subsist while observing the Sabbath. If they were slaves, Gentile masters would not release them from work; and if they were independent and earning their own living, they would still have had to pursue their trade on a Sabbath. It was no doubt because circumcision was a practical possibility for Gentile Christians as the Sabbath was not that it was the centre of controversy.[3]

But, in addition to the great Christological argument

[1] Cf. Justin, *Dial.* xlvii. 1–4 (J. Stevenson 1957, No. 43).

[2] D (Codex Bezae), in place of Lk. vi. 5, which it transfers to follow *v.*10, has: 'the same day, seeing someone working on the sabbath day, he said to him: "My man, if you know what you are doing, you are blest; but if you do not know, you are accurst and a law-breaker".'

If the significance of the Beza *logion* is that it is a deliberate reversal of Num. xv. 32 ff., it is comparable to the deliberate alteration of fast-days in *Did.* viii (so as not to be like the 'hypocrites'); and another possible parallel may be I Pet. iii. 19 ff., if it is deliberately aimed against Mishnaic strictures on the flood-generation (see *Mishnah, Sanh.* 10.3; *Test. Benj.* x.6; Iren. *Haer.* I. xxvii. 3; Epiphan. *Haer.* xlii. 4 (S.-B. i. 964, iv. 1185 f.)). See also Jeremias 1958, 47, and Epp 1962.

[3] For the prominence of the Sabbath law in the Damascus Sect, see E. Lohse, *s.v.* σάββατον etc., *T.D.N.T.* vii. 9. Curiously, there is no mention of it in the *Manual of Discipline* (1QS): see *ibid.* n. 61.

against requiring circumcision, there were other considerations also. Since it concerned males only, it was bound to become less and less significant in communities where women were becoming far more prominent than in non-Christian Jewish communities.[1] Also, besides being, for adults, a drastic step, it was open to fierce obloquy and contempt and would therefore make a great rift between the convert and his pagan friends:[2] was it right, then, to require it? And finally—and more seriously still—it carried with it the obligation to keep the whole law and brought the proselyte under the influence of the Jewish authorities who were themselves antagonistic to Christianity. It might thus afford a route leading straight past Christianity into anti-Christian Judaism. In Acts xv there is a description of a gathering at Jerusalem (the so-called Jerusalem council) at which, in the presence of Paul, a resolution was passed as to the terms on which Gentiles should be admitted to the Church. Doubt has been cast on the historical value of this narrative. What begins as a discussion about the necessity of circumcision ends in a discussion about 'table-fellowship' between Jewish and Gentile Christians. The resolution appears to be an amalgam of religious theory, religious ritual, and morals (it is against idolatry, against eating meat with the blood in it, and against fornication), and represents a compromise to which it is questioned whether Paul could ever have subscribed; and—to add to one's suspicions—not a word is said about it in Paul's letters to Corinth, even when he is actually discussing precisely such problems. But it is possible to exaggerate the difficulties; and it is not impossible that, while circumcision was ruled unnecessary, the basic, so-called 'noachic' requirements[3] were agreed upon, and

[1] So Rowley, cited by Gilmore, ed. 1959, 24, and Rowley 1952–53, 362, 1953–54, 158; and Daube 1956, 106, 113.

[2] See R. Meyer, *s.v. περιτέμνω* etc., *T.D.N.T.* vi. 78 f., and references there. The 'God-fearers'—Gentiles who admired Judaism but had not taken the step of becoming proselytes—seem to have provided a ready field for Christian evangelism; and it may be that one of their reasons for avoiding full Judaism was objection to circumcision.

[3] See commentators *in loc.*

that Paul gave his approval in view of the fact that the sufficiency of Christ was not here at stake. Why he does not refer to it in the Corinthian letters and the letter to Rome is harder to explain. It is noteworthy[1] that in the Corinthian correspondence and Colossians it is not strictly legalistic Judaism but rather syncretism that is the object of attack. So far as our evidence goes, there was no tendency to Judaizing in the Corinthian Church. The clause about abstention from meat with blood in it would not, therefore, have needed to be alluded to by Paul. But the other two clauses of the Jerusalem decree, broadly interpreted as the avoidance of idolatry and of sexual immorality, were basic religious and ethical demands, and one might have expected some reference to them at (e.g.) I Cor. x. 14 and v respectively. Similarly, in Rom. xiv (where tolerance about food tabus is the theme) there is no mention of the relevant Jerusalem decree.

But this still does not alter the fact that a compromise need not in itself have been alien to the Paul who says that he deliberately accommodated himself to circumstances for the sake of the gospel (I Cor. ix. 19-22, x. 33). When Acts xvi. 3 describes Paul as circumcising Timothy, it is simplest to assume that this was because, in his case, there was no question of circumcision's being a *sine qua non* of Christianity. The sufficiency of Christ was not at stake. It was only to 'make an honest Jew' of Timothy, so that he might preach to Jews as one of them. If Paul resisted the circumcision of Titus (if that is what Gal. ii. 3 does mean), it was because in his case the implication would indeed have been that circumcision was a *sine qua non*.

It is against the background, then, of the gradual hammering-out of Christian self-consciousness that much of the New Testament writing becomes intelligible; and the very genesis of certain sections of Paul's letters and of an entire document such as the Epistle to the Hebrews may credibly be traced to this process. The Epistle to the Ephesians, again, whoever was its author, is rightly interpreted as concerned to show that the Christian Church is indeed continuous with Juda-

[1] Goppelt 1954, 125 f., 138.

ism and, at the same time, is not limited by the limitations of Judaism: it is (as has been well said)[1] a splendid *apologia* in the face of the 'scandal of particularity': its claim that the Church has existed always in the mind of God, and is cosmic in its range and embraces the entire human race, is an answer to the objector who sees only a particular group of persons in a particular setting in time and space. Thus it is to non-Christian Judaism as a whole that the much-used words of Isaiah come to be applied:

> He said, Go and tell this people:
>> You may listen and listen, but you will not understand.
>> You may look and look again, but you will never know.
>> This people's wits are dulled,
> their ears are deafened and their eyes blinded,
>>> so that they cannot see with their eyes
>>> nor listen with their ears
>>> nor understand with their wits,
>> so that they may turn and be healed.

(Isa. vi. 9 f.: cf. Mk iv. 12 and parallels, Jn xii. 40, Acts xxviii. 26 f., Rom. xi. 8.)[2]

We turn, next, to the consideration of a special aspect of the process—the use of scripture by the Christian Church.

[1] See Chadwick 1960.

[2] There is an important discussion of the various stages of Christian apologetic to which this quotation bears witness in its various applications, in Lindars 1961; and see the full treatment in Gnilka 1961.

CHAPTER IV

THE CHURCH EXPLAINS ITSELF:
2 The Use of the Jewish Scriptures

AMONG the writings that have been under review, the Epistle to the Hebrews is one for which it is a special temptation to postulate a specific historical setting, since its interpretation depends not a little on the situation its author may be supposed to be addressing. There are those who place it after the crisis of A.D. 70 and as late as possible up to whatever date they assign to I Clement (which shows signs of knowing it). But a very plausible setting may be found in the ardent Jewish nationalism which must have been kindled or enhanced by the opening of the Jewish war in A.D. 66. Certainly some crisis such as might put psychological, moral, and even physical pressure on Jewish Christians to relapse back into non-Christian Judaism seems to make very good sense of this writing.[1] If this is a correct guess, then the way in which the Jewish scriptures are handled in Hebrews may represent a suddenly intensified and highly specialized use. But whether that is so or not, for the birth of much of the New Testament's use of scripture—including the stages antecedent to the Epistle to the Hebrews—it is natural to postulate a prolonged process of gestation. Already, in pre-Christian Judaism, there was a long history of scriptural interpretation, and there were equivalent techniques among the scholars of the Gentile world, notably the grammarians and savants of Alexandria who applied them to the interpretation of Homer. Philo, the Hellenistic Jew of Alexandria, who lived well into the Christian era, was heir to both these traditions.

Thus, in the writings of Paul, for example, we are witnes-

[1] There are, however, those like G. Hughes 1979, who reckon that no persecution situation is required.

sing only special applications of long-established ways of handling scripture. Moreover, these special applications had themselves probably been hammered out in debate, preaching, and instruction before ever they came to be crystallized in the letters. It is one of the merits of 'form-criticism' that it has forced us to strain our eyes—though the illumination is usually inadequate—to see these antecedent stages in the formation of Christian writing. In debate between Jews, Christian and non-Christian, the Jewish scriptures must have played a vital part. The Acts offers us some suggestive pictures of how it might have happened. Its very last scene (xxviii. 23 ff.) portrays an intense debate between Paul and representatives of the non-Christian Jews in Rome. From dawn till dusk, they hammer away at the scriptures;[1] and this is only a more extended description of what is alluded to in earlier chapters also (xiii. 16 ff., xiv. 1 ff., xvii. 2 f., 11, xviii. 4, 11, xix. 8 ff.). Accustomed to think of Paul as the apostle to the Gentiles, we too easily forget his extensive ministry in the synagogue, and the courage that it must have required. The passing allusion in II Cor. xi. 24 to five occasions when he had received the Jewish penalty of scourging (see Deut. xxv. 3, where forty strokes is the maximum, and the *Mishnah, Makk.* 3. 10, where in fact thirty-nine strokes are prescribed) reveals how often he must have come within range of synagogue jurisdiction. Admittedly the offences for which scourging was a penalty mentioned in *Makk.* 3. 1 ff. are scarcely relevant, except that a scholar

---

[1] Would this have been purely from memory? The Hebrew Scriptures were presumably not normally available, except in the synagogues, and then under supervision: individuals would not have private copies of their own. And even if versions into various vernaculars were regarded as less sacrosanct, it is a question how many individuals could have afforded a copy, when copying was slow and costly. In any case, the Scriptures in Greek, which must have been one of the most widely used vernaculars, seem to have achieved something of the sanctity (and therefore, perhaps, inaccessibility) of the original. See Chadwick 1967, 12. The writer to the Hebrews seldom identifies his quotations, and, when he does, he uses only the vaguest of references: see ii. 6, iv. 4. So, Paul refers to I Kings xix as ἐν Ἡλείᾳ (Rom. xi. 2), meaning 'in the passage about Elijah'; and at Mk xii. 26 (Lk. xx. 37), ἐπὶ τοῦ (τῆς) βάτου means 'in the passage about the burning bush'.

might be scourged instead of suffering excommunication (see
S.-B. iii. 530 and iv. 293 ff.). But in Acts v. 40 the apostles are
beaten (δείραντες, and cf. xxii. 19), and it seems reasonable
to conclude that, at any rate in St Paul's day, the penalty was
more widely imposed. In any case, there is no doubt about
Paul's extensive ministry within Judaism.[1] The usual pattern
of events is probably that of Acts xiii. 15 ff.—first, a polite
hearing, but later (vv. 44 ff.) a deeper realization of the
implications of this teaching, accompanied by jealousy,
resentment, and a fiercely antagonistic reaction. There is
plenty of scope here for the development of scriptural debate.

Again, Acts xv draws a (perhaps stylized) picture of a
scriptural discussion within the Church. Here is a wider than
the Pauline circle debating, still with attention to the scriptures, about the conditions for Gentile membership of
Christian Israel—sinister echoes of the debate, still uncon-
cluded, returning in Chapter xxi. Much of the story of the
Church's explanation of itself has to be deduced by attempting to read between the lines of the New Testament—the
end-product of the oral process; and later, we shall see how
the Gospel parables bear traces of such controversy, and how
the Fourth Gospel contains polemic with a similar stamp.
But at the moment we are more particularly concerned with
the use of Jewish scripture in these discussions, and we must
only pause now to note, in passing, that of course a great deal
of other material besides scripture entered in. Controversy
about the Sabbath law, for instance, would no doubt be
conducted not only by reference to scripture but also by
recalling incidents and sayings from the life of Jesus. This is
exactly (we may presume) how such sections of our Gospels
originally began to take shape. Christians in a ghetto, living
shoulder to shoulder with non-Christian Jews, would daily
be driven into controversy over their unorthodox ways, their
novel standards of reference, their altered scale of values.
What was more natural than that they should recall and
recite traditions (or, if they were eye-witnesses, personal
reminiscences) about Jesus healing on the Sabbath or pro-

[1] Might not II Cor. iii. 4 ff. have been constructed out of the substance
of a daring synagogue sermon?

nouncing about its ultimate purpose? How, again, could they help recalling sayings of Jesus bearing on the clean and the unclean—foodstuffs, leprosy-laws, and so forth? Christians in the great pagan centres, correspondingly, would have their own particular problems: they would be faced with difficult decisions about what constituted idolatry, what latitude might be allowed in sexual conduct, how far pagan institutions might be 'baptized' into use for Christians; and might Jewish Christians and Gentile Christians fraternize and participate in an *agape* at the same table? It is not difficult to imagine how self-contained units of Christian teaching came to be hammered out, first orally, then, it may be, as written fly-sheets or tracts—often in several differing though related shapes, according to the contexts in which they were used.

Unless, therefore, we follow Papias quite literally in his assertion that Mark omitted nothing that he had heard from Peter (Euseb. *H.E.* III. xxxix. 15), we may guess that, when he sharpened his reed pen and dipped it in the ink to write, he had already behind him a considerable tradition of Christian speaking and possibly writing,[1] by Peter and many others. He would know recognized patterns of argument and exhortation, of defence and attack, of instruction and challenge—from among which he might select his narrative material and his sayings. The earliest Christian writers were probably already heirs to a considerable body of tradition.

Within this, however, we are considering especially the early Christian uses of Jewish scripture. 'Jesus is Messiah!' the Christians asserted. But what in the world had led them to find the King of Israel in this crucified Jesus of Nazareth, and how could they hope to support such a claim? By most non-Christian Jews—if they had heard about him at all—he

---

[1] It is worthwhile to ask whether the celebrated phrase (Euseb. *H.E.* III. xxxix. 15) ἑρμηνευτὴς Πέτρου γενόμενος may not mean, not that Mark accompanied Peter as his oral interpreter, but that, *in the act of writing* in Greek, he became the interpreter of what Peter had written in Aramaic. See Heard 1954–5, 115. In the same passage of Eusebius, Papias' description of Peter's activity exactly fits the presuppositions of form criticism: 'Peter produced his teaching *as need arose* (πρὸς τὰς χρείας), but not as he would have done if he had been making a compilation of the Lord's sayings.'

must have been thought of as a popular healer and prophet who had taught dangerously subversive doctrines such as to undermine the very structure of scribal Judaism; who might even have made some maniac claims to a special relationship with God; who had perhaps been a scorcerer;[1] and who, in the end, had been brought to book by the Jewish High Court who had managed to get him ignominiously executed, by the degrading torture of crucifixion, as an insurgent against the Emperor's authority.[2] By Jewish law a dangerous false teacher and heretic, by Roman law guilty of treason, disgraced and made an object-lesson: how could Jesus of Nazareth conceivably be argued to be the Lord's Anointed?

[1] For the conception of Jesus as a dangerous false teacher, see p. 56. There are passages relating to Jesus in the Talmud and in later Jewish literature. The Talmudic texts are edited by Dalman as an appendix to Laible 1893; the later Jewish writings are in Krauss 1902; see also Klausner 1929. 'Klausner' (writes Manson 'Life' (1962), where the subject is briefly discussed, 19 f.) 'did succeed in distilling out enough [from these sources] to make a short narrative paragraph', which contains the statements 'that [Jesus] "practised sorcery" [i.e. performed miracles, as was usual in those days] and beguiled and led Israel astray'. See, further, Horbury 1970; Bruce *Jesus* (1974), 54 ff.

[2] The authenticity of the traditions about Jesus' being tried before Jewish courts and the nature of the charge are widely debated. In addition to standard works such as Blinzler 1959, and E. Lohse, art. συνέδριον in *T.D.N.T.* vii, note the following: Winter 1961, Brandon 1967, Bammel, ed., *Trial* (1970), Bovon 1974, Bammel and Moule, edd., 1982, with bibliographies there. That there was a trial in a Roman court is scarcely disputed. The fundamental issues are whether the Gospel accounts of a trial, or trials, before Jewish authorities are authentic, or whether they are not due purely to a Christian desire to exonerate the Romans; and whether the Roman condemnation of Jesus as an insurgent (a 'freedom fighter') was or was not justified. It is difficult to dispose of a Jewish charge—if only because a collision between Jesus and the most religious Jews is so well evidenced by the Gospel traditions. It is impossible (*pace* Brandon) without playing fast and loose with the evidence to establish that Jesus was a supporter of Zealotry, or even that he sympathized with the intentions of the Zealots (see M. Hengel's review of Brandon 1969, and his book 1971). Thus, the hypothesis that Jesus, already condemned on a religious charge, was passed by the Jews to Pilate on a false political charge is still plausible. See Bowker 1978, especially 162 ff., for the view that it was *extremists* among the Jews who brought Jesus to his death.

THE USE OF THE JEWISH SCRIPTURES

In the earliest days, the Christians' convictions seem, as a matter of fact, to have been expressed less as a statement about who Jesus was than as evidence about what God had done in him and to him.[1] God had anointed him with Spirit, they said: that is, Jesus had received the spiritual equivalent of an enthronement ceremony or at least some sort of special commissioning, like the speaker of the words in Isa. lxi. 1,

'The spirit of the Lord GOD is upon me
because the LORD has anointed me;
he has sent me to bring good news . . .'

There were witnesses who could describe the baptism of Jesus as just such a spiritual 'Christing' (Ps. ii, 'You are my son', was a messianic address, and something like it was associated with the baptism of Jesus, even if it was possibly reminiscent also of the suffering servant of II-Isa.); they might even have heard Jesus himself applying Isa. lxi to his ministry (Lk. iv. 18; cf. Acts x. 38). Besides, the exceptional deeds of power accompanying his ministry were evidence that 'God was with him' (Acts x. 38); Jesus himself, when asked by the Baptist's followers whether he was the one they were hoping for, had pointed to these events, and again had linked them with such Isaianic passages (Isa. xxxv. 5, lxi. 1, Matt. xi. 2 ff., Lk. vii. 18 ff.). Once, in controversy with the educated religious men of Jerusalem, Jesus—so the story went—had invoked Ps. cx—a Psalm seemingly referring to a royal (and priestly) personage of even higher dignity than David himself (Mk xii. 35 ff.). Such were the passages most naturally appealed to in order to locate in the scriptures the divine *imprimatur* upon Jesus of Nazareth during his lifetime—scriptures which, according to tradition, Jesus had himself appropriated.

But there was much more even than the great events of his ministry. After his death—so the Christians averred—God

---

[1] 'To the first Church Jesus Christ was not an idea but a sum of events'—Schweizer 1960, 96. But he rightly adds that the *events* were (so far as significant) all *interpreted*, and depended for their significance on the Christian interpretation.

had not allowed his dead body to become corrupt (that was just like Ps. xvi—

> '. . . thou wilt not abandon me to Sheol
> nor suffer thy faithful servant to see the pit'—

Acts ii. 27); he had raised him from the tomb to a position of supreme honour (Ps. cx again!). In view of these overwhelming events—and the Christians had been convinced of them, despite their own despair and loss of all confidence, by the inescapable evidence of their eyes—was it not clear that they were living in the midst of a divine fulfilment of all the hopes of Israel?[1] The Christians began from Jesus—from his known character and mighty deeds and sayings, and his death and resurrection; and with these they went to the scriptures, and found that God's dealings with his People and his intentions for them there reflected did, in fact, leap into new significance in the light of these recent happenings. Sooner or later this was to lead, through a definition of what God had done, to something like a definition of who Jesus was.

But first we must look more closely at the circumstances controlling the early Christian use of scripture. Three main factors are discernible. *First*, pre-Christian Judaism (drawing partly on Gentile traditions) had already developed certain ways of interpreting scripture. *Secondly*, Jesus himself, during his ministry, had used scripture with great originality, and yet with an understanding of traditional methods. And *thirdly*, the early Christians were conscious that the voice of inspired prophecy, long silent, had begun once more to be audible; and they therefore used both scripture and the memories and traditions of the words of Jesus with the creative freedom of the inspired. This third factor, as a matter of fact, interlocks in a striking manner with the second; for the historical Jesus whose exegesis of scripture they recalled was at the same time found to be far more than

---

[1] It is very striking that, with all the parallels between the New Testament use of scripture and its use in the Qumran writings and in other Jewish literature, the note of *fulfilment* seems to be peculiar to the New Testament. CD vii. 10-11 is not far off, but *ml'* appears not to occur in this connexion. See Fitzmyer 1961–62; Moule 1967–68.

a teacher of the days gone by: as the Lord of Faith, he was still with and in and among his people as they continued to expound the scriptures in his name. Thus, early Christian exegesis of scripture (in keeping with what we have already discovered about early Christian worship and the character of the early Christian community as a whole) was a new and creative thing, albeit rooted also in an antecedent Jewish tradition. Christ was found to be more authoritative than scripture, but in the sense of fulfilling and transcending, not of abolishing it.

We must examine these three factors, though the second and third merge into one another.

First, what methods of handling scripture were current in the days of Jesus and of the early Church? It appears that the basis of all methods was an assumption alien to modern critical scholarship, namely, that the Torah (and other scriptures also, in their degree) constituted a divine means of revelation in the sense that it might be treated as a kind of oracle—not historically and, as it were, three-dimensionally, but as a kind of two-dimensional flat surface, from any part of which equally authoritative words might be drawn. A modern Jewish scholar, R. Loewe, has written (1957) that, for all devout Jews alike, it was axiomatic 'that the channel of divine Revelation is Torah'. Given this assumption, it was, of course, necessary to decide how to build a bridge from the authoritative words to the needs and problems of the expositor and his hearers. In the same passage, R. Loewe went on to speak of what was *deducible* from the text of scripture by the application of human reason to it, 'provided only that human reason acknowledges its dependence upon divine grace'.

The whole of Jewish exegesis, comprising a wide range of techniques, represents an attempt to achieve this work of 'deduction'. But, although certain expositors formulated 'rules' for it, the procedures remain arbitrary, since some, at least, of the rules bear no relation to any objective criteria: they are themselves arbitrary. The earliest known rules are attributed to Hillel, who lived at about the time of Christ. Some of his seven rules are sensible enough; but among them are also such arbitrary and dangerous ones as that, when the same phrase is found in a number of passages, then a consideration found in one of them applies to all of them.[1] Thus was built up a long tradition of how this rabbi and that had made texts say things that were not by any means always in the texts themselves.

The activity of investigating the scriptures is known as *midrash*[2] (from *darash*, 'to investigate'); and, within *midrash*, two types of activity are distinguished—*halakah* (from *halak*, 'to walk'), ethical deductions and rules for conduct; and *haggadah* (from *higgid*—hiph'il of *nagad*—'to declare', 'make known', 'expound'), the creating of narratives intended to convey useful or improving lessons.

Behind the use of such techniques and within the general assumption that scripture speaks with God's voice, one may distinguish, broadly speaking, two schools of thought. One school of thought assumes that the accredited interpreters— the 'rabbis', as they are generally but vaguely called[3]—are normative for the understanding of scripture, and that it may only be rightly interpreted from within the collective tradition. The other assumes that an individual may by himself go to scripture and, by using recognized techniques, extract for himself what it is saying. This latter assumption has much in common with the imaginative and allegorical interpretation of Homer and other classical literature by the Alexandrine Greek grammarians and expositors of the Gentile world. For Judaism, it is well represented by Philo, the Alexandrine Jew. It is impossible to be sure what Philo inherited and what he made up for himelf out of his fertile mind;[4] but certainly he is not wont to quote antecedent expositors. He simply tells the reader what the passage means—generally in relation to the individual soul—by

[1] See, for source, etc., Bowker 1969, 315.

[2] Originally, however, *midrash* meant not the activity but the commentary produced: see Ellis 1977, 201.

[3] For the technical names given to different generations of Jewish teachers (Tannaim, etc.), see Bowker 1969, 323. For early Jewish exegesis, see Mann 1940, 1966; Weingreen 1951–52. I owe these two references to N. R. M. de Lange.

[4] See art. 'Philo' in *R.G.G.*

applying imaginative allegory, etymological conceits, and a host of other equally arbitrary devices. He often turns literal regulations for the body or narratives about human events into metaphors concerning the soul.

Within both schools of thought the same devices are used, though not in equal proportions. The net result will be, in the case of the former school of thought, a collective judgment, but, in the case of the latter, an individual's judgment. There are obvious analogies here with the traditions of Christian exegesis: speaking very broadly, the former is more like a Catholic approach, with its emphasis on the Church and tradition, the latter more like a Protestant approach with its individualistic emphasis.

What are the modes or devices in question? Five of them may be readily named and illustrated.

(1) The first is, as a matter of fact, scarcely a 'device'. Indeed, it is the least arbitrary and the most straightforward method possible—that of simply applying to a current situation some basic injunction about moral character or conduct. An obvious example is the *shema'* itself, the ancient Jewish confession of faith made up from Deut. vi. 4-9 (which begins, 'Hear [*shema'*], O Israel, the LORD is our God, one LORD . . .'), Deut. xi. 13-21, and Num. xv. 37-41.[1] This is virtually a reminder of the nature and work of God, and of the proper response from his people, and can be applied directly, in one generation after another. Or again, the Damascus document (copies of which were discovered long before the Qumran scrolls but which is now identified as belonging to the same sect) has:

> And concerning the saying, *You shall not take vengeance on the children of your people, nor bear any rancour against them* [Lev. xix. 18], if any member of the Covenant accuses his companion without first rebuking him before witnesses; if he denounces him in the heat of his anger . . . (CD ix. 2-4, translation in Vermes 1962).

This is a straight application to the community of a Levitical injunction against vengeance and rancour. There is no end to the examples that might be quoted, but these two are sufficient.

[1] Mishnah, *Berakoth* 2, contains regulations for its use.

(2) More arbitrary is the application to current situations of words which, in their original context in history or in the writer's thought, meant something else. Such applications are commonly made with some such assertion as 'This is ...' (like our *id est*, 'that is to say ...') or 'The interpretation is ...' 'Interpretation', in Hebrew, is *pēsher*, or, in Aramaic, *pishrâ*, and this sort of application of scripture has in our own days come to be called '*pēsher*-exegesis' or, for short, simply '*pēsher*'. It occurs all over the so-called commentary on Habakkuk in the Qumran scrolls.[1] A random example is:

> For behold, I rouse the Chaldeans, that [bitter and hasty] nation [Hab. i. 6a].
> Interpreted (*pishrô*, 'its interpretation [is]'), this concerns the Kittim ... (1Qp Hab. ii. 10b-12a).

So, what for Habakkuk was a reference to Chaldeans is turned by the Qumran expositor into a reference to the Kittim (i.e. the Romans).

Or again (though without the word *pēsher*):

> ... the well which the princes dug, which the nobles of the people delved with the stave [Num. xxi. 18].
> The *Well* is the Law, and those who dug it were the converts of Israel who went out from the land of Judah to sojourn in the land of Damascus. God called them all *princes* because they sought Him, and their renown was disputed by no man. The *Stave* is the Interpreter of the Law of whom Isaiah said, *He makes a tool for His work* [Isa. liv. 16]; and the *nobles of the people* are those who come to dig the *Well* ... (CD vi. 3-9a, translation in Vermes 1962).

Here, the mysterious and oracular ancient song from Num. xxi is quite arbitrarily applied to members of the community, by dint of allegorical interpretation and by invoking a phrase from Isaiah, interpreted with equal disregard for its original meaning.

(3) In the same spirit, and representing only a specialized application of the same device, is the arbitrary use of words from scripture as a prediction of something that is now or shortly believed to be coming to pass. This may be illus-

---

[1] Among studies of exegetical methods in these documents, note Bruce 1960, and Betz 1960.

trated from the *florilegium* or anthology from Qumran, in which passages from II Sam. vii are combined with passages from Exod. xv, Amos ix, Ps. i, Isa. viii, Ezek, xliv, and Ps. ii, with a running commentary, so as to designate the rôle of the community and make up a prediction of the coming of Messianic figures. (4Q flor.).

(4) Then, allegory. This is specially associated with Alexandrine schools of interpretation, both pagan and Jewish, and is easy to illustrate from Philo:

> *And Cain went out from the face of God, and dwelt in the land of Naid, over against Edom* [Gen. iv. 16].
> Let us here raise the question whether in the books in which Moses acts as God's interpreter we ought to take his statements figuratively, since the impression made by the words in their literal sense is greatly at variance with truth. For if the Existent Being has a face, and he that wishes to quit his sight can with perfect ease remove elsewhere, what ground have we for rejecting the impious doctrines of Epicurus, or the atheism of the Egyptians, or the mythical plots of play and poem of which the world is full? For a face is a piece of a living creature, and God is a whole not a part ...
> And whence does Cain 'go out'? From the palace of the Lord of all? But what dwelling apparent to the senses could God have, save this world, for the quitting of which no power or device avails? ...
> Well, if God has not a face ...; if he is to be found not in some particular part only, seeing that he contains all and is not himself contained by anything ...; the only thing left for us to do is to make up our minds that none of the propositions put forward is literally intended and to take the path of figurative interpretation so dear to philosophical souls ... (*De Post. Caini* 1-7, translation in C. K. Barrett, *Documents* (1956), No. 184.)

There follows a homily, supported by further allegorization, on the heinousness of voluntarily turning away from God. But this technique is by no means confined to Alexandria. We have already seen something like it in the Damascus document; and R. Longenecker (1975, 47 ff.)[1] calls attention to another instance in the Habakkuk 'commentary',

---

[1] In the same passage he alludes to allegory in the *Letter of Aristeas*, probably, like Philo's works, by a Hellenistic Jew in Egypt.

where 'Lebanon' and 'wild beasts' (quoted from Hab. ii. 17)
stand respectively for the Communal Council (? because
they wore white garments—Hebrew *lābān*), and (never mind
why!) for the simple Jews who carry out the Law. Obviously,
any *pēsher* may, and often does, employ allegory.

(5) The last of the five devices here selected—though
others could be cited—is the use of etymological conceits.
This, again, is one of Philo's methods. In *De Abrahamo*, for
instance, he develops and enlarges upon the difference
between the names 'Abram' and 'Abraham'. Though in fact
they are probably only alternative spellings of the same
name, Gen. xvii. 5 already draws a moral from supposed
differences in meaning—that is to say, the writer of that part
of Genesis itself is acquainted with this way of finding
spiritual lessons in words—and Philo does the same though
with different meanings. (*De Abrahamo* 81 ff.; see the notes in
C. K. Barrett's *Documents* (1956), No. 185.)

In all these uses, except the first, it is broadly true that no
attention is paid to the original meaning or to historical
perspective. The whole is treated in the flat, two-dimensional
way already referred to. Not only so, but in Jewish exegesis
arbitrary alterations are frequently made and embellish-
ments added. This is illustrable from almost any of the
Targums, that is, the interpretative expositions built up
round scripture by generations of 'rabbis'. Like Greek
ἑρμηνεία, *targum* means 'translation' or even (like *pēsher*)
'interpretation'. G. Vermes (1961) has carried out a comparative study of a selection of passages of scripture as they are
presented in certain of the most ancient Targums. To a
modern reader who is not familiar with such traditions, the
free and imaginative embroidering of the biblical stories will
seem extraordinary.

In sum, then, before Christianity came on the scene, there
was already a long history of biblical interpretation in
Judaism, in which a passage of scripture more often than not
was only the starting-point for or vehicle of ideas derived
from elsewhere in scripture or from outside scripture. The
divine authority of scripture is an axiom indeed; but the
authority for what was 'got out of' scripture was really not so

much scripture, as what was recognized and accepted and put into the exposition by a school of 'rabbis' or by their tradition or by an individual scholar. This is the heritage into which the earliest Christians entered. What did they do with it? The answer is, they took it and used it similarly—yet with significant differences.[1] Category (1) in our survey of Jewish methods—the direct application of ethical and moral injunctions—is prominent in the traditions of the teaching of Jesus himself,[2] though he is undeniably represented as also using other methods. As for (2), the most obvious verbal equivalent of *pēsher* in Greek, ἑρμηνεία, is not actually used to denote this particular activity, either in the Greek Old Testament or in the New Testament. In the New Testament, ἑρμηνεία occurs only in connexion with the interpretation of speech in 'tongues' (I Cor. xii. 10, xiv. 26). But the compound verb, διερμηνεύειν, is used at Lk. xxiv. 27 in an exactly comparable way, when the risen Christ 'interprets' the scriptural passages which refer to himself. So, too, ἐπίλυσις, meaning, essentially, 'unravelling', 'decoding', occurs in a significant context at II Pet. i. 20: 'no one can interpret any prophecy of Scripture by himself' (literally, 'no prophecy in scripture is of private ἐπίλυσις). Similarly, the corresponding verb, ἐπιλύειν, occurs at Mk iv. 34, where it is said that Jesus interpreted the parables privately to his own disciples. But, without these particular terms, the thing itself—interpreting scripture—occurs constantly all over the New Testament. An obvious instance is afforded by the 'formula quotations' in Matthew,[3] so called because they are introduced by a formula such as 'then was fulfilled ...' (Matt. ii. 17), or 'in order that what was spoken by the Lord through the prophet might be fulfilled ...' (Matt. i. 23).[4]

[1] Ellis 1977, 206, mentions some more incidental differences. There is a wealth of bibliographical references in the notes to that essay. For valuable bibliography, see also Cranfield 1979, 863, n. 1.

[2] See, e.g., Matt. iv. 4, 7, 10, Mk vii. 6 f., 10, viii. 18, x. 4, 7, 19, xi. 17, xii. 29–31. For discussion of this, see Edgar 1962; Hartman 1972, 151 f.; Mead 1963–64; Longenecker 1975, 69 f.; Thomas 1977–78.

[3] See, especially, Stendahl 1954; Gundry 1967.

[4] For a subtle and elaborate example, see Matt. xxvii. 9 f., with Dunn 1977, 92 f.

There are also such formulae as 'this is that which was spoken . . .' or simply 'that is' (like *id est*),[1] which identify a passage of scripture as relating to some contemporary event. See Acts ii. 16, Rom. ix. 7 f., x. 5 ff., Eph. iv. 9, I Pet. i. 25. The passage Rom. x. 5 ff. is, incidentally, a veritable Christian 'targum': using the 'that is' formula, Paul interpolates a running commentary between words from Deut. xxx, augmented also from Prophetic writings,[2] and himself decides (unless, indeed, he is borrowing from some already existing tradition unknown to us) who is speaking and what is meant.[3]

Thus, our number (2) is amply illustrated in the New Testament. So is the predictive variety of it numbered (3). R. N. Longenecker, in his analysis of Jewish uses of scripture (1975, Ch. I), points out that, in interpretations, it is often assumed that a scripture contains a secret (Hebrew, *raz*) which the writer himself did not understand but which was destined to be solved at some future date. When an interpreter claims that he can now point to the solution in some contemporary or impending event, Longenecker calls this a *raz-pēsher*—an interpretation concerning a secret. Thus, the Qumran Habakkuk commentary, citing Hab. ii. 1 f., declares:

> 'God told Habakkuk to write down that which would happen to the final generation, but He did not make known to him when time would come to an end. And as for that which He said, *That he who reads may read it speedily*, interpreted this concerns the Teacher of Righteousness, to whom God made known all the mysteries of the words of His servants the Prophets' (1Qp Hab. vii. 1-5ᵃ, translation in Vermes 1962).

This idea of a secret not divulged to the prophet who himself wrote about it, but awaiting solution in a subsequent generation, recurs in the New Testament at I Pet. i. 12:

> it was disclosed to them [the prophets] that the matter they treated of was not for their time but for yours. And now it has been openly announced to you through preachers . . .

[1] Bruce 1968.
[2] Ellis 1977, 201.
[3] See Suggs 1967; Jeremias 'Paulus' (1969).

THE USE OF THE JEWISH SCRIPTURES

Throughout the New Testament, indeed, the assumption is that what scripture spoke of relates to Christ and the events round him. It is instructive to compare the use of the same passages by the Qumran sectarians and by Christians and to see how each group appropriated them to its own use. Of these passages used in common by the Qumran sectarians and by Christians there are at least two:

(i) Isa. xl. 3:
> There is a voice that cries:
> Prepare a road for the LORD through the wilderness,
> clear a highway across the desert for our God.

1QS viii. 14-16 (translation in Vermes 1962):
> as it is written, *Prepare in the wilderness the way of ... make straight in the desert a path for our God.* This (path) is the study of the Law which He commanded by the hand of Moses, that they may do according to all that has been revealed from age to age, and as the Prophets have revealed by His Holy Spirit.

Matt. iii. 3 (cf. Mk i. 3 f., Lk. iii. 3 f.);
> It is of him [the Baptist] that the prophet Isaiah spoke when he said, 'A voice crying aloud in the wilderness, Prepare a way for the Lord; clear a straight path for him'.

(ii) Hab. ii. 4b:
> ... the righteous man will live by being faithful.

1Qp Hab. vii. 17—viii. 3a (translation in Vermes 1962):
> [*But the righteous shall live by his faith.*]
> Interpreted, this concerns all those who observe the Law in the House of Judah, whom God will deliver from the House of Judgment because of their suffering and because of their faith in the Teacher of Righteousness.

Rom. i. 17 (cf. x. 6):
> ... a way that starts from faith and ends in faith; as Scripture says, 'he shall gain life who is justified by faith'.

Heb. x. 38 f.:
> ... by faith my righteous servant shall find life ... we have the faith to make life our own.

In the case of both these passages, the interpreters, whether Jews of Qumran or Christians, assume that they refer to their own times and the circumstances and persons that are decisive for them. An impressive example of Christian

83

midrash is detected by P. Borgen (1965) in John vi;[1] and there are in the New Testament also examples of typology and allegory (type (4)—though the line between typology and allegory is not always easy to draw) and of etymological conceits (type (5)). For type (4), I Cor. x and II Cor. iii may be used as illustrations. In I Cor. x, Paul uses (with midrashic embroidering) the stories of the Israelites' initiation into Moses' community and the divine provision of food and drink for them in the wilderness (Exod. xvi, etc.), to warn Christians against imagining that participation in Christ insures them against disaster, any more than membership in the Israelite community and participation in the divine food saved the Israelites. In II Cor. iii, Paul contrasts the only intermittent glory of the Mosaic dispensation, as he deduces it from the story of the veil on Moses' face in Exod. xxiv, with the continuous and increasing glory of the Christian dispensation in which God is constantly present as Spirit; and he draws conclusions about the confidence to which an apostle is entitled.[2] Elaborate allegorizing occurs also in Gal. iv. 21 ff., as does verbal play in Gal. iii. 16. Finally, Heb. vii. 2 provides a good example of etymological fancies in the manner of Philo: Melchizedek, the priest-king of Salem, who comes suddenly on the scene in Gen. xiv without reference to his forbears, is interpreted as symbolic of Christ as eternal and as 'King of righteousness' ('Melchi-zedek') and King of 'peace' (Salem/shālōm).[3]

Thus, the current devices of non-Christian Jewish exegesis were, naturally enough, taken over bodily by the Christians, who, in the early days, were themselves Jews; and what seem, at least to a modern reader, as the sheer arbitrariness and the flat, 'two-dimensional' character of such methods were in no way repudiated by the Christians. The differences at first lay not in technique but in interpretation: whereas

[1] Cf. Dunn 1977, 87, and Smalley 1978, 110.

[2] See Dunn '2 Cor.' (1970); Moule 1972.

[3] Qumran has now yielded rich veins of evidence showing how popular Melchizedek was in Jewish typology and angelology. See especially the Genesis Apocryphon (1Q Gen. apoc. with Fitzmyer 1971) and the Melchizedek fragment from Cave 11 (11Q Melch. with de Jonge and van der Woude 1965–66); also Horton 1976.

non-Christian Judaism such as that of the Qumran sectarians placed one interpretation on (say) the way of the LORD in the wilderness, the Christian Jewish 'sectarians' (as they might at first have been called) placed another interpretation on the phrase. Sometimes, they might even exploit a mistranslation of the Hebrew by a Greek version, as seems to be the case in Acts xv. 17 and Heb. x. 5 (see commentators). Sometimes, the expositor, it would seem, might simply alter or add to his text on his own account, without the authority even of a current version.[1] Sometimes, two widely separated passages are brought side by side so as to obtain a meaning: Acts xiii. 34 f. and Rom. ix. 33 are cases in point. This is reminiscent of the 'rules' attributed to Hillel (see above, pp. 75 f.). Thus, Jerome was justified when he apostrophized Paul in the words:

> The proofs which you have used against the Jews or against other heretics bear a different meaning in their own contexts to that which they bear in your epistles. We see passages taken captive by your pen and pressed into service to win a victory which in the volumes from which they are taken have no controversial bearing at all.[2]

That was meant by Jerome as a compliment; and the so-called *Epistle of Barnabas* exercises the same liberty, in an extreme form, and glories in it (see ix. 9), as does Justin in his *Dialogue with Trypho*. A modern non-Christian Jewish scholar, however, H. J. Schoeps, castigates Paul for abusing the freedom proper to typological exegesis.[3]

It is easy enough, then, to find in the New Testament the old, 'two-dimensional', arbitrary uses of scripture, in which words originally referring to something quite different are

---

[1] This seems to have happened at Rom. x. 11, where πᾶς, 'everyone', appears to be Paul's own addition: see Ellis 1977, 202. In the same passage of Isa. in the LXX, xxviii. 16, ἐπ' αὐτῷ (used by Paul at Rom. ix. 33) is also an addition to the Hebrew text; but whether it is pre-Christian or not is another question. It is found in ℵ A Q, but omitted by B (see Swete's apparatus). On the interesting question of Eph. iv. 8, see Lindars 1961, 52 ff.

[2] *Epp.* xlviii. 13 (to Pammachius); translation from Schaff and Wace 1893, 73.

[3] 1961, 249 f. See also Ellis 1957.

simply commandeered to serve purely as vehicles for a conviction or a message of which the authority (of whatever sort it may be) is derived from elsewhere. The authority may be weighty and authentic: it may be the authority of an overwhelmingly convincing religious experience, or of some self-authenticating saying, or of a supremely convincing person—perhaps of Jesus Christ himself; but the words in which it is conveyed, although seeming to lend the authority of scripture, turn out, in fact, to be only a scriptural vehicle for an alien freight, and not to be speaking with whatever authority may inhere in the passage itself. It is sometimes alleged, indeed, that distinctively Christian interpretations of scripture in the early Church were largely the work of Christian prophets, claiming the afflatus of the Holy Spirit as their authority.[1] Whatever authority their interpretations carried would thus—at least when they were using scripture only as a 'vehicle'—be the authority of their own inspiration.

But for Christians' exegesis the prime authority was their experience of Christ—that is, both of Jesus as he was known (through the traditions or by direct eye-witness) in his circumstances, his character, his teaching, his deeds, and his death, and of Jesus the Lord as he was known as a constant, living presence: Jesus Christ the Lord, of whom they were convinced that he was the coping-stone and consummation of all that ideally the people of God were meant to be and to do, and of the relation that ideally existed between God and his people; of whom they experienced the presence and the releasing, rescuing, life-giving power in their lives.

The exegesis of the Qumran community was controlled by their conviction that they were living in the final period of God's plan for Israel, and that their 'Authentic Teacher' (or 'Teacher of Righteousness', *mōreh hassedeq*) was a specially endowed and chosen teacher. These eschatological and personal convictions they read into scripture. Comparably, the Christians went to scripture already convinced that Jesus had initiated the last period of world history and that, uniquely close to God and alive with eternal life, he was the Mediator of God's salvation. But there is a difference. The

[1] See an examination of this suggestion in Grudem 1978; Hill 1979.

Qumran sectarians did not, so far as any evidence goes, see in their leader the coping-stone and climax and fulfilment of the whole edifice of relations between God and man which is reflected in the scriptures. But in Jesus this is exactly what Christians did find. And this constitutes the vital and decisive distinctiveness of Christian exegesis. While it is undeniable that Christians applied the same arbitrary and artificial devices and, again and again, used scripture in a merely 'vehicular' manner, the incentive for their choice of passages and their interpretations of them was the discovery that, in a historical and 'three-dimensional' way, Jesus actually implemented and achieved in his person, and represented the culmination of, that relation between God and man which is the basic theme of scripture. This genuinely historical and 'three-dimensional' approach to scripture— the lines of divine-human relations converging on Jesus— which has only become deliberate and conscious in 'modern' thought, is, nevertheless, implicit in ancient Christianity in typology, when typology means drawing analogies and tracing connexions between Jesus Christ with his Church, and figures in the Old Testament representing relations between the divine and the human.[1] Thus, however incidentally and arbitrarily a particular passage of scripture may be commandeered as a vehicle, if the expositor is truthfully reflecting the Christian gospel, his exposition will be bearing witness to a real and unforced correspondence between the great types and patterns of relationship and their fulfilment and consummation in Christ, both as an individual (God's beloved Son) and as an inclusive and 'summary' figure (the Son, Israel, whom God called out of Egypt).[2] In this respect, Christian exegesis, using old techniques, proves to be unique and unparalleled. On no other great figure in Judaism, before or since, have all the collective figures and images of the people of God been seen to converge: the suffering Servant of Isa. liii (crushed, extinguished, but creating life and healing for others); the Son of Man of Dan. vii (the loyal people of God, brought

[1] See Dunn 1977, 86.
[2] Matt. ii. 15, iii. 17.

very low but vindicated in heaven); the Son of God of Exod. iv. 23, Hosea xi. 1 (chosen to have a close relation with his Father on behalf of man); the stone of Ps. cxviii. 22 f., rejected by the expert builders but, in the event, vindicated; the stone which, if trusted (Isa. xxviii. 16), becomes the very foundation-stone, but, if rejected, a cause of downfall (Isa. viii. 14). Indeed, over and above such symbols and metaphors, Jesus is seen as, collectively, Israel (for to be baptized 'into' him is to be more than circumcised 'into' the people of God, Col. ii. 11), and, more still, seen as, collectively, Man, Adam (for to be incorporated in him is to be remade in the image of God, Rom. v. 12 ff., Col. iii. 10). These conceptions of Christ, however metaphorical and parabolic, do not represent merely 'vehicular' uses of scripture: they represent, on the contrary, the recognition of Christ as the climax and fulfilment of all that scripture, critically and historically studied, reflects and represents as its ideal. In Christ are summed up the perfection of human response to God (individually and collectively) and God's response to man's need. Most notable is the recognition that the climax which has been reached in Christ introduces a new past tense, a note of fulfilment already achieved. This makes a genuinely Christian eschatology different, in its perspective and centre of gravity, from non-Christian Jewish eschatologies,[1] and it means that Christian faith is not at the mercy of the future tense, if hopes and expectations are deferred or unfulfilled. The 'vehicular' uses of scripture, common to both non-Christian and Christian exegesis, thus became in Christian exegesis only a symptom of something much profounder and deeper—something that the modern historian, whose approach is 'three-dimensional' not 'two-dimensional', can recognize as valid and supremely significant and quite distinctive.[2]

According to the traditions and the representations of Jesus in the Gospels (though each must be critically tested on its own merits) Jesus himself often used scripture in direct and simple ways, but also sometimes availed himself

[1] See Dahl 1971. Also Cullmann 1962, 1967; Ellis 1977, 210.
[2] See Moule 1967–68; 1977, Ch. 5.

of merely 'vehicular' uses of scripture. An extreme example is the Christological argument in Jn x. 34-36, where Jesus is represented as assuming that the phrase 'I said: You are gods' from Ps. lxxxii is addressed by God to those to whom God's message came (that is, presumably, inspired persons), and deducing, *a fortiori*, that the one whom God sanctified and sent into the world (that is, himself) should not be blamed for (*v.* 33) reckoning himself divine. A border-line case is in Mk xii. 26 f. and parallels, where Jesus is represented as drawing from the words 'I am the God of Abraham, the God of Isaac, and the God of Jacob' the conclusion that Abraham, Isaac, and Jacob must be alive, because God is not a God of the dead but of the living. No doubt the phrase need mean no more than 'I am the God to whom Abraham, Isaac, and Jacob once belonged'. Yet, the emphasis of scripture is certainly on God's initiative: it is he who adopts Abraham, not Abraham who chooses him; and there is a profound reality behind the faith that to belong to God and to be called by name by him is to have eternal life. It is a great 'relational' truth even if it is in a perhaps 'vehicular' text. Perhaps most significant of all in Jesus' use of scripture, according to the traditions about him, is the adoption of the human figure of Dan. vii as a symbol for his own vocation and that to which he summons his followers.[1] Incidentally, it is worth while to observe that the traditions represent Jesus' preaching and teaching to the crowds as appealing not to scripture but to analogies drawn from observation of country life or the manners and customs of his day. It is only in debate with the biblical scholars that he is represented as resorting to the scriptures.

Christian uses of scripture, then, although starting from common ground, created in the end a new thing. 'Historical typology came into existence with Christendom'.[2] In other words, the new, Christian phenomenon was the convergence of the Old Testament images and patterns on Jesus. That in him, as both an individual and one who transcended the individual, these patterns became coherent meant that the

[1] For this view, see Moule 1974, 413 ff.; and 1977, 11 ff.
[2] Lampe and Woollcombe 1957, cited by Moody Smith 1972.

history of Israel converged on him and that from him deployed the future of the people of God. It was the coherent organizing of all this into a single inclusive figure, the crown of Israel and the ultimate Adam, that made a completely new thing out of Jewish exegesis.[1] And whatever antecedents there were in the uses of scripture by Jesus himself, it was his living person even more than his remembered words that conditioned its course. To have lived responsively through the events of the ministry, death, and resurrection was to have gained a completely new angle of approach to scripture: or, to change the figure, it meant viewing the map of scripture for the first time as a genuinely three-dimensional relief map illuminated centrally by a brilliant light.

It was from this experience—though doubtless without a clearly articulated account of its implications for scripture—that the apostles and their companions first set out upon their witness, and their task of explanation. And this has brought us back to the point from which we began: the distinctiveness of the early Christian use of scripture is part of the conviction that, in Jesus, God had spoken directly to his people: that thus the voice of 'prophecy'—the immediate witness to the behest of God—had begun to sound again; that God had visited and redeemed his people and that a new understanding of his purposes had been vouchsafed. Therefore the Christians were no longer dependent upon rabbinic traditions for discerning the mind of God or upon the importuning of jots and tittles to yield up a message: they came to scripture from an already given experience, and had only to read in its main contours and its living story the confirmation that what they had experienced was not alien, though so new: it was the climax, the culmination, the 'Amen' to all God's purposes (II Cor. i. 20).

As has been said already, they had intensely difficult questions to answer: it must have seemed a quite preposterous story that they had to vindicate—'Christ nailed to the cross ... a stumbling-block to Jews and folly to Greeks' (I Cor. i. 23). And it was inevitable, that, in the course of

[1] See especially Dodd 1952. Cf. Bruce 1960, 77.

controversy, 'proof texts' should be invoked—in some cases, they may already have been used by Jesus himself. But behind all such adventitious uses of scripture, the Christians had their solid, impregnable experience. Whatever this verse or that might mean (or be tortured into meaning) they now had the key to the whole purposes of God—to sum up all things in Christ (Eph. i. 10). When Luther specified 'Christum treiben' ('to deal with Christ')[1] as the criterion of authentic scripture, he was, in effect, going back to the early Church.

We proceed now to set the main question of this book—How did the Christian writings come into existence?—in the context of scriptural exposition. What, for instance, lies behind such a passage as Rom. ix-xi, St Paul's extended defence of the Christian Gospel in the face of its rejection by the bulk of Judaism? Here we are immediately reminded of a persistent argument against Christianity. If the Gospel is really God's word, how comes it, its antagonists were continually asking, that God's own Israel have rejected it? According to the traditions, Jesus himself met the problem of unresponsiveness by the recognition that, as a matter of fact, this always had been the pattern in Israel. Was not the prophet warned that his message would be rejected? (Isa. vi); was it not the expert builders who rejected the most vital stone? (Ps. cxviii); is there not a famous passage about a stone that would cause downfall in Israel (Isa. viii)? And equally, the scriptural conviction of God's ineluctable purposes affirmed the ultimate vindication of what was temporarily rejected: the vital corner-stone did, in the end, come into its true position; the stone for stumbling over turned out, after all, to be a sure foundation (Isa. xxviii); the stone hewn by no human hands eventually came to shatter the fragile empires of the godless (Dan. ii); the despised and rejected human figure was vindicated (Dan. vii). And it was along these lines that debate developed in the apostolic age. Its results, negative and positive, are expressed in almost lyrical terms, in I Cor. i. 22-25:

[1] See, e.g., the Weimar edition, *Deutsche Bibel* 7, 384 f.

Jews call for miracles, Greeks look for wisdom; but we proclaim Christ—yes, Christ nailed to the cross; and though this is a stumbling-block to Jews and folly to Greeks, yet to those who have heard his call, Jews and Greeks alike, he is the power of God and the wisdom of God. Divine folly is wiser than the wisdom of man, and divine weakness stronger than man's strength.

Peter is shown in Acts iv. 11 appealing to the corner-stone saying:

This Jesus is the stone rejected by the builders which has become the keystone—and you are the builders.

At the end of the Acts Paul's last word to the unconvinced Jews as they leave the long debate is to quote the passage from Isa. vi (Acts xxviii. 25-28);

How well the Holy Spirit spoke to your fathers through the prophet Isaiah when he said, 'Go to this people and say: You will hear and hear, but never understand; you will look and look, but never see. For this people has grown gross at heart; their ears are dull, and their eyes are closed. Otherwise, their eyes might see, their ears hear, and their heart understand, and then they might turn again, and I would heal them'. Therefore take notice that this salvation of God has been sent to the Gentiles: the Gentiles will listen.

But sooner or later the thoughtful Christian disputant is bound to attempt to piece together these fragments of defence. If Israel was all along 'meant' to be unresponsive, then what of its future? If the Gentiles are now invited in, has God's election passed to them? And, if so, what of the constancy of God's promises? A major problem of 'theodicy' has developed; every Christian missionary is confronted by it in some form or another; but no one meets it in such an acute form, or is so well equipped to wrestle with it, as Paul, the rabbinically trained disputer with the Jews on behalf of the Gentiles. And we are fortunate to have, in Rom. ix-xi, the deposit of his conflicts. Gal. iii. 7—iv. 31 is an earlier specimen. The correlative to the *testimonia* for the obduracy of Israel is in the scriptures about God's welcome to the Gentiles. There is little evidence that Jesus appealed much to this during his ministry. Matt. viii. 11, 'many shall come from the east and west ...' (cf. Lk. xiii. 28 f.) may be a reminiscence of Isaianic phrases; but, in the main, a case can be made[1] for a deliberate reserve in this respect, and an application of the 'Gentile' scriptures rather to the post-resurrection situation. Acts xv. 16 f. affords one example; but it is Paul, especially in Rom. ix-xi and xv, who provides them in profusion.

But not all were travelling evangelists or skilled disputants. What of the humble Christians whose circumstances brought them into constant touch with non-Christian Jews—the Jewish Christians still living within the ghetto, or the Gentile Christians just outside it? It looks as though St Matthew's Gospel may represent the climax of a long process of evolving catechetical instruction designed for just such circumstances. It is possible that the Evangelist himself was not a Jew.[2] But in any case, it seems designed as an apologia, to be used by Christians in reply to curious or critical Jews. And its burden is that Jesus of Nazareth can be shown to have fulfilled the scriptural pattern, that he did not undermine the righteousness of Judaism, but, on the contrary, enhanced and completed it, and that to belong to Christ is truly to belong to Israel. And if members of Israel rejected him, so did their forefathers reject the prophets: true Israel has always been a remnant within the larger, degenerate mass. Nowhere else in the New Testament is so extreme an acceptance of precisionist Judaism enunciated as in Matt. v. 19. Verses 18 and 19[3] read:

> I tell you this: so long as heaven and earth endure, not a letter, not a stroke, will disappear from the Law until all that must happen has happened. If any man therefore sets aside even the least of the Law's demands, and teaches others to do the same, he will have the lowest place in the kingdom of Heaven, whereas anyone who keeps the Law and teaches others so will stand high in the kingdom of Heaven.

[1] Jeremias 1958.
[2] See, especially, Nepper-Christensen 1958.
[3] On which, in addition to plentiful earlier discussion, see Ljungman 1954; Nepper-Christensen 1958; Schürmann 1960; Barth in Bornkamm, Barth and Held 1963; Banks 1975.

It is perhaps (see further p. 128 below) intended to show that Christ has no intention to lower the highest standards of Israel but rather to heighten them:

> I tell you, unless you show yourselves far better men than the Pharisees and the doctors of the law, you can never enter the kingdom of Heaven (v. 20).

Yet nowhere is a self-regarding 'priggish' righteousness more ruthlessly attacked than in Matt. xxiii—the great onslaught on the doctors of the law and the Pharisees. It is widely recognized that such strictures are not justified if directed against Pharisaic Judaism in general and without discrimination, even if its unworthy representatives deserved the satire (as do, *mutatis mutandis*, unworthy Christians).[1] But the tone is understandable if it has been influenced by the situation of a Christian 'ghetto' within or near a Pharisaic group.

It is hardly surprising to find in Matthew a high proportion of the 'vehicular', 'pesher'-type uses of Scripture—the 'formula quotations' already referred to. One would expect this, if debate with non-Christian Judaism (as in Justin's *Trypho*) is an ingredient in its composition. A plausible case has been made for the interpretation of Matthew as the result of a 'school' of exegesis.[2] It is quite conceivable (though it cannot be demonstrated) that the better educated Christians, in such circumstances as have been described, should get together as a study-group to see whether they could not, for the benefit of themselves and of less well-educated members of the community, draw up a reply to their critics in their own language and with their own techniques. And if indeed the writer of this Gospel, or (if he was not himself a Jew) one among his circle, was a trained biblical scholar who had become a disciple in the Kingdom of Heaven (xiii. 52)—a converted scribe—here is at least a partial explanation of the phenomena. The only problem is

[1] See Garland 1979, reading Matt. xxiii as an attempt to elucidate the problem of the rejection of Jesus by the Jews and God's rejection of Israel in the war with Rome, and so to turn these judgments on the unfaithful leaders of the Christian Church.
[2] Stendahl 1954.

to explain the inclusion, here and there, of apparent mistakes about Judaism.[1] Perhaps, even if the writer was himself not a Gentile but a converted scribe, there were, in this scribe's group, at least some who did not know their way about Judaism as well as he did. A large number of Christian converts were from among the σεβόμενοι, the Gentiles who reverenced the God of Judaism. It is far from unlikely that these had a hand in the compiling and using of such a document. Or may it be, instead, that the final editor was not a biblical but a 'secular' scribe (exactly as Matthew himself, if a tax-collector, would have been)?

It must be added, at this point, that M. D. Goulder has proposed (1974, cf. 1978) to explain Matthew's Gospel as built up from Mark by 'midrash'. That is to say, Matthew has—for the purposes of providing edifying lections for Christian worship—embroidered his source into an elaborate structure of imaginary stories—of 'midrashim'—in the manner illustrated by G. Vermes (see above, p. 80) from later Jewish sources. While it is impossible to deny that such writing could have been conceived and done within a Christian context, this is decidedly speculative, as is J. Drury's similar proposal for Luke's Gospel (1976); and in the lack of reliable evidence for this, it is more reasonable to believe that Luke meant what he said in his preface about searching out the facts. If so, it follows that the postulate of a source besides Mark, shared in common by Matthew and Luke, makes good sense. Taking into consideration both this fact and the likelihood that the Synoptic Gospels were written primarily to supplement the proclamation of the gospel rather than as alternative sources of edification (see pp. 123 f.), the Goulder-Drury approach is not to be uncritically swallowed. There is extremely little in the New Testament to suggest the wholesale creation of material by the narrators.[2]

If much that went to the compilation of Matthew is correctly placed in the context of strenuous conflict between Church and Synagogue, the same may well be true of St

---

[1] See p. 125, 125 n. 4.
[2] See Dunn 1977, 99f.

John's Gospel. But its use of the Old Testament, though integral to its thought, is less direct, and consideration of it therefore (apart from the passages already adduced) scarcely belongs here. Returning to indications of public debate in the Acts, we are reminded that, besides the debates of Peter and of Paul, a vivid description of a different type of Jewish-Christian apologetic is offered in the account of Stephen in Acts vi, vii. Here is a man, who, like Jesus himself, is accused of a traitorous attack upon the very heart of Judaism—Moses and the Temple. His defence seems, at first sight, extraordinary, if not totally irrelevant. Instead of replying directly, he simply begins to recount the familiar story of the origins of Israel, from Abraham onwards. But after all there is a relevance in this; for he does it in such a way as to indicate that every advance involved the rejection of the traditional and the static; and that at every point the Holy Spirit is the Spirit of progress, of movement, of the refusal to be static; so that the heroes of Israel are all people of gigantic faith, exchanging the known for the unknown, abandoning the security of the familiar in blind obedience to the call of God. Abraham, Joseph, Moses—these are the three mighty men who laid the foundations of Israel by coming out, or going away, and by serving God in the dangerous and the unfamiliar. Accordingly, it is the portable tabernacle rather than the solid Temple that Stephen chooses as his symbol for the true worship of God; and it is Moses, foretelling a future Prophet, and David, debarred from building a static Temple, who are his pointers forward.

In other words, here is a lively defence of the Christian position by carrying the attack behind the enemy's lines: read your scriptures, Stephen is saying in effect, and you will find that it is the scriptures themselves that tell you to look beyond Moses and beyond the Temple (cf. Jn v. 39). Stephen was in all probability a 'Hellenist' (Acts vi. 1 ff.) —that is, a Jew who read his scriptures in Greek translation and who could not or did not speak Semitic languages; and he probably belonged to a synagogue of similar traditions (Acts vi. 9, cf. xi. 19 f.); and it seems entirely possible (although this is only a guess) that his successful disputing and his courageous death may have led to the conversion to Christianity of a group of like-minded Hellenistic Jews from this synagogue. May it not, then, be precisely such a group who are addressed by one of their number in the Epistle to the Hebrews? Its main argument runs in part along the very same lines as Stephen's—that true Judaism lies in advancing forward to Christ, not in retreating back to an entrenched position; that the tabernacle, even if it is preferable to the solid, static temple of Solomon, is still only a copy of the reality, which is the true, the eternal sanctuary in heaven; and that Moses is the pattern of that greater Moses who was to come. It is certainly not impossible, in view of this, that the apparent allusion in Heb. xiii. 7 to martyr-leaders may include Stephen himself.[1] At any rate, this epistle affords us a fascinating example of the final product, the written form, of precisely the kind of debate which is represented as in progress in the trial of Stephen; and it bears witness to yet another 'school' of interpretation, besides what may be postulated behind Matthew. Here is the carefully—indeed brilliantly—constructed apologia of an educated, Alexandrine-type Jewish Christian.[2] He is concerned to help his friends to meet the extreme temptation to relapse back into

---

[1] As a matter of fact, it is not impossible to fit Heb. ii. 3 f. into the same guess. This says that the Christian message was confirmed to the writer of the epistle and his readers by those who had heard it from the Lord himself, and that God added his own witness in signs and portents and various deeds of power and apportionings ($\mu\epsilon\rho\iota\sigma\mu\hat{o}\hat{i}\varsigma$) of the Holy Spirit, in accordance with his will. All this is entirely appropriate as a description of Pentecost, as we find it in the Acts story, by one who, though not an original disciple of Jesus, had been drawn into the Christian Church at that time—exactly as Stephen and his fellow-worshippers in his synagogue might have been. See Acts ii. 3 ('tongues' apportioned or distributed), 19 ('portents . . . and signs'), 36 ('let all Israel then accept as certain ∴ . .').

[2] In Heb. vi. 13 ff. much emphasis is laid upon the assurance provided by the divine oath in the passage about the promise to Abraham (Gen. xxii. 16 f.). The argument leads straight on, however, into the Melchizedek theme (vi. 20 ff.), and one might have expected immediate reference to the divine oath in the Melchizedek Ps. cx. This however, is reserved until vii. 20 f. This suggests, I think, very careful and thoughtful arrangement. The writer wishes to introduce the Melchizedek theme and to follow up first its Genesis-symbolism; he will not allow himself to be diverted to the oath of

Judaism, perhaps under nationalist pressure;[1] and he is using all his (or perhaps their joint) resources of scriptural exegesis to show the finality of Christ and his absolute superiority over Moses and all Jewish approximations. In Num. xii. 8 Moses is described in superlative terms, as the only one with whom God spoke face to face (literally, 'mouth to mouth'). It looks uncommonly as though Heb. iii. 1 ff., with its quotations from this very context, reflects conflict with the proof-text mind of a Jewish opponent, who had been saying 'Your claims for Jesus, even if they are soundly established, place him at best no higher than Moses'. Such an argument is reminiscent of the artificial proof-text method alluded to by a modern writer[2] who says that in face of the Christian doctrine of the virgin birth a Muslim will some-times appeal to Melchizedek's mysterious origin, and urge therefore that Jesus was no better than Melchizedek—thus taking a subsequent leaf out of this epistle's very argument and reversing it! At any rate, it is a familiar fact that this writer does indulge in a good deal of the 'Alexandrine' type of exegesis—depending on words and hints to make his points.[3] There are some applications of scripture which, to a modern reader, appear to be completely arbitrary. Thus, in ii. 13, two phrases from Isa. viii, both originally purporting to be from the lips of the Prophet Isaiah himself, are simply

Ps. cx until he is ready. Then, and not until he has finished with Genesis, this second oath-passage occurs impressively, to pick up that earlier reference to the Genesis oath.

[1] Another motive for relapse, besides the external pressures that might be applied in the name of racial loyalty, might be the more subtle psychological 'urge' to sink back into an old and well-tried way of life. Christianity, after all, must have seemed very newfangled and eccentric and dangerously adventurous. Further, there was the temptation, when Christian Jews were threatened with persecution from Gentiles, to come back under the protection of Judaism, as in the case of that Domnus, to whom Serapion of Antioch addresses a treatise, 'who had fallen away from the faith of Christ, at the same time of the persecution [of Severus], to Jewish will-worship' (Euseb, *H.E.* VI. xii. 1, Loeb translation).

[2] Crossley 1960, 18. Cf. Cragg 1956, 284 f.

[3] Thomas 1964–65, seems to establish that the writer knew a few of Philo's tractates, and, in some instances, was directly opposing Philo's interpretations.

assumed to be spoken by Jesus: 'I will keep my trust fixed on him' (Isa. viii. 17), and, 'Here am I, and the children whom God has given me' (*v.* 18). More startling still, in i. 10 ff., a majestic address to God as Creator of the world in Ps. cii is quietly assumed, without more ado, to be addressed to Christ:

> By thee, Lord, were earth's foundations laid of old,
> And the heavens are the work of thy hands . . .

In view of this, one is hardly surprised if the quotation from Ps. xlv in the preceding verses (i. 8 f.) is (though the syntax is notoriously uncertain)[1] addressed to Christ *as God*:

> Thy throne, O God, is for ever and ever . . .

Within the circle of believing Christians, such uses of scripture, though logically without defence, were undoubtedly acceptable because of the common presupposition of Christ's status and his unique oneness with God.[2] In just such a way, Isa. xlv. 23, on the lips of Yahweh ('. . . to me every knee shall bend . . .'), is transferred bodily to Christ in Phil. ii. 10 f. The Qumran Habakkuk 'pesher' operates in a similar way, when it transfers 'Thou art of purer eyes . . .' (Hab. i. 13) from God to a group of men (1Qp Hab. v. 6, 7).[3] But what is difficult to understand is how the writer to

---

[1] See Porter 1961 and Emerton 1968.

[2] See Westcott 1889, *in loc.* Synge 1959 suggests that the writer to the Hebrews uses a testimony book which was controlled throughout by the equations [cf. Burney 1925–26]: 'In the *beginning* God created' (Gen. i. 1) = in *Wisdom* God created (Prov. viii. 22) = in *Christ* God created; and by the assumption that Scriptural quotations are uttered by God to, or concerning, the Son of God. His proposed situation is that Hebrews was addressed (about A.D. 55) to non-Christian but friendly Jews who ministered to Christians. Similarly Kosmala 1959 learnedly and ingeniously argues for non-Christian Jews as the recipients of what was, in effect, a missionary tract. Schröger 1968, 70 f. mentions the view that Ps. cii can be interpreted as addressed to Christ equally well as to God *because of the Christology* of Heb. i. 2 f. But he prefers himself simply to accept that the χύϱιε (introduced by the LXX) is, for this author, Christ. See also Glasson 1966–67; Thomas 1964–65; and, earlier (from Thomas' bibliography in 1959), Bleek 1835; van der Ploeg 1947; Venard 1934, 23 ff. For the use made in Heb. of Ps. cx, see Higgins 'Old Testament' (1960).

[3] Cf. Bruce 1960, 12.

the Hebrews can venture to use such quotations if he has at least one eye on non-Christian Jewish critics. If, as is here assumed, the Epistle to the Hebrews is addressed to a situation where Christians need ammunition for Christian apologetic, to counter pressure from Judaism, then it would seem that the writer is offering very poor weapons. Of course this may only show that the assumptions about the circumstances are mistaken.[1] Yet, there is so much else in this writing that does seem to point to such circumstances that it would be hasty to jump to this conclusion merely because of what seem to the modern reader to be vulnerable arguments; and, after all, Jn x. 34 uses an equally vulnerable style ('I said: You are gods ...', from Ps. lxxxii) in what purports to be apologetic to Jews; and Justin, in what is undoubtedly intended as a Christian apologia to the Jew Trypho, uses exactly the same methods, and refuses to be deflected even when he himself represents Trypho as making the obvious objections. In *Dial.* lxxiii, Justin quotes Ps. xcvi (LXX xcv). 10, with its notorious Christian interpolation: 'The Lord reigned *from the tree* ($\dot{\alpha}\pi\dot{o}$ $\tau o\hat{v}$ $\xi\acute{v}\lambda o v$)', and bitterly accuses the Jews of having eliminated this phrase! To this, Trypho mildly replies that only God knows whether Justin is right in this allegation. But shortly afterwards (lxxiv. 1), he very justly adds that the Psalm seems to him to refer to the Father, the Creator, whereas Justin has referred it to 'this passible one' ($\tau\dot{o}\nu$ $\pi\alpha\theta\eta\tau\dot{o}\nu$ $\tauo\hat{v}\tauo\nu$) whom Justin is trying to prove to be the Messiah. Justin's reply, inevitably, can only assert that he is right and Trypho wrong. Evidently, Christians did use scripture, even in argument with unbelievers, in this manifestly inconclusive way.[2] These passages in Hebrews i and ii, together with the Moses-passage in Ch. iii, have been singled out for special mention as extreme examples of the arbitrary application of scripture. But throughout this writing the constant and often very subtle application of scripture makes it plausible to postulate for Hebrews, as K.

[1] So G. Hughes 1979.

[2] B. W. Bacon's extremely ingenious rescue-operation (1902) is therefore perhaps inappropriate. He maintained that the LXX had already turned these verses into an address by Yahweh to his Messiah.

Stendahl has postulated for Matthew, a 'school' of Christian apologetic: a systematic re-examination and re-application of the Greek scriptures by educated Christians in debate with scripture-searching non-Christians. And if one of them—their leader—is writing to the rest (cf. xiii. 19), it is natural that he should again go over the ground that they had traversed in their joint studies, reiterating, reapplying, and working them into an ordered whole.[1] It is true that he addresses them throughout as though he was their leader and father in God; and that once (v. 11 ff.) he complains that they are sluggish in understanding and are still children when they ought to be mature enough to teach others. But that still does not make it impossible to postulate previous concerted study under his leadership.

Another interesting phenomenon is one to which B. Lindars (1961) called attention and which J. D. G. Dunn takes up, namely, the multiple use of a single scripture. Certain passages are applied for different purposes and in different ways in different parts of the New Testament.[2] The most notorious example is Gen. xv. 6, the 'justification' of Abraham. This is used by Paul to reinforce his message of justification by faith (Rom. iv. 3 ff., Gal. iii. 6), but by James (ii. 23) to show that faith needs to be expressed in deeds. Similarly, Hab. ii. 4 is used by Paul in connexion with justification by faith (Rom. i. 17, etc.), but in Heb. x. 38 rather differently; and, interestingly enough, the same passage had already been interpreted by the Qumran sectarians with reference to loyalty to their teacher (1Qp Hab. vii. 17-viii. 3; above p. 83). Again, Isa. xlix. 6, apparently applied to Christ in Simeon's Song (Lk. ii. 32), is applied to the Gentile mission of Paul in Acts xiii. 47. By careful attention to 'shifts' such as these, in the application of a passage, it is sometimes possible to detect development in Christian apologetic.

Of all scriptures that Christians of the present day might have expected to be prominent in early Christian apologetic,

[1] The great preponderance of citations is from the Pentateuch and the Psalter. But there are also some from the Prophets and from the Writings other than the Psalms, and signs of a knowledge of apocryphal writings.

[2] Collected by Dunn 1977, 96 f.

Isa. liii is the chief: but in fact it is curiously seldom used in the New Testament. It would appear to combine, as has already been observed, the finest conception of the vindication of the martyr (herein comparable to the vindicated human figure of Dan. vii) with the even finer conception of the redemptive power of the martyr's death, even for his tormentors and oppressors. And, *a priori*, one would have expected that Isa. liii would have been prominent both in Jesus' own interpretation of his mission and ministry and in early Christian evangelism and apologetic. .

But in fact the only explicit quotation from Isa. liii on the lips of Jesus in the Gospels is the allusion, peculiar to Luke, to his 'being reckoned among the lawless' (Lk. xxii. 37)—not a redemptive allusion. Whatever other allusions we may detect in the words of Jesus are in phrases not demonstrably dependent on the words of Isaiah: Mk x. 45 and the words of Institution.[1] And even the New Testament writers themselves make surprisingly little use of the Servant Songs. Outside the New Testament, but within the first century, I Clement xvi cites Isa. liii at length, though even then, it is related only to Christ's example of humility; and *Barnabus* v. 2 cites the 'redemptive' passage. But within the New Testament, how little it is used! Most scholars hear a Servant Song echo in the baptismal Voice (Mk i. 11 and parallels) but it is not demonstrable. Matthew applies Isa. liii. 4 to Jesus' ministry of healing (viii. 17); Acts iii. 13 probably uses παῖς in this sense[2] (Acts iv less probably: see p. 30, above); Philip the evangelist applies Isa. liii. 7 f. (about the humble submission to injustice) to Jesus according to Acts viii. 32 f.; Acts xiii. 47 applies another Servant Song (Isa. xlix. 6) to the apostles; I Pet. ii. 24 has a definite application to the death of Christ of the redemptive words (the solitary instance in the New Testament). But in Paul's writings, where one would expect much, there is little. Unless Phil. ii contains allusions

[1] See Hooker 1959; Moule, 'Defendant' (1967); S. K. Williams 1975. On Mk x. 45 in particular, see Hooker, *op. cit.*, 69 n. 1 and Barrett 1959. *Contra*, Moulder 1977–78.
[2] See Cullmann 1959, 79; though Scobie 1979–80, 418, n. 86, would prefer to link it here with Moses.

to the Hebrew text of Isa. liii (and this, though certainly possible and even probable, is not demonstrable),[1] the only other allusions are in Rom. iv. 25 and x. 16. The former is a definitely redemptive allusion (but how fleeting!); the latter is a citation of Isa. liii. 1 in the interests of showing that Israel's obduracy was all along recognized by scripture as something to be expected and reckoned with.

Thus, a passage of scripture that might have been expected to contribute signally to the formation and shaping of Christian apologetic is singularly rare. One can only surmise that it had somehow been vitiated for this purpose—that it had already been spoilt or blunted as an argument directed to the Jews, by some circumstances no longer clearly discernible to us. Jeremias has argued that Isa. liii had in pre-Christian times been applied by some to the Messiah (or to God's chosen Deliverer in some form), and that it was because the Jews realized too clearly its applicability to Jesus that they reacted against this and began to impose on the passage a quite different interpretation. Later rabbinical interpretations show how the suffering had, by then at least, been applied to the Jews' enemies, and only the exaltation and glory to their own nation or its representative.[2] If such interpretations began to be used very early in the Christian period, it is possible to imagine why Christian apologists seldom appealed much to Isa. liii: they knew in advance how their exegesis of it would be countered by their opponents. But this would still go only a little way towards explaining why the traditions about the words of Jesus himself show so little direct trace of its use by him; for the contents of these traditions are at other points by no means wholly conditioned by what the Church seems to have found useful or interesting for itself; and if Jesus had often quoted Isa. liii, one would expect that, even after it had been largely abandoned by Christian apologetic, it would still survive among his words. Jesus' life, death, and resurrection were

[1] See R. P. Martin 1967.
[2] See Jeremias in *T.D.N.T.* v. 682 ff.; and note especially the apparently messianic interpretation of Isa. lii. 14 implied by one of the Qumran texts (1Q Isa. A): see Bruce 1960, 56.

clearly recognized by the Church (and, the evidence seems to suggest, by himself also) as redemptive: this is the Gospel of Paul, of Peter, of the Epistle to the Hebrews, and of the Johannine writings, even if one leaves out of account the Synoptists and Acts. Yet the only clearly redemptive-suffering passage in the Jewish scriptures is only sparingly used. Here is a phenomenon that still awaits explanation.[1]

Enough, however, has perhaps been said to indicate, by a few selected examples, how the scriptures entered into early Christian apologetic, until sooner or later whole tracts, such as Rom. ix-xi and the Epistle to the Hebrews and Matthew and the Apocalypse—a tissue of Old Testament quotations and allusions[2]—were the result.

Outside and beyond the New Testament one finds other extended examples, such as *The Epistle of Barnabas*, Cyprian's books of testimonies, and Justin's *Dialogue with Trypho*. Comparison of these with the New Testament serves to throw into sharp relief the prevailing sanity and reserve of the New Testament.

But the mention of Cyprian is a reminder that it is relevant to our enquiry to ask whether we are to imagine the Christians of the New Testament period already, like Cyprian and Melito before him (Euseb. *H.E.* IV. xxvi. 12, 13), using 'testimony books'—anthologies of such Old Testament passages as were regarded as significant for Christians. J. Rendel Harris (1916, 1920) answered in the affirmative. Working back from Cyprian's books of testimonies (*Testimoniorum libri* III *ad Quirinum, c.* A.D. 249), and observing such phenomena as the juxtaposition of the 'stone-passages' from Isa. viii and xxviii in Rom. ix and I Pet. ii, he suggested that the evidence pointed to the very early use of such testimony books. More recently C. H. Dodd, followed by J. W. Doeve and others, argued that the New Testament data would be satisfied by postulating simply that, without necessarily using written anthologies at all, the Christians learnt to use

---

[1] Cullmann 1959, 81, discusses why the suffering servant idea was not used in worship and adoration; but a satisfactory explanation of that would still not account for its non-use in apologetic.

[2] See Sweet 1979, 39 f.

whole sections of scripture in the light of the events they had experienced, and that these sections thus came to be associated together in their minds and on their lips. It is difficult, even so, to see, *prima facie*, any reason why written collections should not also have been in circulation, especially in view of the Qumran 'florilegium' and messianic 'testimonia', and M.D. Hooker (1959, 21 ff.) has questioned whether Dodd's claims can be upheld, at any rate, in the case of the Servant Songs.[1]

If written testimony-collections were used, we are confronted once again with the long-debated suggestion that the Hebrew *logia* attributed by Papias to Matthew (Euseb. *H.E.* III. xxxix. 16) were Old Testament *testimonia*. On the whole, however—even if we allow the probability that testimony-books circulated in early days—the likelihood is that Papias meant by *logia* sayings of Jesus, and that what he is describing is something like what critical scholarship has labelled 'Q'—a collection, or a group of collections, of sayings of Jesus, believed to have been drawn upon in the compilation of the Gospels according to Matthew and Luke.[2] That such a sayings-collection should have been associated with Matthew the apostle is not *a priori* unlikely. At any rate, whatever answers are given to the questions whether there were testimony-books and whether the *logia* were Old Testament testimonies or sayings of Jesus, the important fact remains that early Christian writings took shape under the influence of Christian interpretation and

[1] Dodd 1952; Doeve 1953; Ellis 1957, 98 f. On the other hand, the Qumran collections (notably 4Q Test.) must be taken into account: see, especially, Braun 1966, 325, commenting on Fitzmyer 1957. A valuable review of the situation is that by Ellis 1977, with ample bibliography. See also Snodgrass 1977–78, arguing, with reference to 'Stone' testimonies, that Isa. viii and xxviii were already related in Isaiah itself, but that Ps. cxviii was a Christian addition; and Hodgson 1979, adding 4Q Tan. and 4Q Ord. to the Qumran evidence, and indicating tests that might be applied in further investigation.

[2] For the question whether Q is a necessary hypothesis, see p. 127 and Excursus IV. As for the origin of the symbol Q, it is usually assumed to stand for 'Quelle', German for 'source', and this, though it has been questioned, seems now to be decisively vindicated. The curious may consult R. H. Lightfoot 1935, 27, n. 1; Howard 1938–39; H. K. McArthur 1976–77; Neirynck 1978; Silbermann 1979–80.

application of Jewish scriptures. When it is claimed that whole sections in the Gospels were spun out of Old Testament material, this is far out-running the evidence. In the main, the evidence points to the Gospel events as the controlling and decisive factor, to which the Old Testament material is almost always subordinate. Here and there an Old Testament passage may have contributed some circumstantial detail in the recounting of a tradition about Jesus—the two beasts in Matthew's triumphal entry (Matt. xxi. 2, 5) provide a standard instance. Similarly, A. Guilding (1960, 232) attributes the name Malchus in Jn xviii. 10 to the Old Testament lection which her theory finds behind this passage. But it is questionable whether any story of Jesus in the New Testament has been generated, from start to finish, by nothing but an Old Testament passage.

On the contrary, the fact is rather that the choice of Old Testament passages is determined by the Christian events and their interpretation dictated by Christian tradition. Indeed, it is plausibly suggested (by Barnabas Lindars, 1961, 59 ff.) that it was (for instance) the literal fulfilment of what he believes may have been Christ's own prediction that he would rise again 'on the third day' that the Christians first fastened upon; and that it was only secondarily that they attached it to Hos. vi. 2, although it may have been from here that Jesus himself drew the phrase (using it idiomatically to mean 'very soon').

The Christians thus found themselves pushed by the pressure of events into a new way of selecting, relating, grouping, and interpreting what we call 'Old Testament' passages;[1] and, while the scriptures of the Jews undoubtedly exercised a great influence upon the form in which they presented their material, and ultimately upon the very writing and collecting of the Christian scriptures, this influence was evidently subordinate both to the influence of the apostolic witness to Jesus and to the living inspiration of Christian prophets in the Church.

[1] There was as yet, of course, no defined 'canon' of scripture; and the books used by (e.g.) St Paul evidently included some that we now know as 'apocrypha' and even 'pseudepigrapha'.

CHAPTER V

THE CHURCH EXPLAINS ITSELF:
3 The Gospels and the Acts

CHAPTER III contains a preliminary review of some of the basic questions which the Church had to answer as it gradually emerged into an awareness of its distinctiveness. Chapter IV considered various ways in which the use of the Jewish Scriptures by the Christians reflected and clinched this awareness. It is now time to inquire into some of the circumstances leading to the creation of material now in the Gospels and the Acts, and to ask how the units of tradition behind them and the ways in which they were used reflect the questions Who are we? and Who is Jesus? The development of the Gospel tradition can be profitably studied for many other purposes; but in this chapter it seems suitable to look at it from this particular angle: What sort of information does it give us concerning the ways in which the early Christians thought about Jesus and about themselves and about others, and concerning what stages their thinking went through?

During gestation, an embryo is said to go through the main stages of the evolution of the species, recapitulating in a single individual the steps by which that species was brought into existence. So through each of the canonical Gospels it is possible to trace—even if dimly and uncertainly and not necessarily in their true sequence—some of the stages by which their component parts reached their present form. So far as this story can be reconstructed at all, it will constitute part of our account of how the Church explained itself, to itself and to others.

It is here that the technique infelicitously known in English as form criticism (see above, pp. 3 f.) attempts to probe the pre-history of each unit of tradition. The main conclusion is that, undoubtedly, units of tradition underwent modification and adaptation in the course of their transmission,[1] and in these alterations can sometimes be seen reflected some of the varying needs and circumstances and outlook of different Christian congregations. Papias is reported by Eusebius (*H.E.* III. xxxix. 15) to have said that Peter 'used to make the teachings' (which, presumably, means, 'used to recount the teachings of Jesus') 'πρὸς τὰς χρείας—with reference to the needs' (i.e. as occasion demanded, as need arose), and therefore not in chronological order. This is exactly how form criticism has taught us to understand the use and the history of units of tradition: they were applied to each need as it arose. Sometimes it is possible, with at least some degree of plausibility, to reconstruct the demands and needs reflected in the various forms of a unit of tradition as they occur in different Gospels or other early writings. But seldom, if ever, can one claim to have constructed a completely reliable 'genealogy', so to speak, of a unit, so that each stage in its ancestry may be placed in its correct sequence and a fully coherent account be given of the development and changes of outlook in the early Christian communities. Form critical sketches, useful as a hypothesis, are seldom an entirely firm foundation for an account of the New Testament world. E. P. Sanders has demonstrated[2] that most of the criteria commonly employed to determine the sequence of different forms of a tradition are inconclusive; and M. D. Hooker has more than once[3] observed how blunt the tools are—when not simply inappropriate. But there are no others; and one has to rely on cumulative evidence, convergence, coherence, and so forth.

Nowhere are both the value of form criticism and its limitations more clearly evident, and nowhere has more intensive research been applied, than in the elucidation of

---

[1] An extreme example of irreconcilable divergence between two forms of a tradition is provided by the two stories of the death of Judas Iscariot in Matt. xxvii. 3-10 and Acts i. 18 f. See Dunn 1977, 72.

[2] E. P. Sanders 1969.

[3] Hooker 1970–71, 480 ff.; 1972, 570 ff. See also other studies such as Calvert 1971–72, 209 ff.; Hickling 1974.

the parables and of the miracle stories. Regarding the latter, it is widely believed[1] that the so-called 'divine man' (θεῖος ἀνήρ), a wonder-worker with spectacular powers, was a recognisable type, familiar in Hellenistic thought at the time, and that, in Christian tradition, there were whole sequences or *catenae* of miracle stories which cast Jesus in just such a rôle, showing him as supreme among such figures, and able to rival the best of them. Further, it is widely believed that it was Mark, or some predecessor of his, who first transformed material from such sequences of miracle stories into some-
- thing very different.[2] In Mark's Gospel, the miracles are not mere demonstrations of the wonder-worker's success and superiority: they are indications of the presence and of the acknowledgement of God's sovereignty. Never is Jesus mere-ly a supremely successful thaumaturge: rather, he is the Son of Man on his way to the cross, and the wonders are chiefly evidence not of his own superiority but of his obedience to God's design.[3] Thus, the miracle tradition is placed under the sign of the cross and turned into a new thing. But how securely based is the theory that this was new?

Of course there is every probability that miracle stories about Jesus did circulate in the oral period—perhaps in connected sequences or *catenae*—and that they had been modified and adapted in the course of transmission.[4] What is questionable (and certainly not proved) is that these stories were, at any stage, of an 'exhibitionist' kind or were ever circulated in forms which obscured the cross and the destiny of Jesus as the bringer of salvation in God's hard paradoxical way. That this conception was a change, due to editing and adapting, is an insecurely founded hypothesis. Of course the wonder-worker was a well known figure in popular thought, both Jewish and Hellenistic, even if it is questionable whether the particular term, 'divine man', was as familiar as

[1] See Dunn 1977, 71, for a summary.

[2] For the application of the same sort of idea to the Fourth Gospel, see Dunn 1977, 303. For the idea that the Gospels all present *corrections* of false ideas of Jesus, see Talbert, 1977, 98.

[3] See Reumann 1968, Ch. 7.

[4] See Fridrichsen 1972; R. M. Grant 1952; Moule, ed., *Miracles* (1965); Achtemeier 1970, 1972 (*bis*).

has been alleged.[1] But where is the evidence that, in the case of the traditions about Jesus, the wonderful deeds were ever recounted, in the manner of these popular tales, as the 'success stories' of a mere wonder-worker, without relation to the cross? Is it not possible that it was Jesus himself who worked the change in perspective, and that, since he himself was no ordinary thaumaturge, the traditions about him, unlike those about other wonder-workers, carried this paradox in them from the beginning? The nearest that the canonical New Testament comes to making a 'success story' out of wonder-working is, as a matter of fact, in Luke and Acts: and who is to say that it was not Luke who thus brought the original, paradoxical traditions about Jesus' unusual way more closely into line with the Hellenistic style and presented the mighty deeds of Jesus as evidence of the superior 'success' of Christianity in the same category as its rivals?[2] That the miracle stories, like the other units of tradition, underwent adaptation and change is not to be denied: one has only to compare the different versions of a story in the canonical Gospels, and, where it is possible, to look beyond the canonical to the apocryphal Gospels, to be convinced of that. But the 'moral', so to speak, of the forms in Mark's Gospel need not be so different as is usually assumed from that of the forms of the oral period that preceded it. The alleged 'messianic secret', which is frequently associated with the alleged reinterpretation in Mark's Gospel, cannot be shown to have been forcibly imposed upon earlier tradition.[3]

Still less plausible are theories that the Evangelists who followed Mark simply spun midrashic elaborations of his Gospel out of their heads with regard only to edification and

[1] The idea is especially associated with Bieler (1967 etc.), but has been questioned by Tiede 1972 and Holladay 1977.

[2] See Dunn 1977, 20, 180 ff. And, for an original treatment of the handling of the miracle tradition in the Gospels, Hull 1974.

[3] William Wrede's famous theory is open to question, if only because it depends on treating as uniformly messianic the secrecy which, in most instances in Mark, is *not* strictly *messianic*. See Wrede 1971; Dunn, 'Messianic Secret' (1970); W. C. Robinson 1973; Lemcio 1975; Moule 1975 (with bibliography there).

without the use of sources.[1] There is a difference between sheer improvisation and the adaptation of existing tradition (even if there is a blurred borderland between the two); and, in view of all that the hypothesis of sources helps to explain, the burden of proof is on the shoulders of those who deny sources. But however radical or conservative one's guesses may be about the extent of alteration undergone by the traditions before they reached a given Evangelist's formulation, the undeniable fact remains that comparison of the Gospels does reveal alteration. Unless one clings to the improbable thesis that a number of similar but not identical sayings and anecdotes have been preserved, some by one Evangelist, some by another, each having travelled unaltered along a single channel of transmission, one is bound to recognize that, somewhere along its course, a single tradition has fanned out into a number of different versions. This is particularly evident in the parables.[2] It is sometimes possible to make plausible suggestions as to the setting and purpose of each of two versions of a parable. The parable of the lost sheep, for instance, is in the Lucan version (xv. 4 ff.), entirely appropriate to the period of Jesus' own ministry. It constitutes a telling defence of his habit of fraternizing with the unorthodox, the irreligious, the 'drop-outs' and the lost. But in Matthew (xviii. 12 ff.) it seems rather to be intended as an incentive to Christian pastors to bring back straying or lapsed members of the Christian community. Again, each of the versions of the parable of the great feast seems to reflect special conditions—in the Lucan version (xiv. 16 ff.), the successive missions to the Jews and to the Gentiles, in the Matthean version (xxii. 2 ff.), possibly—though this is guess-work—the destruction of Jerusalem viewed as a neme-

[1] Goulder 1974, 1978 for Matthew; Drury 1976 for Luke. Trocmé 1973, 24, is inclined to think of a fairly uniform tradition until the written Gospels began to shape it in different ways. If Riesenfeld, 'Gospel Tradition' (1970) and Gerhardsson 1961 and 1964 were right, the changes would have to have set in after the verbatim apostolic tradition had been left behind.

[2] For the various kinds of alteration undergone by the parable traditions, see Jeremias' *Parables* (1963), 113 f., and Dunn 1977, 73 ff. And, for a useful survey, see Reumann 1968, 159 ff.

sis for the Jews' rejection of Jesus. The later Coptic *Gospel of Thomas* now provides yet another version of this (*Thomas*, Saying 64), as of many other Gospel parables, and invites guesses as to its quite different setting and purpose and theological outlook. Again, whereas in Matt. xiii. 47 ff. there is a parable of a dragnet which seems to mean that ultimately there must be a judgment separating good and bad, in *Thomas* (Saying 8) there is a net which contains plenty of small fish but only one big one which the fisherman keeps— apparently a message about 'priorities' rather than about the last assize. Similarly, there are subtle differences in the parable of the sower in Matthew, Mark, Luke, and *Thomas* (Saying 9), each having its own peculiarities. Once more, it is difficult to resist the impression that Lk. xvi. 8 ff. represents a whole series of morals, attached, at one time or another, to the single parable of the dishonest bailiff:

> . . . For the worldly are more astute than the other-worldly in dealing with their own kind.
>
> So I say to you, use your worldly wealth to win friends for yourselves, so that when money is a thing of the past you may be received into an eternal home.
>
> The man who can be trusted in little things can be trusted also in great; and the man who is dishonest in little things is dishonest also in great things. If, then, you have not proved trustworthy with the wealth of this world, who will trust you with the wealth that is real? And if you have proved untrustworthy with what belongs to another, who will give you what is your own?
>
> No servant can be the slave of two masters; for either he will hate the first and love the second, or he will be devoted to the first and think nothing of the second. You cannot serve God and Money.

Again, the allegorical interpretation of the tares among the wheat (Matt. xiii. 36 ff.) seems better suited to the apostolic age, when 'Church' and 'world', true Christian and spurious Christian, were contrasting but confused elements, than to the ministry of Jesus himself when the antithesis might rather have been disciple over against antagonist, with very little danger of mixture or confusion.

But criticism ceases to be scientific if, on the basis merely of such more or less clear examples as these, it jumps to the conclusion that no allegory can have been dominical, that all the attack and reproof in the original parabolic teaching of Jesus was directed to his opponents, and that Jesus never told parables having reference to the ultimate 'end of the age' or directed to his own disciples' condition. The fact is that a far greater bulk of parabolic teaching, as it stands in the Gospels now, can be fitted quite naturally into a setting within the ministry of Jesus, than critical (but perhaps too *little* critical) scholarship sometimes allows; and that we must not too lightly assume the marks of 'edificatory adaptation' everywhere. Take a seldom noticed instance from Matt. xxiv. 45, Lk. xii. 42.

In these two parallel passages there is a saying of Jesus beginning, in both cases, with τίς ἄρα . . .; 'Who, then . . .?' and continuing, with only small divergences of vocabulary and style, through a full-length parable. (The ἄρα is not translated in the *N.E.B.* of Matt. xxiv. 45; in Lk. xii. 42 it appears as 'Well, . . .') The only substantial difference between the Matthean and Lucan versions is that Matthew's 'Who, then . . .?' is absolutely unheralded, whereas Luke's is introduced by (*v.* 41) 'Peter said, "Lord, do you intend this parable specially for us or is it for everyone?"'. But this small difference is a most remarkable one. In the first place, one is familiar with the idea that it is Matthew, not Luke, who multiplies allusions to Peter. Yet here it is Luke who mentions Peter. Secondly, the direct question about the intended recipients of the preceding saying—are they the disciples or everyone generally?—is arresting and unparalleled (Mk xiii. 37 makes the same distinction, but not in a disciple's question). And thirdly, it is this question alone that lends logic to the ἄρα, 'then', which, in Matthew, without this antecedent clause, is practically pointless. It is true that there is one other instance of such an unintroduced ἄρα in Matthew, namely Matt. xviii. 1, where the disciples ask 'Who, then, is greatest in the kingdom of Heaven?' But this may at least be explained as meaning something like the English 'after all', and as implying antecedent discussion among the disciples.

These considerations together add up to a case for regarding the Lucan version as the closer to the original; or, to put it otherwise, a case against the assumption that Lk. xii. 41, the Peter-clause, is a mere editorial invention. If this is a 'Q'-passage, then Luke's fuller text has perhaps reproduced it more faithfully. The Matthean hanging ἄρα, 'then', is hanging precisely because it is torn from its context.

If this be conceded, then the very setting of the parable goes back to an early source; and the assumption that the question, or even the whole passage (in either Gospel) is a later (and so post-dominical) accommodation to an ecclesiastical situation and to the delay of the *parousia* is to that extent weakened. And yet, if one adopts the opposite assumption—that it is substantially a dominical dialogue from within the ministry—does it yield a conceivable sense? It appears to say: 'This summons to alert readiness (Matt. xxiv. 44, Lk. xii. 40) is directed not to all and sundry but to you, the specially chosen Twelve. You are to be faithful in dispensing whatever it is that you are commissioned to dispense; otherwise you will be caught off your guard'. Is there any conceivable *Sitz im Leben Jesu*, any setting within the ministry, for such a summons?

Perhaps there is. It is notoriously difficult (see pp. 127 f. below) to 'place' Matt. x. 23 (the famous saying—central in Albert Schweitzer's theory of a disillusionment in Jesus himself—about the Son of Man's coming before the cities of Israel had all been visited); but the very fact that it so ill suits a post-resurrection setting with the beginnings of the Gentile mission gives some plausibility to finding some place within the ministry of Jesus for the prediction of a limited (though only a limited) delay of the Son of Man. And in Lk. xix. 11 ff. the parable of the minas is introduced by the preface: '. . . he went on to tell them a parable, because he was now close to Jerusalem and they thought the reign of God might dawn at any moment'. Why this very circumstantial linking of the parable with the approach to Jerusalem, if in fact the purpose of the evangelist was to detach it from the ministry and apply it to a permanent situation?[1]

[1] Cf. Cullmann 1960, 279.

Is it possible, then, after all, that the parable of the unfaithful servant has been too hastily assumed to have been shaped to the needs of ecclesiastical office-holders? Is the hanging ἄρα, 'then', pointing to the genuineness of the Petrine exordium (preserved by Luke, not by Matthew with his Petrine interests!), a possible clue to the historicity of injunctions given by Jesus during his ministry to the Twelve to be faithful in their dispensing of the message of the Kingdom? It is far from a demonstration of the case, but it is perhaps enough to demonstrate the insecurity of the opposite assumption if it be based only on such arguments as are here called in question.

Another example of the questionable wisdom of assuming the adaptation principle too readily is the parable of the sower in Mk iv.[1] It is often said[2] that the parable proper (*vv.* 3-9) is more or less original and authentic, but that the allegorizing interpretation (*vv.* 14-20) represents an addition and adaptation by early Christian teachers and preachers— not to mention the further reflections in *vv.* 21-25. Further- more, it is either held that the difficult *vv.* 10-13 are not dominical, but reflect a rather later predestinarian attitude regarding unbelieving Jews (and appeal is made to the vocabulary of these sections to support the hypothesis of their alien character); or else that the verses, though domi- nical, are misplaced, and belong in a different context.

But there are weaknesses in such assumptions. First of all, what did the original parable mean, if not what it is made to mean in *vv.* 14-20? The answer offered by C. H. Dodd is that it meant: 'Can you not see that the long history of God's dealings with His people has reached its climax? After the work of the Baptist only one thing remains: "Put ye in the sickle, for the harvest is ripe"' (1978, 135). J. Jeremias' answer is similar: 'In spite of every failure and opposition . . . God brings forth the triumphant end which he had prom-

---

[1] The five paragraphs which follow are borrowed, with only small adjustments (by kind permission of the S.C.M. Press) from what I wrote in *Religion in Education*, spring 1961, 61 f. Add, now, Moule 1969; Boucher 1977.

[2] From at least the time of Jülicher 1899, i. 118 ff. See Klemm 1969.

ised' (1963, 150). But this brief message is better conveyed by such parables as that of the leaven and the mustard seed. Why all this circumstantial detail—path, rock, thorns, good ground (all, moreover, perfectly natural, unforced features)—if that is all that was intended? Surely it is actually more scientific to recognize the simple fact that this realistic picture of a sower at work presents, without the slightest forcing or squeezing (how different from the frigid, laboured allegory of, e.g., Hermas, *Similitudes*, ix. 17 ff.!), a vivid analogy to the varied response with which the teaching of Jesus was met. In other words, here is a parable about the reception of Jesus' own parabolic teaching—a parable so circumstantial that it happens also to be a ready-made allegory.

'Parable', as it is commonly distinguished from 'allegory' by writers on this subject, presents a genuine, straight analogy—say, from the realm of physical life to that of human character. But this particular parable chances to be also an unforced allegory: there are good, natural analogies in its details as well as in its broad effect. Is that unthinkable for the original teaching of Jesus?

Then, next, even the difficulty of the bridge-passage, *vv.* 10-13, has been exaggerated. First, it is quite gratuitous to assume that the categories of 'those outside' and 'those inside'[1] are meant to be rigid and 'predestined'. What about Mk viii. 18, where the disciples themselves are clearly being classed as deaf and unseeing? Surely the simplest view is that men are 'outside' or 'inside' according to their response. It is impossible to convert or persuade by mere dogmatizing or ranting. No amount of mere statement, no 'spoon-feeding' (as every teacher knows) will achieve this end. There is nothing for it but to sow 'seed-thoughts'—to set something germinating in the hearers. If they respond, they begin to be 'inside', they 'come for more'; if they pay no heed—or for as long as they pay no heed—they are self-excluded. Hence the use of parables. We are being perversely literalistic if we imagine that the free quotation from Isa. vi ('that they may look and look without seeing . . . lest they turn . . .') is really

[1] On 'those without' see also van Unnik, 'Rücksicht' (1960), 223, n. 6.

intended to mean that parables are used *in order* to exclude, deliberately to make the message difficult for all except the favoured few. As in its original setting in the Book of Isaiah, so here, it is most naturally taken as an arresting, hyperbolical, oriental way of saying 'Alas! many will be obdurate'. (Even the most rugged of prophets might justly lose his faith, were he really summoned to preach *in order to* fail!) And secondly, the linguistic difficulties of this bridge-passage almost disappear if *vv.* 10-12 are recognized as a generalization (like *vv.* 33 f., and, like them, using the imperfect tense): to those who did ask for explanation, Jesus used always to say, 'To you is granted the secret, which is hidden from the rest as long as they stay outside'. This is a grammatically sound interpretation, and it accounts for the generalizing plural, 'parables' (*v.* 10), as contrasted with the particularizing singular which follows (*v.* 13) when 'this parable' is considered.[1]

This leads straight into the 'allegory' (*vv.* 14-20), where it is, after all, not really surprising to find several words which are seldom or never used elsewhere in the Gospels and which remind us more of Paul's vocabulary. This phenomenon need only mean that the themes in question happen not to recur. The words are perfectly suitable to the theme; the theme fits the parable naturally; and neither seems to be incompatible with the actual ministry of Jesus.

This is perhaps enough to warn us that the recovery of the precise use made of the parables of Jesus by Christian evangelists and teachers of the apostolic age is no easy task, and that the critical scalpel, invaluable and indispensable though it is, cannot by itself ever decide for us when the authentic 'lowest layer' has been reached. What we can reiterate, with conviction, is that the parables were undoubtedly used and adapted freely, and that the Christian Church was much too confident of the living presence of the Spirit of prophecy to attempt to abide by a rigid authoritarianism in its attitude to the traditions. The very reshaping

---

[1] It has to be admitted, however, that Marcan usage does not justify pressing the iterative meaning of the imperfect tense. See D. Wenham 1972–3.

and adaptation of a parable might be the work of the Spirit of Jesus in the Christians: the test of authenticity was adherence not to the original words, but to the truth of the message as a whole. Incidentally, it is possible that *The Gospel of Thomas*, for all its manifestly doctrinaire adaptations, may also preserve traces of an ancient stream of tradition (possibly from the Gospel according to the Hebrews)[1] which had run parallel to those which flowed into the canonical Gospels; and H. Koester's re-examination (1957) of evangelic matter in the Apostolic Fathers[2] points (even if one does not accept the extremes of his position) to independent channels of tradition. At all events, even if edificatory midrashim were not created (as it has already been suggested they were not), evangelists and teachers were using and adapting genuine traditions freely and uncritically, with an eye chiefly upon their main task of edification.

Thus, if the data were sufficient, various stages of tradition might be plotted along a 'trajectory' leading up to the canonical documents and out beyond them into the post-canonical literature.[3] The New Testament documents, it has been well said,[4] are *'traditions . . . caught at various moments . . . in the course of their development'* (the italics are the author's own); they represent 'teaching and practice frozen in writing at particular points . . .' It is possible that material from the parables has left its mark, even earlier than on the written Gospels, on the Pauline epistles. If this is a correct reading of the facts, it suggests that long before the canonical Gospels were universally recognized, teachers and preachers were using the gospel tradition to illustrate or drive home their lessons. The language of I Cor. vii. 35, 'I am thinking . . . of your freedom *to wait upon the Lord without distraction*' (πρὸς τὸ εὐπάρεδρον τῷ κυρίῳ ἀπερισπάστως), is so strongly reminiscent of the Lucan narrative of Martha and Mary (Lk. x. 39 f.,

[1] On the affinities of *The Gospel of Thomas*, see Montefiore 1961 and Turner and Montefiore 1962.

[2] Earlier, the well-known study, *The New Testament in the Apostolic Fathers* (Oxford, 1905), had been rather more ready to allow for direct dependence. See further Nock 1960, 68.

[3] See J. M. Robinson and Koester 1971; and cf. Reumann 1968, 20 f.

[4] Dunn 1977, 61.

'Mary, who *seated herself at the Lord's feet* . . . Martha *was distracted* . . .', Μαριάμ, ἣ καὶ παρακαθεσθεῖσα πρὸς τοὺς πόδας τοῦ κυρίου . . . ἡ δὲ Μάρθα περιεσπᾶτο) that one cannot help wondering whether Paul was not holding this picture in his mind as he chose his words, knowing that his Corinthian friends also had it in theirs. If there is any truth in the idea, it would mean that he may actually have illustrated a desirable attitude by recounting the anecdote. Again, the parables of growth seem to be in mind, not only in the embryo parable of II Cor. ix. 10 (God gives growth to grain: he will also make almsgiving produce fruit) but in the phrases in Col. i. 6, 10 (yielding fruit and growing), so naturally fitting a background consisting of the parable of the sower.[1] In Acts xx. 35, Paul is represented as actually appealing to an otherwise unknown saying of Jesus ('Happiness lies more in giving than in receiving'). In I Thess. v. 21 occurs a parabolic saying which recurs in more explicit form in Clement of Alexandria, *Strom.* I. xxviii. 177, 'be good bankers, rejecting some things but retaining what is good' (ἡ γραφὴ . . . παραινεῖ· γίνεσθε δὲ δόκιμοι τραπεζῖται, τὰ μὲν (?) ἀποδοκιμάζοντες, τὸ δὲ καλὸν κατέχοντες), which may well be a genuine saying of Jesus; and the identification of the metaphor by Clement as drawn from banking lends plausibility to the interpretation of what follows in I Thess. v. 22 in the same vein: 'have nothing to do with anything counterfeit' (ἀπὸ παντὸς εἴδους πονηροῦ ἀπέχεσθε: perhaps referring to the rejection of bad coins). It is actually appropriated in this sense by Basil, *Hom.* xii. 6, '. . . and like an approved banker, he will retain what is approved but will keep clear of every bad type' (καὶ ὡς δόκιμος τραπεζίτης, τὸ μὲν δόκιμον καθέξει, ἀπὸ δὲ παντὸς εἴδους πονηροῦ ἀφέξεται, cf. id. *In Isa.* 47).[2] Thus the complete metaphor may be a dominical parable in embryo. Again, in I Tim. vi (though this, of course, could be

---

[1] The *hysteron-proteron*, yielding fruit before growing, might be explained as a reminiscence of the Hebrew of Gen. i. 28 (where, addressed to *persons*, it is not an anomaly: they are to be productive and thus to multiply their race). But the fact remains that the LXX there does not use καρπός or καρποφορεῖν, and the Gospel parable is the closer parallel to Col. i.

[2] Resch 1906, 116 ff., collects no less than 69 citations of this saying from the Fathers.

later than the writing of the Gospels) there are not a few echoes of Gospel sayings and settings.[1] It must be emphasized that these are only straws in the wind, impressive only for their individual slenderness and fragility. Thus, to take one example of the great lacunae in the evidence, II Tim. i. 12, 'I know who it is in whom I have trusted, and am confident of his power to keep safe what he has put into my charge', which seems to clamour for an allusion to the parable of the money in trust, offers no evidence for any awareness of it whatever. Conversely, we are at a loss to know what picture lies behind such a metaphor as 'cutting straight' in II Tim. ii. 15 (ὀρθοτομοῦντα—is it ploughing, stonemasonry, or what?). But collectively and cumulatively there is enough, all the same, to leave us in little doubt that early preachers and evangelists used material, such as eventually came into the Gospels, to illustrate and drive home their points—material both from the sayings of Jesus and from his life and work.[2]

However that may be, there are certainly other categories of tradition, besides the parables and the miracle stories, that appear in various documents at various stages of their transit. 'Wisdom-sayings' and 'I-sayings' (that is, sayings with the opening formula 'I say to you . . .') seem to occur at a different stage of development in Matthew from the stage at which they occur in Luke.[3] Apocalyptic material appears alike in the epistles and in the Gospels and in the Apocalypse.

All in all, many categories of oral tradition can easily be

[1] See Excursus II.

[2] See Moule 1952; and note further the following: Phil. iv. 12 has some of the vocabulary of the parable of the Prodigal Son in Lk. xv (I owe this observation to the late Dr G. S. Duncan); II Pet. i. 13, 15 is reminiscent especially of the Lucan version of the Transfiguration story; Rev. iii. 3, 20 has the thief, and the knocking at the door, and II Tim. ii. 19 (ἔγνω κύριος τοὺς ὄντας αὐτοῦ, καὶ ἀποστήτω ἀπὸ ἀδικίας πᾶς ὁ ὀνομάζων τὸ ὄνομα κυρίου) might be regarded as a (reverse) reminiscence of Matt. vii. 21-23. See also Enslin 1930, 116, n. 18; Hawkins 1909, 196, n. there cited; Spicq 1952, 100, n. 2; Stanley 1961; Riesenfeld, 'Parabolic Language' (1970); and Bruce, 'Paul' (1974).

[3] See Suggs 1970.

conceived of as having been brought out for specific purposes—πρὸς τὰς χρείας, like Peter's teaching according to
Papias (above, pp. 71 n. 1, 108). Christians in conflict with
non-Christian Jews might recount stories of how their Master
broke sabbath traditions, or challenged a pentateuchal law
in the name of an equally pentateuchal fundamental principle. Christians engaged in healing and exorcizing might
recall narratives of Christ's triumphant victories over evil,
not by secret formulae or magical recipes but in the name of
God's sovereignty and at the cost of total obedience to God's
design. Faced with the question of their own relation to the
authority of governments, Jewish or secular, they might have
recourse to traditions about the sayings of Jesus on these
matters. Wondering whether to join resistance movements
and resort to violence in the name of freedom, they might
recount incidents from the last days before the crucifixion.
They had to make up their minds about their attitude to the
material world and its systems: were these so transitory as to
be negligible? Was the end of all things so near that they
need only hold on, keep vigilant, and wait? What had the
Master said about the future? In all these areas—particularly in the last, that of apocalyptic (where reflections of
historical circumstances and fluctuations in hopes can often
be plausibly detected by comparison of the versions)—it is
possible to detect details in the wording and the shape of the
relevant parts of the different Gospels that seem to point to
adjustments and developments within the Christian communities. But it is sometimes difficult to prove the post-
dominical character of a section, and, as has already been
said, the sketching of the circumstances and vagaries of this
period is more a matter of seizing on hints and collecting
cumulative evidence than of establishing hard data.

When one comes to the stage of the first documents and to
the work of the writers of the Gospels themselves, a new set
of criteria comes into play. 'Redaction criticism'—the study of
how each Evangelist selects and edits his material—has
become prominent in New Testament research, and is
sometimes illuminating.[1] But, once again, the assured facts

[1] See Fortna 1976.

are too scanty for most guesses to be really firmly grounded. Who can confidently practise redaction criticism when even the order and literary dependence of the Gospels is disputed? But it is worth while to see where hypotheses about the character and the purpose of each Gospel lead.

It is usual to relate the Gospels of Matthew and Mark primarily to Christian worship, and Luke-Acts to apologetic.[1] But there is much to be said for finding apologetic as a prominent motive in all three Synoptic Gospels and perhaps also in St John's Gospel, in the sense that they constitute works of 'explanation'. Not that Matthew and Mark are at all likely to have been written as tracts for the unbeliever to read: they are undoubtedly Church-books. But even so they are most easily to be explained as instruction, certainly for believers in the first instance, but with special reference to unbelievers: aids to Christians in explaining their faith and defending it when occasion offered.[2]

The attempts to relate Matthew and Mark primarily to worship are not wholly convincing. Carrington's theory that Mark follows a lectionary system does not seem to stand up to closer scrutiny; and although Kilpatrick makes possible the thesis that Matthew represents the adaptation of Christian traditions for reading at worship, Stendahl's thesis that it represents rather the work of a school of exposition is more plausible.[3] And, when one comes to think about it, it is obvious enough that, once someone had accepted the *keryg-ma*, he would need a filling out of it and (as it were) an 'embodiment' of the Jesus who had been thus briefly proclaimed as Lord. The evangelistic message of Paul, as we deduce it from references in his epistles, would have lacked the power to hold the affections and loyalty of the believer if it had never been reinforced by a portrait of the Lord in his

[1] See, e.g., for Matthew and Mark, Kilpatrick 1946; Carrington 1952 (*contra* Davies 1956) and 1960; Goulder 1974 and 1978; for Luke-Acts, Easton 1955.

[2] Moule 'Intention' (1967).

[3] There are wise reviews of the possibilities in S. E. Johnson 1960, 21 ff., Filson 1960, 10 ff.; and see Davies 1964, *passim*. More recently, see Kingsbury 1976.

words and deeds;[1] and, what is more, it would have been virtually impossible to explain Christianity to an enquirer or defend it against an antagonist without some circumstantial account of 'how it all happened'.[2] It is all very well to say to the Jerusalem crowd very soon after the crucifixion that the Jesus whom they crucified (or let be crucified) has been made Lord and Christ (Acts ii. 36); but hearers remoter in time or place would necessarily ask, Who is this Jesus, and how came he to be crucified by his own people? And even the already converted would very soon ask, What is known about his story? What sort of words and deeds are connected with him? Why did he fall foul of his own people? It is in the context of such inquiry that the Gospels seem most likely to have taken shape.

But this view that the Synoptic Gospels (with the Fourth Gospel the matter is different) are likely to have been ancillary to the proclamation of the apostolic gospel about Jesus, crucified and raised from death, rather than intended to be themselves independent and complete proclamations, is supported by more than mere probability. A comparison of Lk. i-xxiii on the one hand with Lk. xxiv and the Acts on the other, demonstrates that, if one may assume one and the same writer for both, he was deliberately holding back, in his representation of the circumstances of the ministry of Jesus, something that, according to his account, becomes explicit after the resurrection—namely, the acknowledgement of Jesus as Lord. Luke refers to Jesus as 'Lord' (κύριος) when he is writing, as a narrator; but, until the resurrection, he almost never represents any human contemporary as so referring to him. (The vocative, κύριε, a familiar polite

---

[1] Cf. Dodd 1927, pointing out that Paul's ethics gain their concreteness and find a ready point of attachment in the figure of the historical Jesus, who loved us and died for us and is to be imitated. See also Mitton 1973, Ch. 4. (It is worth-while, in passing, however, to recall how little interest there appears to have been in antiquity in a *literal* portraiture of persons—whether pictorially or by description. The famous description of Paul's appearance in the *Acts of Paul and Thecla*, iii, is exceptional, and in any case is comparatively late. Is the lack to be traced primarily to the Hebrew antipathy to visual representation?)

[2] See Stanton 1974; Klijn 1972.

address in Greek, is not, in itself, significant in the way in which other cases of the word, used in reference to Jesus, are.) As soon, however, as Easter comes, then the disciples are heard saying 'The Lord has risen indeed' (Lk. xxiv. 34), and thenceforward the designation is normal.[1] Without arguing over historicity, this proves that at least one writer deliberately held back, in his Gospel, the proclamation of Jesus as Lord which he recognized as part of the full Christian gospel. This should make one slow to assume that the Synoptic Gospels are to be treated as though they were intended to be, in themselves, more than ancillary teaching, to support and explain the more explicit announcement of Christian faith.[2]

As for the characteristics of the respective Gospels, Matthew's has already been touched upon in a previous chapter. It is frequently called the Gospel for the Jews. But, while it may indeed represent the interests of Jewish Christians, it might fairly be called the Gospel *against* the Jews, in the sense that it contains material that seems to reflect Christian apologetic and defence against Jewish criticism, particularly, perhaps, from Pharisaic Judaism. Long ago, Theodor Zahn called it 'an *historical apology of the Nazarene and His Church over against Judaism*';[3] E. P. Blair, more recently,[4] said '. . . it is obvious that the church [to which the Gospel belonged] was locked in bitter struggle with the synagogue . . .' There have even been attempts (see p. 93 above) to show that the writer himself was not a Jewish but a Gentile Christian. Be that as it may, a dialogue seems to be reflected in the Gospel. The Jewish critics said: Your master was no Messiah (answer—yes, he was: of Davidic descent, fitting into the pattern of prophecy (Matt. i. 1 ff., and *passim*)); or, Your Master was no true Israelite—he undermined the Law

[1] Details in Moule, 'Christology' (1966).

[2] Again, cf. Mitton 1973, 61, for the absence from the Synoptic story of what he calls kerygmatic affirmation.

[3] 1909, ii, 560 (italics are the author's). Cf. Schmid 1959, 24 f. Zahn, *contra* Schmid, even thought that Matthew might have been intended for reading by non-believing Jews. Hummel 1963 constitutes an important investigation.

[4] 1960, 161.

(answer—on the contrary, he set more rigorous standards than the Jewish rabbis (Matt. v. 17-20)); or, The Nazarenes' claim to be true Israel is false (answer—no, it is on the confession of Jesus as Christ that the assembly of Israel is built (Matt. xvi. 18)); or, What business have you to be going out to the Gentiles? (answer—the Lord, it is true, kept carefully within Israel during his own ministry, and directed his disciples accordingly; but his long-term sayings and his commission were universalist (Matt. viii. 11, x. 5, 23, xv. 26, xxviii. 19)). Here are just the sort of arguments that might have been used in such conflict, and it is easy to see Matthew as a textbook for Christians living very near (if not in) a Jewish ghetto: 'near' rather than 'in', if, with D. Hill,[1] we believe that 'the Jewish Christianity evidenced by the Gospel is a Christianity which has just severed connection with the Jewish communities, but which expresses itself in forms and categories borrowed from Judaism'. J. A. T. Robinson, however, places the Gospel in a situation before Judaism and Christianity became 'two estranged and separated camps'.[2] On the other hand, there are those who question the accuracy of the knowledge of Judaism displayed in this Gospel. J. W. Bowker argues[3] for an accuracy in Mark's portrayal of the Pharisees and the Scribes which contrasts with a tendency in Matthew, as in Luke, to 'generalise or "explain" the references to Jewish parties'.[4] The data are perplexing.[5] Is it possible that Matthew represents the work

[1] 1972, 41, referring to Daniélou 1964–77, i, 7 ff. Cf. Hare 1967, who places Matthew after the failure of the Jewish mission.

[2] 1976, 103. He appeals to Reicke 1972, 133: 'The situation presupposed by Matthew corresponds to what is known about Christianity in Palestine between A.D. 50 and ca. 64'.

[3] 1973, e.g. 51.

[4] Again, would the high priests and Pharisees have gone to Pilate on the day after the Preparation, xxvii. 62? Is the combination of Pharisees and Sadducees in iii. 7, xvi. 1, 6 ff. plausible? For other difficulties, see Garland 1979, *passim*.

[5] In addition to literature already cited, note, *inter alia plurima*: K. W. Clark 1947 (Gentile bias); Goodspeed 1959 (arguing for the tax-collector Apostle as author); Trilling 1964 (?Hellenist); Strecker 1962; Bornkamm, Barth and Held 1963: C. W. F. Smith 1963 (suggesting that the parable of the tares may reflect an influx of segregationist, 'Qumran-type' Christians

of a thoughtful group of Christians (Stendahl's 'school')—a kind of 'study-group' (cf. p. 94, above)—comprising both Jews and Gentiles, who had together assembled the traditions (including Mark) and formulated the arguments and presented a portrait of Jesus such as would help them and their community in standing up to non-Christian Jews? Not all of them would necessarily have learnt to understand the details and nuances of Jewish traditions and parties. Here is a body of Christians 'explaining' themselves as true Israel, *vis-à-vis* near neighbours who spit out their name as unclean. The target of attack is the 'hypocrite' which (for this community) means the non-Christian Pharisaic Jew, just as the *ethnikos* is the non-Christian Gentile.

No doubt we are bound to find room, in any account of how Matthew came to be and what it was for, for the persistent early tradition of a Semitic writing by the apostle Matthew.[1] The most often quoted form of that tradition is that in Papias (*apud* Euseb. *H.E.* III. xxxix. 16), which speaks of 'the oracles' (τὰ λόγια), translated from the Semitic original by each reader as best he could. It seems to be widely agreed that the Gospel as we know it does not offer any clear evidence of being, as a whole, and in its more distinctive parts, a translation, and includes material which it is difficult to attribute to one of the Twelve. But it is difficult to see how the tradition of a Semitic and apostolic original sprang up at all if there is absolutely nothing behind it. It is simplest, probably, to postulate a Semitic apostolic sayings-collection—perhaps (as was said above, p. 105) the very one (usually called 'Q') which it appears Luke also used; and to assume that, at however many removes from the original, this contributed to the traditions drawn into our present Gospel. It still remains possible to see the Gospel as

who needed to be answered); Albright and Mann 1971 (a Levite—perhaps Matthias); Merkel 1973–74 (strongly denying Gentile authorship); Kingsbury 1976; Cope 1976. On the study of the use of the Old Testament in Matthew since Stendahl (1954), see Gundry 1967, Rothfuchs 1969, Cope 1976.

[1] See the texts collected by Nepper-Christensen 1958, 73, n. 1, 210 f. (Euseb *H.E.* III. xxiv. 6, xxxix. 16; V. viii. 2, x. 3; VI. xxv. 4; Jerome, *De Vir. Ill.* iii, *In Matt.* II. xii. 13, *Contra Pelag.* III. ii).

it now stands as a collection of 'explanations' for Christians to use among themselves for edification and in conflict with opponents.

If 'the oracles' are identified with some such early Semitic source lying behind both Matthew and Luke, then it is conceivable that Papias' allusion to diverse Greek versions ('each reader translated them as best he could') may help to explain some of the differences between Matthew and Luke in these parallel passages.[1] This is not, of course, to deny that many differences—perhaps the majority—may be traced to the theological and other predilections of the editors or collectors (in their common use of Mark this is virtually demonstrable); it is only to suggest that some of them may be accounted for as variant renderings of a common Semitic original. This would hold good in some measure at least, even if an extreme position were adopted, postulating (as is the tendency in Scandinavian scholarship) oral traditions rather than anything so rigid as a document ('Q').

One thing is clear about the enigmatic Gospel according to Matthew as we now have it: it embraces a considerable breadth of tradition, and no one absolutely consistent outlook can be extracted from it. It may be that the actual writer himself (or writers, if it was a group) had a consistent policy and outlook—for instance, approval of the evangelization of the Gentiles and a defence of the Christian Church as true Israel without making them proselytes. But respect for the traditions, and a desire to preserve them even when they could not be fitted into the scheme, have evidently weighed heavier than the desire for consistency. Hence particularist or rigorist sayings stand side by side with liberal and universalist ones. Perhaps the most glaring discrepancy is constituted by the presence within this Gospel of the famous saying in Matt. x. 23 'before you have gone through all the towns of Israel the Son of Man will have come'. Either the evangelist identified the coming of the Son of Man here with the Resurrection, despite other passages in which it seems clearly to relate to the remoter future; or he is interpreting

[1] See Excursus I.

the mission-charge of Matt. x without any relation to the context in the ministry of Jesus in which he has himself placed it, and applying it instead to his own contemporary situation; or he is faithfully preserving a saying found in his traditions, which (whether genuinely dominical or not) had ceased to have any relation to his own day; or, finally, the saying originally related to the 'coming of the Son of Man' in the crisis of the Jewish war.[1] These are difficult choices; none of them is very easy to believe.

There is another Matthean saying, already touched on (above, pp. 93 f., 124 f.), which is notoriously difficult to fit convincingly into the scheme—the 'rigorist' one in v. 19 about not only the permanence of the law and the prophets, but the importance of observing details of the law. But it is possible that this was deliberately retained by the Evangelist from his traditions, in order to rebut charges levelled by Jews against Christians of undermining the high standards of Pharisaic Judaism. It would be as much as to say, Jesus himself set a maximum, not a minimum standard. Is not this a more likely explanation than the one more usually offered[2] that it reflects strictures on antinomianism within the Matthean community? May it not rather be ammunition brought out from the armoury of the *logia* (though in this case not also used by Luke) against non-Christians who are attacking the Christians (as St Paul was attacked) for ruining Judaism?

If we view Matthew as a collection of traditions by a Christian group who may have had a definite viewpoint of their own and a definite defence to maintain against Jewish antagonists, but who yet were more anxious to preserve the traditions than to observe consistency everywhere, we shall perhaps be seeing it in its true light. It need hardly be added that its careful arrangement in topical sections makes plausible the idea that it was planned for the instruction of believers in their faith and its vindication. This is a manual (in this respect something like the *Didache*), a catechist's book: but it is for instruction in apologetic quite as much as in religion and morals.

[1] See Feuillet 1960–61.
[2] E.g. by G. Barth in Bornkamm etc. 1963, 64–73.

THE GOSPELS AND THE ACTS

Mark's Gospel, in a seemingly simpler manner but with great profundity, also furnishes material for explanation and defence. It shows how jealousy and antagonism arose; it shows how popularity and 'success' culminated in total desertion and martyrdom; but, more profoundly, it presents an interpretation of honorific designations such as 'the Son of God' and 'the Christ' in terms of 'the Son of Man'. More than anything else, perhaps, the theme of Mark is Jesus as the Son of Man.[1] The tenacity with which the definite article ('*the* Son of Man') adheres to the phrase in the traditions of the sayings of Jesus in all the Gospels suggests that the original Aramaic phrase must have been such as to 'fasten' this definiteness. ὁ υἱὸς τοῦ ἀνθρώπου is perfectly correct Greek: there is nothing linguistically barbarous about it, as is sometimes asserted. But it is a clearly 'deictic' phrase: it does mean '*the* Son of Man'. Now, if (as is maintained by some) it was impossible in the Aramaic of Jesus' day to represent this deictic phrase—'*the* Son of Man'—unambiguously merely by using the word for man in the emphatic state (nāšâ'), yet it was certainly possible to represent it unambiguously in other ways (e.g. by using both 'son' and 'man' in the emphatic state and connecting them by the preposition *dᵉ* ('of'));[2] and unless what lies behind the Greek versions of the traditions contained such a phrase, the consistency of the use of the article in the Greek form is hard to explain. Still harder would it be to explain how the

[1] See Hooker 1967; Lemcio 1975.

[2] See Moule 1974. *Pace* Vermes 1978, the definiteness in the Greek form of the tradition—ὁ υἱὸς τοῦ ἀνθρώπου—could be represented in Aramaic. I am indebted to the Reverend A. Gelston for information about this matter, though he must not be held responsible for my conclusions. It is noteworthy that exactly the phenomenon I am postulating actually occurs in the Ethiopic of the Similitudes of Enoch (which are probably later than the time of Jesus—see Knibb 1978–79, Mearns 1978–79, J. H. Charlesworth 1978–79): at I Enoch, xlvi. 1, Daniel is virtually quoted, and 'a man' (anarthrous) is mentioned as in Daniel vii; but thereafter, with reference to this figure, deictic phrases are consistently used. For important essays on the Son of Man theme, see Pesch and Schnackenburg, edd., 1975, Black 1976–77, Bowker 1977 and 1978, 139 ff. But long before, the line I have followed was indicated by Dodd, e.g. 1952, and Manson 'Son of Man' (1962), though without making my point about the definite article.

post-Easter Church could have invented the phrase (everywhere in the Jewish scriptures it is in the indefinite form—'sons of men' or 'a son of man') and artificially attributed sayings containing it to Jesus. (It is another matter, if it did occur in genuine sayings, to introduce it subsequently into sayings that did not originally contain it: in one or two cases that may well have happened.[1]) Therefore, it is hard to avoid the conclusion that Jesus used a phrase referring to some recognizable son of man—'*the* (well known) human figure'. The only document known to have been current at the time containing an allusion to a distinctive and appropriately significant human figure is Dan. vii. There, whatever its antecedents may have been in earlier stages of its compilation,[2] the figure ('one like a son of man') is interpreted as representing the loyal Israelites who had been oppressed by 'the little horn' (representing Antiochus Epiphanes) but who are vindicated in the court of heaven before God Almighty. For that human figure a favourable verdict is delivered, and he is given an everlasting kingdom. Thus Daniel's son of man—'*the* Son of Man whom we know from Daniel'—is a symbol of the vindication in heaven of a loyalty which on earth has led to lethal opposition. And it seems to be this symbol that Jesus used to interpret his relation to God and God's Son and as God's royal vicegerent. Titles such as 'Son of God' and 'Messiah', which were normally titles of privilege, are reinterpreted[3] in terms of that honour and vindication which are to be had only by the surrender of all privilege and on the further side of suffering and martyrdom. And it is Jesus' acceptance of this principle, for which a favourable verdict is pronounced in heaven, that constitutes him, as the Son of Man, judge of all the world.[4] God's verdict in vindication of the loyal sufferer *is* God's verdict on the world: Christ's vindication is the judgment of the world.[5] And if there is one theme that specially char-

[1] Matt. xvi. 13 looks like one such case, and so, perhaps, Lk. vi. 22.
[2] Emerton 1958.
[3] For this, again see Lemcio 1975.
[4] J. A. T. Robinson 1957.
[5] Summary in Moule 1977, 11 ff.

acterizes Mark's Gospel, it is this reinterpretation of 'honour' and 'shame'. Since William Wrede's epoch-making work on the messianic secret first published in 1901, it has been customary, as has already been observed, to associate Mark with this secret, and even to claim that the enigmatic abruptness of ending with 'for they were afraid' at xvi. 8 would be in keeping with it. But, strictly speaking, secrecy about *messianic* status is mentioned only once, that is, at Mk viii. 30. Elsewhere in the Gospel, the secrecy-motif is concerned with Jesus' cures or his designation as Son of God (see above, p. 110 n. 3). Thus, Mark presents Jesus as a self-effacing wonder-worker who did not want to parade his powers, and as a supremely exalted figure who interpreted his exaltation in terms of service, suffering, and death, with vindication only on the further side of it all, when the Son of Man would 'come with clouds'—that is, both come to God to be vindicated (as in Dan. vii), and thus also come to the world in judgment. Mark is not nearly so pointedly anti-Judaic as Matthew: it is suitable for the training of Christians generally, in explaining, whether to Jews or Gentiles, how it all began, and why Christians hold Jesus to be Christ and the Son of God. It opens[1] with a 'pesher'-style applica-

[1] It is tempting to postulate a mutilation of Mark at the beginning as well as at the end. If one removes 'The beginning of the gospel of Jesus Christ the Son of God'—which is the sort of heading that any scribe might supply, if presented with only a mutilated exemplar to copy—, then the Gospel starts with a relative adverb, καθώς, 'just as', which is no less abrupt and improbable as a beginning than γάρ (xvi. 8) is as an ending. K. Aland 1969 and 1979 'Schluss' demonstrates that the earliest available manuscript evidence is entirely silent beyond that γάρ; but is it impossible that mutilation took place even before any copies were made, yet was not mended even if the Evangelist was still living? And if the original autograph was on a codex and not a roll (Roberts 1939, 255–57, 1954, 1979, 47, 76), then it only requires the bottom sheet to be lost for beginning and end to go at one stroke. (Even a roll seems to have been easily damaged at the beginning: Roberts 1939). Craigie 1922 suggested this. Later, S. C. Neill, in a letter some years ago (but see also Neill 1976, 77), mentioned his guess that the opening of the Gospel was lost; and a paper by Way-Rider (forthcoming) has independently worked the idea out in more detail. Despite all efforts to defend the view that the Gospel was meant to end at xvi. 8 (Creed 1929–30, Lohmeyer 1937, R. H. Lightfoot 1950, K. Aland, *ut sup.*, etc.) or, conversely, to find Mark's hand in part

tion of scripture (for which see p. 78, above)—including the very scripture in Isa. xl ('the voice of once crying . . .') which we now know (p. 83 above) was being used also in the Qumran circles (1QS, viii. 12-16), combined with another scripture (Mal. iii. 1 or Exod. xxiii. 20); these are declared to apply to the circumstances of John the Baptist. And throughout this Gospel Old Testament *testimonia* occur. Mark fills out the apostolic *kerygma* with Old Testament evidence and vivid narrative.[1]

Luke and John, each in its own way, are different again. It is easier to imagine them as devised actually to be put into the hands of an opponent or a doubter, and not as dependent on verbal mediation by the Christian. If Matthew and Mark are instructions to help Christians to explain themselves, both to themselves and to others, Luke-Acts, at any rate, is a single individual's direct address to a catechumen (as Theophilus may have been) and to others of his type—the people on the fringe, the outsiders who are looking inquiringly within; possibly even, through them, to really antagonistic readers also.[2] Not that it does not contain magnificent material for the building up of the Christian body; but if we

(Linnemann 1969) or all (Farmer 1974) of xvi. 9 ff., it remains difficult not to believe that something has been lost. See W. Knox 1942.

[1] On Marcan studies, see R. P. Martin 1972.

[2] C. H. Roberts, in his Sandars Lectures at Cambridge, February 1961, pointed out that the first Christian books found on rolls, in contrast to the usual Christian codex, are Luke and Acts—pointing, possibly, to their design for a non-Christian public. He hazarded the guess (contrary to my guess later in this paragraph) that the d-text might represent this 'public' edition, and the b-text a more restrained revision for Christian use. Dibelius 1956, 89 f., traces the wide variations in the text of Acts to its 'secular' currency. Roberts 1963 added: 'In spite of the fact that there is no known example of a book of the N.T. written on the recto of a roll (i.e. written on a roll for choice), it seems to be almost certain, on internal evidence, that both Lk. and Acts were published in roll form; if so, by the end of the second century they had fallen into line and appeared only as *codices*'. See now his Schweich Lectures (1979). Seccombe 1978, 297, suggests that Luke is intended to be evangelistic. He ends his dissertation with the words: 'This study would certainly add weight to the opinion that Luke was addressing well-to-do hellenistic God-fearers who were attracted to the Christian movement, but hesitant as to whether such a newcomer on the scene could possibly be authentic, and afraid of what might be the

are looking for primary purposes, it looks like something outward-aiming. It is most improbable that it would have been produced in many copies. Most likely the single autograph was handed to a single individual, Theophilus, only later to be copied (and perhaps embellished, as in the d-text). It is possible, admittedly, to exaggerate the apologetic character of Acts. From time to time it is described as though its one object was to prove to the Roman authorities (through His Excellency Theophilus) that Christianity has as much right to exist as Israel—or rather, that Christians alone *are* true Israel.[1] It is doubtful (cf. p. 174, below) whether Luke would have done exactly what he has done if that had been his single aim. Without denying this motive as a contributory element, it is nearer the mark to see the Acts as, in the main, a grand vindication of the will of God. It is the story of the minute but mighty mustard-seed; it is the narrative of the Holy Spirit championing and vindicating the cause of Christ in such a way that prison-bars go down like clay before the divine decree; or, if a witness of the Gospel does lay down his life, then it turns out positively to be to the furtherance of the very cause that the enemy is trying to extinguish. The whole story runs to its climax through storm and shipwreck, the plotting of evil men and the attack of the serpent: nothing can prevent the 'chosen vessel' from achieving God's design.[2]

Here, then, in the synoptic Gospels and Acts, each with its peculiar emphasis, may be found the deposit of early Christian explanation: here are the voices of Christians explaining what led to their existence—how they came to be: telling the story to themselves, that they may tell it to others, or even telling it directly to those others.

What may be said about the genesis and purpose of St

cost to them socially and economically if they were to declare themselves publicly and unreservedly for Christ and his church.'

[1] For the subtle tensions in the Acts between the presentation of Christianity as continuous with Israel and as discontinuous, see especially Lampe 1969 and O'Neill 1970.

[2] Chadwick, *Circle* (1959), 16. A valuable estimate of the purpose of Luke–Acts is to be found in Barrett *Luke* (1970); see also I. H. Marshall 1970.

John's Gospel, the great enigma?[1] If we had an authoritative answer to this question, we should probably be able to
point, within the span of a single Gospel, to examples of
almost all the circumstances which generated the New
Testament writings: liturgy, confession of faith, self-
understanding, controversy within and without the Church,
catechesis, and all the rest. The Fourth Gospel is so complex
and the circumstances of its composition so obscure that
speculation is rife but clear conclusions virtually impossible.
There is a judicious and comprehensive survey of the
theories in S. S. Smalley (1978, Ch. III), ending with his own
tentative theory. He suggests (pp. 119 ff.) that three stages
may be discerned behind its composition. First, John the
apostle (who was 'the beloved disciple') 'moved from Palestine to Ephesus, where he handed on orally to a disciple or
disciples of his ... accounts of the deeds ... and sayings of
Jesus, and of his death and resurrection'. Secondly, 'the
disciple or disciples of John ... committed to writing the
traditions preserved by the beloved disciple', and interwove
explanatory discourses. This is the stage at which 'what we
now recognize as "Johannine" thought emerges, by develop-
ing the seminal theological ideas handed on by the apostle
himself'. Thirdly, 'the Johannine Church at Ephesus, after
the death of the beloved disciple, published a finally edited
version of the Gospel', including, among other parts, the
prologue, based on a community hymn, and an epilogue, Ch.
xxi. 'The whole Gospel thus assembled then carried an
authenticating postscript (Jn 21: 24 f.) ... '[2] J. A. T. Robinson (1976, 254 ff.), on the other hand, is inclined to doubt
theories of compilation that drive a wedge between the
apostle in the early Palestinian days and the completion of
the Gospel, and to keep it all very close to the apostle both in
contents and in date.

In any case, there is considerable plausibility, as more
than one investigator has recognized, in detecting in some of

[1] For a lucid exposition and assessment of the various traditions about
the connexion of persons named John with Ephesus, see Bruce 1977–78.
[2] A more complicated redaction theory is proposed in Brown's great
commentary (1966, 1970).

the polemic passages, such as that in Jn viii, reflections of conflict between Church and Synagogue after the ministry of Jesus, even if there is much to be said for finding there also a nucleus of authentic tradition from debate between Jesus himself and his opponents.[1] Equally, it is plausible to find reflexions of liturgical practice, whether or not Bultmann was right in postulating an interpolator who introduced sacramental teaching contrary to the original Evangelist's anti-sacramental stance.[2] Not only is Jn vi, as it now stands, irresistibly eucharistic in its associations (whatever explanation may be offered for the absence of any narrative of the Last Supper), but Ch. iii contains, in its present form, phrases which sound baptismal, and Ch. ix looks uncommonly like a narrative told with one eye on the circumstances of Christian baptism[3] in the face of Jewish antagonism: enlightenment (which at least in later days was associated with baptism) comes from washing in water which is (like Christ himself) divinely 'sent' (*v.* 7). Perhaps even baptismal anointing ('chrism') is hinted at by the ἐπέχρισεν ('smeared') of *v.* 11 (though in *v.* 6 it is ἐπέθηκεν, simply 'applied'). There follows the simple Christian witness, 'once I was blind, now I can see' (*v.* 25); and ultimately this is found to imply the basic Christian confession—belief in Jesus (though, *si vera lectio*, as 'the Son of Man'). The inevitable result of 'enlightenment' is ostracism and excommunication from the synagogue (*vv.* 22, 34).[4] Thus, although the order of events is not accommodated precisely to the pattern of baptism, the scattered phrases and the total picture add up to an impression that genuine dominical tradition is being retold in the light of prevailing conflicts. It is easy to believe the same of Chapters vii and viii, as well as

---

[1] Dodd 1963 makes an impressive case for early, authentic traditions, without denying subsequent developments. Martyn 1968 traces subsequent disputes between Church and Synagogue. Harvey 1976 traces Jewish juridical settings in the Gospel's presentation of its material.

[2] Bultmann 1971; and see Smalley 1978, 136 ff.

[3] *Contra* Dunn *Baptism* (1970), 188.

[4] Not necessarily a sign that this was written after the introduction of the ban on heretics into the Eighteen Benedictions: see J. A. T. Robinson 1976, 273. See also Carroll 1957–58, 19 ff.

of other less extended passages here and there.[1] In such ways as these, good traditions of the controversies of the Lord's life-time may have been re-set in such a way as to continue topical in a later Palestinian community, or, later still, for the cosmopolitan populace of Ephesus[2] where the mystic and the biblicist Jew, the dualist philosopher and the ebionite might have jostled one another; and the story of the Word of God incarnate, with his creative words and his luminous deeds, had messages for them all.[3]

An even more general comment must be added in this hasty sketch of where St John's Gospel belongs in the Church's self-explanation. This Gospel, unlike the others, answers the question, 'What must I do to be saved?' The others mainly confine themselves to the story of discipleship, and may, as we have seen, be ancillary to the preaching of the gospel; the Fourth Gospel speaks in terms not only of following and imitation, but of belief and incorporation. What is less often noticed is that it also answers the question 'What must *I* do ...'—it is an extremely individualistic message. Whereas St Paul sees Jesus as the New Humanity, the incorporative Body in which all are organically connected limbs, the one in whom the resurrection of all mankind has actually taken place, St John sees Jesus as the source of life, to be connected with whom is, for each individual, life eternal. He sees the Holy Spirit in each heart as the presence of the Lord, and he can speak already of fulfilment in this realm precisely because he does move on the individual level. He does not deny a general resurrection at the last day or a coming of the Lord at the end. But he is concerned with the individual's faith and contact with the Lord of life now. Here is a Gospel that—to that extent—

[1] In addition to Martyn 1968, see Dodd, 'Johannine Dialogue' (1968).

[2] But it is strange that, whereas in vi. 4 the Passover has to be glossed as a Jewish Festival, in x. 22 the Feast of Dedication gets by without any gloss at all.

[3] But the old controversy over the question for whom this Gospel was intended still goes on. On the meaning of xx. 31 see, *inter alios* Dodd, *Interpretation* (1953), 9; Riesenfeld 1965. More generally, Dodd 1953, van Unnik 'Purpose' (1960), J. A. T. Robinson 'Destination ... of St John's Gospel' (1962), Higgins *Fourth Gospel* (1960).

could be readily accepted by the Gentile mind. Perhaps, again, it is the evangelist's explanation of Christianity to the cosmopolitan people of Ephesus, Jew and Greek alike.[1]

In all four Gospels, the passion narrative is a prominent and proportionately large component part. In none of them is it told in such a way as to make the redemptive aspect of the death of Christ particularly obvious, although the Old Testament allusions make it clear that the whole story is treated as the fulfilment of God's design of salvation for his people—so much so that its very opponents unconsciously help to weave the pattern. Once again, then, it is an explanatory or an apologetic purpose that seems to underlie the telling; and this indeed seems to be served not only by the Old Testament allusions but also by what is ostensibly straight narration. It is precisely the apologetic purpose that has, according to numerous authors,[2] grossly distorted the trial narratives of the Gospels. Thus, it is alleged that Jesus was really in sympathy with those, such as the Zealots, who were for using violence to throw off the Roman yoke, and that Pilate was, on his own terms, justified in sentencing a potentially dangerous instigator of 'freedom fighting'. The Gospels, it is alleged, in asserting Jewish complicity in his death, only reflect a period when the Christians were trying to ingratiate themselves with the government by as far as possible exonerating the Romans. This, quite apart from the difficulty of dismissing so much that is circumstantial as though it were mere fabrication, does less than justice to the evidence, indicated above (pp. 56, 72) that Jesus' way of life and teaching were already recognized during his ministry as dangerous to Pharisaic Judaism; and, in its measure, the story of St Paul also, as it is presented in the Acts, is extremely difficult to discount as evidence that the Christian position is basically such that it must rouse opposition from the Jewish side. It makes much better sense of the trial

[1] See Moule, 'Individualism' (1962), 1970.
[2] E.g., Winter 1961, 1962–63; Brandon 1967. On the other side, see Blinzler 1959; Bammel, ed., *Trial* (1970); Hengel 1969, 1971; Catchpole 1971 (with ample bibliographies). Also see van Dyen 1961, and Bammel and Moule 1982.

narratives—whatever their undeniable difficulties and dis-
crepancies in detail—to accept the motive of Jewish antagonism as historical. A credible story emerges if only we may
assume that the Jewish gravamen was 'blasphemy' (or some
form, at any rate, of false teaching), but that the Jews did not
choose (even if they had it in their power) to execute the
sentence of death, but preferred instead to get Jesus crucified
by the Romans as a rebel. This would be intelligible as an
attempt on the part of the Jewish leaders to remove a
popular but dangerous figure without incurring unpopularity for themselves. At any rate, one of the primary motives
behind the stories of the trials and the crucifixion is likely
enough to have been simply that of explaining how Jesus
came to be crucified although Son of God and Messiah.

CHAPTER VI

THE CHURCH EXPLAINS ITSELF:
4 The Reign of Christ

IT is a mistake to attribute the development of Christian understanding in the New Testament age and in the immediately subsequent period primarily to the delay of the return of Christ.[1] To do so is to pay too little attention to the decisive function of the past tense in the Christian proclamation: The Word became flesh; God has raised up Jesus from among the dead. Whatever the early Christians expected of the future, and however gravely they found themselves mistaken, they were held much more firmly by the *fait accompli* than some interpreters have allowed. The juxtaposition of Advent and Christmas in the Church's calendar with the hint that Christ's 'coming' is not two but one and indivisible is suggestive.[2]

It is not impossible that, in the earliest days, the followers of Jesus may have imagined that they, with Jesus, were already living in the New Age. Pharisaic belief, in at least some forms of its expression, seems to have held that at the end of history, at the dawn of the longed-for New Age, the righteous would be together raised from death[3] and transformed into denizens of a new world-order. Similarly the

[1] Werner 1957, assuming that Judaism at the time of Christ was dominantly apocalyptic, regards 'consistent eschatology' as a criterion of genuineness in reconstructing the teaching of Jesus. He allows himself such sweeping assertions as (14): '... the message of Jesus has only to show agreement in one single characteristic element with the apocalyptic conception of the future Kingdom of God, and the proposition of a Kingdom of God being already realised in the present is rendered thereby completely problematic'.

[2] See J. A. T. Robinson 1957.

[3] Sometimes the hope is very literalistic, sometimes in more sophisticated forms. See W. D. Davies 1970, 298 ff.

early Christians, convinced that Jesus was alive, not in the sense of being merely brought back to mortal life (as they believed of Lazarus and others), but in the sense that he had been brought through and beyond death into the life of the New Age, may have imagined that, *ipso facto*, they too, as his companions, had been taken with him into the New Age. It is difficult to find any cogent evidence for this, but it is conceivable: one might appeal to Acts ii. 16 f., which quotes (but freely adapts!) Joel and implies that 'the last days' (not in Joel) had begun. However, if so, they must very quickly have been disillusioned by the discovery that death was still a reality and that sin had certainly not been eliminated, even within the ranks of committed Christians.[1] Even if the story of the death of Ananias and Sapphira (Acts v. 1 ff.) could be explained as an attempt to rationalize what 'ought' not to happen to Christians in the New Age,[2] such devices could not remain plausible for long. In the earliest datable Christian documents, the Pauline epistles, Paul has certainly come to terms with the death of Christians: indeed, in I Cor. xv (cf., possibly, II Tim. ii. 18), he may actually be battling with a false notion that Christians were already beyond mortality—a notion springing from a dualism (incompatible with a seriously incarnational Christology) which disparaged physical life and the material world. Very early in the Church's life, then, Christians must have realized that, even if 'rescued' by Christ, as Paul puts it, 'from the present evil age' (Gal. i. 4), they were still living within its ambit. It was indeed still 'present': the old age still overlapped the new, and was 'a most unconscionable time dying'. Apart from sophisticated dualistic speculations, there cannot for long have been illusions on that score.

But this did nothing to reduce the eager expectation that very soon the kingship of Christ would be decisively confirmed. Jesus himself (whether or not conceiving it in terms of his own kingship) evidently expected some final assertion

---

[1] The Epistle to the Hebrews and I John have their own ways of dealing with sin after conversion. See Telfer 1959 and Carlston 1969.

[2] Menoud 1950.

of God's sovereignty within his own generation.[1] Paul seems never to have abandoned this expectation, even if he gave up expecting himself to survive until that day.[2] And although St John's Gospel refers to the coming of the Holy Spirit as a 'Paraclete' in terms which seem to imply that, in a sense, this coming is to be Christ's own coming—his coming in the resurrection—, yet the same Gospel also includes references to a time still in the future when the dead will hear the voice of the Son of God and will come out of their graves for judgment (v. 28 f., etc.). However many redactors one postulates for the Gospel, at least it remains true that the final redactor did not eliminate either type of element as incompatible with the other; and, despite the frequent assertions of scholars that the Fourth Gospel represents the abandonment of futurist eschatology in favour of a fully realized eschatology in terms of the Spirit's presence, the Gospel in fact uses 'realized' language only with reference to committed individuals.[3]

Thus, that Christ would come soon is an expectation which appears even in the latter writings of the New Testament. It is present in almost every stratum. Outside Paul and John, one immediately thinks of such passages as I Pet. i. 7, iv. 7, v. 4, Heb. i. 2, ix. 28, x. 37, and, of course, Rev. I.7, xxii. 20, etc. And although it is often said of Luke and Acts that here the expectation is pushed into a siding and provision made meanwhile for a long period of Church history without serious concern for the coming, this is not easy to sustain with chapter and verse.[4]

It is logically plausible enough to postulate evolutionary theories of a diminuendo in the hope of the coming and of a progressive adjustment of Christian thinking to successive stages in the delay; but it is difficult to substantiate this.

[1] There is no getting round γενεά in Mk xiii. 30 etc. See such different writers as Beasley-Murray 1954, 260, 1957, 101, and Barrett 1967.
[2] See especially commentators on II Cor. v.
[3] See Moule, 'Individualism' (1962), 1970.
[4] See Barrett *Luke* (1970), I. H. Marshall 1970, etc. Cf. Seccombe 1978, 254: 'For Luke discipleship means unreserved attachment to Jesus in hope of the coming Kingdom; the Christian life means living now with that Kingdom as the ultimate value and goal of one's life.'

There is no cogent case to be made for a chronological sequence from the earliest tiptoe expectation through a Pauline compromise[1] to a fully realized eschatology in John, or, alternatively, to an ecclesiastical and institutional present, in Acts and the Pastoral Epistles,[2] as a substitute for the eschatological future. Actually, it is precisely in one of the latest documents (according to most chronologies), namely, II Peter, that concern over the delay of the coming is displayed in an extreme form. So far from having settled down to a 'catholicism' and institutionalism in lieu of the hope, II Peter asserts merely that God's time-scale is different from man's. E. Käsemann sees here a betrayal of the authentic tension between the 'already' and the 'not yet';[3] but the point remains that time had not altered the pattern of expectation.

It appears, then, that the expectation of Christ's return was held, in varying degrees of intensity and in different forms, throughout the New Testament period, and that there is no justification for attributing any substantial development in doctrine to the exigencies of accommodation to the delay.[4] On the other hand, C. H. Dodd's appealing attempt[5] to show that Christ himself taught that the decisive event had happened with his own ministry and that, *within human history*, there was nothing further to expect except variations on that theme, has not fully justified itself either. It is not possible, without straining the evidence, to eliminate the future tense from the teaching of Jesus about the sovereignty of God and the final 'coming' of his own vindication, as critically reconstructed from the Synoptic traditions—think only of the Lord's prayer!—, nor even from the Fourth Gospel. It is true that an impressive case has been

[1] Observe that, on the contrary, Rom. viii (containing a vigorous non-apocalyptic eschatology comparable to that of Ephesians, in terms of the Spirit's presence and a future in which God's sons will find full realization) cohabits with xiii. 11 f. ('It is far on in the night; day is near').

[2] Again, the present and future in reality cohabit in all these writings.

[3] Käsemann, 'Apologia' (1964).

[4] Dodd, 'Mind of Paul' (1953), does not establish a change in the pattern of Paul's thought so much as in its emphasis.

[5] Dodd 1978.

made for the view that Jesus' message about the kingdom or sovereignty of God did not, after all, depend on apocalyptic Judaism as is so often assumed. Dependence is, perhaps, itself a misleading word: Jesus' teaching, explicit and implicit, was highly original. But, so far as analogies do exist, and in so far as Jesus was drawing on antecedent views, the closest seem to be not in apocalyptic writings but in certain of the Targums, where God's reign is not tied to time-schemes but is flexible as to tenses.[1] The Targums, though in their present forms too late, incorporate ideas that may well have been abroad at the time of Jesus. Yet, if one pressed the temporal flexibility in this illuminating analogy too far, one might be in danger of reducing the sovereignty of God to a private and individualistic affair: it would then be only a variation on the theme of individual obedience––'assuming the yoke of the kingdom of heaven'––in Jewish piety;[2] and this, if it stood alone (as in F. T. Palgrave's beautiful poem, 'O thou not made with hands ...'), would eliminate the historical and corporate dimensions in the work of God, and would make nonsense of the appeal to the nation in the ministry and message of Jesus.[3] In their measure, however, and with these reservations, the Targumic conceptions reinforce the case for refusing to assume that Christian hopes stood or fell with the success of an eschatological time-scheme.

If, then, the future tense runs virtually throughout the New Testament's formulations of the Christian gospel, it is the more impressive that hope deferred so seldom made the heart sick. If II Peter is not representative of the New Testament in its way of answering the taunt about the delay of the coming, it is clear that some driving force held the Church of those days as a whole steadily on its way, when the non-return of Christ might have been expected to becalm it. As in the Rime of the Ancient Mariner, there was a mysterious, invisible mover. What was this? It was the past

[1] See Chilton 1977–78 and 1979; Koch 1978–79. And, for the terminology, Lattke 1975.
[2] E.g. *T. B. Berakoth* 13a.
[3] For which see especially Caird 1963, 142 f., and 1965.

tense—the conviction that Christ had already come—not so as never to come again (as a consistently realized eschatology would have it), but so as to establish decisively the conviction that God had visited and redeemed his people, had given them the Holy Spirit's presence in a new way, and would bring them through to the consummation, whatever and whenever that might be.

As a matter of fact, even pre-Christian and non-Christian Jewish apocalyptic hopes had never been at a loss to reconcile their confidence in God's sovereignty with the non-arrival of the hoped-for age: their ardour was no more dependent on an immediate fulfilment than was that of the Christians.[1] And for Christians, the decisive fact of Christ was the sheet anchor. It has been suggested that Acts iii. 20 f. should be interpreted to mean that thus far Jesus had come only as the Suffering Servant and that his royal manifestation was still in the future, and that this was an early form of Christian eschatology which was soon outgrown.[2] Whether that is so or not, and whatever nuances of difference may be detected between different formulations, the balance between past, present, and future and the consistently firm anchorage in the past seems to be characteristic of Christian hopes as they are reflected virtually throughout the New Testament.[3]

Accordingly, there are no grounds for regarding the early Christian hopes reflected in the New Testament as invalidated, as though depending for their essentials on a literal expectation that was not fulfilled. Doubtless the Christians went through perplexities and anxieties. Doubtless crude literalism had to give way before realities or else accept an increasingly large credibility-gap (cf. II Peter). But the firm support of the Word made flesh, leading to the realized presence of the Spirit, had all along been normative; and this

[1] 1Qp Hab. vii. 7-14 shows the Qumran sect wrestling with the same problem. See Strobel 1961 and Bauckham 1980; Schillebeeckx 1979, 121.

[2] J. A. T. Robinson, 'Most Primitive?' (1962).

[3] On all this, O. Cullmann has constantly had wise observations to make. See, among much besides, Cullmann 1962 and 1967—the latter containing a discussion of the views of Dodd, J. A. T. Robinson, and Werner (see p. 38).

remained. The Christian gospel is not exhortation or appeal to expectation: it is the proclamation of an event. Yet it is a divine event, always recognized as involving the 'vertical', the 'eschatological' as well as the 'lateral' and the historical. It remains, then, briefly to review some of the forms taken by Christian response to what (at least from outside) looked like the cult of an absent Lord. 'Where is your Messiah?' must have been a question often thrown at Christians.

Just as the grosser idolaters had pointed derisively at the Jews' empty shrine until they were forced to exclaim 'As for our God, he is in heaven' (Ps. cxv. 3), so the non-Christians, both Jew and Gentile, naturally asked the Christians what had become of the King whom they alleged to have been raised from death. And, within their own hearts, the Christians had to meet the same question. If Christianity was to explain itself, one of the foremost difficulties that it had to explain was the invisibility of the Christians' Lord, and the patent fact that his reign of peace was not yet implemented. The New Testament Christian, asked or asking himself, 'Where is your King? Why is not his reign evident?' replied that the Kingdom, though indeed inaugurated, was not yet consummated. The clearest expression of this is in I Cor. xv. 25, 'he is destined to reign until God has put all enemies under his feet' (the allusion is to Ps. cx); and its conclusion (*v.* 28) that when this is achieved, then Christ himself will be subjected to God, appears (in terms of later credal formulations) to be 'subordinationist' (cf. I Cor. xi. 3, where there is a kind of hierarchy, 'God-Christ-man-woman'). But, though more faintly, the same idea seems to make itself just audible in Rev. xi. 15, where the sovereignty of the world is declared to have 'passed to our Lord (God) *and his Christ*'—implying some consciousness of a distinction. So in Matt. xxv. 31 ff., there may be some relics of an awareness of 'the kingdom of Christ' as distinguishable from 'the Kingdom of God'.[1] If so, however, Rev. iii. 21 shows how, side by side with such a notion, the conception of the equal kingship of Christ and of God can occupy the thoughts ('I myself was victorious and sat down with my Father on his throne'); and it is doubtful

[1] See Dodd, 'Matthew and Paul' (1953).

whether even those Pauline passages indicate more than a recognition that the Church is living in an interim-stage, waiting for the consummation and implementation of Christ's victory which is God's victory. The Pauline formula which usually describes Christians as 'in Christ' rather than 'in God' is comparable: and, significantly, the sole instance of his using the remarkable formula, 'hidden with Christ in God' (Col. iii. 3) is in a context of eschatological expectation. (I Thess. i. 1 and II Thess. i. 1, with the formula 'in God . . . and . . . Christ'—*N.E.B.*, 'who belong to God . . . and . . . Christ'—are exceptional.)

Relevant to the same issue is the New Testament attitude to the conquest of the demonic powers by Christ. Cullmann has argued[1] that Christians of the New Testament period saw the cross as the conquest of the malign powers, who thenceforth were reduced to obedient servitude—so much so that now it was a positive duty for Christians to obey and be subject to them as servants in Christ's kingdom. C. D. Morrison, on the contrary, argues (1960) that, although, on the New Testament showing, Christ always had been and was eternally supreme over the 'powers', his death, in itself, made no difference to their temporary ascendancy, but only relieved Christians, as such, from the necessity of submitting to their tyranny. The most problematic verse for Morrison's position is Col. ii. 15 ('on that cross . . . he made a public spectacle of them . . .'), which seems very explicitly to define the cross as the occasion of the triumph over the powers. But in the main his position is convincing. In any case, what matters for the moment is that Christian speculation about these demonic angel-powers bears further witness to the sense of an interim-stage, awaiting the final consummation.

Closely related to the same issue is the sense that the evangelization of the world must be achieved before the consummation can come. The Acts narrative seems to run along this pattern (Acts i. 11, ii. 33, iii. 19 ff.), although, curiously enough, Lk. xxi. 24 speaks not of the evangelism of the Gentiles but (apparently) simply of a necessary quota of years during which the Gentiles must domineer over Jeru-

[1] Cullmann 1957.

salem: '. . . Jerusalem will be trampled down by foreigners until their day has run its course' (cf. Rev. xi. 2). Contrast with this the Matthean parallel: '. . . this gospel of the Kingdom will be proclaimed throughout the earth as a testimony to all nations; and then the end will come' (Matt. xxiv. 14—whether Mk xiii. 10 means the same is another matter).[1] At any rate, Paul clearly saw the evangelization of the Gentiles as the essential step towards the consummation: '. . . this partial blindness has come upon Israel only until the Gentiles have been admitted in full strength; when that has happened, the whole of Israel will be saved . . .' (Rom. xi. 25 f.).[2]

Such variety as there is in the New Testament formulations of this interim-idea depends on the variety of situations addressed. There will be more to say about this when we come to consider error and heresy within the Church. But for the time being it is worth while to observe that there were two extremes in misunderstanding which had to be met. First, there were those who said that the resurrection (of Christians) had already taken place (II Tim. ii. 18; cf. I Cor. xv and ? II Thess. ii. 2 and I John, *passim*).[3] This was presumably a dualistic type of thinking:[4] denying the reality or the importance of the material world and concentrating on the private religious experience of the individual soul, these heretics maintained that by baptism they were already made partakers of the risen life and that there was nothing further to follow. (They could quite easily have misunderstood the outlook represented by John in this sense.) In reply, Christians who were loyal to the apostolic witness maintained that the visible, resurrection-body of Jesus was the first-fruits and guarantee not of escape from this world, but of its redemption, and that they looked for an event still in the future—the raising of all God's people together into a new life, 'the emancipation of the body' (not 'from the body', Rom. viii. 23). They affirmed

---

[1] See Kilpatrick 1955.
[2] See Munck 1959.
[3] Cf. Schweizer 1960, 112, and see 28, n. 1.
[4] Many would call it 'gnostic'; but the fact remains that there is no evidence for gnostic 'systems' until later. See Nock 1964; Yamauchi 1973.

the expectation of an ultimate redemption of the whole people of God as against individualistic notions of prior escape.

Secondly, there were the 'scoffers' who said, 'You can wait forever and nothing will happen. Things are going on exactly as they were before. There will never be an end to the world'. The real mistake here is to make time the determining standard at all. The very form of the scoffing bears witness to a misunderstanding of the real issue. For the Christian's hope is not to be measured primarily in terms of lapse of time but in terms of the continuous working out to its completion of a *datum* already given—namely the incarnation.[1] New Testament eschatology at its deepest level concentrates upon entering into, implementing, loyally expressing that which is already given, which is Christ: it does not say, 'How long will it be before the whistle blows for the end of the game?' but, 'Where ought I to be now, to receive the next pass?'[2] In other words, the fact that the kick-off has taken place, that the game is on, and that we have a Captain who can lead us to victory, is all that matters. Yet, once the false question was formulated, it was difficult to avoid an answer in its own terms; and II Pet. iii. 8 shows us the application of Ps. xc. 4 as an *ad hominem* reply: God's time-scale is different; to him a thousand years are as a single day; therefore you cannot blame him for delay!

Whenever time-scale considerations come in, we seem to find unprofitable judgments. If the scoffers traded on 'delay' to draw false inferences, the opposite extreme—the oppressive sense that 'the time is short'—seems to have led Paul to some of his least enduring judgments. Both the expectation of a *parousia* the day after tomorrow and its postponement *sine die* seem to have led to unfruitful conclusions. But neither of these is characteristic of New Testament thought, which concentrates far more on the *datum*—on the fact that already the kingship of Christ has been established, already the

---

[1] See, again, J. A. T. Robinson 1957, where this point is finely made, even if one does not go all the way with some of the argument.

[2] This metaphor appeared in the first edition, to the surprise of my sporting friends, though it has much more recently turned up in a book by a colleague (where it receives high marks from a reviewer!).

Kingdom of God has been inaugurated, and that the responsibility of the children of the Kingdom is to act here and now
as those who are charged to bear witness to its reality.[1] And
always at moments of Christian worship, time and space are
obliterated and the worshipping Church on earth is one in
eternity with the Church in the heavenly places:

> ... you stand before Mount Zion and the city of the living
> God, heavenly Jerusalem, before myriads of angels, the full
> concourse and assembly of the first-born citizens of heaven, and
> God the judge of all, and the spirits of good men made perfect,
> and Jesus the mediator of a new covenant, whose sprinkled
> blood has better things to tell than the blood of Abel. (Heb. xii.
> 22 ff.)

Thus, the future (in detail) was never the primary concern; it
was the past leading to the present that occupied the
attention of Christians when they were really Christian. And
consequently, it is a mistake to read the New Testament as
though the 'delay of the *parousia*' were a conditioning factor
of essential importance—still worse to measure the chronological sequence of the writings by supposed developments
depending upon it. There may be—there probably are—
developments in *emphasis*:[2] but the general programme of
expectation varies little; and even changes in emphasis are
an unreliable measure of chronological development.[3]

It is, perhaps, appropriate to add a coda on Christian
apocalyptic writing. Apocalyptic eschatology needs to be
recognized as a particular mode of eschatology. All Christian
doctrine is inescapably eschatological, because of the Christian conviction of the finality and absoluteness of Christ as

[1] Cf. Schweizer 1960, 22 f.: 'It is possible that for a while the
expectation of the approaching *parousia* suppressed any other questions.
But we must say that this expectation has not exercised any substantial
influence on the earliest summaries of the Church's faith.' Käsemann
1969, 105, writes: 'John's saying to the effect that judgment is already
taking place in the present is already foreshadowed in essence within the
community after Easter, even though, analysed from the standpoint of the
history of religion, the Fourth Gospel expresses it in different forms.' See
also Cullmann 1960, 276, pointing out that in very few New Testament
passages is the 'problem' of the delay of the *parousia* discernible as a *motive*.

[2] See Dodd, 'Mind of Paul' (1953).

[3] See Moule, 'Influence' (1964).

the 'ultimate' or 'final' one (ὁ ἔσχατος). Let it be said in parenthesis that the neuter, the *eschaton*, is not used in the New Testament eschatological sayings, except in the complex phrase 'the end of these days' in Heb. i. 2, and 'the end of the times' in I Pet. i 20 (cf., perhaps, II Pet. iii. 3). For the New Testament, it is a Person, Christ, who is the final one. Eschatology, however, is not necessarily nor always apocalyptic. Apocalypse—literally 'unveiling'—, the anticipatory raising of the curtain to display the final scene, is a way of conveying, pictorially and in symbol, the conviction of the ultimate victory of God. And this particular form of teaching tends to take shape at times of stress or of tense expectancy, when the human resources of believers are more than ordinarily exposed in all their futility and helplessness, and when the human or demonic forces of tyranny seem to be making their last desperate bid for supremacy. Then it is that the seer is given to see, dramatically and in vast images, thrown up in boldest black and white on the screen of his vision, that

> Though the cause of evil prosper,
> Yet 'tis truth alone is strong;
> Though her portion be the scaffold,
> And upon the throne be wrong,
> Yet that scaffold sways the future,
> And, behind the dim unknown,
> Standeth God within the shadow,
> Keeping watch above his own.

Exactly so the seer of Dan. vii had seen the frail, defenceless human figure[1] vindicated and invested with glory in the face

---

[1] It is, of course, true that 'the human figure' ('one like unto a son of man') of Dan. vii is not described as crushed: indeed, at his first and only appearance, he is already invested with glory (*v.* 13). But the fact that, in the interpretation of the vision, he stands for 'the saints' against whom the tyrant makes war and prevails (*v.* 21), and the extremely probable application of the whole scene to the Maccabaean martyrs, warrant, I believe, the interpretation of the symbol as meaning the triumph, *through suffering and eclipse*, of those who have no armour but their inflexible loyalty. Cf. Dodd 1952, 117, n. 2; Bowker 1978, 146.

of the bestial powers who stamped on him and crushed the
life out of him:

> I was still watching in visions of the night and I saw one like a
> man [literally, like a son of man] coming with the clouds of
> heaven; he approached the Ancient in Years and was presented
> to him. Sovereignty and glory and kingly power were given to
> him, so that all people and nations of every language should
> serve him; his sovereignty was to be an overlasting sovereignty
> which should not pass away, and his kingly power such as should
> never be impaired.... As I still watched, that horn was waging war
> with the saints and overcoming them until the Ancient in years
> came. Then judgment was given in favour of the saints of the Most
> High, and the time came when the saints gained possession of the
> kingly power. (Dan. vii. 13f., 21f.)

Such was God's message through apocalyptic to the
Maccabaean martyrs and their generation. And in the New
Testament, besides many apocalyptic phrases and sections
interwoven with the rest, there stand out three main examples: the Revelation—a long, sustained piece of apocalyptic
writing—the Gospel apocalypses (Mk xiii and the various
parallels), and II Thess. ii.

Speculation on the origins of these three or more apocalypses is rife. The attempt of Caligula to introduce his image
into the Temple, and the beginning of persecution in connexion with Emperor worship are the obvious crises by
which to account for these manifestations; and these, and
additional circumstances, call for further consideration in
the next chapter.

CHAPTER VII

THE CHURCH UNDER ATTACK

ACTIVE hostility to the Christian Church is a matter which is clearly relevant to our enquiry into the circumstances which led to the formation of the New Testament; for the attacks of opponents both give rise to certain types of document embodying defence or counter-attack, and also afford, from time to time, clues to chronological order and circumstances. The basic Christian Creed, 'Jesus is Lord' or 'Jesus is Christ' might well find a setting in a persecution context as well as in a baptismal;[1] and elaborations of that confession may be indicative of various particular periods.

When we were considering the Church's explanation of itself, we found that it was *vis-à-vis* Judaism that such explanation was, in the main, required. And similarly the thesis of this chapter (which is concerned not so much with question and reply as with active attack and defence) is that Judaism bulks by far the largest among the antagonists of Christianity which have left their stamp upon the New Testament. It is, of course, a familiar fact that Christians were persecuted by the Roman government: everyone knows about Nero. What is less commonly recognized is that it is not possible to establish that this is reflected anywhere at all in the New Testament except in certain limited passages of the Revelation. J. A. T. Robinson (1976, especially 142-150 and 221 ff.) goes into the details. What emerges is, first, that

[1] See Cullmann 1949, 27, where I Cor. xii. 3 is discussed in the light of such persecution as tried to make the Christians renounce their confession κύριος Ἰησοῦς in favour of Κύριος Καῖσαρ and to say ἀνάθεμα Ἰησοῦς. I would doubt whether one needed to look as far as Caesar-worship. If it is a persecution context, Acts xxvi. 11 is a more plausible one, where, before his conversion, Paul the scourge of the Nazarenes tries to compel them to blaspheme. But it is not easy to place I Cor. xii. 3 in a context of persecution at all. A different view is offered by van Unnik 1973.

Nero's notorious brutality to Christians described by Tacitus (*Ann.* XV. xliv) took place some considerable time after the disastrous fire in Rome (perhaps in A.D. 65, if the fire is rightly dated in 64). Tacitus alleges that the Christians were used as scapegoats for whoever was the real incendiary, but Tacitus' accuracy has been challenged.[1] Secondly, that although Peter may well have suffered crucifixion in or at about the same time as this persecution, there is no reason to associate the execution of Paul with the same occasion. These observations provide a corrective to what is often said about the date of Nero's persecution and about the deaths of Peter and Paul. But, for the present purpose, more important is a further fact that emerges from Dr Robinson's reinvestigation of the question, namely, that there seems to be no cogent evidence for the actual death of any Christians as martyrs *in a state persecution in the province of Asia* before the time of the celebrated correspondence between the Younger Pliny and Trajan (*Epp.* x. 96 and 97, *c.* A.D. 112). The alleged persecution under Domitian, to which the relevant passages of the Apocalypse are usually referred, cannot be established;[2] neither can any part of the Apocalypse be securely given a Domitianic date.[3] The death of many Christians under Nero in Rome in the sixties is well authenticated (see Tacitus *Ann.* XV. xliv and 1 Clem. vi). So is the death of a few in Asia under Trajan, though the Emperor discouraged Pliny from going further. But within the New Testament period, the death of any Christians in a state persecution in Asia cannot be established for certain. It is impossible to be sure that Antipas (Rev. ii. 13) and the anonymous of Rev. vi. 9-11, vii. 13-17 were put to death in such circumstances. Rev. xiii. 15 is a virtually explicit

---

[1] See, e.g., Canfield 1913, 43 ff. Sulpicius Severus, *Chronic.* II. xxix, is shown to be slavishly dependent on Tacitus. See Hare 1967, 72, n. 1.

[2] Cf. Sweet 1979, 24 ff.; though Chadwick 1967, 26 writes: 'The customary oath "by the genius of the emperor" became officially obligatory. There is good evidence that this created a crisis for the Jews. It is probable (though not quite certain) that the Church was no less embarrassed.'

[3] Fitzmyer 1977–78, 312, is inclined to accept J. A. T. Robinson's early dating of the Apocalypse, though critical of the rest of his dating.

reference to the death-penalty for what is there evidently a refusal to conform to the Emperor-cult, and there is some reason to believe that there was actual legislation against Christians in Rome under Nero (see Tertullian, *Apol.* v. 3, and Sulpicius Severvus, *Chronic.* II. xxix. 3 (though n.b. p. 153 n. 1 above), *apud* J. A. T. Robinson 1976, 234). But there is no direct evidence that the death-penalty was actually incurred under this law (and Sweet 1979, 208, takes Rev. xiii. 15 as hypothetical rather than actual), or that, in any case, anything outside Rome is intended (this last qualification applies even more obviously to Rev. xvii. 6). One can only say that it certainly reads like an urgent message for Christians actually caught in state persecution.

Postponing, then, further consideration of the question of Christians *vis-à-vis* the Emperor-cult, we return to the antagonism of Judaism to Christianity. It is a tragedy that Christians, themselves in origin an off-shoot of Judaism, should first have been persecuted by Jews and subsequently turned into ruthless persecutors of Jews, even to attempted genocide.[1] But all this—cause for deep penitence—does not alter the fact that, within the New Testament, the indications (and critical examination suggests that they are not due to mere tendentiousness) are that Jews more often than Gentiles were the persecutors of Christians or instigators of persecution—though seldom, if ever, on a large scale, and not often to the length of taking life.[2] The Christians were quick to realize that the persecution of a minority by the majority of the religious community to which they belonged was a phenomenon already deeply embedded in the Jews' own history: which of the prophets had not their forefathers

[1] And early Judaism had its own martyr roll of honour, from Maccabaean times to Rabbi Hananiah, defending his Torah-scroll, and beyond. See Leipold und Morenz 1953, 197. (I owe this reference to C. H. Roberts.) Jews were harried by the Roman government from time to time, as is evident from Horace (slightly earlier than the New Testament period), Juvenal, and Philo (*Legatio* and *Flacc.*); and there is the famous passage in Suet. *Claud.* xxv. 4 about the expulsion of Jews from Rome (cf. Acts xviii. 2).

[2] See Hare 1967. I Pet. ii. 12 is one of the rare exceptions, where it is Gentiles who are the opponents.

persecuted (Acts vii. 52)? To make the situation more complicated, it appears that the non-Christian Jews were most prone to persecute the Christians when Judaism was itself under attack by the Roman imperial authorities. The times when there was most tolerance were precisely the times when external pressure was at its least. Relations between Christians and Jews were strained to breaking-point most naturally when it was dangerous for the one to acknowledge any contact with the other.[1]

In the New Testament there are allusions to persecution, whether as forecasts or as narratives of events, in the Gospels and the Acts; and the other documents chiefly concerned are II Thessalonians, the Pastoral Epistles, Hebrews, I Peter, and the Revelation. It will be well to look at these in turn.

All four Gospels contain allusions to impending antagonism against Christians, both on the private level, within households, and, publicly, on the level of both Jewish and Gentile courts (Mk xiii. 13 and parallels, Matt. x. 22, Lk. xii. 11, xxi. 12, Jn xvi. 2).[2] It is relatively immaterial, for our purposes, whether or not these allusions are genuine prophecies or whether they sprang, *post eventum*, from the actual occurrences. In either case they stand for the recognition of the element of conflict at the heart of the Christian situation. The Fourth Gospel actually depicts the excommunication, during the ministry of Jesus, of the blind man who had received his sight. For refusing to declare Jesus a sinner, he is banished from the synagogue (ix. 34). It is by no means certain that this necessarily reflects a situation after the ban on heretics had been introduced into the synagogue (see p. 135 n.4 above).

---

[1] See the very suggestive essay by Reicke 1953. 'He distinguishes three phases: (i) the thirties, when the young church was attacked both by the Jerusalem authorities and by the "Zionist" diaspora; (ii) the forties, when there came, first, Herod Agrippa I's persecution, favouring legalistic Jews, and then, under the Procurator, a corresponding recession of the stricter Judaism; (iii) the fifties, which saw the Zealot terrorism blaze up and the fuse lit which kindled the conflagration culminating in A.D. 70' (from my review in *J.T.S.*, n.s., 5 (1954), 91 ff. (93)). See also Smallwood 1976.

[2] Lk. xii. 11, xxi. 12 does not mention *sunedria* although there were Sanhedrins even in the diaspora, because the Gentile Christian was more familiar with *synagogues*—so Strobel 1956.

But if there is no inherent reason for declaring it to be anachronous (xii. 42 mentions excommunications again in passing), it certainly uses terms which make a type for all baptizands out of this blind man, who receives his sight through washing, at the behest of Jesus, in water described as (divinely) 'sent', and then is expelled by the Jews; and later in the same Gospel, excommunication and even death are promised to the faithful followers of Jesus (xvi. 2). (See above, p. 56).

Whether or not these allusions are *post eventum*, it is difficult to deny that Jesus himself was brought to book before both Jewish and Gentile tribunals. E. Stauffer even maintained that, long before his trial—indeed, during much of his ministry—the Jerusalem hierarchy and the rabbinic authorities had been systematically spying on him, setting traps for him, and collecting evidence against him as a teacher of error, and that he eventually came under their discipline on these grounds (see Stauffer 1957, Ch. 10, 1960, Ch. 6).[1] In that same Chapter ix of St John, the Jews are said to have agreed (*v.* 22) that anyone who confessed Jesus as Messiah should be banned from the synagogue.

Whatever the historical status of these allusions, the pattern of Jesus' own life, with its provocation of fierce antagonism and its undeviating courage, was recognized by Christians as the norm for the lives of them all:

> Run the great race of faith and take hold of eternal life. For to this you were called; and you confessed your faith nobly before many witnesses. Now in the presence of God, who gives life to all things, and of Jesus Christ, who himelf made the same noble confession and gave his testimony to it before Pontius Pilate, I charge you to obey your orders irreproachably and without fault until our Lord Jesus Christ appears. (I Tim. vi. 12-14.)

> Remember Jesus Christ, risen from the dead, born of David's line. This is the theme of my gospel, in whose service I am exposed to hardship, even to the point of being shut up like a common criminal; but the word of God is not shut up. And I endure it all for the sake of God's chosen ones, with this end in view, that they too may attain the glorious and eternal salvation

---

[1] See, however, a critique of the evidence by Kümmel 1966, 293 (with reference to Stauffer 1957, Ch. 10).

which is in Christ Jesus.

Here are words you may trust:

'If we died with him, we shall live with him;
If we endure, we shall reign with him.
If we deny him, he will deny us.
If we are faithless, he keeps faith,
    For he cannot deny himself'.

(II Tim. ii. 8-13)

Yes, persecution will come to all who want to live a godly life as Christians, ...

(II Tim. iii. 12)

From the very beginning, therefore, some measure of suffering had to be assumed as the Christian's lot. Indeed, it had already been the lot not only of Jesus himself, but of John the Baptist, and of all the messengers of God before them. The story of the persecution of Christians is continuous with the story of their predecessors under the old dispensation, and they had ready to hand a considerable Jewish literature of martyrdom. In the books of Daniel and Judith, and in the Maccabaean stories, they could read of Jewish witness before the heathen; while in the legends of the Prophets were the patterns of heroes suffering at the hands of their own people. The writer to the Hebrews found solace in both. And simultaneously with the rise of the Christian literature, Philo the Jew was writing his indictment of Flaccus and his account of the deputation to Caligula, monuments of the contemporary Jewish witness in the face of pagan opposition.

So in the Acts the narrative of actual persecution begins: and from start to finish it is instigated by the Jews. When the Gentiles do join in, it is only in the unthinking manner of excited mobs (once, at least, their indiscriminate violence recoils upon the non-Christian Jews who are attacking the Christians, Acts xviii. 17), or because they momentarily imagine that their political peace is threatened. It is the Jews who are really the aggressors. (This is written, as has already been said, in full and penitent realization of the terrible reversal of the rôles in later history, when Jews suffered indescribably at the hands of Christians, as well as at the hands of secularists or men of other religions.) If one asks

157

what New Testament references to the persecution of Christians are inescapably and demonstrably to be referred to Gentile action, there are extraordinarily few. Even one reference in addition to I Pet. ii. 12, noted above, which at first looks explicit, tells us little to the contrary. This is I Thess. ii. 14, addressed to Christians at Thessalonica, who are suffering, it says, at the hands of their own fellow-countrymen (ὑπὸ τῶν ἰδίων συμφυλετῶν)) just as the Jewish Christians had suffered at the hands of Jews. Some commentators *in loc.*, such as Milligan and Rigaux, are not prepared to interpret συμφυλέται rigorously in a racial sense, but think that it need only be a term of locality (so the 'Ambrosiaster' reads *concivibus*), and, if so, might actually include Jews. It would then, presumably, be necessary to interpret Ἰουδαῖος also locally, as 'a Judaean'. At most, even if we do assume here the persecution of Gentile Christians by Gentile non-Christians, there is no reason to interpret it in a sense contrary to the circumstantial account of this persecution at Thessalonica in Acts xvii. 5, where Jews are expressly named as the instigators of others—as with the martyrdom of Polycarp a century later (see Stauffer 1955, note 65, citing *Mart. Polyc.* xiii. 1). The reason why, in this same passage in I Thess. ii, the final doom is said to be overtaking the Jews has been interestingly discussed by E. Bammel (1959), who conjectures that it was the expulsion of Jews from Rome that led Paul to think that the final dénouement was imminent. If this is correct, it throws a significant sidelight on the interrelation between the persecutions of Jews and Christians.

There is no need here to dwell at length on the stories of persecution in Acts. It is enough to recall that, over and above the Thessalonian persecution just mentioned, all the others in Acts, from the persecution conducted by Paul before his conversion to the persecutions suffered by Paul and others, are uniformly traced to Jews or Jewish instigation, except a joint attack by Jews and Gentiles at Iconium (xiv. 5), and the attacks at Philippi (xvi. 19 ff.) and Ephesus (xix. 23 ff.). The one at Philippi starts for purely mercenary reasons and significantly ends with a complete vindication of

the apostles and abject apologies from the Roman authorities. So at Ephesus, it is commercial anxiety that precipi-
tates the attack, and it is civic authority that declares it
unjustified. When Roman local judicial procedure does come
upon the scene, it is (with the special exceptions of Philippi
and Ephesus) invariably the result, as with the trial of Jesus
himself, of agitation by the Jews; it invariably leads to a
verdict of 'not guilty', and if a Roman official, such as a Felix
or a Festus, does try to play into the hands of the Jews, it is
confessedly unconstitutional and immoral. The allusion to
Roman beatings in II Cor. xi. 25 (τρὶς ἐραβδίυθην) need not
fall outside such situations as these.

So far, then, as our only New Testament narratives go,
there is no predisposition to expect other than Jewish origins
for persecution. And if it is objected that the Acts is biased
in this respect, because it is a studied apologia to the Roman
government, the burden of proof rests with those who try to
discredit its reliability here. What do our other documents
reflect?

Within the Pastoral Epistles, II Timothy is the only one
containing more or less direct allusion to persecution. In II
Tim. i. 8, ii. 3, iv. 5, Timothy is bidden accept his share of the
suffering involved in the preaching of the Gospel; in ii. 9-12,
he is reminded of the apostle's own sufferings as typical of
confessional Christianity, and again in iii. 11 they are
mentioned, with the corollary (v. 12), 'Yes, persecution will
come to all who want to live a godly life as Christians'. But
although the apostolic example admittedly includes imprisonment, which, as we know, was generally not Jewish but
Roman (Acts v. 18, xii. 4 are exceptions), it has to be
remembered that in so far as it was Roman it was protective
custody rather than penal. The point of the example,
therefore, is simply that the apostle is suffering for his
Christian witness even to the length of imprisonment: there
is no necessary implication that what Timothy is facing is
Roman persecution. On the contrary, the apostle's own
predicament is traceable entirely to Jewish antagonism; and
indeed Gal. v. 11, vi. 12 had already expressly referred to
'persecution' for not 'preaching circumcision'. The same

applies to the allusion in I Tim. vi. 13 to the example of Jesus himself, who, before Pontius Pilate made his noble confession. The point need lie in no more than the courageous witness before a high authority; it is no necessary deduction that Timothy is himself facing persecution from the imperial authorities. That the threat of such persecution is by this time a real one may, however, be surmised, unless other evidence drives one to an earlier date, from the Christology of these epistles. It is well known that they use terms and titles for Christ (e.g. 'God our Saviour'[1] and his 'appearing') which, far more explicitly than those of the acknowledgedly Pauline Epistles, seem to have an eye upon the rivalry of an imperial cult. It is not difficult to believe that the menace of this rivalry is here throwing its shadow over the Christian consciousness: but it is impossible to be confident about this.[2] In Tit. iii. 1 Christians are still urged to be obedient to government authorities.

What of the persecutions alluded to in the Epistle to the Hebrews? The most explicit allusion is in x. 32 ff., where the readers are bidden recall the former days when, after their enlightenment (i.e. their conversion and baptism), they endured a great Marathon of sufferings, whether they were actually themselves made a spectacle as they endured insults and afflictions, or whether they took the side of others who were being subjected to such treatment; for indeed—it continues—they had shared the sufferings of the prisoners and had submitted to the seizure of their property. Further, that there were still, at the time of writing, Christians suffering imprisonment and distress is indicated by xiii. 3, where the readers are exhorted to remember such and to enter with them into their distresses; by xiii. 18 f., which hints that the writer himself may be a prisoner, though

[1] On this title see Mbiti 1973.

[2] See, however, Nock 1960, 64 f., questioning whether the Christian *euangelion*, good news, was meant in conscious rivalry to the 'good news' of the Caesar cult and whether there is not a misunderstanding of the pagan use of *Soter* ('which is very far from having in its ordinary usage the exalted connotation which it had for the early Christians') in the application of 'Erlösungsreligion' to the Caesar cult. See further Morrison 1960, *passim*, and especially 92 f.; and for the meaning of *Soter*, 134 f.

expecting release; and by xiii. 23 which announces that
Timothy 'has been released'. Finally, in xii. 4, in the course
of an extended exhortation to the patient endurance of
disciplinary suffering, they are reminded that in their conflict
and struggle with sin they have not yet reached the point of
shedding their blood; and xiii. 7, the allusion to their leaders'
faithful departure from life, looks uncommonly like an
allusion to the martyrdom of their original leaders.

All this, whatever its obscurities in detail, at least yields a
clear picture of Christians suffering violence and put in
prison, both in the past and present, with the possibility of
martyrdom ahead of them, and perhaps its example behind
them. So far as can be seen, this would all be satisfied, in
every detail, if one postulated, as has been suggested already,
that the origins of this Christian group lay in the circle of
Hellenistic Christianity in Jerusalem to which Stephen had
belonged and of which he had even perhaps been the founder
and martyr-hero. If, as the Acts tells us, a severe persecution
had ensued, leading to a dispersion—a Christian 'diaspora'—there is every reason to believe that many members, perhaps now re-assembled somewhere outside Palestine, would have cause to look back on the seizure of their
property, on imprisonments (such as Paul himself inflicted in
his rôle as scourge of the Nazarenes, Acts viii. 3, ix. 2, xxii.
19, xxvi. 10 f., Gal. i. 13), and on other sufferings; while at the
present time they would be still liable, like Paul the Christian
apostle and many other contemporaries or near contemporaries, to similar treatment. There is no trace here of any
circumstances that need have lain outside the scope of
Jewish violence or even Jewish constitutional procedure
against heretics within their midst. There is not the slightest
hint of anything that requires state persecution to account
for it. Even if we assume that the writer was, and Timothy
had been, in Roman custody, this still need be in no way
different in origin and circumstances from St Paul's Roman
imprisonment to which he was driven by Jewish opposition
(Acts xxviii. 19).[1]

[1] Dr J. A. T. Robinson, who was kind enough to read the revised
version of this chapter, remarks that he finds my proposals for the setting

As for I Peter, this is a well-known storm-centre of dispute. Here and here only in the New Testament we meet express allusion to potential suffering ὡς Χριστιανός, 'for being a Christian' (I Pet. iv. 16), and that, in contrast with suffering as a murderer or a thief or a criminal (κακοποιός—or 'a magician'?) or as ἀλλοτριεπίσκοπος. The last term is of uncertain meaning; but it is sufficiently clear at any rate that, whereas the Christians are warned against the scandal of becoming involved in penalties for ethical misconduct, they are told not to be ashamed if the charge is simply that they are (to use the opprobrious or scornful term invented by their opponents) Christianoi. Indeed, they are to welcome it as a chance to bring honour to God for the name (ἐν τῷ ὀνόματι τούτῳ). It is not surprising that this has been interpreted as a reference to some situation in which it was actually an indictable offence to be a Christian, and the celebrated correspondence between Pliny and Trajan (c. A.D. 112 has been appealed to as the closest parallel.[1] Pliny (Epp. x. 96) actually inquires 'whether punishment attaches to the mere name (nomen ipsum) apart from secret crimes, or to the secret crimes connected with the name' (flagitia cohaerentia nomini), stating that he had, in fact, condemned some simply for persisting in the claim that they were Christians, because he believed that 'in any case obstinacy and unbending perversity deserve to be punished'. The Emperor replied that, although they were not to be sought out, yet, if properly accused and convicted of being Christians, they must be punished unless they recanted. The distinction here drawn between 'the name itself' and crimes associated with the name seems at first sight to provide a striking parallel to the passage in I Peter. And it has been noted further[1] that the

of Hebrews incredible. He thinks that the reference is to Rome and to the deaths of Peter and Paul. He believes that the harassment which the readers suffered earlier when they were newly enlightened was from internecine attacks by the 'old believers' on the new, which may well have led to the expulsion of Jews from Rome in A.D. 49, impulsore Chresto (Suet. Claud. xxv. 4). See J. A. T. Robinson 1976, 206 ff., where a very closely reasoned and attractive case is made for this view, which may well be right.

[1] J. Knox 1953.

exhortation in I Pet. iii. 15 f. to give one's Christian witness boldly but with meekness and deference (ἀλλὰ μετὰ πραΰτητος καὶ φόβου) is reminiscent of Pliny's objection to the opposite qualities, *pertinacia et inflexibilis obstinatio*, in the Christians whom he condemned. It must be observed in passing that *pertinacia* and *obstinatio*, if they mean inflexible adherence to the Christian confession, are not really incompatible with meekness and deference, and that the Christians condemned by Pliny do not in fact seem to have shown any qualities other than I Peter approves, though it may well have looked like reprehensible stubbornness to Pliny. The main question is whether I Peter reflects a situation in which to be a Christian was itself an indictable offence.

That to be a Christian might lead to suffering is clear enough (although in I Pet. iii. 13 f. this is declared to be unlikely). That the suffering was inflicted by opponents who at least included Gentiles is shown by ii. 12. The only question is whether the suffering in view is the constitutional sentence of a Roman or a Jewish court, or is the rough justice of unofficial action. It can, of course, be argued that, since in I Pet. iv. 15 f. 'as a Christian' is parallel with 'as a murderer', etc., it follows that being a Christian is an indictable offence comparable to being a murderer. But it is questionable whether this is a fair inference. The word 'suffer' can include both the penalties of a sentence in a court and the sufferings (say) of victims of mob violence; and the phrase in I Pet. iv. 15 f. might mean: 'do not get into the courts for criminal conduct or even suffer unpopularity or violence for antisocial behaviour of any sort; but if you suffer unpopularity or violence for being a Christian, there is nothing to be ashamed of—rather it is an opportunity to bring honour to God for the name'. More probably still, however, even the charge of murder and the rest is not meant to reflect a constitutional indictment in court but is typical of the taunts of popular spite, that Christians are murderers, cannibals, fornicators, and atheists (see, e.g. *Mart. Polyc.* iii. 1; Tacitus, *Ann.* XV. xliv. 25; Tertullian, *Apol.*, *passim*); and that what the writer means is that Christians must give no handle whatever for calumnies of this sort: they must be beyond reproach in conduct; their only offence must be their allegiance to Christ.

Thus, on careful scrutiny, there is nothing even here to warrant the assumption of a setting or a date in which Christianity was an officially indictable crime; and the conditions are satisfied by precisely the circumstances we have already seen in the Acts: Jewish agitation leading to general unpopularity and suspicion, and then to mob violence, if not to Roman intervention. It remains, however, possible that at the time of this writing pagan opposition to Christianity is gaining in intensity, even without official backing, as it becomes more evident that the Christians will not acquiesce in the imperial cult. Long before any official Roman persecution *eo nomine* need be invoked,[1] one may imagine situations in which some Christian communities were threatened, others actually subjected to unofficial persecution, private antagonism, and mob violence: and, as a matter of fact, a case can be made for I Peter's containing two letters of encouragement, one addressed to Christians under the threat of such attack, the other especially designed for Christians in the actual flame.[2]

There remains the Apocalypse. It is widely recognized that Rev. xiii contains allusions to the emperor cult, veiled as thinly as possible—perhaps too thinly for prudence. Moreover, the titles of Christ in this writing seem (like those in the Pastoral Epistles already mentioned, but to an even clearer degree) to reflect a studied rivalry with the Emperor. Yet even here it is a remarkable fact that, as distinct from other parts of the Apocalypse, the letters to the seven churches (Rev. i-iii), unless it be in the one allusion to a Christian martyr at Pergamum 'where Satan lives' (ii. 13), reflect only Jewish antagonism. From within the Church, they reflect plenty of scandalous concessions to Gentile immorality: the Christian communities are clearly battling against the inroads of terrible antinomian licentiousness; but

[1] For a discussion of the grounds for Nero's persecution of the Christians, see Momigliano 1934, 725, 887 ff.

[2] Hart 1910, and Moule 1956–7. For further discussion, see Selwyn 1950, Kelly 1969, Best 1971, J. A. T. Robinson 1976, 140 ff., Elliott 1976, Bovon, 'Foi' (1978).

so far as danger from without goes, it is entirely located in the bitter antagonism of Judaism—those who call themselves Jews but are in reality the synagogue of Satan (ii. 9). Not a scrap of evidence can be extracted from these letters—if we were to confine ourselves to them—that persecution connected with the imperial cult has begun, unless we believe (and why should we?) that Antipas' death can have been for no other cause. From Chapter xiii one does gain a different picture. Rev. xiii. 16 seems to suggest actual civic disability or boycotting of some sort attaching to a refusal to accept pagan ways. But this is not to be found in the seven letters, and even Chapter xiii might be no more than a predictive lampoon on the essential antagonism of the state to a deviant group, a warning painted (as J. A. T. Robinson 1976 suggests) with colours borrowed from Nero's persecution in Rome. Certainly the allusions to the killing of Christians (ii. 13, vi. 9, vii. 14, xii. 11, 17, xiv. 1-5, 13, xvii. 6, xviii. 24, xix. 2, xx. 4) constitute evidence of persecution, as does the whole tone of the Apocalypse as an 'exhortation to martyrdom'; but the date, the place, and the degree of officialdom that should be attached to such references remain uncertain. What weight should be given to words like 'butchered' (ἐσφαγμένοι, vi. 9) on the one hand, which might suggest mob violence, and 'beheaded' (?) (πεπελεκισμένοι, xx. 4) on the other, which sounds more like a constitutional or quasi-constitutional execution? It certainly does not follow that we are witnessing a concerted persecution in Asia or even anything on the scale of the outburst in Rome under Nero. All in all, the New Testament contains very little that points clearly to more than mob violence, still less to the organized enforcement of the imperial cult. Such persecution as is evidenced is usually, by, or at the instigation of, Jewish opponents. In the words of Munck 1959, 55:

> The old notion of an initial period free from persecution, succeeded under Nero by continuing persecution on the part of Rome, must ... give way to the conception that the church was persecuted from the beginning, first by Jews, who did so partly through their own courts or by bringing charges before Roman courts, and partly by rough and ready means such as murder,

and later by the Roman state. The transition to this later period is perhaps also due to the Jews, for the action against Paul seems to be intended to draw the attention of Roman authorities to the fact that Christianity is not a Jewish sect but a new religion which, like any new oriental religion, was not covered by the law.

But we have still to consider the question what attitudes were adopted by Christians towards the imperial cult, quite apart from any matter of pressure or persecution. This involves the attempt to enter a world of ideas unfamiliar to the modern mind—at least in the West. Judiasm of the New Testament period is a special case, and, still more, Christianity; but of non-Jewish and non-Christian cultures of that period it seems to be true that terms which we reserve for worship of God alone tended to have a less limited application, and that, correspondingly, the line between the gods and men was less sharply drawn. Take, for instance, the Greek verb προσκυνεῖν, 'to do obeisance'. Such writers as D. J. Horst 1933 and M. P. Charlesworth 1935[1] show that, for a Greek from the days of Herodotus until at any rate the first two centuries of the Roman principate, it signified not *per se* an act of worship but rather of supplication, and that, if it was regarded as an inappropriate gesture before a human being, this was not because it was impious but because it was servile: it was despicable, perhaps—'foreign' and 'un-Roman'—but not blasphemous. Philo. *Legatio* 116, calls it βαρβαρικὸν ἔθος, something that cultured nations do not do. Hence Mordecai's refusal to 'kotow' to Haman in Esther iii. 2, etc.; while Nebuchadrezzar's abject gesture towards Daniel (Dan. ii. 46, etc.) enhances a special hero's dignity. In the New Testament, to be sure, 'obeisance', προσκυνεῖν, is expressly rejected, as appropriate only to God, by Peter (Acts x. 26) and by an angel in the Apocalypse (xix. 10, xxii. 9). It is perhaps significant, incidentally, that in the Gospels, while it still occurs as a gesture of servility in the parable of the two debtors (Matt. xviii. 26), it appears, by Matthew at least, to be regarded as appropriate before Jesus.[2] But the

[1] See also Nock 1928 (*bis*) and Mastin 1973.
[2] See Moule 1977, 175 f.

main point, although the matter is a complex one, is that roughly speaking the uses of προσκυνεῖν suggest (among other evidence) that the polytheistic world was less concerned about the distinction between men and gods than about the degree of adulation appropriate to a benefactor, whether human or divine, whereas monotheists might begin to ask questions about its appropriateness to any mortal.

And yet, even within monotheism this immediately needs qualifying. Koester (1966, 188) states that 'the Emperor cult did not have any serious religious implications throughout the first and second . . . centuries'; and Morrison (1960, 99) summarizes what was generally believed by all, *including Christians*, to the effect that '. . . *the ruler was both divine by appointment and human by birth*' (his italics); and, among the early Emperors, he distinguishes between the fanatics, Gaius and Nero, and the others who did not in the same way claim personal divinity. Thus, the practical distinction is not so much between different theories of divinity as between situations which allow one's attitude to remain imprecisely defined and situations which force a decision. Jews and Christians alike, when courageous enough, took a stand if and when the imperial cult required a discriminatory action such as offering incense. It was Domitian (A.D. 81-96) who demanded the style 'Master and God';[1] and it is under him that the provincial *concilia* in Asia Minor, which were concerned with the encouragement of the worship of Rome and Augustus and the supervision of richly endowed games accompanying the religious festivals, are likely to have become a menace to religious liberty. Dio (LXVII. xiii) tells of a certain Juventius Celsus (cf. Pliny, *Epp.* vi. 5. 4) who was accused of conspiracy and only escaped by worshipping Domitian. But Trajan, who succeeded Domitian, adopted a very different attitude, as we know from the famous correspondence with the younger Pliny, already men-

---

[1] Suet. *Dom.* xiii. 2; Dio LXVII. iv. 7. In addition to works already mentioned, note: Pauly-Wissowa, *Real-Encyclopädie, Suppl.* IV (1924); *Cambridge Ancient History*, xi (1936), *s.v.* 'Emperor-worship'; R. M. Grant 1955; Taeger 1960; Frend 1965; Osborn 1973; and bibliography in Cullmann 1959, 197, n. 3.

tioned (*Epp*. x. 96, 97). Thus Domitian is peculiar within the New Testament period; and while it is not unlikely that the Fourth Gospel reflects a consciousness of the rivalry between Caesar and Christ (xix. 12—you cannot favour Jesus and be a friend of Caesar; xx. 28—Domitian's very style, 'my Lord and my God!'), this in itself does not necessarily imply organized persecution.

What is implied, however, is a unique position for Jesus in the hearts and minds of Christians. The mere description of him in exalted terms might, in certain contexts, have meant no more than that, like the Emperor, he was hailed as a great benefactor, someone of heroic stature, even a Saviour. What makes it impossible to interpret the Christians' meaning as going no further than this is not the mere use of titles (although even these are in fact used in ways and in contexts which give them a special significance), but the fact that Jesus is accorded a place in relation to God which is unthinkable, especially in monotheistic terms, for one who was only human. He is found to be the sum of Israel, the sum even of humanity (he is ultimate Adam), in its ideal relation to God; but also he is found 'on the Creator's side', as it were: he is life-giving, he is the source, with God, of spiritual blessing; he is the environment in which Christians live their lives.[1] This, essentially, is why Christians who refuse to say Κύριος Καῖσαρ, 'Caesar is Lord', or to offer incense on the altar of *Roma et Augustus*, will have Κύριος Ἰησοῦς, 'Jesus is Lord', as their basic confession of faith.[2] In Judaism, Philo, it is true, did speak of Moses as divine, θεῖος; but he did so with the utmost care and reserve and qualification, and only in an exceptional context.[3] To Jews and Christians alike it was unacceptable to accord a man fully divine honours. Within the first century of the Christian era, the two most shocking years, in the eyes of world monotheism, both Jewish and Christian, must have been A.D. 40 and 70. In A.D. 40, Caligula made plans for the erection of his statue in the

[1] See Moule *Origin* (1977).

[2] Cullmann 1949. And see the interesting study of the worship of Jesus in apocalyptic Christianity by Bauckham 1980–81.

[3] Holladay 1977.

Temple (Josephus, *B.J.* II. 184 ff.)—an insane act of provocation[1] which was deferred by the courage of Petronius until the danger was mercifully averted by the emperor's death. But the very intention must have inflicted a deep wound on the sensibilities of Jew and Christian alike; and whatever may be the date of the relevant phrase in Mk xiii. 14, it would certainly have been recognized as particularly significant just then. B. W. Bacon made an exceedingly ingenious attempt to arrange Mk xiii and the Matthean and Lucan parallels in their relative order round this crisis,[2] but whatever one makes of the dating of these documents, and of the other most obviously relevant passage, II Thess. ii, there is no doubt that the year A.D. 40 must have seemed a religious crisis of such magnitude that many Christians may well have thought that the challenge to Christ had reached its climax and the End was imminent.

We must digress for a moment to consider II Thess. ii:

> And now, brothers, about the coming of our Lord Jesus Christ and his gathering of us to himself: I beg you, do not suddenly lose your heads or alarm yourselves, whether at some oracular utterance, or pronouncement, or some letter purporting to come from us, alleging that the Day of the Lord is already here. Let no one deceive you in any way whatever. That day cannot come before the final rebellion against God, when wickedness will be revealed in human form, the man doomed to perdition. He is the Enemy. He rises in his pride against every god, so called, every object of men's worship, and even takes his seat in the temple of God claiming to be a god himself.
>
> You cannot but remember that I told you this while I was still with you; you must now be aware of the restraining hand which ensures that he shall be revealed only at the proper time. For already the secret power of wickedness is at work, secret only for the present until the Restrainer disappears from the scene. And then he will be revealed, that wicked man whom the Lord Jesus will destroy with the breath of his mouth, and annihilate by the radiance of his coming. But the coming of that wicked man is the

---

[1] This would have been tantamount to a claim very different from that formulated by Morrison 1960 (see p. 167 above) as acceptable to Christians among others. (See especially Morrison, p. 133, on Gaius and Nero.)

[2] Bacon 1925, 53 ff.

work of Satan. It will be attended by all the powerful signs and miracles of the Lie, and all the deception that sinfulness can impose on those doomed to destruction. Destroyed they shall be, because they did not open their minds to love of the truth, so as to find salvation. Therefore God puts them under a delusion, which works upon them to believe the lie, so that they may all be brought to judgement, all who do not believe the truth but make sinfulness their deliberate choice.

(II Thess. ii. 1-12.)

Other suggestions apart,[1] there are two main rival interpretations of this passage which claim attention. One, recently revived, is that what prevents the arch-antagonist of Christ from openly showing his hand is the fact that the necessary evangelization of the world (Mk xiii. 10-14 (?), Matt. xxiv. 13-15) is not yet complete. 'That which restrains' (*N.E.B.* 'the restraining hand') is, on this interpretation, the missionary situation, the impenitence or non-conversion of areas of the pagan world: God in his long-suffering is waiting for them to be brought to the truth (cf. Lk. xviii. 7 (possibly), Acts xvii. 30 f., Rom. ii. 4, I Tim. ii. 4, II Pet. iii. 15). But, even if this might otherwise be plausible, it is extremely difficult to see how the masculine ὁ κατέχων (*N.E.B.* 'the Restrainer') can be fitted into this sense: it will have to mean the apostle and his missionary colleagues, in so far as they have not yet achieved their task! The alternative interpretation (going back to Tertullian and many others after him)[2] is to take the restraining power to be the Roman law and order, which prevents the outbreak of state persecution (or of persecution by Jews—so E. Bammel 1959) against Christians; and the masculine, the one who restrains, might then be the Emperor himself (Claudius) or some governor to whom the allusion would be recognizable. It was indeed after the removal of such restraints and in the reign of Claudius' successor, Nero, that the great antagonist did really come out into the open.

---

[1] For an exhaustive review to date, and a completely new theory, see Giblin 1967.

[2] Tertullian, *Apol.* xxxii; *De Carnis Resurr.* xxiv; Lactantius, *Inst. Div.* VII. xxv; Ambrosiaster, *in loc.*; Augustine, *C.D.* XX. xix; Chrysostom *in loc.*; etc.

And this interpretation still seems the more plausible, though by no means wholly satisfactory.[1]

At any rate, the future denouement referred to in II Thess. ii is described in terms which may well have gained significance from the attempt of Caligula, so nearly realized, only some ten years earlier, to do just what is here predicted. And, returning now to this Caligula crisis, we have to admit that, at such a time, instead of drawing together in face of the common threat to their common faith in one God, Jew and Christian are more likely to have been conscious of estrangement. If the Jews were in for persecution, they had no desire to be embroiled with the doubtfully loyal sect of the Nazarenes; and if the Christians' faith was menaced, they, on their part, could not meet the danger on exactly the same terms as their Jewish neighbours, for their allegiance to the one God was couched in terms quite alien to the Jews—the Lordship of Jesus Christ.

But that crisis passed, and even as soon after it as the writing of Romans, Paul was able to declare that the state derives its authority from God and that a mark of a good Christian is that he should be a law-abiding citizen. Indeed, this would not in any case have seemed to be contradicted by Caligula's madness.[2] The famous saying of Jesus, 'Pay

[1] *Contra* Cullmann 1962, 164 ff. Excellent survey in Best 1972, *in loc.*

[2] Cf. Morrison 1960, 105: 'There is no reason to believe that Paul's view of the State would be lightly altered by troubled circumstances; he had suffered and Jesus had been put to death at the hands of the State, but Paul was peculiarly impressed by the hand of God in it all'. Cf. Philo's panegyric of Augustus and Tiberius, side by side with his attack on Caligula in *Legatio*. See also Bammel 1960. He observes that Rom. xiii. 1 ff. is practically alone in the Pauline writings and rare in the New Testament altogether (I Pet. ii. 13 ff., Tit. iii. 1 are the only parallels), and that it carries a Jewish rather than a Christian (let alone Pauline) stamp, though it goes beyond anything in Jewish Wisdom Literature. The explanation of its presence he finds in the situation at the time of writing. The Jewish community in Rome, though themselves demonstratively loyal to the Emperor, were continually being upset by turbulent elements coming in from Palestine. Hence the repressive measures and the expulsion of the Jews from Rome in A.D. 49. Not until A.D. 54 were Jews and Jewish Christians beginning to be able to return; and then, in their sense of insecurity, the Jews would be anxious to make the Christians scapegoats for anything that went wrong. Hence Paul's particular concern to

Caesar what is due to Caesar' (Mk xii. 17 and parallels) was
still as appropriate as when it was first uttered. Even more
noteworthy, in view of the discussion above, is the occurrence of similar sentiments in I Pet. ii. 13 ff.—

> Submit yourselves to every human institution for the sake of
> the Lord, whether to the sovereign as supreme, or to the
> governor as his deputy. . . . For it is the will of God that by your
> good conduct you should put ignorance and stupidity to silence;

and in I Clement lxi. 1 f. (despite the references to persecution in i. 1)—

> Thou, Lord and Master, hast given them [our rulers and
> governors] the power of sovereignty through Thine excellent and
> unspeakable might, that we knowing the glory and honour
> which Thou hast given them may submit ourselves unto them,
> in nothing resisting Thy will![1]

If the Epistle to Titus is late, the exhortation to obedience in
Tit. iii. 1—

> Remind them to be submissive to the government and the
> authorities, to obey them. . . .

is also noteworthy, as is the injunction to prayer for rulers in
I Tim. ii. 1 f.

But far more striking than the passing of the crisis of A.D.
40 and the maintenance of a Christian ethic of state loyalty is
the remarkably small trace left upon the New Testament by
the major crisis and disaster of the Jewish war and its
culmination in A.D. 70. One reason for this is perhaps to be
found in the fact (as B. W. Bacon pointed out) that 'it was
the Synagogue, not the temple, which was the real opponent
of the Church; and the effect of the disappearance of the

emphasize the Christian affirmation of the State's rights and responsibili-
ties. Much more characteristic of Paul's own thought, however, is
(according to Bammel) I Thess. v. 3 where εἰρήνη καὶ ἀσφάλεια (a good
Roman slogan, *pax et securitas*) is held up to ridicule in the light of
apocalyptic. The Rom. xiii attitude, he holds, is far from central in Paul's
thought. Travis 1970, 128, n. 43, queries whether there is evidence that
'peace and security' was actually a slogan; but in any case it no doubt
represents the way in which the blessings of the principate were hailed.

[1] J. B. Lightfoot's translation.

worldly-minded Sadducees, with their outworn sacrificial
ritual in the temple, largely divorced from the true religious
life of the people, was really on the whole to strengthen
essential Judaism' (1925, 81).[1] But it would be an over-
simplification if one imagined that all that A.D. 70 did to
Jewish religion was to remove an outworn 'establishment'.[2]
It would probably be nearer to the mark to say that Judaism
was only saved, when the virtual removal of the Temple
system might completely have wrecked it, by the dedicated
labours of such as Johanan ben Zakkai and others, in turning
Judaism into a religion of writings and of a tradition such as
could survive independently of sacrifice.[3] There may be a
more direct explanation for the paucity of references in the New
Testament to the disaster of A.D. 70. What if most of the New
Testament was written before that date? This suggestion was
made in the first version of this book, and J. A. T. Robinson
(1976) has, since then, taken it up in detail and asked whether
any part at all of the New Testament can be proved to be later
than A.D. 70. Perhaps it is worth while to print again such
reflexions on this question as were offered in the first version.
They do not go so far as Dr Robinson, but they go a long way
towards his position. They assume that the Pastoral Epistles,
the Johannine Gospel and Epistles, and the Revelation are
probably later than A.D. 70 (though see Excursus II for an
alternative suggestion on the Pastorals); had they mentioned
II Peter and Jude, it would also have been in the post-70
category. They run (with small changes) as follows: It has yet
to be demonstrated beyond doubt that Matthew's Gospel is

[1] Morton Smith 1960–61, 355 f., maintains (but is he right?) that G. F.
Moore (1927) misrepresents the situation when he suggests that Phari-
saism was *representative* Judaism. Rather, the Pentateuch, the Temple, and
the *'amme ha' aretz* were the real backbone of Judaism. Daniélou 1964–77, i,
9 f. contrasts 'the Judaism contemporary with Christ, that of the
Pharisees, Essenes and Zealots' with 'the rabbinical, legalistic Judaism
developed after the fall of Jerusalem' which early Christianity was
concerned to combat. Is he right in these distinctions?

[2] Clark 1959–60 even argued that sacrificial worship in fact continued
after A.D. 70. See p. 175 n. 4 below.

[3] See Le Déaut 1976, 217 ff.; and, for Johanan ben Zakkai, Neusner
1970. See, further, observations by Morton Smith, 1960–61; W. D. Davies
1964, 259.

later;[1] even if it is, there is less scope here for signs of the situation if (as is here maintained) that Gospel was a genuine attempt to reconstruct the story of Christian beginnings. Luke-Acts may or may not be later. The notorious allusion to the siege of Jerusalem (Lk. xxi. 20) is not proof positive that the words were written after the event.[2] And even if the Acts is concerned, if not primarily yet *inter alia*, to demonstrate that Christianity is true Judaism and should thus be unmolested by the state and had in fact always been acquitted by Roman law, this proves little or nothing as to its date. As a matter of fact, this particular aspect of its apologetic may easily be exaggerated: if Christianity as true Judaism had really been its primary theme, would its author have gone to such pains to underline the abolition of circumcision as a rule? As for the Epistle to the Hebrews, it has already been argued (above, pp. 68, 97, 160 f.) that it fits best in a period before—perhaps shortly before—A.D. 70. The Pastoral Epistles and the Johannine Gospel and Epistles are of uncertain date: probably after A.D. 70 (though see Excursus II for an alternative theory for the Pastorals), but it is difficult to say how long after. The Apocalypse may be before A.D. 70. If it were later, one might certainly have expected not only a reference to the vindication of God's martyr-prophets in the city where their Lord was crucified (Rev. xi. 8), but a description of her destruction on the analogy of the doom-song on Babylon-Rome in Chapter xvii. One might, however, perhaps argue that it was

[1] Note that Rengstorf 1960, 106 ff., argues that Matt. xxii. 7, usually taken to be a *post-eventum* reference to the destruction of Jerusalem, need not be more than the use of a 'topos' already well-established in Rabbinic literature.

The story of the coin in the fish's mouth (Matt. xvii. 24-27) is connected by both Clement of Alexandria (*Paed.* II. i. 14. 1) and Irenaeus (*Haer.* V. xxiv) with the incident of the tribute-money; but they confuse the temple-tax with the imperial poll-tax. 'This could the more easily happen after the destruction of the Temple in A.D. 70, when the Temple-tax was replaced by the *fiscus Iudaicus*'—T. W. Manson in an unpublished paper on 'Render to Caesar ...' (where he cites Juster 1914, i. 377 ff., ii. 282; Schürer 1901, ii. 314 f.; Dalman 1928, iii. 182 f.) See further, Horbury 1982

Possibly the correct deduction from the non-juxtaposition of the two incidents in Matthew itself is that it was before A.D. 70?

[2] See Dodd, 'The Fall of Jerusalem' (1968). But *contra* O'Neill 1970, 1 ff.

not the judgment on Jerusalem, but the vindication of God's Israel over 'the synagogue of Satan' that really concerned the Christian. It might be a different matter if we had any literature from the Jewish Christians who escaped to Pella— if indeed this is a historical event.[1] It is hard to believe that a Judaistic type of Christianity which had itself been closely involved in the cataclysm of the years leading up to A.D. 70 would not have shown the scars—or, alternatively, would not have made capital out of this signal evidence that they, and not non-Christian Judaism, were true Israel.[2] But in fact our traditions are silent: either, as has been said, there is less of the New Testament than is generally imagined that belongs to a date later than A.D. 70, or else, when the disaster fell upon the centre of Judaism, the spiritual core of its adherents consolidated so rapidly the already familiar argument that the heart of their religion was not in sacrifices but in prayer and almsgiving,[3] that the Christians found little change of front in their essential opposition, and therefore found little occasion to appeal to the destruction of the Temple in their apologetic.[4]

[1] See Munck 1960.

[2] As a matter of fact, even demonstrably later literature is also strangely reticent on this issue. Even Justin (*Dial.* lxxxix. 2) just stops short of using this argument. But we find it in Hippolytus *Jud.*; and Sulpicius Severus, *Chronic.* II. xxx (*c.* A.D. 400), says that by destroying the Temple Titus, far from destroying Christianity, 'furnished a daily demonstration to the world that they [the Jews] had been punished on no other account than for the impious hands which they laid on Christ' (information kindly furnished by H. W. Montefiore). The Jews' retort was that, on the contrary, it was the apostasy of the Christians that had brought down wrath (see A. L. Williams 1935, 137, n. 7).

[3] E.g. 'He who prays in the synagogue is as one who offers a pure *minhah*', R. Phinehas (*c.* A.D. 360), in the name of R. Hoshaiah (*c.* A.D. 225), *T. J. Berakoth* 8d, four lines up (cited in *T.D.N.T.* vii, 824).

[4] Clark 1959–60, 121, n. 3, argues that Jewish sacrificial worship continued on the temple site until A.D. 135. His strongest evidence is certainly Josephus, *Ant.* III. 224–236 (*c.* A.D. 94), *Contra Apionem* (a few years later), II. 77 and 193-8, and the unique Hebrew document discovered in Nablus *c.* 1900, based on a fourteenth-century chronicle and describing a pilgrim going to sacrifice in the High-priesthood of Amram (A.D. 120–130). He thinks that II Esdras (IV Ezra) is between A.D. 70 and A.D. 135, and if so, i. 31 is a Christian addition shortly after A.D. 70.

For Jews and Rome, see further Morrison 1960, 137.

Outside the New Testament, I Clement is also silent about A.D. 70. J. A. T. Robinson (1976) 327 ff., asks why this, too, may not, after all, be because it was written before the fall of Jerusalem. At all events, it was before the fall of Jerusalem that Paul, more than any other Christian of his generation known to us, succeeded in establishing a Gentile Christendom independent of its geographical origins.[1] Jesus Christ himself becomes the Temple, the Place, the Land.[2]

To conclude. The New Testament as a whole reflects plenty of attack from antagonists, but little that was official or state-organized. What can be identified is mainly Jewish rather than imperial; and the manner and degree of it varies from place to place and from situation to situation. Relations between Christianity and Judaism depend in part on the relations at any given time between Judaism and Rome. These are the main factors to be borne in mind when trying to discern the genesis of 'persecution-documents'.

[1] See Chadwick *Circle* (1959), with comments by W. D. Davies 1964, 320, n. 1.
[2] Cf. W. D. Davies 1974.

CHAPTER VIII

BUILDING THE SUPERSTRUCTURE
AND CONSOLIDATING

FOR the study of Christian beginnings there is value in that architectural metaphor which distinguishes the foundation from the superstructure. It is this which has attached the word 'edification' to a certain type of Christian activity; and although that word has unhappily been spoilt (like too many good words) by association with what the rebellious call 'trying to do them good', it stands for an important distinction within Christian procedure—the distinction between foundation and superstructure. 'I am like a skilled master-builder', wrote Paul (I Cor. iii. 10), 'who by God's grace laid the foundation.' That foundation, he immediately goes on to say, can be nothing other than Jesus Christ. No structure is a Christian structure which is not so founded. The Christian community is not reared on exhortation but on declaration: not on fine ideals, but on witness to a Person. When, at Caesarea Philippi, Peter declared that Jesus was the King of Israel, he was bearing witness to what he had thus far observed in Jesus. It was only a preliminary finding; it was, as directly appeared, a distorted estimate; but it was the start of an estimate which was corrected and deepened by the resurrection, and which constituted the foundation of the Christian faith. It turned out that the apostles' witness to what they had seen and discovered to have been done by God in and through Jesus was the rock upon which the whole edifice was reared.

Evangelism is thus the laying of the foundation. But what follows upon it is of course the rearing of the superstructure—the work of 'edifying', and consolidating, both the individual convert and the community corporately. And this prolonged task was the cause of much that has come to form part of the New Testament—indeed, of far more than was produced by evangelism, which has left less written deposit.[1] Literature was not then a primary propaganda-medium. The initial 'propaganda' was mostly spoken. But much that followed came to be written. It is therefore to the words, the phrases, and the whole sections that reflect the work of upbuilding and (to change the metaphor) 'pastoral care'—shepherding—that we now direct our attention.

If the work of evangelism, in some form, must needs be always the beginning, the mode of that evangelism and the nature, scope, and time-scale of the response vary widely. In Acts ii the response to Peter's preaching at Pentecost is represented as immediate, and we are told that large numbers were baptized forthwith. As for the gaoler at Philippi, so far as the narrative goes it sounds as though he and his household were baptized there and then, in the night, on no more secure a basis than the desire for 'rescue' from peril and the assurance that to be 'rescued' he need only believe on Jesus (Acts xvi. 30 f.). Such sudden conversions, without background, training, or instruction may sound precarious. But it would be arbitrary to say that there can never be situations in which it is right to receive into the Church first and give detailed instructions and 'edification' afterwards.[2]

In other words, we are here confronted with the perennial tension between two ideals: on the one hand, there is the ideal of what later came to be called 'the gathered church'—that is, a Church composed only of 'converted' individuals, gathered out of their setting by the election of God and the careful sifting of the evangelist. On the other hand, there is the 'mass-movement' type of ideal, in which whole clans, whole populations, are swept in collectively. The rights and wrongs of these conceptions of evangelism depend very largely upon the social structure and other conditions prevailing in any given instance. The 'gathered church' ideal is primarily applicable in a context where the individual is already accustomed to act independently—that is, in a society where

[1] For an important study of evangelism in the early Chruch, see E. M. B. Green 1970.
[2] For Jewish catechesis for proselytes, see Daube 1956, 106 ff.

some degree of sophistication obtains, and where some measure of individualism has resulted: still more obviously, in areas which are already nominally Christian. The opposite extreme is presented by societies which are still essentially tribal in structure. A well-documented study of such conditions in India some years ago is to be found in J. W. Pickett 1933. There he writes (p. 22):

> The distinguishing features of Christian mass movements are a group decision favourable to Christianity and the consequent preservation of the converts' social integration. Whenever a group, larger than the family, accustomed to exercise a measure of control over the social and religious life of the individuals that compose it, accepts the Christian religion (or a large proportion accepts it with the encouragement of the group), the essential principle of the mass movements is manifest.

More recently, D. A. McGavran 1959 wrote (p. 23):

> Except in individualized, urbanized, homogeneous populations, men and women exist in social organisms such as tribes, castes, and kindreds. They have an intense people-consciousness and tribal loyalty. Churchmen holding Gathered Church convictions proclaim a universal Gospel to them and invite them as individuals, regardless of what others do, to choose Christ. To them this sounds like being urged to leave their own and join the Christian 'tribe'. ...

Now, curiously enough, in the New Testament we hear scarcely anything of prolonged, individual catechumenates; yet, on the other hand, neither is there direct evidence of any collective, corporate units larger than the household. We are confronted, therefore, with a delicately balanced situation. There is no clear evidence within the New Testament that Christianity advanced into any primitive tribal areas, unless it be North Galatia. If it is South Galatia that is meant, then 'Galatians'—so far as Paul's converts went—need only mean the town-dwellers of Derbe, Lystra, and Iconium—vernacular-speaking, admittedly, but worshippers of Zeus, not primitive animists (Acts xiv. 11 ff.). Apart from these—even assuming these to be in any way exceptional—Paul's work seems to have lain in the Hellenized cities and to have reached no lower in the scale of education and intelligence than the household slave. There is no evidence for the penetration of Christianity into the labour-slave-gangs of the great estates, or the mines.[1] I Cor. i. 26-29, whatever its stress upon the ignorance and obscurity of the majority of converts in Corinth, certainly need not be read so as to imply the completely inarticulate and illiterate.

Thus we are led to conclude that, for the New Testament, the household is generally the largest unit. It is possible, as has been suggested, that the recipients of the Epistle to the Hebrews may have been a more or less homogeneous group which had originally formed a synagogue or a section of a synagogue. But it seems to have been the household (including slaves and servants as well as relations) that formed the largest evangelized group, and the 'house-church' that represented the normal manner of such a unit's growth and expansion.

Not that there is extensive direct evidence even for this assertion. All that can be said is that, while we hear in the New Testament of the conversion of individuals (and that in large numbers, on the day of Pentecost and shortly afterwards), we also hear of the conversion of the households of the 'official' in Jn iv. 53, of Cornelius (Acts xi. 14; cf. x. 2), of Lydia at Philippi (Acts xvi. 15), of the gaoler (Acts xvi. 31 ff.), of Crispus, the Corinthian synagogue-official (Acts xviii. 8), and of Stephanas (I Cor. i. 16; cf. xvi. 15); while Onesiphorus' household is alluded to, evidently as a Christian group, in II Tim. i. 16, iv. 19, and in Tit. i. 11 false teachers are described as upsetting whole households, and there is evidence for the existence of house-churches (Rom. xvi. 5,[2] I Cor. xvi. 19, Col. iv. 15; Philem. 2). As a matter of fact, even in Pickett's study of the Indian mass movements, one of the most arresting conversion-stories is that of Ditt, the Chuhra hide-dealer in the Punjab, who, on being individually converted, returned to his village and converted first his wife, his daughter, and two neighbours, and later four other men. It was only then that the movement in his

[1] See Judge 1960, 51 ff. (esp. 60), and 1961.
[2] Minear 1971 believes that Romans reflects a number of different house-groups. But see Cranfield 1979, 820 ff.

area gained momentum (see *op. cit.* 43-45. This was in about A.D. 1900).

New Testament evangelism, then, represents neither the typical mass movement type of primitive tribalism nor the purely individual, 'gathered church' ideal. Its background was the family life and synagogue group of Judaism or of a near-Judaic pattern, unless there were cases when, in the relatively atomized, sophisticated life of the Levantine city, it took the form purely of house-churches, 'gathered' from an amorphous society. And it is in such a setting that we have to place the process of edification which is the subject of our inquiry. As has already been remarked, we hear almost nothing of a prolonged catechumenate. Apollos is scarcely an instance. He was already himself an evangelist when he was taken and further instructed by Aquila and Priscilla (Acts xviii. 24-28); it does not appear whether, in the end, he was given specifically Christian baptism, like the 'disciples' (perhaps Apollos' converts) found by Paul at Ephesus (Acts xix. 1-7). Apart from this, there are indications, indeed, that there were recognized courses of 'training for beginners'; but whether, as in the later Church, baptism was the climax to which such courses led, or whether the New Testament practice was first to baptize and then to instruct,[1] is harder to establish. The only direct evidence, as we have already seen, points to the latter. In Gal. vi. 6 the catechumen is bidden share his goods with his catechist, which seems to imply a substantial period of instruction; but we are still not told whether or not baptism had already taken place.

In three passages in the New Testament, the metaphor of 'milk' as the diet of the immature is used. In I Cor. iii. 1-3 the metaphor is applied, first to the Corinthians' condition—a natural one—when they were first evangelized, and then, by way of reproof, to their unnatural continuance in a state of spiritually arrested development (evidenced by selfish rivalry and partisanship). This yields no evidence as to the nature and place of catechetical teaching. In Heb. v. 11-14 the milk metaphor is applied, again by way of reproof, to the

---

[1] See a striking instance of this in Java, in Bentley-Taylor 1961, 43. I owe this reference to K. N. Sutton.

failure of those who are addressed to grow up, beyond their elementary grounding, into maturity in the Christian faith; and in vi. 1 f. there follows a very interesting definition of what this grounding consisted of: it was 'elementary Christian teaching' (ὁ τῆς ἀρχῆς τοῦ χριστοῦ λόγος); it was a 'foundation' (θεμέλιος) 'consisting of' (? or, less probably, 'upon which was to be built') 'repentance from dead (i.e. useless or fatal?) deeds; faith in God; teaching about lustrations (βαπτισμοί), (? and about) the imposition of hands, the resurrection of the dead, and eternal judgment'. Fairly clearly, this is catechesis. But again, whether it in fact wholly preceded or in part followed baptism (? and the imposition of hands), who can say? Finally, I Pet. ii. 2 urges the hearers to long for the unadulterated spiritual milk (λογικὸν γάλα) that will enable them to grow into salvation. For those who believe that this represents an address to baptizands on the verge of baptism, it will mean, no doubt, the further training which will follow baptism and might also contain an allusion to the ritual administration of literal milk at baptism as a symbol of the milk and honey of the promised land they were now entering (cf. Heb. vi. 4). But if it be interpreted rather as a recall of Christians who are facing persecution to the great basic experience of their baptism in the past, it will be a reminder of and a recall to their essential nourishment, and will imply neither reproof for immaturity nor the actual imminence of baptism itself (see above, pp. 37 f.).

So we are left unable to be certain whether or not, before the end of the New Testament period, the later system of a prolonged catechumenate before baptism had developed. It seems entirely possible that an individual was often baptized as a member of an entire household, after a single hearing of the very minimum of 'Gospel', and only subsequently given detailed instruction. But about the content of the instruction, whenever it was given, there is fortunately more evidence. Even without specific evidence, it would go without saying that, sooner or later, after baptism if not before, the initial evangelism must be followed by a process of detailed instruction—of 'edification'. And this rearing of the superstructure, this upbuilding, would, according to the stage at which it occurred, comprise more or less of the basic proclamation, the foundation Gospel. In other words, if we maintain the familiar distinction between *kerygma* and *didache* too rigidly, we shall not do justice to the real nature of all Christian edification, which builds, sometimes more, sometimes less, but always at least some of the foundation material into the walls and floors.

In the main it is, of course, true that the foundation is laid by the proclamation of what God has done in the life, death, and resurrection of Jesus ('There can be no other foundation beyond that which is already laid; I mean Jesus Christ himself', I Cor. iii. 11), and the challenge to acknowledge Jesus as Lord; and that there then follows detailed instruction about the implications of this, both for doctrine and conduct.

But, to illustrate how subtly foundation and superstructure interlock, it may be observed—however paradoxical it may seem at first sight—that in the New Testament it is in the epistles that one may hear more echoes of the work of evangelism than in the Gospels—or, at least, than in the Synoptic Gospels. For the Synoptic Gospels, at any rate, contain virtually no post-resurrection, evangelistic 'appeal': they do no more (essentially) than state the facts; they do not embody the 'Believe, repent, and be baptized' of the pentecostal appeal (Acts ii. 36, 38). The epistles, by contrast, although all addressed to the already evangelized, and, to that extent, speaking retrospectively, nevertheless contain a great deal more reference to the meaning and the means of becoming a Christian—hearing, believing, becoming incorporate in the Body of Christ (e.g. Rom. i. 2-4, I Cor. xv. 1 ff., Gal. iii. 1-5, Eph. ii. 8, 13, Col. i. 6, 13 f., 21 f., ii. 6 ff., I Thess. i. 9 f.). Thus, in a sense, the rôles are reversed: it is the epistles which echo the initial challenge (albeit as a recollection of what happened to the Christians originally); whereas the Synoptic Gospels, viewed from this angle, embody rather that filling out of the initial challenge which was bound to follow. Even when the evangelistic appeal had been accepted and the convert baptized, there followed the stage when the catechumen (for he was still such) must be given some conception of the character of the God to whom, in Christ, he had yielded his life: bare *kerygma*, without personal content, would lack the power to stir and move, which the Gospels, by bringing the character of Jesus to life, do possess.[1] The contents of the Gospels are thus necessary, if the convert's faith is to be concrete and his love glowing. The Fourth Gospel to some extent combines both functions, for it alone of the four Gospels both presents a narrative 'portrait' of Jesus and also answers the question 'What must I do to be saved?' But even so, its reply is strangely lacking in corporate and ecclesiastical content. The Johannine Epistles go a little further; but it is Paul who alone provides an adequate answer, though, as has just been said, it needs reinforcing by the living portrait of Jesus' character.

Paul speaks in terms of hearing and responding with trust; of divestiture of the old humanity and investiture with the new; of coming to be incorporated in Christ; of receiving the power of the Holy Spirit. And all this is for him clearly 'focused' in Baptism and Holy Communion (Rom. vi. 1 ff., I Cor. x, xi. 17 ff.). Only on such conditions may a Christian look to receive the moral fibre and stamina to become what in reality he now is: it is to the Holy Spirit that he owes his life; it is by the Holy Spirit that he must now let his conduct be shaped (Gal. v. 25). Only on such conditions, perhaps, can the Sermon on the Mount be faced. J. Jeremias *Sermon* (1963) proposed to see in the Sermon on the Mount in its present form in Matthew a body of teaching intended for Jewish Christians, already converted, already 'overpowered by the Good News'. He saw it as a catechism for baptismal candidates or newly baptized Christians (p. 24).

We have, then, to recognize an interlocking of foundation and superstructure something like this:

(A) Initial proclamation: Jesus, approved by miracles and deeds of goodness, was handed over by the Jews to Pilate and killed; but God raised him from among the dead and made him Lord and Messiah. All this was according to the scriptures.

---

[1] See Dodd 1927; also Filson 1941, and Stanton 1974.

(B) Initial appeal: therefore repent, be baptized, and you will receive the Holy Spirit.

(a) Extension of proclamation: Jesus' life and miracles and deeds of goodness were such as the following (extended examples). His clash with the Jews, his sentence and execution followed the following pattern (details). The resurrection was manifested like this (narratives). The relevant scriptures are appropriately inserted throughout.

(b) Extension of appeal: repentance, baptism, and the coming of the Spirit *mean* (a new life, a transfiguring of outlook, the wearing of the new humanity, etc., etc.); they involve (details of character and conduct); they are related to Judaism and pagan religions as follows (discussion of the relevant issues).

Thus, into foundation (A) and ground-floor (B) alike are introduced materials of character (a) and (b). In any case, again and again the initial impact must, in actual life, have come neither from the hearing of 'Gospel' material nor from the direct 'appeal', but from the quality of the Christian community, as family or as house-church, into which an outsider would begin to be drawn by friendship, and only then would hear the explanations.[1] In such cases, (Aa) and (Bb) may occur in any or in no order. In I Tim. iv. 13, Timothy is bidden to give his attention to (public) reading (? of the Jewish scriptures), to exhortation, and to teaching: all three, side by side. Nevertheless, it is safe to assume that standard instruction for enquirers—newly baptized or preparing for baptism—did, like the proclamation, the *kerygma*, settle into a certain more or less regular pattern. Instruction, *didache*, both as the repent-and-be-baptized appeal and also as instruction in the meaning and morals of the Christian life, found for itself its own sequences and chapters; and it is possible to reconstruct something of its appearance from the material scattered about the New Testament. It is true that the New Testament contains no elementary handbook of

---

[1] See R. R. Williams 1954–55, pointing out that Eph. iv. 4-6, which manifestly contains 'credal' elements, is nevertheless not in the order of credal logic (God–Christ–Spirit–Church) but in the practically reverse order of experience.

instruction (such as *The Didache* may be). But it does contain a good deal of instruction addressed to the already Christian communities, and it seems probable that much of this, with only minor differences, represents what had already been given to them at the beginning. At any rate, this instructional and edificatory material often looks like a reminder, a recall to what they already knew: sometimes, indeed, it is explicitly so described—just as, correspondingly, the celebrated little summary *kerygma* in I Cor. xv. 1 ff. is, in so many words, a reminder of what they had heard at the beginning:

> And now, my brothers, I must remind you of the gospel that I preached to you; the gospel which you received, on which you have taken your stand, and which is now bringing you salvation. Do you still hold fast the Gospel as I preached it to you? If not, your conversion was in vain.
>
> First and foremost, I handed on to you the facts which had been imparted to me: that Christ died for our sins, in accordance with the scriptures; that he was buried; that he was raised to life on the third day, according to the scriptures; and that he appeared to Cephas, and afterwards to the Twelve. Then he appeared to over five hundred of our brothers at once, most of whom are still alive, though some have died. Then he appeared to James, and afterwards to all the apostles.
>
> In the end, he appeared even to me.

There is sufficient literature on the codes of household ethics—the *Haustafeln*, to use the German term—to make it unnecessary here to go into much detail about these.[1] In Acts xx, in his moving farewell to the Ephesian elders at Miletus, Paul is represented as committing them to the Lord and to the message about his graciousness which can build them up and give them a share in the promised land with all God's people (*v.* 32). That is a striking description of just that merged *kerygma*-and-*didache* which we have been considering; and we may assume that much the same is intended in the allusion in Rom. vi. 17 to the τύπος διδαχῆς,

[1] The literature, covering decades of research, includes the following: Klein 1909, Weidinger 1928, Carrington 1940, Hunter 1940, Selwyn 1958, 194 ff., Seeberg 1966, Lillie 1974–75 (bibliography, p. 183), Schweizer 1976, 159 ff., 1977, Dunn 1977, 141 ff.

the outline or mould of teaching to which the Romans had been 'entrusted' by their evangelist, whoever he may have been. And precisely this kind of τύπος seems to be exemplifed both by the brief summaries of the Gospel in I Cor. xv. 1 ff. and II Tim. ii. 8, and by the rules for domestic and family life (the *Haustafeln*) of the epistles, which contain injunctions to each member of the household springing directly from the baptismal fact of incorporation in Christ. That there seems to be a certain uniformity in the 'headings' relating to baptismal divestiture and investiture, and the resulting conduct, not only as between the Pauline Epistles but also when I Peter and James are brought in, argues for a widely recognized τύπος. And the fact that parallels to some of the ethical material can be found, not only within Judaism[1] but also in Stoic and other pagan writers, is only natural. Christianity began within Judaism and quickly spread in Graeco-Roman society; and borrowings from both were to be expected. What is striking is the degree to which the distinctiveness of the ἐν κυρίῳ, 'in the Lord', permeates and sets its stamp upon the Christian ethical instruction.[2] It is against membership in the Christian community that conduct is tested. The measure of what is right becomes 'that which is fitting' (ὡς ἀνῆκεν) 'with the Lord as one's standard' or, possibly, 'for one who is incorporate in the Lord' (ἐν κυρίῳ), Col. iii. 18; cf. I Cor. vii. 39 ('provided the marriage has the Lord's approval' or 'is within the Lord's fellowship').

But one feature of far-reaching importance, which is common to all the ethical teaching of the New Testament and to that of the immediately succeeding period also, must

---

[1] See Zöckler 1904, 1–12, 19–44; Vögtle 1936; Wibbing 1959.

[2] In I Thess. iv. 1 ff. the tradition received from the apostle concerns 'how to behave and to please God' (τὸ πῶς δεῖ ὑμᾶς περιπατεῖν καὶ ἀρέσκειν θεῷ) and is spelt out in ethical injunctions, closely bound to religious devotion; and similarly in II Thess. iii. 6 conduct according to the tradition received from the apostle (? and his colleagues) (περιπατεῖν κατὰ τὴν παράδοσιν ἣν παρελάβετε παρ' ἡμῶν) is contrasted with disorderly behaviour (ἀτάκτως περιπατεῖν), which bears witness to the element of instruction on *conduct* in the tradition or traditions (παραδόσεις, plural, in II Thess. ii. 15).

here be mentioned. Most Christians at the time must have had very little opportunity to exercise any direct influence on public affairs.[1] Let alone the fact that of course they had no vote in the appointment of Roman administrators, it seems unlikely that they could have become involved much or for long even in local administration (as Greeks and Hellenized Egyptians for instance, were in Alexandria[2]). The Christian way of life was as peculiar, in the eyes of the pagan world, as Judaism—and even more unintelligible. This does not mean that the Christian ethic was individualistic. On the contrary, New Testament Christianity is nothing if not social: the Semitic traditions on which it arose are themselves strong in corporate sense; and, still more, it was quickly found to be impossible to describe Christ himself otherwise than as an inclusive, a corporate personality. To become a Christian, therefore, was *ipso facto* to become an organ or limb of that Body, and the Christian Church is essentially the household of God (see Gal. vi. 10, Eph. ii. 19, I Tim. iii. 15, Heb. iii. 5 f., x. 21). Indeed, for all its corporate sense in the Old Testament, Israel was never so fully organic a concept as in God's Israel, the Church. Perhaps one must add, in all honesty, that the alienation from the rest of society, forced upon Christians by their way of life, must have been an added incentive to find the social dimension within their own community.[3] For all this, it remains true that, strong as the corporate sense was within the fellowship of the Church, the kind of activity in society at large which, in our day, is known as Christian socialism, leading to 'Christian action', was simply not a possibility.

The question of slavery is a signal instance. Everyone knows what a battle had to be fought in Parliament by Wilberforce and others in the nineteenth century to secure the abolition of slavery in the British colonies. For Christians

---

[1] Perhaps it should be added, in all fairness, that the Stoics, despite their boast that the world was their *polis*, may not have done much better: Schweizer 1960, 104, calls this only 'a retreat from active political life and an admission that he can no longer exercise any practical influence on this "polis"'.

[2] I owe this observation to C. H. Roberts 1963.

[3] Again, I owe this observation to C. H. Roberts 1963.

in the first century to take any direct action for the abolition of what was part of the very structure of society was plain impossibility: there was no machinery except bloody rebellion—and that was not the Christian way. Besides, this weapon had in fact failed when, periodically, it had been tried by pagan slave-heroes such as Spartacus. Stoicism had influential members; and although it may too often have been content to proclaim ideals in general, it did sometimes practise them on the individual scale, and it did influence the imperial legislation.[1] But for Christians the only way of advance, apart from purchasing the freedom of individual slaves (cf. e.g. Ignatius, *Ad Polyc.* iv. 3), was to change the relations between individuals. This they did, and nowhere is it more remarkably reflected than in the New Testament Epistles (see especially Philemon). And the same principle applies, *mutatis mutandis*, to all New Testament ethics. The Sermon on the Mount is essentially concerned with individual character and action. The sex-ethics of the Epistles and Gospels are related entirely to individual action within the framework of already existing law and custom. Nothing else would have been realistic.

The result is not only that present-day readers look in vain to the New Testament for directions in social ethics, but also—paradoxically enough—that, in the New Testament period itself, Christianity seemed, to outside observers, to be cut off from religion. For paganism, religion was emphatically an integral part of the civic life. For Jews, religion was nationalism and was partly expressed in external ways that symbolized a national allegiance. But Christians, refusing to join in the pagan imperial cult and yet possessing no tangible sacrifices, no priesthood, no place of worship of their own, seemed to be atheists. They could show none of the recognizable badges of a religion. Their political community ($\pi o\lambda i\tau\varepsilon v\mu a$), as Paul put it, was in heaven (Phil. iii. 20), and it was not available for demonstration (cf. above, p. 145).

Thus in two directions this deeply corporate way of life appeared to be something individualistic—or, if corporate, then at any rate withdrawn from public life: it took no part in

[1] See Ehrhardt 1959, ii, 18.

civic action, and it possessed nothing that the ancient world could recognize as a cultic system. Elsewhere there were religious confraternities—Greek ἑταιρεῖαι and Semitic *ḥaburoth*—within a larger cultus; here, although there were fellowship meals, they seemed to lack the visible background of cultus. But the outsider was mistaken. Within its own communities, the Church was not only aware of the organic unity of limb with limb in the Body of Christ, but was extremely active in 'social welfare'; and, for those who had eyes to see, it had both altar and Priest (see, especially, the Epistle to the Hebrews; cf. pp. 51 f. above).

Further, it needs to be strongly emphasized that what has just been said about the Christians' inability to participate actively in politics does not necessarily mean that they showed a lack of concern for them.[1] On the contrary, in many cases they took a very lively interest in all that went on. A Jehovah's Witness today may watch the Gadarene stampede of the nations without dismay, because he believes that they are irretrievably doomed and that their downfall must bring in the new age. An extreme sectarian today may renounce membership in all societies except that of Christ, citing II Cor. vi. 14—vii. 1 ('Do not unite yourselves with unbelievers; they are no fit mates for you . . .') and seeming to forget I Cor. v. 9-13 which explains that when St Paul said (perhaps in this very passage, II Cor. vi. 14 ff., if that is a fragment from an earlier letter) that the Christians were not to mix with the immoral, he meant immoral *professing Christians*, not the immoral among non-Christians: to avoid the latter they would have had to leave the very world! But, in contrast to such attitudes, most New Testament Christians seem to have believed that the Kingdom of God must show itself in connexion with and not independently of the kingdoms of this age. A good case can be made for tracing this to the teaching and example of Jesus himself. The outlook of Revelation, admittedly, is more detached; but for Paul, the rule of the Emperor was part of the divine system of law and order (Rom. xiii. 1), and the Kingdom of God could not be conceived of in a vacuum, independently of the events

[1] See Schmidt in Ehrhardt 1959, ii, 20, n. 1.

of history. But the Church's rôle was not yet to take overt political or social action. It was still to grow within the body politic as a (usually unrecognized) revolutionary force. It was leaven, like the Kingdom of God of which it was the agent. The only point, within the New Testament period, where it inevitably came out into the open was in relation to idolatry, and so to Emperor worship. Here, 'passive resistance', even, if need be, to the length of martyrdom, was the only course for the loyal. But until the Roman authority demanded something that the Christian could not conscientiously give, because it conflicted with his ultimate loyalty, it was his duty, as an obedient member of society, to promote that law and order which, in principle, belonged to the God of peace whose very act of creation was itself a triumph over anarchy (cf. I Cor. xiv. 32 f. and Rom. xvi. 20). God is a God of 'cosmos', orderliness; the principle of authority, and ordered society, is part of the divine structure of things (cf. I Cor. xi. 3). Human authority therefore goes wrong only when it assumes the supreme authority which belongs to God alone: 'pay Caesar what is due to Caesar', but also, 'pay God what is due to God'. New Testament Christianity thus proved itself to be revolutionary but not anarchical. Revolutionary, because the recognition of a divine, ultimate authority always, in the last analysis, must overturn the secular lust for absolute power; but not anarchical, because it renounced violence, and, when its ultimate loyalty clashed with the secular demand, it still accepted the principle of authority and submitted to the penalties imposed by the secular authority even when they were irresponsibly imposed. Its weapon, in other words—when it was true to itself—was not the sword but the cross.[1]

Here, then, was the focus of extremely vital instruction for the new convert. Having renounced Satan and made Jesus his Lord, was he not to refuse to pay taxes, was he not to reject all civic authority? Might it not be his positive duty to join revolutionary bodies like the Zealots, and use force to overthrow the secular power—the arm of Satan? No, said the

[1] On the agonizing tension between these two, see J. A. T. Robinson 1960, 43 ff.

Christian catechist. God's whole creation owes its coherence to the principle of orderly, stratified, authority: God-Christ-Man-Woman; God-the Powers-the Subjects;[1] and if sin and disobedience have introduced dislocation and chaos, it will not be mended by anarchy, but by costly, suffering obedience. This is the very principle of the incarnation. Therefore, although 'the children of the kingdom' are indeed free (in the sense that to them belongs the true citizenship and that they are not a subject people), yet they pay taxes as their contribution to the principle of orderliness (Matt. xvii. 24 ff.); they obey civic authority, not for fear of the sanctions, but as a positive contribution to the same principle (Rom. xiii. 5, I Pet. ii. 13-15); and if they should be forced to disobey because of a head-on collision of loyalties, then they will without question accept the cost (Revelation). Above all, they must never make themselves liable to penalty for immoral conduct: ethically they must be exemplary.[2]

This brings us to the situations reflected more than once in the New Testament—the situations in which pagan standards in sexual conduct conflict with Christian. Was a convert to make a clean break with his past by renouncing his pagan partner? If he did, might he marry again, within the Christian community? Or was sex itself evil, and must the Christian renounce it totally? One can see these questions being dealt with tentatively, sometimes inadequately, by Christian pastors; and there is clear enough evidence of gross moral failure within the Church, necessitating severe disciplinary action. (See especially I Cor. v, vi. 12 ff., vii and the Pastoral Epistles.)

Another problem, that of the right attitude for Christians to the participation with pagans in eating meat that had been consecrated to idols, bulks large in I Cor. viii-x; but whether instruction along these lines formed a regular part of catechesis it is impossible to say. That it was, according to

[1] Cf. Morrison 1960, *passim*.

[2] On the consciousness that failure to exhibit Christian conduct and qualities brought discredit on the Name of Christ, see van Unnik 'Rücksicht' (1960). In the New Testament there are: Rom. xiv. 16, I Cor. x. 32 f., Phil. ii. 15, Col. iv. 5, I Thess. iv. 11 f., I Tim. iii. 7, vi. 1, Tit. ii. 8, 10, I Pet. iii. 17, iv. 14 ff.

Acts xv, dealt with in general terms by the Jerusalem council, only adds to the uncertainty: what had become of this decree when Paul wrote I Corinthians? Why does not the question figure at all in the other Paulines (unless it be in Rom. xiv) and in I Peter? It is difficult to imagine a Gentile-Christian community in which it would not be a problem; yet Acts xv (generally) and I Cor. viii-x (in great detail) are the only clear allusions to it. The parallel food-problem—whether Gentile Christians were to be expected to observe Jewish tabus in their common meals with Jewish Christians—is also dealt with in Acts xv and is perhaps hinted at here and there (Gal. ii. 11 ff., Rom. xiv, Col. ii. 16?), but otherwise it is not mentioned—not even in Rev. ii. 24, which in some other respects recalls the decree of Acts xv. One may readily imagine that, as the Christians became progressively distinct from Judaism and more and more Gentile in membership, this soon ceased to be a live issue: table-fellowship with someone possessing a sensitively Jewish conscience ceased to arise.

In addition to the ethical problems confronting the Christian, about which instruction was offered in the catechetical tradition, there were what may be called the matters concerning quality of character. Strictly speaking, there are no 'cardinal' virtues in Christianity, for Christian character does not 'hinge' round the disciplined practice of virtue: it is a spontaneous growth, it is a crop of qualities springing from the seed of new life divinely sown (see Gal. v. 22, Eph. v. 9, Phil. i. 11, Heb. xii. 11, Jas iii. 18); or—more characteristically described—it is life in the new age, resulting from incorporation in the new humanity which is Christ (see Rom. xiii. 14, II Cor. v. 17, Gal. iii. 27, Eph. iv. 20-24, Col. ii. 11 f., iii. 9 ff.). *Agape* is not a virtue among other virtues so much as an impulse, divinely implanted: it is God's love for us in Christ, reflected and responded to. And what in other systems might be called virtues are the shape spontaneously taken by *agape* in the Christian community (I Cor. xii. 31—xiii. 7).[1] Therefore, although in fact many Christian

[1] On *agape* the fullest treatment is to be found in Spicq 1958–59 (abridged Eng. trans. 1963, 1965), though see the important critique in

qualities seem to coincide with those on the Stoic list, the difference is a radical one. The Stoic virtues are the proud struggle of the human spirit to conform to nature and to gain the mastery over weakness; the Christian virtues emerge after the recognition of sin and the confession of human helplessness: they are the result of committal to God and dependence upon him. It is not by chance that ἀνδρεία, 'courage', so prominent in pagan ethical systems, is a word never occurring in the New Testament (the verb ἀνδρίζεσθαι occurs once, I Cor. xvi. 13). The courage of the Christian martyr is not the result of the steeling of the soul to endure; it is the by-product of self-forgetfulness and abandoned loyalty—sheer dependence upon the Lord. By the same token, the Christian character is notable for just that warmth and graciousness of which the Stoa might actually have felt ashamed.[1] Catechetical teaching about character accordingly consists largely of a recall to baptism, and only derivatively of an enumeration of those qualities of graciousness, forbearance, and sympathy which are the crop springing from the baptismal seed of the Spirit (e.g. I Pet. i. 23—ii. 3, cf. Gal. v. 22). It contains, however, plentiful warnings against a relapse into the indiscipline and immorality of pagan days.

One of the most impressive features of the new life, for the recent convert, must have been the deliverance from fear—fear of witchcraft and evil spirits and the forces of evil. The typical exhortation therefore speaks in terms of the realm of darkness from which the Christian has been rescued into glorious light, of the conquest of the powers of darkness and

Joly 1968. Further to *agape*, see Schlier 1970; Furnish 1972; Piper 1979. On various aspects of New Testament Ethics and their Jewish background, the following may be consulted (a very small selection, in alphabetical order): Bonsirven 1935, abridged ed. 1964; Clogg 1944; Daube 1956 *passim*; W. D. Davies 'Ethics' (1962); Dodd 1927, 1951; Enslin 1930; Flew 1934; Furnish 1968, 1979; Herbert 1963; Houlden 1973; Jessop 1960; J. B. Lightfoot 'Paul and Seneca' (1888); Lofthouse 1939; Manson 1960; L. H. Marshall 1946; C. H. Moore 1920; Radford 1931; P. Richardson 1979; Schrage 1976; C. A. A. Scott 1934; Snape 1938; Spicq 1965; Wilder 1950, 1956.

[1] See Spicq 1958–59, iii, 262, n. 3.

of this age, of the slavery from which Christ releases into the freedom of the new creation (Rom. viii. 35 ff., xii. 2, xiii. 12-14, xvi. 20, I Cor. viii. 5 f., xii 2, Gal. iv. 8 ff., Eph. *passim*, Col. i. 13, I Thess. i. 9, I Pet. ii. 9, etc.). The hag-ridden world of superstition looms up very clearly behind the catechumen. Yet, now that he is released from fear, he finds that among the chief dangers of the new life are rivalry, partisanship, disunity; and much catechesis is concerned with meeting these, as may be seen towards the end of Romans, Galatians, Ephesians, Colossians, and throughout I Corinthians and Philippians.

Thus the New Testament material reflecting primitive Christian catechisms[1] ranges from the repetition of the Gospel foundations, through specific ethical problems, to the building up of character in the common life in the Body of Christ. And there is no reason to be surprised if similar material was used again and again even in the later stages. Every Christian, however mature, profits from a recall to his baptismal vows and his earliest instruction in the Christian way. And this brings us back to the subject of the Christian homily. This has already been mentioned in the chapter on worship (pp. 40 f.). It need only be repeated here that catechetical instruction on the meaning of baptism and the conduct springing from incorporation in Christ are so integral to the whole Christian life that one is not surprised if it is impossible to be sure whether, for instance, material in I Peter represents a baptismal homily, or epistolary instruction for the already baptized. Both alike have the same content.

Much more specific are the passages relating to false teaching. These are prominent in many of the New Testament writings, and, while some are evidently addressed to a single, given situation, there are others which may well represent recurrent difficulties. The various types of error

[1] For the next phase in this fascinating study, outside our period, the reader is referred to H. Chadwick's edition of the *Sentences of Sextus* (1959), where he writes (pp. x f.): 'The interest governing the present study has lain in the affinity and difference between Christian morality of the second century and that of the surrounding world. The work is set forth, therefore, as a contribution to the much discussed question of the continuity and discontinuity between the early Church and contemporary society ...'.

attacked may be fairly succinctly catalogued. There is the tendency to rely upon human action as meritorious, instead of constantly casting oneself on the mercy of God alone[1]— one of the chief dangers attacked by Paul (see especially Romans, Galatians, and Phil. iii). At the opposite extreme is antinomianism—the assumption that the mercy of God condones licentious living or a selfish unwillingness to act charitably and that the spiritual life is, in any case, not concerned with the physical realm—also attacked by Paul (e.g. Rom. iii. 5 ff., vi. 1 ff.), but taken up with special vigour in James (ii. 14 ff.). Behind both this antinomianism and the opposite extreme of legalism stands a false doctrinal position often combated in the New Testament—the dualism which regards the material world, as such, as evil; and this, in its turn, naturally fraternizes with a false Christology which does not allow for a real incarnation but either places Jesus in the (Arian) position of a demi-god, or reduces him to the wholly human level, or splits him into two not really united aspects.

With this kind of error goes, indeed, a generally weak grip upon the historical. As G. Stählin points out in his article μῦθος in *T.D.N.T.*, the New Testament uses this word 'myth' in a pejorative sense: it signifies a divorce from the reality which had been historically manifested, and most of all in the incarnation (I Tim. i. 4, iv. 7, II Tim. iv. 4, Tit. i. 14, II Pet. i. 16). For the New Testament, 'truth' is not abstract: it is in Jesus. Thus the myth-mongers are vigorously assailed in the Pastoral Epistles and II Peter.[2] II Peter and Jude are both much occupied with combating extreme licentiousness masquerading as religion (II Pet. ii, Jude throughout); and

[1] In the original version of this book, I called it a 'Judaistic' tendency. This is correct only if 'Judaistic' is carefully distinguished from 'Jewish'. The fact is that 'legalism' is a phenomenon that appears within both Judaism and Christianity, and wherever men rely on their own efforts and aim at their own justification. For criticism of exploiting so-called 'Jewish' legalism as a foil for Christianity, see E. P. Sanders 1977, *passim*.

[2] See Miegge 1960, 103 ff. Outside the New Testament, 'myth', otherwise defined, may be used in far from pejorative senses. It can stand for metaphorical modes of speech such as, in certain contexts, are the best or only modes available. See J. Knox 1964, Wiles 1977.

the same danger seems to be reflected in parts of the letters to the seven Churches in Rev. ii and iii.

But Christological error bound up with moral laxity receives its classic refutation in I and II John. For the first time in the New Testament, clearly defined doctrinal tests are laid down (I Jn ii. 22 f., iv. 2 f., v. 5), and those who do not conform have been expelled, or, at any rate, have left (I Jn ii. 19). Paul could speak scathingly of a false gospel (Gal. i. 6-9); he could call false apostles Satan's ministers (II Cor. xi. 13-15); he could call for the excommunication of a moral offender (I Cor. v). Rev. ii. 9, 24 and iii. 9 stigmatizes false teaching as Satanic. But not till I John is specifically defined doctrinal error ascribed to Antichrist, or Christians encouraged to slam the door on the unorthodox (II Jn 10 f.). This extreme attitude seems to have been due to reaction against that insidious type of dualism just referred to. In reply, the Johannine Epistles urge that Christians do not sin (I Jn iii. 9), or, if they do, they must confess it and seek forgiveness (I Jn i. 8—ii. 2); and that Christ did come in flesh (I Jn iv. 2) and 'through blood' (I Jn v. 6)—that is, he really suffered physically. In their arrogance, these spiritual 'élite' had evidently un-churched the rest. I John is concerned to reassure the ordinary members of the community that the real tests[1] are in conduct, in love, in the presence of the Spirit, and in a sound creed.

Another agitating problem, which assumed larger proportions in the sub-apostolic era, is the question of sin after baptism, and of perfectionism.[2] The Epistle to the Hebrews is the New Testament writing that seems to exhibit the clearest signs of this (see vi. 4 ff.; but also I Jn v. 16 ff.).

Thus individual instruction for catechumens, homilies addressed to groups of worshippers, and special admonitions in the face of particularly critical situations can all be seen to have contributed content and form to different parts of the New Testament. Catechesis implies catechumens and catechists: it implies a 'pastoral' situation; and sooner or later a pastoral situation calls for administrative organiza-

---

[1] Cf. Law 1909.
[2] See Telfer 1959.

tion and doctrinal definitions of some sort. It requires some guarantee that the teaching will be authentic and properly given, and that those under instruction—and, indeed, Church members at any stage—will be properly looked after. But organization and concern for orthodoxy are always liable to lead to institutionalism and ossification and authoritarianism. A great bug-bear of German Protestant New Testament scholarship is *Frühkatholizismus*[1]—the beginnings of 'catholicism' in the sense of institutionalization and sacramentalization; and many see it rearing its head in the Pastoral Epistles, if not in Luke and Acts and elsewhere. The concern of the present inquiry, however, is not primarily the history of Church order, but the understanding of circumstances that actually led to the writing of the various parts of the New Testament. Is any part of the New Testament attributable to the need for order or the beginnings of the bureaucratic mind? It is arguable that the Pastoral Epistles are, in large measure, of this character. I Timothy and Titus contain directions about the qualities needed in elders or overseers (πρεσβύτεροι or ἐπίσκοποι) and their assistants (διάκονοι); I Timothy also contains directions for selecting such widows as deserved relief; all three of these epistles evince a concern for sound teaching, decorum, and order, and contain references to discipline. There is a passage, too, in I Peter (v. 1-5) about Church leaders and discipline; and the Johannine Epistles reflect conflict over both orthodoxy and authority.

For such reasons it is possible to view these documents as arising from a concern for Church-order; and it is often proposed to place them all late in the New Testament period on the ground that, in the earlier decades, no such institutionalism had yet arisen.[2] But the matter is not quite so simple. It is true that the main Pauline Epistles seem to reflect a spontaneous or 'charismatic' leadership in the local communities, rather than constitutionally appointed officers. The word presbyter does not occur in the Pauline *corpus*

---

[1] 'Emergent Catholicism' in Perrin 1974. See Dunn 1977, 341 ff.; and, for a careful definition, Conzelmann 1969, 289 f.

[2] See Dunn 1977, 197, 351 ff. *Contra* J. A. T. Robinson 1976, 67 ff.

except in the Pastorals, and, although the Acts, as well as referring to elders in Jerusalem, represents Paul and his assistants as appointing elders in their Churches, it is often said that Acts is late and unreliable and anachronistic. Philippians is the only Pauline letter outside the Pastorals to mention overseers (ἐπίσκοποι) and (as an office) assistants (διάκονοι). On the other hand, presbyters are not intrinsically unlikely to have become an institution in Christian communities in early days. They were, of course, already an institution in Judaism and other cultures (indeed, wherever a γερουσία or senate—a council of elders—obtained), and the ἐπίσκοποι or overseers are not recognizably different. And there is nothing in the organization implied by the Pastoral Epistles that absolutely necessitates a late date. There is generally someone with the authoritarian and organizational tendencies in most movements, even at an early stage.

However, whether early or late, the writing of the Pastoral Epistles does seem to have been occasioned by the need for order, authority, and stability; and the Johannine Epistles provide evidence for a crisis not only in doctrine (already noted) but also in authority. The writer of II and III John, who styles himself 'the elder', is bitterly at odds with some leader named Diotrephes (III Jn 9). Whether Diotrephes is an orthodox leader and the elder a 'deviationist',[1] or whether the elder is the rightful authority (a Bishop or a 'presiding Bishop'?) and Diotrephes a rebellious underling, it is impossible to be sure. Certain it is that there was conflict; and that, in the Johannine Epistles, there is an inward-turned, protective exclusiveness, and an antagonism against innovating ('from the beginning', ἀπ' ἀρχῆς, is a refrain, I Jn i. 1, ii. 7, 13 f., 24, iii. 11, II Jn 5 f.; the one who goes ahead instead of 'staying in the teaching'—in other words, a 'modernist'—is condemned, II Jn 9). This is not a common note in the New Testament, though there is also Jude 3 with its phrase 'the faith which has been handed down to God's people once for all' echoed, substantially, by II Peter. Both Jude and II Peter are essentially attacks on

[1] Käsemann 1951.

false teaching (apparently insolent and immoral perversions of the Christian faith), and both of them were actually occasioned by this danger: Jude 3 says so in so many words. They join the Johannine Epistles in the category of defence against attacks from within, and in their reactionary appeal to an established doctrine. In these respects, they would certainly fit well into a late stage in the New Testament period. G. W. H. Lampe (1973) offers a sketch of the doctrinal threats to the Christian faith, particularly from 'Judaizers', in the late apostolic and sub-apostolic periods, including evidence from these Epistles. Yet, there is a certain freshness, too, in the Johannine Epistles, and, with the appeal to tradition, a sense of spiritual renewal, which marks them as alive and supple.[1] Institutions and orthodox creeds, if they are here being fought out and moulded, have not yet ossified or become dead.

[1] Dunn 1977, 198.

CHAPTER IX

VARIETY AND UNIFORMITY IN THE CHURCH

IT has often been alleged, since F. C. Baur's influential work (especially 1845 = 1873–5), that the history of the early Church can only be understood in terms of sharp conflict between Paul and the Jerusalem leaders. Paul is portrayed as fiercely at odds with Peter and with James the Lord's brother, who, in Acts xv, appears as the president of the Jerusalem community. This was one of the foundation principles of the so-called Tübingen School in its reconstruction of the story, and some form of it lies behind much thinking today. On this showing, Acts is an eirenic attempt, many years after the event, to paper over the cracks. Now, Acts xv certainly does represent Paul as present and at least tacitly concurring when the 'Jerusalem decree' was agreed, whereas there is not a hint of it in the Pauline epistles, even when it would have been most germane (I Corinthians). Equally, it is undeniable that Gal. ii. 6, 9 refers, in what sound like sarcastic tones, to the 'pillar' apostles at Jerusalem; that in Gal. ii Paul refers to interference at Antioch by a person or persons 'from James', and records a sharp controversy that followed, between himself and Peter; and that in both I and II Corinthians he is more than once on the defensive against (apparently) attacks on his apostolic standing. But there is not sufficient evidence to establish doctrinal warfare between Paul on the one side, and Peter and James (and John) on the other. In Gal. i. 8 f., Paul fiercely denounces the preachers of an alien gospel— which, he says, is no gospel. But when it comes to the controversy with Peter in Ch. ii, it is not that Paul disagrees with Peter on any principle. Paul's gravamen is that Peter is not being consistent with his own convictions and his accepted principles. And as for James, there is no evidence that he commissioned or sanctioned those whom Paul attacked as false preachers (Gal. ii. 5, 12), or (in II Cor. xi. 13-15) as Satan's ministers.[1] On the contrary, Gal. ii. 9 shows James, Peter, and John entering into a concordat with Paul. It may be sarcasm, again, when Paul speaks in II Cor. xi. 5 of the 'super-apostles' (οἱ ὑπερλίαν ἀπόστολοι), but there is no evidence that, in their case, he opposes their teaching. Paul is certainly arguing for his own equal authority; but he shows no sign of trying to combat their teaching. And when it is said, as it frequently is, that Paul was inconsistent with his own principles, this is to misunderstand those principles.[2] He hotly condemned any 'gospel' that impugned the sufficiency of Christ, and that implied that baptism into the death of Christ needed reinforcing by circumcision. To this he made no concessions whatever (Gal. ii. 4 f., v. 2, vi. 12; cf. Col. ii. 10 f.). But his principle otherwise, when this was not at stake, was to go all the way in accommodation and tolerance (Rom. xiv, xv, I Cor. ix. 19 ff., x. 33). Such intransigence and such tolerance belong together in a perfectly logical way; and as for Paul's battles for his authority, these are not to be confused with purely doctrinal issues. In any case, the threat to Paul's 'gospel'—to his teaching and his doctrinal stance—came (so far as the evidence goes) not from the leaders themselves, such as Peter and James, even if James' doctrine, especially his Christology, may have been very different from Paul's, but from the unnamed Judaizers—the more zealous and less thinking adherents of the conservative wing (cf. Acts xxi. 20 f.).[3] Even if one connects the Epistle of James with this James the Lord's brother, and interprets it as a manifesto of a strongly Judaistic wing in the Church, this provides, in itself, no evidence for actual conflict with Paul. Paul would have accepted all James' strictures on 'faith without works' (Jas ii. 14 ff.).

But if substantial evidence is lacking for doctrinal conflict between Paul and the Jerusalem apostles, this is not for a

[1] See Barrett 1973, *in loc.*
[2] Dunn 1977, 254 f.
[3] *Pace* Dunn 1977, 256.

moment to deny the fact of diversity in the early Church. At
the present time, a bewildering variety both of liturgy and of
doctrinal stance confronts any worshipper who travels round
from place to place, even within such traditions as the
Anglican and the Roman, where over many previous generations there was comparative uniformity. But in this respect
the Churches of today are nearer to those of the New
Testament period. In the New Testament period, before
there was a written (let alone an authorized) liturgy, and
before there were any generally recognized formularies of
doctrine, the Christian who journeyed would have met
extreme variety.

According to Acts xvi. 15, Lydia, a woman who dealt in
purple dye-stuffs and whose base was at Thyateira in the
Province of Asia, in western Turkey, was brought, with her
whole household, to Christian faith, through Paul's ministry
of preaching at Philippi. When this happened she was
presumably on an extended sales tour over the Aegean cities.
If we had travelled with her on such a tour and on similar
tours along the chain of Levantine coastal cities and inland
from them, and had gone with her to the little Christian
group or house-church in each place, what should we have
found? We should have encountered a wide range of doctrine
and practice among communities who all, nevertheless,
claimed some attachment to Jesus of Nazareth. Somewhere
in Judaea we might have found the circle of James the Lord's
brother still worshippping in a Christian synagogue consisting of practising Jews who also believed in Jesus as God's
Messiah, but who may have gone only a very little way
towards formulating a doctrine of Jesus as divine: the
Ebionite type, entertaining a diminished Christology.[1] In
Samaria, who knows what kind of a Christian colony there
might be? One, possibly, which highly honoured the name of
John the Baptist (whose mission had been vigorous in those
parts and whose tomb, perhaps, they boasted), and which
treasured traditions many of which are now embodied in the

[1] For the extra-biblical evidence about James, see Euseb. *H.E.* II. xxiii.
4 ff., III. v. 2; and, in addition to standard discussions of this in
Dictionaries etc., note one by Hyldahl 1960.

Fourth Gospel. They would see in Jesus the one who had been destined to come—the prophet like Moses.[1] Cosmopolitan Antioch (even to judge from no more than the references to it in the New Testament, let alone its later history) would present within itself a considerable range of different types of community—Gentile, Jewish, Judaizing, Hellenizing—with different shades of Christology; while the Lycus valley, if we followed that route, would present a strange amalgam of oriental astrology, Jewish legalism, and Christian beliefs (see Colossians and commentaries thereon). By journey's end, we would be prepared for the seething diversity of Ephesus where the Pauline churches were to be quickly invaded by antinomianism, Judaizing Christianity, and influences of a Johannine type (see Acts xx. 29 f., ? Ephesians, Rev. ii. 1 ff., and the Gospel and Epistles of John). If we then took ship from Miletus to Alexandria, it is hard to say what we should find. There is a strange silence in the New Testament about Christianity in Egypt.[2] But C. H. Roberts challenges W. Bauer's theory (1971) that the early Egyptian Church was mainly gnostic, and explains the obscurity of the early Church in this area rather by the dominance of the Jews till

[1] For John the Baptist's connexion with Samaria, note the tradition of his burial there (for which see Jerome's Latin version of Eusebius' *Onomasticon s.v.* 'Someron' (Migne XXIII, 920): 'dicunt autem nunc pro ea Sebasten vocari oppidum Palaestinae, *ubi S. Joannis baptistae reliquiae conditae sunt*' (the italicized words correspond to nothing in Eusebius' text), and Theodoret *H.E.* III. iii, where, under Julian the Apostate, they opened ἡ θήκη of John the Baptist, burned his bones, and scattered the ashes). For his connexion with the Fourth Gospel, see *inter alios,* J. A. T. Robinson, 'The Others' (1962); and for an exposure of the thinness of the evidence for rival 'Baptist sects', see *id.,* 'Elijah, John and Jesus' (1962), 279, n. 2.

For Samaritan eschatology, and the interpretation of Deut. xviii. 15 ff. in terms of the Ta' eb (the 'returning' or 'restoring' one), see Montgomery 1907, 245 ff., Jackson and Lake 1920, 406, Merx 1909, Cullmann 1959, 19, Macdonald 1964, 362 ff.

[2] This is where Brandon 1957 wanted to find the asylum for non-Pauline Christianity. Certainly C. H. Roberts' account of the early Church in Egypt is congruous with Brandon's thesis to the extent that Roberts 1979, 71, concludes that the original Christian mission to Egypt, addressed to the Jews, and particularly to the Jews of Alexandria, came from the Church in Jerusalem and was Jewish in emphasis rather than Pauline.

Trajan's time.[1] At any rate, if, eventually, we found our way to Rome, there all sorts and kinds would jostle one another—Judaizing Christian synagogues, the most liberal of liberal 'gnosticizing' sorts, looking more like a mystery cult than the Israel of God, Petrine congregations, Pauline congregations, and all the rest (cf. Phil. i. 12-17, and the implications of Rom. xv. 20).[2]

What was the minimum constituent of a Christian community? How far away from the apostolic *kerygma* must one stray to be altogether outside the fold?[3] What are we to make of the 'disciples' at Ephesus who knew only John's Baptism (Acts xix. 1 ff.)?[4] Or, what should we say (to take an instance from much later and from a remote field) of the account given by the seventeenth-century Jesuit missionary Matteo Ricci of what a Chinese Jew told him when asked if he had any knowledge of the Christians in the towns from which he came? He did not even recognize them by that name, but when explanations were made by signs he acknowledged that there were certain foreigners who had come to China with their ancestors and worshipped the cross. Why they worshipped the cross neither he, nor, so he believed, they themselves could say; and their only name was 'men who do not eat animals with uncloven hoofs', because 'while the Moors and Jews and the whole of China eat the flesh of horses, mules and other such beasts of burden, they follow the custom of their native land and do not eat it . . .' (A. C. Moule 1930, 4 f.). To have gone so far from a consciously accepted Christian confession is obviously to have left the essentials far behind; but what is the limit? Is the test nothing more than baptism in the name of Christ?

The answer to which the main stream of the early Church was feeling its way is reflected in the canon of the New Testament. As will be seen (see Chapter X), the writings ultimately excluded from the canon were mainly those

[1] See Roberts 1979, Ch. 3.
[2] But see Judge and Thomas 1966, for the theory that no recognizable *Church* existed in Rome before Paul himself started preaching.
[3] See Bauer 1971; Dunn 1977.
[4] See Käsemann, 'Disciples of John' (1964).

which, even when claiming some apostolic connexion, presented an estimate of Jesus out of accord with the apostolic estimate now reflected in the New Testament collectively. This means that there must have been a commonly recognized norm of Christian confession forming itself on the basis of the apostolic *kerygma*. Judged by this standard, any estimate of Jesus which did not acknowledge his historical existence and his real death would be out; so would any which did not acknowledge the transcendent aliveness of Jesus and the continuity between the transcendent Lord and Jesus of Nazareth, and the decisiveness of his fulfilment of God's plan of salvation as Christians read it out of the Scriptures of the Old Testament. In other words, a dualism which denied either the historical humanity or the absolute 'transcendence' of Jesus would be disqualified. This test finds explicit expression in I and II John.

But within these limits there is a wide range of emphasis; and the writings of the New Testament help to make it articulate for us. As mountain-tops stand up from the ocean bed to form islands and to be, for the voyager, the only visible expression of the submerged continent beneath, so the writings of the New Testament give us some idea of the range and variety of the less articulate Christianity within the ambit of the apostolic confession. Outside that ambit, the apocryphal New Testament[1] articulates the vagaries of belief and speculation standing up in the alien seas into which so many voyaged. But the two submerged continents are more nearly continuous than the distinctions above water might suggest. If apocryphal writings are fairly clearly separated from orthodox, that only indicates the difference between the leaders on either side: the masses beneath them were quite likely to be found merging.

If we ask what factors helped to shape the variations and to give different and distinctive characters to different colonies of Christians, it may be well to begin from a consideration of social and economic conditions. Not that the New Testament writings can be divided into those for the poor

[1] For the New Testament apocrypha, see Hennecke-Schneemelcher 1963, 1965; and James 1953.

and those for the rich, or even, very satisfactorily, into those for the simple and those for the learned. But such a picture of social structure as can be reconstructed, certainly contributes to our understanding of the range of thought and feeling in our documents.[1]

When one is asking about the social and intellectual standing of New Testament Christians, one passage inevitably springs to mind—I Cor. i. 26 ff.:

> My brothers, think what sort of people you are, whom God has called. Few of you are men of wisdom, by any human standard; few are powerful or highly born. Yet, to shame the wise, God has chosen what the world counts folly, and to shame what is strong, God has chosen what the world counts weakness. He has chosen things low and contemptible, mere nothings, to overthrow the existing order.

If one adds to this the fact that, in the Pauline Epistles, there are several allusions to slaves as members of the Church, one is tempted at first sight to conclude that, at this stage, Christian communities were ignorant and illiterate. But such a conclusion needs qualification. In the first place, even if the more intellectual and better educated were few, many of them were probably good teachers; and in a genuinely Christian community there is a humility that renders mutual learning quick and easy—the intellectuals ready to learn from the silent witness of the less articulate, and vice versa. The intellectuals need not all have been arrogant, like those attacked in I Corinthians and Colossians. Paul, with his penetrating intellect and vivid style, must have managed to communicate at least something of his understanding of the meaning of Christ. It is true that he did not suffer fools gladly; his letters must often have gone over the heads of his hearers. To catch the full meaning of such a passage as I Cor. xv or Col. i at first hearing would imply considerable mental agility, even given an intimacy (no longer ours) with the circumstances to which the letters were expressly addressed; and there is no guarantee that great minds always rightly estimate the capacity of others. The slaves, shopkeepers, and smallholders in Paul's congregations probably

[1] See, again, Judge 1960, 1961.

admired but at certain points gaped at the apostle's storm of words—or slept, like poor Eutychus (Acts xx. 9). All the same, much of his teaching would, in the end, get through and 'stick'. He was utterly dedicated to the communication of the gospel, and spared no pains (I Cor. ix. 23).

Aquila and Priscilla, again, were able to instruct Apollos, himself a finely educated person and a good teacher (Acts xviii. 26 ff.). The writer to the Hebrews—another great teacher (unless he be the same?[1])—commanded a brilliant style and a subtle mode of argumentation, which he expected his readers or hearers to follow. They must (unless he hopelessly misjudged them) have been steeped in the Greek Old Testament and in certain techniques of exposition—so much so that commentators rightly observe that they seem to have constituted a smallish group of highly educated persons, a little 'clan' of trained biblical thinkers. The suggestion has already been made (pp. 96 f. above) that they may all at one time have belonged to a single synagogue.

Again, if it is right to trace, behind Matthew's Gospel, a 'school' of Christian exegesis (p. 94 above), that, too, points, at some time in the New Testament period, to what might be called a kind of Christian higher education, privately developed within the Christian communities: a 'scribal' Christianity.

But if such thinkers and writers, early or late in the New Testament period, are exceptionally literary and subtle, and were the chief teachers in their communities, yet even the less literary—indeed, the illiterate—need not have been uneducated. Even the original followers of Jesus, though described in Acts iv. 13 as ἀγράμματοι, which strictly, and normally in the papyri, does mean 'illiterate', need not have been without a good verbal (aural) education.[2] Thus, the

---

[1] See H. W. Montefiore 1964, 1 ff.

[2] See careful documentation of ἀγράμματος in Jackson and Lake 1933, *in loc.* In John vii. 15, the Jews ask contemptuously concerning Jesus πῶς οὗτος γράμματα οἶδεν μὴ μεμαθηκώς; 'How did this fellow get his education when he had no teacher?' (R. E. Brown's translation, 1966 *in loc.*); but commentators agree that 'knowing letters', which, strictly, could mean ability to read, probably refers here to Jesus' superior ability to dispute with experts. Roberts 1979, 65 and n. 5, quotes from P. Oxy. xxxiii. 2673

better educated and more intelligent must have helped the rest, in a community in which a fair level of intelligence may have obtained; for it is a mistake to assume that even the slaves were necessarily illiterate. Sadly, the Christian gospel seems not to have penetrated to the lowest menials among the slave population—the ones whose lot was no better than that of beasts of burden.[1] Therefore, the slaves that do appear in the New Testament were probably on a much more intelligent level. In Egypt a vast amount of clerical work was done by slaves, and even remote villages yield up fragments of Greek books as well as more incidental documents.[2] As for Jewish Christians, if they came from conscientious Jewish families, they would probably have memorised the Torah and other parts of the Scriptures, and would, at least to that extent, have been educated.[3]

So we have to picture communities in which there was a considerable ingredient of education and good intelligence, but which were virtually devoid of 'influence' in the social and political senses.

Returning to the Jewish element in Christian communities of the New Testament period, the Epistle of James might throw light on the social status of a certain type of Christian

(dated Feb. A.D. 304) where a *lector* of the former village church of Chusis is described as μὴ εἰδὼς γράμματα. Roberts takes this to mean that 'he did not know Greek, and must have read the lessons to his flock in Coptic'. What did Jesus write on the ground (Jn viii. 1 ff.)?

[1] See Judge 1960, 60; Aristotle, *Politics* I. ii. 4 ὁ δοῦλος κτῆμά τι ἔμφυχον; *Eth. Nicom.* VIII. xi. 6. ὁ γὰρ δοῦλος ἔμφυχον ὄργανον, τὸ δ' ὄργανον ἄφυχος δοῦλος (!). To do him justice, however, Aristotle is only concerned with indirect agencies, and is not using ὄργανον pejoratively.

[2] So Roberts 1963; and now see *id.* 1979.

[3] It is difficult to come by hard facts about education at this period, whether Jewish or Gentile; but see *T.B. Baba Bathra* 21a; *T.J. Kethuboth* 32c. 4; also Josephus *Contra Apionem* II. 204; *Ant.* IV. 211; *Test. Lev.* xiii.2; Philo, *Legatio* 115, 210 (quoted by Ellis 1975, 305); N. Morris 1937; Bertram 1932, and art. παιδεύω in *T.D.N.T.*; Marrou 1956; Jentsch 1951; Barclay 1959, Ch. 1; Gerhardsson 1961, Ch. IV; van Unnik 1962, 41, n. 6; Judge 1966; Philadelphia Seminar on Christian Origins, Minutes (typescr.), vol. VI, Set 2 (12 Nov. 1968), pp. 3 f., and bibliography; Hocht 1977–78 (arguing that Paul regarded his tent-making or leather-work as demeaning).

congregation, if only we could be sure about its provenance, purpose, and date. Were there really extremes of wealth and poverty within this Christian community, or are these allusions rhetorical and general? And what sort of community would it be, anyway, to which a writer would name Jesus only twice, and refer scarcely at all to any distinctively Christian attitudes?[1]

Beyond such extremely uncertain hints, it is difficult to find positive evidence of Christianity having, in the New Testament period, won any lasting allegiance from the influential or wealthy: Clemens is too common a name for it to be even likely that the one named in Phil. iv. 3 might be otherwise identifiable. That he was 'Clement of Rome' is unlikely enough; as for the attempt to make him into the Flavius Clemens who was a relation of the Emperor Domitian, this labours under vast difficulties, one of the least being the necessity of making Philippians post-Pauline. (See J. B. Lightfoot's demolition of the theory, 1888 in loc.) The Erastus of Rom. xvi. 23 was 'the oikonomos' (i.e., perhaps Treasurer) 'of the city' (i.e., probably Corinth); but there is no need for such an officer of a provincial city council to have been a man of more than local eminence, if of eminence at all.[2] It is true there are one or two Christians named in the New Testament who seem at least before their conversion to have had some connexion with the Jewish or semi-Jewish aristocracy of Palestine. Such are Manaen, who had belonged to the court circle of Herod Antipas (Acts xiii. 1), and

[1] As well as commentaries (most recently, Adamson 1976), see: Shepherd 1956; Souček 1958; W. D. Davies 1964, 401 ff.; Via 1969; J. A. T. Robinson 1976, 118 ff.; Lorenzen 1977–78. See also p. 219 n. 2 below.

[2] See Cadbury 1931 (an examination of the possibility of identifying with a New Testament Erastus the Erastus of a Corinthian inscription discovered in 1929, and concluding against identification). He argues (47 ff.) that in the Roman period οἰκονόμος in such a context may well have corresponded with arcarius (as it is translated in the Vulgate), and adds (p. 51) 'The arcarius was invariably a slave or of servile origin, though he may often have been wealthy'; (p. 57) '... the associations of arcarius or οἰκονόμος do not imply social pre-eminence such as wealth and station bring, and those commentators are probably wrong who cite Erastus as an exception to Paul's description of the first Corinthian Christians ...' See also Judge 1960, esp. Ch. V.

Joanna whose husband Chuza held responsible office in the household of some Herod, probably, again, Antipas (Lk. viii. 3).

But otherwise, it appears that the most influential Christians were only locally influential while the majority were, in the eyes of the world, nonentities, nobodies, often slaves. On the other hand, it is only fair to reiterate that there is equally no evidence of Christianity having reached the lowest of the low, namely the pathetically degraded land-slaves or condemned criminals who worked in the forced labour gangs on the great estates or in the mines and factories—unless, indeed, there were one or two who had been converted to the faith before being taken prisoner and forced to join such a labour gang.[1] But even so, their chances of reaching their fellow slaves would be slender in the extreme. The New Testament allusions to slaves, where they are sufficiently explicit, imply the household slaves, whose lot, equally intolerable in principle, was generally in fact mitigated by at least some sense of 'belonging' to a small and intimate community and did not necessarily reduce them to a completely mechanical, sub-human condition. At least some of these may have been educated persons.

All this adds up to the conclusion that, if one were compelled to generalize, one would say that the social level of most Christian communities was probably towards the lower end of the scale without touching 'rock bottom'. If the Christian Gospel had never reached down to the bottom it is because the labour-gang type were virtually incapable of being reached.

But, within the social limits just defined, there was, in fact, almost certainly a considerable range of variety, as between one local group and another. The geographical situation and condition of the towns and villages in question no doubt had its effect. Corinth and Athens, Alexandria, Ephesus and

---

[1] The only actual instance of this in the New Testament period, however, is that of John on Patmos, if this is how his situation is to be interpreted. But this cannot be demonstrated to be penal exile, still less condemnation to work in the mines. See again Judge, *op. cit.* 60. The evidence for the later persecutions is collected by J. G. Davies 1958.

Antioch, and, above all, Rome, were commercial centres of great importance. Philippi and Laodicea, on main roads, must have been cosmopolitan towns. On the other hand, little country communities must have been on a more primitive level of culture. The level of intelligence and quickness in Church meetings at a place like Corinth must have differed from that at some outlying village in its early Christian days much as a London youth organization might differ in speed of uptake and smartness from a club for village youths in some tiny rural community. And there would be differences in material prosperity also. But the wealth of a particular locality only implies the possibility of wealthy members being enlisted to a community: it of course does not guarantee it. And in fact the Philippian Christians were desperately poor—and (as so often happens in such circumstances) wonderfully generous (II Cor. viii. 2). At Corinth there may have been some relatively rich Christians (I Cor. iv. 8?). The Jewish Christian communities in Palestine were poor enough to be in need of alms from the Gentile Churches. In the community addressed by James there may or may not have actually been poor being ground down by the wealthy (see above p. 210).

As for the writers of the New Testament themselves, much could be said about the varieties of style among them.[1] If one were to summarize the facts very briefly, it might be said that Hebrews and James, though in different ways, both show a command of idiomatic Greek; that Luke is versatile—capable now of imitating the self-conscious and rather ornate style of contemporary historians, now of writing biblical (Septuagintal) Greek, and now of accepting distinctly un-

---

[1] See Robertson 1931, N. Turner 1963, and, especially, 1976, with bibliographies. Morgenthaler 1958 is indispensable. Among numerous individual studies, in addition to those in N. Turner 1976, note: Excursus I, pp. 276 ff. (Matthew); C. H. Turner 1923–28, Kilpatrick, 1956 (*tris*), Lindsey n.d., Introduction (Mark); Cadbury 1919 (Luke); Abbott 1906, Kilpatrick 1960 (John); Nägeli 1905 (Paul); Harrison 1921 (Pastorals); Charles 1920 (Revelation). Sometimes small words provide important pointers to individuality. For instance, a concordance shows the strange distribution of so ordinary a word as σύν (though compounds with συν- straddle the groupings).

Greek, Semitic sources into his scheme; that Matthew seems nearly always to use careful and correct Greek, though he does not indulge in the literary flourishes occasionally displayed by Luke nor attempt to conceal Semitic idioms in his sources; that parts of Mark are written in the idiom of one more familiar with a Semitic tongue than with Greek; that Paul, or his amanuenses, wrote in a variety of styles, sometimes very strongly Semitic, sometimes rather less so, but nearly always tense and brilliant and lively;[1] while the Gospel and Epistles of John are in a peculiar style, mainly correct, superficially simple and unadorned, but in fact complicatedly charged with meaning and more Semitic than Greek in essential character. The Apocalypse stands alone as the only New Testament writing containing considerable sections of quite barbarously ungrammatical writing, which, nevertheless, achieve a profoundly moving effect.

But to return to the main theme: given such intellectual activity (even among a minority) as seems evidenced by Hebrews and Matthew and the Pauline Epistles, it is not surprising that rivalry and faction showed themselves also. The *locus classicus* for this is, of course, I Cor. i-iv. J. Munck (1959) has argued that what is indicated by I Corinthians is not necessarily a radical partisanship running right up from the foundation apostles, and that it is possible grossly to exaggerate the cleavage implied. What Paul is castigating, he thinks, is rather the Corinthians' tendency to treat their leaders like Greek sophists and side with one of them against the rest.[2] Whatever one thinks about this in detail, it is true that there is nothing here to prove a conflict between Peter and Paul (see above, pp. 201 f.). But the false apostles of II Cor. xi. 13, though not the great leaders, represent a serious threat, as does the 'different gospel' of Gal. i. 6; and Phil. i. 15 ff. certainly compels us to recognize deliberate partisanship in some quarters. And the *a priori* likelihood is certainly that there would be a variety of emphasis, tendencies, outlook, and approach in different groups of Christians,

[1] Cf. Moule 1981.
[2] Cf. Dahl 1967.

which would ultimately harden into distinguishable schools of thought.

This consideration of the social and intellectual stratification of the Christian communities has thus led to two conclusions: that the average level was low though not as low as it would have been if the slave-gangs had been included; and that correspondingly high must have been the respect accorded to the giants of intellect and of spirituality—the Pauls and the Johns—and the temptation to follow the exciting vagaries of sectarians who exaggerated the respective tendencies of these giants. It is not surprising, therefore, if we find marked differences in emphasis and tone as between the representative writings of different localities and various traditions. Moreover, the very fact that different types or genres of writing exist makes it inevitable that subsequent developments will follow diverse lines. J. M. Robinson and H. Koester 1971 is an interesting attempt to trace out a 'trajectory' on which each of the distinguishable New Testament types of writing may be placed: Wisdom literature, gnomic writing, apocalypse, etc.—each has its path, and on that path later specimens of the same type of writing may be identified. The marvel is—and this is the main 'moral' of this chapter—that the basic Christian convictions persist with such remarkable consistency through such diversity.

When Christian thought is traced out beyond the New Testament period, it is well known that certain broad distinctions are found setting in as between such centres as Antioch and Alexandria: Antioch, with its tendency to stress the literal and the historical, and with them the humanity of Jesus; Alexandria, with its tradition of allegory and symbol and its greater stress on the transcendent. It is all too easy to contrast these two emphases in a mechanical manner, without allowing for subtle interchanges and variations. For instance, one of the elementary qualifications that would need to be made, were we attempting to describe this period, would be the recognition that even the Antiochene thinkers did not rest content with the plain, historical sense of scripture. If they differed from the Alexandrines, it was not so much in rejecting other senses as in preferring 'typology', which recognizes the importance of historical events as such, to allegory, which would reduce everything to timeless truths.

But if we look back to the roots of this broad divergence in New Testament times, we can already discern its beginnings. Here, too, however, definition is made difficult by the number of different factors already contributing to the thinking of the New Testament Christians. Suppose we start by a too extreme simplification. Abandoning cautious qualifications for the moment, and attempting a kind of caricature, we might say that Jewish Christianity, with its strongly monotheistic presuppositions and its readiness to welcome earthly rulers and prophets in the name of God, might be expected to hold on to the 'fleshly'—τὸ κατὰ σάρκα—in Jesus and to ignore or belittle his divinity. These were, in fact, the tendencies of what soon came to be called Ebionism (from the Hebrew word for 'poor', used proudly for a Franciscan poverty and simplicity or used derogatorily for a poverty of doctrine, a *psilosis* or attenuation in Christology). The Ebionites were among the Judaizing types of sub-apostolic Christianity, and their tendency was towards 'adoptionism'—the theory that Jesus, the human prophet, came to be 'adopted' as God's Son in a supernal sense and won his way up, as it were, by outstanding goodness.[1] Caricaturing the opposite wing, one might call it typically pagan, and say that it started from polytheistic presuppositions and was familiar with the ideas of the demigod and of the pre-existent saviour who descends into the material world to rescue those who respond or who are predestined. When converted to faith in Jesus, such a type will stress Christ's pre-existence and his descent from heaven, and, by concentrating on his supramundane origin, may lose grip upon his real humanity. If the 'Jewish' error leads to adoptionism, the latter is the road to monophysitism—the obliteration of the human in the transcendent.

But in fact neither of these types ever existed in an

[1] But see Schweizer 1961, 37, for warnings against tracing a direct connexion between New Testament phrases and adoptionism.

unadulterated form. To draw them thus as clearly contrasting shapes is to caricature. We know, better even than previous generations of New Testament students, that already by the time of Christ the strongholds of monotheistic Judaism had been deeply penetrated not only by Hellenistic but also by oriental thought. There is dualism (even if not a fully metaphysical dualism) in Qumran; there is, perhaps, a certain Epicurean rationalism about Ecclesiastes. Hellenistic ideas are certainly *a priori* far from unthinkable in James the Lord's brother: so far as *that* goes, there is no reason why he might not have written the Epistle. Dualistic ideas are not totally alien to Paul, although his firm grasp on the incarnation (or rather the grasp of Christ on him) precludes, again, a fully metaphysical dualism.

We shall not, therefore, expect to find anywhere—least of all in the New Testament—the reflection of 'pure' Ebionism or 'pure' transcendentalism. But tendencies in one direction or another may be looked for and are worth tracing; and it is of real importance to ask to what extent the writings ultimately held within the New Testament canon show a consistent controlling conviction which both includes complementary tendencies and excludes really incompatible elements in such a way as to produce coherence.

One very substantial contribution towards an answer to this question is the remarkable fact that the earliest datable documents of the New Testament already reflect an understanding of Christ which demands at one and the same time the recognition of his real humanity and of a relation between Christ and God which implies eternal and transcendent existence. The earliest documents of the Christian faith that can be fairly securely dated are the main Pauline Epistles—those to the Romans, to the Corinthians, to the Galatians, and (in all probability) to the Thessalonians, though the Paulinity of II Thessalonians is questioned.[1] Some would make I Thessalonians the earliest of all, others Galatians. But even confining ourselves to Romans and I and II Corinthians, we have evidence from about A.D. 55 for an understanding of Christ which cannot be defined without

[1] See Bailey 1978–79.

reference both to his historical being and his transcendent status. This means that the latter is not something that begins to belong to Christian faith only when Christianity has had time to borrow, syncretistically, from pagan ideas. The thing is inherent in the earliest Christian religious experience available to us—and that, the experience of a converted Pharisaic Jew.[1]

It is symptomatic of this same fact—the coherence, from the beginning, of an understanding of Christ as both human and divine—that Dunn's (1977) careful and impressive examination of unity and diversity in the New Testament, while it brings out the remarkable range of variety and difference between different types of New Testament faith, reaches the conclusion, time and again, that through all the diversity runs the unifying recognition that the transcendent Lord is continuous with the historical Master.[2] A study of the New Testament documents gives the lie to the theory that 'high' Christologies are only a fantasy-creation at the end of a long evolution away from 'low' Christologies of the earliest days. Divine and human cohere in the earliest known Christian experience; and this paradox coheres, in its turn, with the mysterious figure reflected in the traditions collected in the Gospels.

It is this which is essentially the apostolic gospel; and the criterion of 'apostolicity' was the main criterion by which what ultimately became the 'canon' or 'norm' for Christian doctrine, was tested. The criterion of faithfulness to the apostolic *kerygma* did in fact admit within the canon only those writings which kept sufficiently close to the Christ-event to achieve this coherence. Once begin to speculate and to dogmatize about what must be or may have been, and any extremes may set in; but to keep close to the apostolic witness is necessarily to affirm that the Gospel

'is about [God's] Son: on the human level he was born of David's stock, but on the level of spirit—the Holy Spirit—he was

[1] See Moule 1977.
[2] For the relation between the historical Jesus and the risen Christ of Christian proclamation, see the collection of essays edited by Ristow and Matthiae 1961.

declared God's Son by a mighty act in that he rose from the dead: it is about Jesus Christ our Lord' (Rom. i. 3 f.).

The real humanity, and, with it, the inclusive, representative person, such that (as Paul saw) his resurrection *is*, in anticipation, the resurrection on the Last Day—these are the two elements in the apostolic *kerygma* which give coherence to all the diversity within the New Testament. As R. Williams 1979, 13, well says:

> It seems more than a little presumptuous to try to reduce the enormous diversity of New Testament models of Christian life to a single pattern; but if it can be done at all, it is because the New Testament churches and their writers existed in virtue of one revealed, lived and acted model: the life, death and vindication of Jesus of Nazareth. Their unity is a unity of direction and vision, not of formulation ...

But at its margins the New Testament sails dangerously near to the excluded area: the Epistle of James might, for all the signs it shows of Christology, be near-Ebionite; II Peter makes startling concessions to Greek ideas of divine nature:

> ... you may escape the corruption with which lust has infected the world, and come to share in the very being of God (i. 4)

and the Fourth Gospel, if it were the only Gospel, might leave us with an almost monophysite Christ, and a markedly individualistic religion (see pp. 136 f., 147 above). It is the central conviction which holds together these diversities and which also draws the circumference where it does.

How much better our understanding of the New Testament would be if we possessed more information about Judaistic Christianity![1] James the Lord's brother remains a too little known character. In Acts xv we find him, at the head of Jerusalem Christianity, deciding for the non-circumicision of Gentile converts, and clinching his argument by what seems to be a Greek mistranslation of the Hebrew of Amos (Acts xv. 17). In Acts xxi he is counselling Paul to demonstrate his own allegiance to the ritual law. According to Hegesippus (*ap.* Euseb *H.E.* II. xxiii) he is so

[1] See Hort 1894; F. C. Grant, 1960; Daniélou 1964–77.

Jewish as to be expected by the Jews to denounce the
Nazarene faith, and is martyred for refusing to do so.[1] In
apocryphal legend he is visited by the risen Lord himself
(Jerome, *De Vir. Ill.* ii). Whatever we make of the Epistle of
James, it is not out of character with many of these hints. It
betrays a considerable acquaintance with the Greek moral-
ists and sophists; it is so Jewish as to stress the Law and
almost obscure the Gospel. And although it scarcely mentions Jesus, yet, try as one will, one cannot eliminate from its
texture a certain number of phrases which seem to be
stubbornly Christian in form. Is it, then, perhaps, an
attempt by a Jewish Christian to conciliate non-Christian
Jews? But if so, it is by one who still actually belongs within
their synagogue, and is that conceivable? Is it not, then,
rather the extreme example within the New Testament of
Judaistic Christianity, reflecting a community whose members still worshipped in synagogue style, and threw a
characteristically Jewish stress on character and conduct,
but confessed Jesus as God's 'glory' (ii. 1) and believed
themselves re-born by the Christian Gospel (i. 18)? Yet, if so,
we have to date it, nonetheless, at a period when an
antinomian interpretation of Christian liberty had already
set in (Jas ii. 14 ff.)—whether through Paul's disciples or not
is not clear. Whichever way we turn, the interpretation of the
Epistle is beset by problems. But at any rate it reflects a type
of Christianity as different as can well be imagined from the
Pauline or Johannine, yet one that confesses Jesus as Lord
(i. 1, ii. 1), believes in rebirth by God through the Gospel
(i. 18), and looks forward to a dénouement (v. 7).[2]

[1] See p. 203 n. 1.

[2] See above, p. 41 n. 1. In a discussion of Jewish diaspora homilies
Thyen 1955, 14 ff., takes James to be a synagogue homily worked over very
slightly by a Christian. But on such a hypothesis it is difficult to explain
why the working over was both so slight and so subtle. Paul Feine's study
1893 (again, see above, p. 41 n. 1) contains much that is still of value. He
argued for the possibility that all the allegedly non-Jewish allusions in
James could have reached a Palestinian Jew such as the Lord's brother
through Jewish apocalyptic sources. On the whole, more recent discover-
ies (especially the Qumran literature, etc.) go to support this view. But see
also Schoeps 1949, 343 ff., placing it as late as the first half of the second
century.

At the opposite extreme to the tendencies exhibited in James, there must have been a temptation so to identify Jesus with the Spirit or the Wisdom of God as to minimize his historical particularity. As a matter of fact, however, it is remarkable how difficult it is to illustrate this end of the spectrum from the New Testament itself. The *Logos* in St John is notoriously (and no doubt to the pagan reader shockingly) portrayed as having become flesh, σάρξ (i. 14); and although the Fourth Gospel does lean sometimes in a docetist direction (Jesus' questions are artificial ones, framed for the sake of the disciples, vi. 6, cf. xi. 42), yet nothing is clearer than the evangelist's determination to stress the reality of the incarnation: the 'scandal of particularity' and of materiality is never avoided but positively embraced (vi. 52).[1] The Epistles to the Colossians (i. 15 ff.) and to the Hebrews (i. 1 ff.) both contain what is a 'logos-doctrine' in all but the actual terms; yet they too are as clear as can be about the reality of the earthly life. And although later writers like Justin confuse Word and Spirit, the New Testament very strikingly confines 'Spirit' almost entirely to its account of God's dealings with his People in the 'new creation', using the Logos and Christ, not Spirit, in its allusions to the universe and cosmogony. Christ and Spirit are sometimes interchangeable—or nearly so—within the Church, but never outside it.[2] And all this probably bears witness to the successful avoidance, in the New Testament, of that dualism, so common in the pagan world and in heretical Christianity, which treated matter as evil—essential Manichaeism. The doctrine of matter and of creation is the real touchstone: and, for all its range of diversity, the New Testament does not founder on the Manichaean rock.

Part of the New Testament's diversity is due precisely to the variety of alien positions which are combated: it debates from a single platform, but from different corners of it; and so far as it does lean over towards any extremes, it is because the writers, at those points, recognize particularly clearly

[1] This, with great respect to Käsemann *Testament* (1968). See Bornkamm 1968, 104 ff., Smalley 'Testament' (1973), 1978, 55 f.; Dunn 1977, 298 ff.

[2] Moule 1978.

what are the positions that are being occupied by error and recoil violently from them.[1] Paul sees especially vividly what principle is involved in the superficially good or harmless stress on Jewish legal rectitude, and therefore goes so far as to say that if Christians get themselves circumcised Christ will be useless to them (Gal. v. 2). James sees the selfish laziness which claims that correct belief is sufficient without corresponding conduct (ii. 14 ff.), and I John throughout attacks the dangerous position which holds that once baptized the Christian is secure, whatever his morals: and both James and John are led to extreme statements—faith without conduct is dead (Jas ii. 26); a Christian cannot sin (I Jn iii. 9).

It is not unlikely that Christian congregations originally founded by one or other of these great protagonists would tend (rather like denominations today) to retain and exaggerate or stylize the particular emphases with which the Gospel had originally been presented to them. There may well have been distinctive stamps upon, respectively, Pauline, Petrine, Johannine, and Jacobaean churches. According to the Acts, Philip the evangelist and probably Barnabas (with John Mark) also engaged in independent evangelism (Acts viii. 26 ff.; cf. xxi. 8, xv. 39), and, for all we know, their churches too may have stood for something distinctive. It would be particularly interesting to know more about the Gospel in Samaritan territory: is it not likely that here, too, there were particular characteristics (see pp. 203 f. above, and 204 n. 1)? But everywhere there hangs a curtain of obscurity; and all we can say is that the traditions that accumulated in any given centre must have to some extent been selected, moulded, and applied in accordance with the local tendencies, and that this explains the diversity of emphases in the Gospels—both internally and in relation to one another.

Turning, then, to look more closely at the diversity of emphases within the New Testament, we shall do best to offer a crude, rough-and-ready classification of types, leaving it to further study to break them down and qualify them

[1] Moule 1959, 'Influence' (1964); J. M. Robinson 1965, 148 f.

more precisely.[1] And it will be well to recall frequently how much wider is the gulf that separates the New Testament as a whole from non-canonical writings than the distances between different parts within the New Testament itself. Even the so-called Apostolic Fathers are (with the partial exception of the letters of Ignatius) separated from most of the New Testament by a considerable gap in outlook and approach.[2]

First, then, there is the broad distinction between the Epistle to the Hebrews and, one might almost say, the rest of the New Testament. Hebrews, more than any other part, presses into service the Platonic conception (adopted also by Philo) of a supra-sensible world of absolute reality over against a sensible world which is only its reflection or copy (though even in Paul there is II Cor. iv. 18, v. 7, Col. ii. 17); and entertains a conception of Christ as the Hero and Leader—the Pioneer whom Christians are to follow to the heights. Neither idea is consistently carried through: the Christian tradition is too strong to allow it. This shadow-world which is but a copy of the transcendent is not so Platonic but that in it the decisive act of history takes place—the purgation of sins; and Jesus is not really only a Hercules toiling upwards to the stars, for he is already the pre-existent utterance of God. The writer to the Hebrews makes bigger concessions to Greek ways of expression than Paul or John; but there is never a doubt but that, in common with all apostolic Christianity, he takes time seriously and thinks of history as significant and of this world as an important arena of divine action, and that he sees Jesus as infinitely more than a hero winning immortality. Perhaps Paul, and even John, are more firmly on the Hebrew side of the line; but Hebrews, for all its concessions, never surrenders 'the scandal of particularity'. Indeed, it is clear enough that throughout the treatise, it is non-Christian Judaism that is being combated by being claimed, absorbed, and transcended; and even if it is a Philonian, Alexandrian

[1] See especially Dunn 1977.
[2] See Torrance 1948, though it is a question whether, on his showing, James ought not to have joined the ranks of the Apostolic Fathers.

Judaism, it is nothing like a genuinely Greek philosophy or a rootless gnosticism.[1]

Then, secondly, there is the broad distinction between, on the one hand, the Pauline emphasis on the essential powerlessness of man—his complete helplessness to save himself[2]—and, on the other hand, the tendency of the Epistle of James to see religion as duty and kindness and to credit man with the ability to resist temptation—a stress by no means alien to the Christ of the Synoptic Gospels, especially Matthew's. Corresponding to this contrast is the Pauline and Johannine conception of Christianity as incorporation or 'abiding' in Christ over against the conception of discipleship, imitating, following, which runs (not unnaturally) through the Synoptic accounts of the ministry of Jesus, but finds a place also in Hebrews.[3] In the New Testament as a whole, Christ is both pattern and power (for this useful terminology, see Alexander 1910, 105 ff.); but there is more of pattern and less of power in some of the writings than in others. The Pastoral Epistles (as a whole, though they may be composite of Pauline and deutero-pauline material) look, at least in some respects, like a confluence of the two streams—a second-generation Christianity which repeats the Gospel of the free grace of God ('not by works . . .', Tit. iii. 5) but which, in a more widely Christianized setting, finds it not unnatural to think of man's ability to keep the law (? I Tim. i. 8 ff.).

Thirdly, one may distinguish an attitude of despair about the present and of eager expectation of a coming reversal

[1] On the Epistle to the Hebrews, besides the Commentaries, note Spicq 1950, Barrett 'Eschatology' (1956), Héring 1956, Kosmala 1959, G. Hughes 1979. I owe a good deal in this paragraph to the work of A. S. Browne (towards a Cambridge Ph.D. degree).

[2] For this motif also in the Dead Sea Scrolls, see Schulz 1959, suggesting that Paul himself inherited the idea of justification by faith from an anti-Pharisaic Qumran-stream of tradition which might have come early into the primitive Church. But see Jeremias 1965, 66 ff., for a difference between Qumran and Paul. Relevant also in E. P. Sanders 1977, *passim*.

[3] But A. S. Browne (as in note 1 above) has taught me that this needs careful qualification.

from an attitude which concentrates on the here and now and accepts a positive estimate of human history. If so, it is, however, important to recognize the complexity and interaction of attitudes involved. Apocalyptic eschatology is not, as such, necessarily dependent on an assumption of the shortness of the time before the 'End', nor even necessarily dependent on pessimism about this world (cf. pp. 149 ff. above). The main concern of apocalyptic is simply to portray, in symbol and picture, the conviction that ultimately God is in control and that, whether soon or late, his loyal people will be vindicated: it is an 'unveiling' of hidden reality. Thus, the message of Revelation is not dependent on its 'Behold I come quickly'. Its belief in the shortness of the time does, of course, add intensity to its appeal, and encouragement to its exhortations to endure; but the ultimate reality to which it bears witness is independent of the duration of the interval. On the other hand, there are eschatologies (whether couched in apocalyptic symbols or in plain prose) which do depend on the shortness of the time; and these stand in contrast with those which have come to terms with a prolonged period of human history or even evaluate it positively. Of the latter stance, Luke-Acts is, in some respects at least, an obvious example—so much so that Luke is sometimes blamed for resolving the essential tension between the 'already' and the 'not yet'.[1] It is not that Luke-Acts is not as explicit as anybody about a Day of Judgment and the coming of Jesus. But he also recognizes and, as it were, 'regularises', as part of God's design, the interim period in which the Holy Spirit is sent to guide and empower the worldwide expansion of the Church. In the narrative of the Acts Luke turns into a formal period and gives chronological value to the mere statement that, in the words of the 'Little Apocalypse' of Mark xiii, the gospel must 'first' ($\pi\varrho\hat{\omega}\tau o\nu$) be proclaimed to all the nations (v. 10).

Attitudes which depend on the assumption that the time is short and which devalue the present are rare in the New Testament, if only because incarnational faith by definition sets a positive value on this world. But Paul himself, though

[1] Conzelmann 1960. But see I. H. Marshall 1970.

mainly exhibiting just such a positive attitude, does say, in I Cor. vii. 29–31:

> What I mean, my friends, is this. The time we live in will not last long. While it lasts, married men should be as if they had no wives; mourners should be as if they had nothing to grieve them, the joyful as if they did not rejoice; buyers must not count on keeping what they buy, nor those who use the world's wealth on using it to the full. For the whole frame of this world is passing away.

In I Cor. xv. 58, however, Paul is affirming the permanent value of work in this age; and in Romans, while eagerly looking forward to a new age, he is not in the least escapist but entirely positive towards the present as a medium in which God's glory may be affirmed (e.g. Chapters viii, xii, xiii). And the Captivity Epistles, Philippians, Colossians, and Ephesians, whether Pauline or deutero-Pauline, are clear about the Christian's use, not rejection, of this life. The Christian may groan (Rom. viii. 23, II Cor. v. 4) and long for change; but he still believes that the present is to be used for God, not rejected or evaded (Eph. v. 15 f., Phil. iv. 8, Col. iv. 5 f.). II Pet. iii is the most explicit attempt in the New Testament to explain delay by contrasting a human with a divine time-scale; and it is explicit in its devaluation of this world. But it is far from typical of the New Testament.[1] Outside the New Testament, *Barnabas* iv. 4 still hangs on to a temporal calculation (τὸ τέλειον σκάνδαλον ἤγγικεν, περὶ οὗ γέγραπται).

There is an eschatological contrast also between the Fourth Gospel and other parts of the New Testament. But it would be over-simplifying to say that John exhibits a fully 'realized' eschatology over against the 'futurist' eschatologies of other writers. Of course Jn v. 24 and I Jn iii. 14 speak of having already passed from death to life. But that does not mean that either writing has given up the 'ordinary' expectation of an 'End' in the future. What it does mean is that Johannine thinking, in the Gospel at any rate, is not much concerned either with past or future. Its real focal point is the

---

[1] Käsemann 'Apologia' (1964).

relation of the individual to God in Jesus Christ (see above, pp. 136 f.). For the individual who loves God and does his will, who believes in Jesus as the Son of God and abides in the real Vine, eternal life is already realized; and the Gospel scarcely concerns itself with the corporate gathering up of God's purposes or the course of the Church's perfecting: that is the theme, far more, of the Epistle to the Ephesians, which has a very strong forward looking, futurist hope, although its goal is in terms of maturity and fulness of growth, not in terms of apocalypse (Eph. iv. 11-16; cf. Rom. viii.). A fourth pair of contrasting tendencies, thus, might be the individualist over against the corporate. In the Johannine Epistles there is a mediating position: they are more corporate, and therefore also more concerned with a future End, than the Gospel; but the corporate ideas in I John are less comprehensive and universal than in Ephesians.[1]

A fifth contrast might be found in the intuitive genius of St John (well summed up in the famous story of the dying John simply saying over and over again, 'Little children, love one another'—Jerome, *In Ep. ad Gal.* vi. 10), and the vigorously intellectual genius of Paul. Paul argues, where John affirms; and John simply utters resonant, suggestive, poetic words, where Paul labours to explain.

Sixthly, there are varieties in the interpretation of authority and Church-order. As has already been said, Christians of the New Testament period recognized the revival of the Spirit of prophecy; and their ultimate authority was always God in Jesus through his Spirit in the Church. But there were varieties of mediation. In Paul almost everything is represented, from the rabbinic interpretation of scripture to the authority of vision and audition in prophetic ecstasy. But in the Pastoral Epistles inspired scripture and sound Christian traditions seem to be the main oracles.[2]

Similarly, it is possible to trace, behind the New Testament, the form both of 'charismatic' communities, and constitutional ministries. Some depended upon no clearly

---

[1] See Moule, 'Individualism' (1962), 1970; Dunn 1977, 118 f., 202.
[2] See Schweizer 1961, 77 ff.; Barrett 1963.

defined order of ministry but upon the spontaneous leadership of inspiration; others were organized round an articulated ministry of elder-overseers and assistants (presbyter-episcopi and deacons)—perhaps even a triple ministry of 'apostolic men', overseer-presbyters, and deacons; and there may sometimes have been other constitutionally recognized officers corresponding to Jewish types such as scribes and sages.[1]

It is a familiar fact that the Christian scribe appears in Matthew (xiii. 52; cf. xxiii. 34), and it is possible that this Gospel, in its miscellaneous traditions, also reflects a variety of community ideals, some charismatic, some constitutional, some acceptable to the Evangelist himself, others alien to his outlook. E. Käsemann (1969) has pointed out that Christian theology, in some of its early phases, represents a conflict between opposing schools, all alike appealing to the authority of the Spirit, but in very different ways—'enthusiasm' (in the technical sense of that word) with miracle-working (reflected perhaps derogatorily in Matt. vii. 22–25), a Jewish and rabbinical type of organization (note Matt. xxiii. 8-10), legalistic Judaism (for which some might quote Matt. v. 17-20, though it can be otherwise interpreted), and, at the opposite extreme, the kind of liberalism and universalism for which perhaps Stephen stood. Different outlooks, embodying different structures of society, criss-cross confusingly in the dim background of the New Testament, within Jewish Christianity as well as in Gentile Churches. In the last analysis, a good deal of it can be expressed in terms of varying eschatologies. Some groups perhaps saw the conversion of the Jews as the first necessity before any further spread of the Gospel; others, led by St Paul, looked for the reverse process: only when the full complement of the Gentiles had come in would all Israel be saved (Rom. xi. 25). Some looked to human labour, others expected a supernatural intervention. To postulate this diversity of organization and of expectation goes some way towards accounting for the

[1] In addition to older treatments of the origins of Christian ministry (e.g. J. B. Lightfoot 'Ministry' (1888), Lietzmann 1913, articles ἀπόστολος etc. in *T.D.N.T.*), see Barrett *Signs* (1970).

diverse traditions that seem to be reflected in such a writing as St Matthew's Gospel.[1]

It would be easy to go on multiplying these rough-and-ready antitheses; but they all need modifying and refining, and these are only mentioned as examples of the type of phenomenon that may be watched for—not as the 'antitheses of what is falsely called knowledge'! If we return, for a moment, to the types of error that are attacked in the New Testament, they will serve as a foil to, and in part an explanation of, these varying tendencies. But again, they can be treated only in a broad way, as a mere preliminary to proper investigation.

An obvious one, already touched on, is the effort after merit, attacked by Paul. It is not true that Paul thought of faith as saving from sin. He is sometimes represented as replacing 'works' by 'faith'—as though, whereas a man cannot save himself by his deeds, his faith (if only he can summon up enough of it) will save him. But what in fact Paul is saying is that nothing at all that comes from man's side can make fellowship with God possible: nothing of man's 'own', that he 'possesses', can qualify him to enter the Presence. It is only when he flings away all attempts to qualify, and accepts what God offers as a free gift (as an act of 'grace' or gracious generosity) that he can be brought into fellowship with God. But fellowship is a personal relationship; and the offer of restored fellowship therefore requires the outgoing of the entire person—his whole-hearted response—if it is to be entered into. Faith is, for Paul, this commitment to God's goodness and faithfulness which is not the ground of, but simply the response to, God's gift. Paul thus radically opposes—rules out altogether—human merit and deserving. Judaism, it is true, also seems to have thrown much emphasis upon the antecedent love and mercy of God in the covenant. All Jews, as such, are within the covenant: initially, and in that sense, they are secure of God's salvation by God's sheer grace. But to stay within the covenant, they must 'keep the rules': hence, adherence to the Mosaic requirements is important; and if, as a consequence,

[1] See pp. 127 f.

a merit begins to be made out of keeping the regulations meticulously, then a kind of 'legalism' does result. And it is this that helps to explain the conflicts reflected in Galatians and Romans, whether the legalists there attacked are Christians or non-Christian Jews. But Paul is in conflict also with even the more moderate Judaism because, as a Christian, he no longer assumes the basic 'savedness' of a Jew as such— not even within the covenant: all men are in a position of helplessness; all alike depend solely on God's mercy; and this can be responded to only by trust (the Pauline 'faith'). Paul, having started as a very orthodox and precisionist Jew (Phil. iii. 5 f.), continued, after becoming a Christian, to be by no means indifferent to the observance of Jewish ritual and custom (it is unlikely that the hints in the Acts (xviii. 18, xx. 16) are fictitious—so circumstantial yet so incidental); but he leaps out like a lightning-flash against any threat to the sufficiency of Christ. Thus, while conforming to Jewish rules in things indifferent to this matter (Rom. xiv, xv, I Cor. ix. 19 ff., cf. Acts xvi. 3), he refuses to conform where the heart of the gospel is at issue (Gal. ii. 11 ff., cf. i. 6, v. 2-12, vi. 11 ff.).[1]

On the other hand, there is another error, which at first sight looks like the opposite of legalism or reliance on human merit and correctness—the error that came to be called antinomianism. If nothing that man can do is of avail, then why trouble about conduct? Why not sin recklessly and offer the more scope to God's generosity? Such blasphemy Paul had actually encountered (Rom. vi. 1)—indeed, he had even himself been accused of holding such a position (Rom. iii. 8). He says tersely that its condemnation is well deserved. It constitutes, of course, a failure to recognize the meaning of fellowship with God as involving the whole personality and total response: it is a fatal departmentalizing of human nature. But it took various forms, some at least of them more sophisticated than the formulation derided by Paul, as may

---

[1] Cf. pp. 63 f. For an important re-examination of certain types of Judaism and a defence of them against some of the Christian interpreters of Paul, see E. P. Sanders 1977. For a detailed study of Paul's position in the Galatian and Corinthian letters, see Drane 1975.

be seen from what is attacked in the Epistle of James and the Johannine Epistles. James is attacking people who claim that they are saved because their beliefs about God are orthodox: they are good monotheists. So, replies the writer, are the demons (Jas ii. 19)! What matters is that the belief should issue in a good life: 'the kind of religion which is without stain ... is ... to go to the help of orphans and widows ...' (Jas i. 27). In the Johannine Epistles we witness an attack upon another form of antinomianism. It is fairly clear that it was sharply 'dualistic', regarding matter as evil and spirit as distinct and separable; and from this its exponents seem to have made two deductions. First, they evidently could not accept that 'the Word became flesh'—that was, for them, too crassly material; and secondly they refused to regard conduct as relevant to initiation. They believed themselves, evidently, to have become initiates with the true, saving knowledge. What did it matter that they took no trouble to show practical kindness to others or were loose in their morals? It will be recognized that these antinomians were really as far from the Pauline (indeed the Christian) position as the legalistically minded. The latter tried to win merit by good deeds; the antinomians regarded their knowledge and their initiation as securing them. Both alike were relying on something other than the free and undeserved graciousness of God. And although from time to time Paul had been and has been tarred with the antinomian brush, nothing is in fact less fair to his position.

By now it has become evident that Christians, holding to central, distinctively Christian emphases, were being compelled to walk a tightrope. Beneath were chasms—the disconnecting of Christ from God, the disconnecting of the Lord Christ of Christian worship from the historical Jesus, the disconnecting of creation from the Creator, the disconnecting of belief from conduct, the disconnecting of the gracious approach of God from the human response. Did their spokesmen waver or falter? Paul has often been called one-sided and charged with failure to recognize the value of good deeds; but nothing is clearer, in fact, than that he strenuously called for good deeds, but as part of man's response of trust to God's initiative, not as a *means* of acquiring God's favour. The Pastorals, whatever their origin, look like a compromise, a crystallization of Pauline doctrine in a setting of organized Church life. I Peter does not stress the grace of God over against human effort, but its exhortation to good deeds is no stronger than Paul's. II Peter is much nearer to the recognition of the attainability of salvation by human effort (i. 5 ff.) and the Greek idea of attaining to deification (i. 4), but even so there is the phrase to 'grow in the grace . . . of our Lord' (iii. 18). The Apocalypse is simply a call to Christians to hold on and remain loyal. Jude is chiefly occupied with attacking antinomians, but there is his noble and unforgettable doxology:

> Now to the One who can keep you from falling and set you in the presence of his glory, jubilant and above reproach, to the only God our Saviour, be glory and majesty, might and authority, through Jesus Christ our Lord, before all time, now, and for evermore. Amen. (Jude 24 f.).

Only James is nearly without allusion to the grace of God in Jesus, and concentrates on the attainment of such a character as will lead to salvation.

All this, if the New Testament were representative of the generality of Christians at that time, would indicate that, if one travelled from centre to centre, one might find varieties of emphasis, but seldom any abandonment of the unique, distinctive Christian Gospel of the undeserved graciousness of God actually effected in history in Jesus Christ—in other words, the continuity of the Lord of Christian worship with Jesus of Nazareth.[1] But in fact one suspects that the *communis sensus fidelium*, expressed in the 'summit' pronouncements, which became the New Testament, was more tenacious of the central verities than were the uninstructed and obscure local members. One suspects that in some communities Jesus was looked back to as an example rather than looked up to as Lord—followed as Rabbi rather than dwelt

[1] Cf., again, Dunn 1977.

in as limbs dwell in a body,[1] that what we should call purely 'humanistic' ideas of him were cherished; while elsewhere he was thought of as the Saviour of a mystery religion, scarcely historical at all; that in some places sermons on the atonement were seldom heard; that sometimes Baptism and the Eucharist were treated as little more than charms to safeguard the members of the Church, while in others little doctrine was ever heard, only exhortations to good living.[2]

If so, it is the more remarkable that the differentia of the faith did ultimately survive and come through; and it is to the Church's pastors and teachers that we must look for part of the explanation. It is their leaders' writings that stand out from the undifferentiated masses, and that help to preserve the faith. For although in respect of organization and of ministry also, there was almost certainly, as we have seen, a considerable variation from congregation to congregation, the leadership of each congregation must usually have included some responsible person called and commissioned and entrusted with the Gospel. It is noteworthy that the Acts more than once alludes to this care: in xiv. 23 and xx. 32 the verb παρατιθέναι is used of 'committing' a Christian group to the Lord or to the Gospel; and correlatively in II Tim. ii. 2 the same verb is used of entrusting reliable men with the well-authenticated facts of the Gospel—that which, correspondingly, is called παραθήκη, 'a deposit', 'a trust' in II Tim. i. 14. The sense of responsibility for receiving, preserving, and handing on the authentic Christian Gospel is strikingly strong throughout the epistles (I Cor. xi. 23, xv. 1, Gal. ii. 2, Col. i. 5 f., I Thess. ii. 2-4, I Tim. ii. 7, II Tim. ii. 8, Heb. ii. 3, Jas i. 18, 21, I Pet. i. 23-25, I Jn ii. 20, 27, Rev. ii. 25). That is presumably why the Pauline lists of functions within the Christian ministry begin with apostles. It is the ministry of witness to the facts which stands first. Without the *datum*, no deduction. Then come the prophets and teachers—those who, within the community which is built

---

[1] Cf. Schweizer 1960, 77 ff.; but I believe that he allows too little for the possibility that the Synoptists are consciously reconstructing a 'preresurrection' scene.

[2] Moody 1920 has much to say on this.

upon the rock of the confession of Christ, are able to discern and expound God's will, and inculcate the facts and conduct attaching to the faith. Once again, although there may have been considerable variation in the manner of worship as between different congregations, the worship (it seems probable) revolved round one and the same narrative of the Last Supper with the breaking of the loaf and the sharing of wine or its equivalent.

Thus, wherever one went throughout the ancient world, the Christian community would be distinguishable as at least having at its head men who preserved a single Gospel, and led the worship of God in the name of the same Lord Jesus. And one further factor in the maintenance of the unity and purity of the faith must have been the inter-communication between one centre and another. A little later we get a picture of the elaborate care taken by Ignatius of Antioch to write to and then meet the Christians at the chief centres on his triumphal progress to martyrdom. But even in Paul's day messengers travelled rapidly between the towns, and it is remarkable that, as may be seen from his letters, so close a contact was maintained.

Thus, despite all their individuality and distinctiveness, despite the probably extreme vagaries of the 'underworld' of Christian communities from which they sprang, despite the considerable range of variation between the levels of language and style represented in the New Testament, its various writings speak with a nearly unanimous voice of a single Gospel and of one Lord. J. M. Creed spoke (1964, 122) of 'a common attitude of faith towards a Messiah, who in the fullness of time had actually appeared upon the stage of history', which united believers, although they 'were not yet in possession of any one accepted theory as to his person or his relation to God'. One only needs to compare an extra-canonical writing such as *The Gospel of Thomas*[1] with the New Testament to recognize this. H. E. W. Turner well

_____
[1] Translation by R. McL. Wilson in Hennecke-Schneemelcher 1963, 511 ff.; or in R. M. Grant and Freedman 1960; or in Bruce *Jesus* (1974), 112 ff.

sums up the contrast when he points out[1] that, in *The Gospel of Thomas* we miss completely 'the tang of historical reality', the Cross, the doctrine of grace, and 'the robust personalism of New Testament religion' (as contrasted with the unitive mysticism of *Thomas*). Such were some of the distinctive aspects of the Christian good news which the struggling Churches preserved—a phenomenon hard to explain in purely rational terms. Call it, rather, part of the evidence for the aliveness of Jesus Christ and for the power of the Spirit of God.

[1] Montefiore and Turner 1962.

CHAPTER X

COLLECTING AND SIFTING
THE DOCUMENTS[1]

THE story of the formation of what is known as the New Testament 'canon' is a story of the demand for authority. The Christian Church set out with a preposterously unlikely tale: that a person who had recently been executed by the Romans at the instigation of the Jewish religious authorities had been brought through death to an aliveness that brought life to others, and was the very corner-stone of the entire building called 'Israel'. Where was their evidence for this, and what was their authority? Probably the most immediately cogent evidence was the very existence of this group of 'Nazarenes', so confident and convinced in their witness to the events, bound together in such transparently sincere brotherhood, attended by such unmistakable signs of God's power and presence. The early chapters of the Acts describe the impact of such a community suddenly making itself felt in Jerusalem. The whole population was shaken: a large number were convinced. It was difficult to believe that such a faith—not derivable from Pharisaic expectations—and such results sprang from hallucination or a huge mistake.

But, more particularly defined, the authority for the Christian statements about Jesus was the expressly authorized eyewitness of twelve men at the heart of the witness of a still larger number. That, at least, appears to be the theory implied by Acts i, and it is compatible with the Gospel tradition and with certain hints in the Pauline Epistles.

[1] In addition to the relevant sections of Introductions, note: Westcott 1875; Zahn 1888–92; Gregory 1924; Harnack 1925, 1926; Souter 1954; Mitton 1955; Filson 1957; Cross 1960, Chh. IV, V; K. Aland 1962; Hennecke-Schneemelcher 1963, 19 ff.; Sundberg 1968, 1973, 1976 (*bis*); Käsemann, ed., 1970; Dunn 1977, Ch. XV.

According to the Gospels, Jesus himself had in his lifetime chosen and commissioned them to be with him and to be sent out as heralds of the Kingdom of God (Mk iii. 13 ff. and parallels). One of them, Judas Iscariot, had turned traitor; but the remaining eleven are claimed, in the Acts, to have received a further express commission from the risen Master to be his witnesses, and a new twelfth, Matthias, was afterwards selected by lot as between two chosen from among the other eye-witness disciples. It was agreed (Acts i. 21 f., and cf. Jn xv. 26) that a condition for election should be that a new member must have been with the Twelve all the time from John the Baptist's mission until the ascension— that is to say, he must have been an intimate participant in the whole ministry of Jesus and a witness of the resurrection and its sequel. His evidence must cover the scope of the *kerygma*—the Christian proclamation. The use of lots (Acts i. 23 ff.), representing divine guidance, was evidently intended to be the equivalent of the express commissioning by Jesus. Thus was repaired the body of the Twelve, all intimate participants in the ministry of Jesus and witnesses of the resurrection, and all authoritatively commissioned to give such witness.[1] I Jn i. 1 again alludes to the eye-witness evidence (cf. II Pet. i. 16). It is natural to see in the number twelve a deliberate allusion to the tribes of Israel: it was as much as to say 'Here *in nuce* is the real Israel's witness to the world'. It is possible also to see in the Acts narrative of the solemn restoration of the eleven to twelve a hint of the intention to underline the true, inner Israel's appeal to the wider, less loyal Israel in the Church's mission: here is a concentrated, twelvefold appeal to the twelve tribes themselves.[2] In this respect it is comparable to the mission of Yahweh's Servant to the rest of Israel in Isaiah.

However that may be, the Twelve evidently constituted the earliest Christian 'canon' or measuring-rod—the standard by which the authenticity of the Church's message was

[1] Authorized witness is the specific function of the Twelve. There is virtually nothing in the Acts about any function of leadership, as such, belonging to them (*pace* Dunn 1977, 106 f.).
[2] See further Rengstorf 1962.

to be gauged, for the duration of their lifetime. They are the pillars of the whole structure (for the metaphor, though with different scope, cf. Gal. ii. 9, I Tim. iii. 15), and to such one must refer one's preaching (cf. Gal. ii. 2). But there is no sign that the Twelve were intended to be perpetuated by succession. Here was no caliphate: if there was a caliphate anywhere in the Christian Church, it was in the line of James the Lord's brother, not of the Twelve.[1] They were (again, according at least to the theory implied by Acts i) regarded as essentially a dominically chosen and commissioned foundation body, expressly authorized to give eye-witness evidence of the decisive events. As such they were, by definition, irreplaceable in any subsequent generation. Whereas the removal of Judas by apostasy was met by the special lot-casting for Matthias, none of the subsequent depletions, by martyrdom or natural death, were made up. The Twelve were no self-perpetuating body: they were simply the initial authority for the Christian claims about Jesus.[2]

Alongside this authority, and indeed as an integral part of it, there ran also the authority of the Jewish scriptures. The 'argument from scripture', that is, the demonstration that what the apostles bore witness to was no isolated phenomenon, but could be shown to be the culmination and fulfilment of God's design for his People already sketched in scripture, has already been discussed in some detail (Chapter IV). It is enough here to recall that what the apostles had seen was claimed to be 'according to the scriptures', and that the very form in which they framed their evidence was itself sometimes influenced by scripture. The witness of the Twelve was at once a confirmation of scripture and was confirmed by scripture.[3] The way was already being paved

---

[1] See Ehrhardt 1953; also Stauffer 1952.
[2] W. L. Knox's speculations 1925, 169, about James the Lord's brother in some sense taking the place of his namesake the martyred apostle are thus misleading. 'The mere death of an apostle need not have created a vacancy . . . but apostasy is a different matter.'—Dodd 1952, 58, n. 1 (on p. 59). The whole note is very instructive.
[3] Is this the intention of II Pet. i. 19?

for the recognition of the apostolic witness as itself material for authoritative writing.

St Paul's efforts to establish his own claim to apostolic status seem to imply the same criteria as those defined in Acts i. 21 f., in however abnormal a form. In I Cor. xv. 8 he reckons the appearance of the Lord to him on the Damascus road among all the other post-resurrection appearances, though at a different time; in I Cor. ix. 1 again he appeals· to the fact that, in this sense, he is an eye-witness of the resurrection; and in Gal. i. 1, 11 f. he makes it clear that his commission as an evangelist came directly from the Lord. The peculiarity of his commission is that it is expressly to the Gentiles (Gal. i. 16, ii. 2; cf. Acts xxii. 21, xxvi. 17), and that he is outside the body of the Twelve—a thirteenth[1]—and never knew Jesus intimately, if at all, during his earthly life. But his claim remains that he is an eye-witness of the risen Lord and personally commissioned by him to bear that witness.

Thus, to challenge the Christian message was to doubt a body of living eye-witnesses authorized by the Lord himself; and, so long as they or even their close followers still lived, one can readily understand the preference expressed by Papias (about A.D. 150) for the living voice rather than for writings. 'For I did not suppose', said he, 'that information from books would help me so much as the word of a living and surviving voice (ζώσης φωνῆς καὶ μενούσης), Euseb. H.E. III. xxxix. 4. (Loeb translation).[2] Admittedly, Papias himself nevertheless valued at least three of the written Gospels (for Matthew and Mark, Euseb. H.E. III. xxxix. 15 f.; for John, an argument prefixed to a ninth-century Latin ms. of the Gospels in the Vatican library[3]); but it remains true that the Christian community was in essence not 'bookish': it had been called into existence by a series of events well

[1] See A. Richardson 1958, 314, n. 1.

[2] Cf. p. 52, above.

[3] See Filson 1957, 152, for further reservations on Papias' evidence for the valuation of oral tradition. For the ms. in question, see J. B. Lightfoot 1889; also Harnack 1893, 68. For Papias' knowledge of the Gospels, see R. M. Grant 1943.

remembered; it lived under the continued personal guidance, as it believed, of the central figure of those events; and the time would not be long, so it imagined, before he would return to sight. Its authority was 'the Lord and the Apostles'.[1] The only book it needed was the collection of scriptures already recognized by the Jews, in which the Christians now found explanation and confirmation of their own convictions, while, conversely, they found the scriptures explained and confirmed in an entirely new way by the recent events.

But the last of the Twelve died before 'the consummation of all things', and it began to become evident that the Church must continue for an indefinite time in an imperfect world. Where were the guarantees to be found for the authenticity of its claims, after the accredited eye-witnesses had ceased to be available, and when even their immediate followers were growing scarce? The answer lay inevitably in written records. With the appeal to 'the Lord and the Apostles' begins an inevitable process of development leading to accredited writings.[2]

What did books look like at this period, and how general was literacy? The answer to the first question seems to be that important, and especially sacred, books had usually been in roll form, until the Christians adopted the codex form (essentially the form of a modern book) for their own sacred writings. Codex (*caudex*) is Latin for a tree-stump, and then a slab of wood; and hence a slab or tablet for writing—the wax-coated board for note-taking; and then, eventually, the term was transferred to the flat, rectangular piles of paper, or, in some cases, parchment, constituting what we now call a book. By association and derivation, therefore, the codex tends to be used for the more incidental, transitory jottings, as contrasted with the *biblion* (or Latin *volumen*), the

[1] Whatever may be intended by the controversial phrase τὰ βιβλία καὶ οἱ ἀπόστολοι (if indeed this is the right reading) in II Clement xiv. 2 (see the discussion in Köster 1957, 67 ff.), this homily certainly uses λέγει (εἶπεν) ὁ κύριος elsewhere (iv. 5, v. 2, etc.): so that ὁ κύριος and οἱ ἀπόστολοι may justly be said to be its two sources of authority. For the date of II Clement (first half of second century?), see Altaner 1960, 103.

[2] Cf. Hennecke-Schneemelcher 1963, 24.

roll, containing the treasured, sacred writings. And although the word *biblion* is merely derived from the word for the papyrus reed, from the pith of which paper was made, in fact it came to denote the form (roll) rather than the material. And although rolls were sometimes written not on papyrus but on animal skin—parchment or vellum—while many a codex was made of paper (that is, papyrus) leaves, yet, while *biblion* tended to mean a roll, *membranae* (skins) tended to mean a codex.[1] The two words occur together in II Tim. iv. 13. T. C. Skeat (1979) has advanced reasons for believing the sense of the phrase in this passage to be 'Bring the *biblia*—I mean the *membranae*'. If this is correct (and Skeat's evidence for so translating μάλιστα (δέ?) is strong), then *biblia* must here be used as a general word for books (of any sort) and *membranae* be a particular word, meaning the parchment notebooks. If, however, the previously accepted meaning for μάλιστα could stand, and the phrase could mean 'Bring the *biblia*, but particularly the *membranae*' (i.e. if you can't bring them all, at any rate bring the latter), then there would be a case for imagining that the *biblia* might be the Jewish Scriptures (albeit probably in Greek translation) and the *membranae* the apostle's own writings (perhaps notes or records)—almost, one might say, the unconscious beginnings of Christian Scripture. But to indulge in this romantic interpretation against the evidence about the meaning of μάλιστα would be irresponsible. At any rate, it appears that it was in the Christian communities that the codex came into its own, so that eventually it superseded the roll as the recognized form for permanent—even sacred—writings.[2] That this took place earlier than used to be thought is

[1] See Roberts 1949; 1954; 1979. Also Quinn 1974, 383.
[2] See Katz 1945, Roberts 1954, 1979, 47. Note, *ib.* 76: 'we do not know of any copy of any of the Gospels written on a roll'; but (*ib.* 89) *non*-canonical Gospels are found indifferently on roll or codex. H. Chadwick, however, points out (in a letter 17 March 1980) that, as late as the eighth century, the roll was still regarded as the right form for the official, signed *acta* of councils. He cites as evidence *actio* iv of the Seventh Ecumenical Council (Nicaea II, 787), Mansi XIII (1767), Coll. 41, 42; and compares *actio* xiv of the Sixth Ecumenical Council (680–81), Mansi XI (1765), Col. 890.

important for New Testament criticism. The displacement of leaves in a codex is a possibility, as it is not in a roll; and the date of the use of the codex is relevant, therefore, to the discussion, for instance, of the possibility of displacement in St John's Gospel, and the question about the beginning and end of Mark (see above, p. 131 n. 1). On the other hand, as we shall see (below, p. 261), certain theories about the order of books in the New Testament canon depend upon the assumption of roll form.

As for literacy, Paul, the possessor of those 'books and parchments', was of course well educated, and so were his assistants who acted as his amanuenses. But what the state of education was among others is difficult to determine (see above, p. 209); and how many Christians at that time owned any books privately (even a Greek version of the Scriptures, for instance) it is impossible to say. Some Gentile Christians may well have been acquainted with the Jewish Scriptures only by hearing them read or quoted in homilies or liturgy or catechism. Others, who had been 'God-fearers' on the fringe of the synagogue, might have heard them in that context already. But everywhere there must have been a considerable degree of dependence on sheer memorizing.[1]

Whatever, then, the extent of literacy in the Christian communities, it is likely that memory played a big part, and that it is against a mainly 'un-bookish', though not illiterate, background that we have to picture the formation of a Christian literature, and the ultimate selection from it of authoritative writings. One of the obvious consequences of such a situation is the natural leadership that would be acquired in a given community by anyone sufficiently well equipped both with good character and learning to hold what few books might be available and to communicate their contents. (In I Tim. iv. 13, when Timothy is bidden to attend to reading this means, no doubt, reading aloud to his congregations.) Another consequence is, of course, that

[1] See a valuable survey of the book situation by Roberts 1970. See also Leipoldt und Morenz 1953, esp. 115 ff., appealing, *inter alia*, to Acts viii. 28 and Philo *Vit. Contemp.* 25, for the availability of at least parts of scripture to individuals.

Christian assemblies for worship and religious instruction would be the most natural seed-beds for such communications. Thus we may confidently assume that the messages of Christian writings took root largely through the ears of the faithful and of enquirers and catechumens, and in the context of worship and religious instruction.

But what were the factors that controlled the writing, and then the selection or rejection, of the various Christian books? Such evidence as we possess suggests that before the last of the apostles had died, there were already in existence various written documents containing sayings of Jesus and perhaps certain anecdotes in his life, and at least one full-length Gospel—St Mark's. It is difficult to establish more than this. The earliest (and most plausible) tradition about Mark places the writing even of his Gospel after Peter's death (though that would not mean after the last surviving apostle's death): the traditions which put it within Peter's life-time look suspiciously like 'improvements'. The direct apostolic authorship of St John's Gospel, maintained by tradition, has been very widely disputed. And Matthew, in its present form, can hardly have been written by an apostle.[1] So far as full Gospels go, therefore, we cannot be certain of more than that Mark's Gospel was written well within the natural life span of the apostolic generation—though in fact the most plausible dating of Matthew, Luke, and John places them also within this era.[2] But it is not unlikely that Mark used already existing written sources besides spoken traditions. Of the existence of widely current traditions, whether written or spoken, at a very early stage there can be no doubt. One may already detect in the Pauline or near-Pauline Epistles echoes of just such traditions about Jesus as later find their way into the Gospels (see pp. 118 ff. above). Thus a missionary like Paul already had access to traditions, oral or written, such as the evangelists ultimately drew upon. Even much later, in the sub-apostolic

---

[1] See the evidence for the traditions about Mark and Matthew in any good N.T. Introduction; and see Streeter 1930, *passim*. See also pp. 122 ff., above.

[2] Cf. now J. A. T. Robinson 1976. For Mark, Excursus IV below.

writers known as the Apostolic Fathers and in *The Gospel of Thomas*, there are traces of similar traditions still running free, and possibly running parallel to the Gospels we know rather than through them.[1] Thus is built up a picture of a great reservoir of traditions, some spoken, some already written down,[2] on which the early preachers are already drawing and from which ultimately the full-length Gospels are going to crystallize. Once again, it is the assemblies for worship and religious instruction that are the most likely reservoirs. The use of a writing in worship may be the antecedent stage to its recognition as canonical.

In due course, the first full-length Gospel appears. As we have seen, it is in essence probably intended as more circumstantial documentation for the basic *kerygma*, the Christian proclamation. If we accept the priority of Mark over the other canonical Gospels, we do not know positively of any full-length Gospel earlier than Mark's, though it is possible that he had predecessors, perhaps in Aramaic, or even Hebrew.[3] After him, in due course, there came to be a great spate of Gospels. But it is noteworthy that of these the now canonical Gospels of Matthew, Luke, and John are still plausibly dated earlier than almost any other we know of (whatever may be implied by Lk. i. 1 with its reference to

---

[1] See Köster 1957; Montefiore and Turner 1962.

[2] Roberts 1963, asks: 'It was natural for Paul to write frequently: wouldn't it be equally natural for some remote, or infrequently visited, churches to have κήρυγμα in writing at a very early date?'

[3] There is a large literature on the question whether Hebrew was not freely used as well as Aramaic for certain purposes; and, incidentally, how far Greek was used in normally Semitic-speaking circles (e.g. by Jesus himself). The following is a selection: Segal 1907–8 and 1927; Grimme 1935–36; Birkeland 1954; Nepper-Christensen 1958, 101 ff.; Grintz 1960; Emerton 1961; W. D. Davies 1964, 417, n. 2 (with valuable bibliography); Black 1968, 1969; Carmignac 1969 (arguing for Hebrew as the original language of the Lord's Prayer); Barr 1970; Fitzmyer 1970; Emerton 1973–74; P. E. Hughes 1974. Torrey 1952 (cf. *id.* 1958) suggested that the mixed Hebrew and Aramaic list of canonical scriptures in Bryennios' *Didache* manuscript, discussed by Audet 1950, lying as it does in the ms. between II Clement and the *Didache*, was probably of Christian origin, and that therefore Aramaic was the religious language even for Greek-speaking Christians before A.D. 70.

'many' predecessors); and many of the others,[1] whether still extant or known through references and quotations, are not Gospels in the same sense at all, but are either anecdotes about Jesus or mythological romances, or sayings-collections.[2] Perhaps in the end it was really not so much a matter of selecting as of recognizing that only four full-length Gospels were available from within the apostolic period. And if it be asked why these maintained their independence, instead of suffering fusion (as in Tatian's *Diatessaron*) or instead of one alone coming out as sole survivor, the answer may be found in the authority of local churches or in some other prestige. The one of the four that most nearly went under was Mark, because of its brevity and because of the fact that its substance was so largely included in Matthew; but, perhaps because it was connected with Peter or because it was connected with Rome or because of both, it held its own. And each of the other three evidently represented an influential centre of Christianity. Not that they all immediately gained universal recognition. Towards the end of the second century, Luke was still only hesitantly recognized, and John was to meet much opposition

---

[1] Jerome alludes to an *evangelium juxta* (or *secundum*) *Hebraeos* (*Contra Pelag.* III. ii and *De Vir. Ill.* ii), and in the former passage says that many affirm that it is *juxta Matthaeum*. But it is notoriously doubtful how far (if at all) there really was a Semitic antecedent to Matthew: and in any case Nepper-Christensen 1958, 64 ff. has cast grave doubt on almost every sentence of these two *testimonia* from Jerome. There is but slender evidence, then, that even this Gospel (if it ever existed) was prior to the canonical ones. When Luke refers (i. 1) to 'many' predecessors, does he mean more than Mark and whatever other component parts he employed?

[2] It is striking that comparison of the Coptic *Gospel of Thomas* with the Greek Oxyrhynchus sayings suggests that the Greek sayings may represent earlier sayings-collections used by the writer of *The Gospel of Thomas*. If so, we are presented with an instance of non-canonical sayings-collections circulating and being absorbed into a subsequent writing, rather as we may assume happened earlier in the compilation of the canonical Gospels. See Bartsch 1960. But there is the important difference (noted by Bartsch) that the Synoptic antecedents are *not* mere collections of sayings detached from their narrative settings. The sayings-collections behind *The Gospel of Thomas* are not therefore closely comparable. Miegge 1960, 121 f., points out that, whereas orthodox Christian writing moved in the direction of 'theological meditation', the apocryphal writings with Gnostic leanings moved in the direction of 'mythological imagination'.

until as late as about A.D. 220.[1] But the point is that what ultimately emerged was not a single Gospel but four—neither more nor less. Marcion and Tatian both tried, in their different ways, to establish a single Gospel, but did not carry the whole Church with them.[2] The process of selection was well under way before ever it began to be consciously reasoned about or rationalized: owing to a variety of causes, some of which have just been mentioned, the four-Gospel canon slid into existence almost furtively. It was certainly not the arbitrary decision of a single Christian body, still less of an individual. Its formal declaration, when it was made,[3] was only the recognition, by the Church collectively, of a conviction that had long been silently growing on their consciousness. Perhaps at least one or two of these writings had been regularly used in assemblies for worship long before they were officially described as authoritative.

As it happens, much the same could be said of the recognition of the Jewish scriptures also. We have to remember that there is no known official pronouncement embodying a Jewish 'canon' of scripture until near the end of the New Testament period (although there is evidence of long debate before this). The Synod of Jamnia (Jabne) in A.D. 90 is usually claimed as the occasion of this pronouncement; and a very interesting discussion of it by P. Katz (1956)

---

[1] See Schneemelcher 'Canon' (1963), 33, after Bauer.

[2] According to W. Bauer's thesis (1971) the Roman Church and other Churches in its sphere of influence, for long recognized only Matthew and Mark, accepting only with hesitation Luke (discredited by heretical use) and abandoning direct opposition to John only c. A.D. 200. He thinks Papias recognized only Mark and Matthew; Justin did not regard John as authoritative; Ignatius used not John but Matthew.

This differs from Harnack (see, e.g., 1925), despite many points in common. Harnack too saw the fixing of a four-Gospel canon as a compromise, and saw John as playing a decisive role in the process. But he thought that the opposition to the 'Alogi' led to the championing of the Fourth Gospel in the East at a time when the other Gospels were so well established that they could not be ousted.

[3] For the ultimate determination of the Canon of the New Testament, see the bibliography for this chapter. The date usually given is that of Athanasius' 39th Paschal letter (*Epist. Fest.* XXXIX), A.D. 367.

attributes to this synod also the present arrangement and division of the Hebrew Bible, arguing that this was not an ancient order at all, but that (contrary to generally held opinion) it is the arrangement of the books in the Septuagint that represents the earlier Hebrew order. However that may be, the Synod of Jamnia seems to represent the first official Jewish canon—and even that was official only for a section of Judaism: there was no such thing as an ecumenical organ of Jewish opinion, and doubtless the Jews of the Alexandrine and other dispersions continued to be without a defined 'canon' of scripture.[1] The 'Sanhedrin' of Jamnia (and thus of the *Mishnah* Tractate *Sanhedrin*) is not the lineal descendant of the Jerusalem Sanhedrin of the pre-70 period; it consisted not of priests and elders but of rabbis. Tractate *Sanhedrin* is not to be incautiously used as evidence for the Jerusalem Sanhedrin.[2] Jamnia represents a new departure. It is the remarkable achievement of Johanan ben Zakkai and his successors in establishing Judaism as a religion of the Law so as to meet the virtual abolition of the sacrificial system with the destruction of the Temple and the fall of Jerusalem in A.D. 70 (see above, p. 173).[3] But however new and special the idea of a canon of Jewish Scriptures was, its formation may well have added some momentum to the corresponding (though otherwise occasioned) Christian process.

If we ask what criteria the Church *believed* it was applying (whether in fact it succeeded is another matter), we shall find that they are criteria dictated by controversy with heretics or disbelievers.[4] The most obvious one is 'apostolicity'. If not actually written by one of the Twelve, a Gospel (to confine our inquiry for the moment to this category) must at least have some kind of apostolic *imprimatur*: it must be shown to come from some close associate of an apostle, and, if possible, with the apostle's express commission. Conse-

---

[1] One wonders what relation, if any, to Jamnia may be assumed for the use by a Christian of the phrase πᾶσα γραφὴ θεόπνευστος in II Tim. iii. 16. Was it known by this time precisely what 'scripture' comprised?

[2] Lohse in *T.D.N.T.*, *s.v.* συνέδριον.

[3] See the brief review of the circumstances by R. Le Déaut 1976.

[4] See the study by Stendahl 1962.

quently, it must necessarily belong to an early period, and would be expected (one may suppose) to show signs of at least derivation from the primitive Aramaic-speaking Church. A corollary of this, itself constituting another criterion, was that no genuinely apostolic Gospel could contain an interpretation of Jesus contrary to what the *communis sensus fidelium* had come to recognize as authentic. That sounds like a very slippery norm, and Bauer and Dunn and others have questioned whether, at this early stage, there was anything approaching to the idea of 'orthodoxy'. Yet, it does seem to be a fact that, by the time, for instance, of I and II John, certain convictions about incarnation had been established in circles which were influential enough to be eventually represented in the canon: Jesus was truly 'in flesh'—that is, he was known as a man of flesh and blood, a descendant of David—, yet also was truly 'Christ'—that is, in the sense in which 'Christ' is used in I John, the one raised from death and vindicated as, in a unique sense, God's Son (I Jn ii. 22 f., iv. 2 f., v. 5 f., II Tim. ii. 8, Rom. i. 3 f.). In other words, the conviction that seems to run down the middle of Christian thought is that the living Lord of Christian devotion is continuous with the Jesus of Nazareth who was crucified under Pontius Pilate (see above, pp. 216 f., etc.) Some of the apocryphal Gospels threaten or contradict this central position; and although all that survive seem to be later than the canonical Gospels, it is a question whether they would not have been rejected by mainstream Christianity even if they had been as early as the Gospels that became canonical. The story of Serapion, told on pp. 251 f. below, is significant in this connexion.

Finally, a Gospel presumably needed to be a Gospel. It is true that the Coptic document self-styled *The Gospel of Thomas* (see above, p. 12) is not a Gospel in this sense, being virtually nothing but a collection of sayings, almost devoid of narrative. But this is considerably later, and its adoption of the title 'Gospel' is hardly representative of Christian usage. It appears that what mainstream Christianity recognized as a necessary part of any normative collection of documents was a Gospel in the sense of a narrative of the

earthly ministry of Jesus (or at least a sequence of anecdotes), presented in such a way as to follow the pattern of, or
else be ancillary to, the apostolic proclamation—the proclamation of Jesus as God's special emissary, crucified, and
raised, all being in accordance with the design of God's
relation with his people found in the Jewish Scriptures.
Already, before the writing of the first Gospel, there were
evidently a number of fragmentary documents in circulation—sayings-collections, collections of miracle stories,
perhaps, and of conflict-stories; but these could not stand on
their own feet as whole Gospels.

Now, when the Church came consciously to apply these
tests, it was sometimes one of them, and sometimes another
which was uppermost. The original apostolic contact was
clearly a primary demand; but it was not always possible to
test this as rigorously as might have been desired; and
alongside came the additional test of usage: Had the book
proved its worth? Had it survived the critical sense of the
Christian tradition?—for it is possible that certain writings
had already asserted themselves as eminently useful and
sound before evidence for apostolic contact was discovered.
In some few instances it may even be that the latter was a
post-hoc rationalization. But in such cases the *communis
sensus fidelium* had already been so soundly informed by
authentic tradition that its own *imprimatur* was in fact
sufficient.

It must be added, in all fairness, that we have, in Christian
antiquity, at least one instance of an author being very
severely penalized for a work which, though perfectly orthodox (at any rate by the standards of his period), turned out
to be a fiction. This is the story told by Tertullian in *De
Baptismo* xvii of the priest of Asia who admitted to having
written the *Acts of Paul* (which includes the *Acts of Paul and
Thecla*) and was deprived of office (presumably on the charge
of passing off fiction as though it had been history). This
gives the lie to the idea that the early Church never exercised
any historical criticism, but relied entirely on its sense of
what was orthodox and edifying.[1] The unsuspecting priest

[1] Ironically, it is II Peter, widely believed to be pseudonymous, which

had done it in all good faith, meaning to enhance the honour of the apostle; and he had written anonymously, not attempting to assume the authority of another. How much severer (it might have been supposed) would the Church have been towards one who was caught impersonating (say) an apostle! On the other hand, it is one thing to write fiction as though it were history and quite another to communicate teaching in someone else's name. This latter was a time-honoured technique and scandalized nobody unless the teaching was either maliciously intended (cf. II Thess. ii. 2, iii. 17)[1] or heretical (cf. the case of *The Gospel of Peter*, below, pp. 251 f.). Yet even in the realm of teaching, if they did indulge in what has just been called a *post-hoc* rationalization, one may assume that it was not consciously thought to be a rationalization. The acceptance of Hebrews as Pauline is an instance. There were at first some doubters in the East and many in the West.[2] But it was indispensable; it was compatible with Pauline doctrine; and the prevailing opinion of the Eastern Churches was eventually accepted—that it was Pauline (Moffatt 1918, 431). And it must be remembered that Hebrews was not accepted without challenge. As late a writer (in our time scale) as Tertullian, *De Pud.* xx, attributes Hebrews to Barnabas, and, though preferring it to Hermas, does not treat the work as scripture (Gregory 1924, 222 ff.; cf. Moffatt 1918, 437).[3]

Moreover, it must be remembered that Hermas, the writer of the popular *Shepherd*, did not, even as a teacher, try to write under another name; and it is noteworthy, further, that in the ante-Nicene era, forgeries were relatively rare and often detected. 'No one in this period made much use of most

itself formulates just this criterion of historicity, when the writer says (i. 16), 'It was not on tales artfully spun ($\sigma\varepsilon\sigma\sigma\phi\iota\sigma\mu\acute\varepsilon\nu\sigma\iota\varsigma\ \mu\acute\upsilon\theta\sigma\iota\varsigma$) that we relied ...'

[1] But II Thess. iii. 17 represents the stress of dangerous circumstances: by the time of the Pastorals, things may have been different. See, however, the inquiry by Bailey 1978–79 (pp. 143–5 being on pseudepigraphy).

[2] Cf. Sundberg 1973, 40.

[3] On the idea that Hebrews was rejected in the West because it played into the hands of the Montanists, see Grässer 1965, 193, n. 247.

of the forgeries we later encounter in such quantities.' (R. M. Grant, 1960, 23.)

Nevertheless, even though the early Church was much more alert against 'forgery' than is sometimes supposed, we have to recognize a two-way traffic: the living community was indeed constantly subject to check and correction by the authentic evidence—by the basic witness, first of accredited eye-witness apostles and later of the written deposit of that witness; yet also the documents which soon began to circulate in considerable numbers were themselves in some measure subject to check and correction, whatever their origin, by the living community—simply because it, by that time, contained within it, or among its leaders, a sufficiently firm and uniform tradition to constitute it corporately a preserver of tradition. One may see the living community's control operating in the Johannine Epistles, where appeal is made to authentic, early, eye-witness tradition against the opinionated interpretations and assertions of men who were running contrary to these. Something similar, though without the allusion to eye-witness, is to be seen in the Pastoral Epistles. The further one goes in time from the original sources of evidence ('that which was from the beginning', I Jn i. 1, etc.) the more precarious becomes the claim of the Church, in its own right, to test the evidence. But until there is a recognized body of authentic documents to appeal to, there is no other way; and this is how we see the Church proceeding before the establishment of the canon of Christian scriptures. The claims of documents seem, until then, to have been checked by that tradition of orthodoxy which was generally diffused through the living, worshipping communities.[1] That tradition, in its turn, however, was subject to the check of apostolic eye-witness as long as the apostles were available; and before the death of the last

---

[1] Very important here is the fact that Gnostic writings, such as *The Gospel of Truth*, are now available to demonstrate what sort of doctrinal criteria the Church must have used in excluding them. See van Unnik *Gnostic* (1960), 68, 90, 91. Note, further, that the inclusion of the Paulines and the exclusion of (e.g.) Clement shows that the Church had not lost its appreciation of what Paul stood for.

apostle, as we have seen, there had already begun to exist at least some soundly attested apostolic documents.

At this point it is worth while to observe that a distinction has been drawn, by K. Aland (1961) between an earlier period (to about A.D. 150) and a later. In the earlier period, the prophetic afflatus was recognized, and a teacher could stand up and speak in a Christian assembly in the name of the Spirit and in the name of some great apostolic leader, and be accepted. This (Aland suggests) is how some writings that we should be tempted to call pseudonymous came to be openly accepted: they were *bona fide* utterances of formerly known (though now anonymous) speakers in the name of apostolic men. But when the afflatus waned, and the Church became conscious of living in an era separated from that of the apostles, the more literary tests of authority began to come in, as did also deliberate forgeries.[1]

Such extra-canonical documents styling themselves 'Gospels'[2] as we actually possess are all of a suspect character. The two most recently recovered—the probably Valentinian *Gospel of Truth* and *The Gospel of Thomas*—must certainly have been rejected for their contents, even if on other grounds they had seemed to carry impressive claims. As a matter of fact, neither of them is a Gospel in the sense of comprising the *kerygma*, and *The Gospel of Truth* has not even the semblance of apostolic authority either. There is no known extra-canonical Gospel material which is not (when it can be tested at all) in some way subject to suspicion for its genuineness or its orthodoxy: many of the recovered fragments are in some sense 'gnostic' in tendency.[3]

The stock example of the application of the test of orthodoxy, as against that of apostolic attribution, is the story of Serapion, bishop of Antioch in about A.D. 200,

[1] There is a well-documented essay on 'epistolary pseudepigraphy' in Guthrie 1961, 282 ff. See *id.* 1962, for criticism of Aland. See also a sharp exchange between K. Aland, Falsche Verfasserangaben, and Brox, both 1979; and Brox 1975 and 1977.

[2] C. H. Roberts 1963 asks whether the use of the word at this stage may not reflect the recognition of the genre, and therefore of the canonical Gospels.

[3] See, e.g., Jeremias 1964; Gärtner 1961; Haenchen 1961.

quoted by Eusebius (*H.E.* VI. xii). The Greek of the passage is by no means lucid; but this much is clear, that Serapion had, without reading it himself, sanctioned the use, in the Christian commmunity of Rhossus (a small town in Cilicia), of a writing calling itself *The Gospel of Peter*. Subsequently, however, he discovered (still possibly not at first-hand—the Greek is very odd) that, while the greater part of this Gospel was 'in accordance with the true teaching of the Saviour', there were heretical additions which had apparently been used by heretical teachers to lead the Christians of Rhossus astray. Against these he warns them, since, whereas 'we receive both Peter and the other apostles as Christ' (cf. Matt. x. 40, Gal. iv. 14), 'the writings which falsely bear their names we reject, as men of experience, knowing that such were not handed down to us'. Serapion's treatise from which Eusebius quotes was called περὶ τοῦ λεγομένου κατὰ Πέτρον εὐαγγελίου ('concerning the so-called Gospel according to Peter'), and it seems to be clear that the grounds for this stricture, 'so-called', were entirely its heretical character, not any research into its origin. The fragment of this very Gospel which was discovered at Akhmim in the winter of 1886–87 confirms Serapion's judgment: or, if it is impossible to prove that it is strictly docetic or otherwise heretical, at least its extravagances mark it as spurious and well on the way to heretical fancies. It breathes an entirely different atmosphere from that of the canonical Gospels.[1]

Thus, while the earliest Church was shaped and controlled by the evidence of all the eye-witnesses, and especially the authenticated Twelve, there came a brief period when this evidence had become so entirely a part of the life and thinking of the leaders of the Church that they automatically refused to assimilate into their system what was contrary in doctrinal tendency to the now indigenous standards. This brief transitional period, between the earliest stage, when presumably the eye-witness test was constantly applied, and the later stage of confidence when even what claimed to be apostolic witness was itself subjected to the doctrinal test, may perhaps be illustrated by parts of the Pastoral Epistles.

[1] See Maurer 1963.

These betray an awareness of 'orthodoxy'; and although the 'faithful sayings' cited in the Pastorals are not sayings of Jesus and do not in any sense represent a 'canon', yet the very phrase shows an instinct for classification into true and false.[1] Moreover, a good deal of prominence is given in these Epistles to the need for careful transmission of the apostolic teaching; it is a precious deposit, entrusted by God to the apostle, and by the apostle to his chosen disciple, to be handed on by him to carefully chosen men. The 'pattern or mould of teaching' ($\tau \acute{u} \pi o \varsigma\ \delta \iota \delta \alpha \chi \widehat{\eta} \varsigma$) of Rom. vi. 17, and the 'traditions' ($\pi \alpha \rho \alpha \delta \acute{o} \sigma \varepsilon \iota \varsigma$) of II Thess. ii. 15, iii. 6 (cf. I Thess. iv. 1 f.), are on their way, via the 'sketch' or 'outline' ($\dot{v} \pi o \tau \acute{v} \pi \omega \sigma \iota \varsigma$) of sound teaching (II Tim. i. 13) and the $\pi \alpha \rho \alpha \theta \acute{\eta} \varkappa \eta$ or 'deposit' (I Tim. vi. 20, II Tim. i. 12, 14; cf. ii. 2), into the 'canon' of approved writings.

The recognition in the whole Church of the four Gospels as alone authentic is difficult to date. There are scraps of evidence that they circulated independently for a considerable period after their first appearance. Thus, to judge by the textual history of the manuscripts of Mark, this Gospel was by far the most heavily corrected by scribes; which probably means that it had a longer independent history than the others.[2] Indeed, there are signs that it was early recognized as the first Gospel, despite the later traditions which placed Matthew on the pedestal of primacy,[3] and, if so, it may well have circulated independently. But as soon as Matthew did rise to the highest place in popularity, then, for the same reason, it may be presumed to have been often copied by itself (though, as has just been implied, less often than Mark

---

[1] See Excursus III.

[2] See Kilpatrick 1957, 96; and note, with S. E Johnson 1960, 30, the interesting case of the solitary Mark in the University of Chicago Library (Chicago MS 972 = Gregory-Eltester catalogue Codex 2427, see K. Aland 1963, p. 189), described by Willoughby 1946 and by Casey 1947. For separate mss. of John, note the famous Rylands fragment p[52] (description by Roberts 1935), and the Bodmer fragment p[66] (V. Martin 1956, 1958); and note the Bodmer fragment p[75] of Luke/John (V. Martin and Kasser 1961). Brief descriptions in Metzger 1968. Also, Roberts 1963 believes that p[64], the Magdalen College Matthew, was probably a separate book.

[3] F. C. Grant 1957, 64 ff.

had been separately copied). Thus, 'for the Syrian Church *the* (written) Gospel long continued to be that of Matthew, as it had been elsewhere'. (Bacon 1900, 38).

As for Luke and John, there is much *a priori* likelihood that they both circulated for some time among the particular persons or groups for whom, respectively, they were first intended. Many of the Gospel echoes in the Epistles seem to be exclusively Lucan, suggesting, perhaps, that Luke alone was the Gospel for the Pauline circle;[1] and R. G. Heard, in a posthumously published article (1955), points out the evidence afforded by a comparison among themselves of the 'old Gospel Prologues' for the independent circulation of the Prologue to Luke even in the fourth century. With regard to John, it is a well-known matter for discussion whether even Justin Martyr (*circa* A.D. 150) knew it.[2] There is an echo of what we know as a Johannine saying ('unless you are born again, you will certainly not enter the Kingdom of the heavens') in *Apol.* i. 61, but if Justin did know the Gospel, it has not influenced his theology. On the other hand he cites a

[1] Though of course if Luke wrote the Pastorals, this would remove some of the significant statistics! See Excursus II below.

[2] On Justin's sources, see Bousset 1891; Heer 1914; Buckley 1935; Baumstark 1935. Westcott 1875, 166, n. 1, cites as the chief passages: Jn iii. 5-8, I *Apol.* i. 61; Jn i. 13, *Dial.* lxiii; Jn i. 12, *Dial.* cxxiii; Jn xii. 49, *Dial.* lvi; Jn vii. 12, *Dial.* lxix. Of these, Jn i. 12, 13, vii. 12 are very faintly echoed, if at all. See also Sanday 1876, Ch. IV. J. N. Sanders 1943 examines a wider range of passages, concluding (31): 'The most reasonable conclusion from this examination of the passages ... which appear to show traces of the influence of the Fourth Gospel seems to be that certain passages are most naturally explained as reminiscences of the Fourth Gospel, while there are few, if any, which can be certainly said to be dependent upon it'. Osborn 1973, 137, writes: 'While there is only one quotation from the fourth Gospel—and this could well be part of the baptismal liturgy "Except ye be born anew, ye cannot enter the kingdom of heaven"—there are many coincidences of thought and expression'. Osborn's list in the latter category goes far beyond Westcott's.

From the Synoptic Gospels, Osborn 1973, 127, lists 10 exact quotations in Justin, 25 slightly variant, and 32 variant. He holds that a strong case can be made for Justin's using a harmony, or making one for himself (125 ff.). After all, Tatian was Justin's pupil (126), though the phrase ἐν τῷ εὐαγγελίῳ γέγραπται (*Dial.* c, quoting a 'Q' saying, Matt. xi. 27, Lk. x. 22) does not necessarily indicate a single Gospel book (130).

'Q' saying ('All things are committed to me ...', Matt. xi. 27, Lk. x. 22) with the formula ἐν τῷ εὐαγγελίῳ γέγραπται, 'it is written in the Gospel' (*Dial.* c).

Rather earlier (? *circa* A.D. 130) *The Epistle of Barnabas* (iv. 14) uses γέγραπται, 'it is written', to introduce a phrase known to us as Matthean ('many are called, but few chosen'). But it must be admitted that γέγραπται need not imply the concept of authoritative scripture; and Köster, 1957, 126, questions whether even this saying can be pinned down to an exclusively Matthean origin. However, the main point is that here are sufficient hints to suggest a period during which the four Gospels were in existence separately and were used, perhaps, only locally.

But if there was a period when each group or area recognized only one or two Gospels in writing, there came a time when the four emerged into equal recognition. Cullmann (1956, 39 ff.) argues that there were two conflicting motives for the four-fold canon: (i) the conviction that no one Gospel presented the fullest possible witness to the Incarnate; (ii) the desire of each Evangelist to make a single Gospel which should include his predecessors' witness. The result was reduction—though not reduction to only one. In briefest summary, Cullmann's argument may be outlined as continuing thus: in view of the spate of manifestly gnostic and false writings, it was natural to treasure *all* of the few really apostolic ones. Then (unlike the attitude of the earlier period) came the desire to champion *one* versus the rest. Marcion's is the best known attempt. But it is a docetic tendency to conflate into one, or to choose one against the rest: it is a genuinely historical insight to recognize a plurality in human witness. Irenaeus himself, claiming that four is a divinely rather than a humanly chosen number, really looks in the same (mistaken) direction as docetism. He ought to have seen that the *scandalon* of human diversity should be accepted as such. The earlier Church was right—to accept all that was thought to be truly apostolic, and to see it as mediating through human diversity, the one divine event. (The Muratorian Canon itself is not far from such a recognition when it says '. . . though various ideas are taught in the several books of the Gospels, yet it makes no difference to the faith of believers, since by one sovereign Spirit all things are declared in all of them . . .';[1] yet, in the preceding section the concept of a single, supreme Gospel has already appeared in the legend of John, of whom it was revealed to Andrew that John was to write all things in his own name.) It was probably from the middle of the second century that it became usual to speak of 'the Gospel *according to* Matthew' etc. (reflecting a notion of a single proclamation evidenced by a plurality of witnesses).

Our earliest extant manuscripts—the Chester Beatty papyri and the Sinaitic Syriac—take us back to A.D. 250 or earlier for the four together; but *The Gospel of Peter*, the fragment of which, already mentioned, shows signs of the use of all four, cannot be much later than A.D. 150, since it was well established at Rhossus when Serapion found it; and Tatian's famous *Diatessaron*—his conflation of the four into a single Gospel—gives us a similar date for the joint recognition of at least the four (even if there are obscure traces of a fifth or of an independent tradition in his conflation—unless these are due simply to the use of a different text).[2] By about A.D. 185, Irenaeus is proclaiming that it is as inevitable that there should be four Gospels as that there should be four winds and four corners of the earth. If this is polemic, as it well may be, the target of his attack is probably heretical opinion: there is nothing to suggest that any considerable section of the orthodox Church would have wished to deny

[1] Translation from J. Stevenson 1957, No. 124.

[2] See Metzger 1966, 1977. Tatian was a pupil of Justin's. Hitherto, only one tiny fragment in Greek of his *Diatessaron* has been found (publ. by Kraeling, 1935). Otherwise, our sources are (for the East) Ephraem's commentary on the *Diatessaron* (c. A.D. 360) in Armenian translation; Arabic translations from Syriac; some later versions; and scattered quotations in the Syriac and Armenian Church Fathers; (for the West) the harmony, with Vulgate text, in *codex Fuldensis* (before A.D. 546); later versions; scattered quotations. There are apocryphal additions and the canonical material is occasionally coloured with ascetical touches. It is these phenomena that Messina 1951 and others are trying to account for. See an interesting discussion in Montefiore and Turner 1962. Jerome (*Epp.* cxxi. 6) alludes to Theophilus of Antioch's similar work, but of this we have no other trace. See further Baarda 1961–2.

his assertions. After Irenaeus follows Clement of Alexandria and thereafter plenty of evidence to confirm the recognition of the four alone. But it is to be noted that until this mid-second-century date there is remarkably little sign of this. Hermas, *Visions* iii. 13, misses a golden opportunity of mentioning the four (unless one can indeed believe that the four legs of the bench are meant to symbolize the Gospels[1]), and it is a matter of considerable uncertainty whether the recognition of the canonical Gospels can be detected in the Apostolic Fathers generally. But at least it can be said with confidence that the four-fold canon is well established before our earliest official lists of accredited books. Also (to judge by Justin's attitude) Gospels generally (no matter how many) tended to carry more weight, as the apostles' 'reminiscences', ἀπομνημονεύματα,[2] than other writings. Before Justin, Ignatius had said that he took refuge in the Gospel as in the flesh of Jesus and in the apostles as in the presbytery of the Church (*Philad.* v. 1). But the margin of time between such vaguely defined independent or partially independent circulation of Gospel material and the solid unity-in-quaternity[3] of the fourfold Gospel canon appears to be slender. It looks uncommonly as though something which we do not know about acted as a rather sudden incentive to the collection.

This brings us to Marcion. Did that interesting heretic find four Gospels already recognized together by about A.D. 140, and did he deliberately drop off Matthew, Mark, and John (as well as the unacceptable parts of Luke)? Or was it rather that the catholic Church, after seeing what havoc Marcion wrought by his one-sided use of documents, brought the four Gospels together to restore the balance and

---

[1] Strongly denied by Koester 1957, 254. See further C. Taylor 1892.

[2] See Heard 1954-5 with some discussion of the meaning of the word and of Heard's article by Hyldahl 1960. See also Osborn 1973, 123 f., 135, 138. Of earlier writers, note Lippelt 1901.

[3] There may be something to be learnt from the parallel and contrast offered by the convergence and conflation of various accounts of *Israel's* 'Gospel'—the story of the exodus and the covenant—within the Pentateuch.

make a fourfold harmony? This is the same problem as confronts us for the whole New Testament canon: was Marcion's the first canon, and is the orthodox canon the catholic Church's subsequent reply? Or did Marcion play fast and loose with an already existing canon? There is at present no conclusive evidence for the existence of a pre-Marcionite catholic canon. Marcion may have been the catalyst we have already hinted at. We cannot be certain.[1]

Even the evidence of the famous Gospel prologues[2] is inconclusive. These are to be distinguished from the brief descriptive prologues to the *Epistles* which de Bruyne believed to have originated with Marcion himself. The oldest *Gospel* prologues, by contrast, were believed by de Bruyne to be anti-Marcionite. R. G. Heard,[3] however, questioned this conclusion, at any rate for the prologue to Luke, which, he argued, is independent of the prologues to Mark and John (that to Matthew is not extant)[4] and is free from anti-Marcionite material; and Regul (1969) has altogether abandoned de Bruyne's thesis as indefensible. Once again, then, little if any light can be shed on the relation of the canon to the heretic.

But meanwhile, how had the epistles and other writings fared? One of the most elusive problems in the history of the New Testament canon concerns the origin of the collected letters of Paul, the Pauline *corpus*. Even when it did first emerge, it was not complete: some Pauline writings had already been lost (or at any rate were omitted). I Cor. v. 10 appears to refer to a previous letter of which, at most, a fragment may be detected in II Cor. vi. 14–vii. 1. In II Cor. vii. 8 allusions are made to a severe letter which, though it may conceivably be I Corinthians itself, is more likely identified either with II Cor. x ff. or with a completely lost

---

[1] See Blackman 1948; Regul 1969.

[2] Huck-Lietzmann-Cross 1951, vii f. See de Bruyne 1907; 1928; W. F. Howard 1935–36; R. M. Grant 1941; Regul 1969.

[3] Heard 1955 and further literature there cited; and now Regul 1969, with a radical rejection of de Bruyne's thesis.

[4] The 'Monarchian Prologues' (for description and references, see Jackson and Lake 1922, 242 ff.), which do include Matthew, are not to be confused with the ancient, so-called anti-Marcionite ones.

letter.[1] In Col. iv. 16 a letter 'from Laodicea' is mentioned, which evidently means a letter from Paul which is to be passed on to Colossae from Laodicea in exchange for the letter to the Colossians. This 'Laodiceans' is also either totally lost, or is to be identified with what we now know as 'Ephesians' (or else, as has been conjectured by E. J. Goodspeed, with 'Philemon').[2] Conversely, that some of the letters ultimately included in the canon as Pauline are not by Paul falls only just short of demonstration. The Epistle to the Hebrews, though eventually included in the Pauline canon, was regarded as not of Paul's workmanship by several writers of antiquity (cf. p. 249 above), and now is widely acknowledged to be un-Pauline; and a large number of scholars regard the Pastoral Epistles as at least in part post-Pauline; while varying degrees of suspicion are cast on other Epistles, especially on II Thessalonians and Ephesians. Thus, some were irretrievably lost, some may have eventually been added from the Pauline circle rather than from Paul himself. It was a deeply ingrained tradition in Jewish circles that certain genres of writing should, as a matter of course, be written under the name of their representative authors: Law was by Moses, Wisdom by Solomon, Psalms mostly by David;[3] and at least during K. Aland's 'earlier period' (see above, p. 251) this may have held good for Christians also. But the question still remains: who or what prompted a collection of Pauline Epistles in the first instance?

As with the four Gospels, so with the Pauline Epistles, we know that they existed before ever they were presented in a single collection. Not only so, but there is some evidence in the manuscript tradition, comparable to that mentioned above for the Gospels, suggesting that they actually circulated for a time separately (and this, it is to be noted, applied to Eph. i).[4] And the appearance of the collection can be

[1] See commentators; also Hurd 1965.

[2] Goodspeed 1927, 1933, 1956. For theories finding a plurality of letters in Philippians, see Beare 1959; Rahtjen 1959–60, replied to by Mackay 1960–61.

[3] See Brockington 1953.

[4] See Zuntz 1953; and a suggestive footnote in Beare 1953, 601.

plausibly, if not with certainty, placed within a fairly short period. Acts shows no trace of a knowledge of the Pauline Epistles, whereas I Clement (generally dated about A.D. 95) does, and thereafter there are enough echoes to show that they were at least beginning to be known. Yet, even so, evidence for the knowledge of one or two Pauline Epistles is not evidence for the existence of a collection, a *corpus*; and as with the Gospels, so with the Pauline corpus, Marcion is the really important landmark. He, we know on the evidence of Tertullian, used a collection of Pauline Epistles. Was it then he, in fact, who created it?

Two particularly interesting things we learn from Tertullian about Marcion's *Apostolicon* or collection of the apostle's writings: that he knew our Ephesians as 'Laodiceans', and that his collection contained the following letters (probably in this order): Galatians, I, II Corinthians, Romans, I, II Thessalonians, Laodiceans, Colossians, Philemon, Philippians. That is, Marcion (if 'Laodiceans' is 'Ephesians') used the nine great Paulines (and Philemon).

What may be learnt by comparing the order in other known lists? The best-known of these is the Muratorian Canon (Stevenson 1957, No. 124), usually dated towards the end of the second century,[1] whose catalogue is: Corinthians, Ephesians, Philippians, Colossians, Galatians, Thessalonians, Romans (in that order), and also (though not necessarily in this order) Philemon, Titus, I, II Timothy. The Muratorian Canon goes out of its way here to mention also the Epistles to the Laodiceans and Alexandrines, falsely, it says, attributed to Paul 'in connexion with' (*ad*) the heresy of Marcion. A brilliant conjecture by J. Knox (1942) relates Marcion's and the Muratorian orders as follows, in two steps: (a) Marcion, using an already established list with Ephesians at its head, transposed Ephesians (Laodiceans) and Galatians, bringing Galatians to the head because it was specially important for his own doctrinal purposes. (b) Assuming that the letters of the already established list were contained in two rolls of roughly equal length,[2] the two most

[1] *Contra*, Sundberg 1973.
[2] Brownlee 1964, 247 ff. wrote: 'The gap between Chapters thirty-three

substantial components, I, II Corinthians and Romans, will probably have been placed one in each roll. This might make one roll contain Ephesians and Corinthians; the other all the rest. And if one divides the Muratorian Canon into two sections on this principle and reverses the orders of the two sections, one gets exactly Marcion's order (with the one alteration already noted in (a)). Is it possible, then, that these two lists are the result of rolling up the two rolls in opposite directions? This, though an exceedingly ingenious guess, is only a guess as the author himself is the first to admit. And, as has already been remarked (pp. 239 ff. above), it is by no means clear that the writings catalogued in the Muratorian Canon would have been on rolls and not in a codex—in which case the theory would fall to the ground.[1] If we deny ourselves the luxury of Knox's theory, we seem to be left without a clue as to the relation between the heretical and the (presumably) orthodox list: and in that case we still do not know which came first—whether Marcion first collected his *apostolicon* and later the orthodox Church decided to make theirs, or whether Marcion tampered with an already existing list.[2] The situation here is the same as with the Gospels.

and thirty-four in the complete Isaiah scroll (1Q Isa[a]), together with orthographic peculiarities of each half, points to the practice of bisecting the Book of Isaiah into two scrolls: (1) Chapters i-xxxiii and (2) Chapters xxxiv-lxvi. ... The ancient practice of bisecting books is well discussed by H. St John Thackeray in his Schweich Lectures of 1920, *The Septuagint and Jewish Worship*, Appendix VI, pp. 130–6. This was done, at times, for the convenience of handling by a purely mechanical division of large works into two scrolls; some of the better constructed books of antiquity, however, were so composed as to yield a natural literary division at about the mid-point of the work. ... In the scroll, each [half] consists of twenty-seven columns, and the point of division lies between two sheets of skin, so if it were not that they happen to be sewed together they could easily circulate as two separate scrolls. An unprecedented gap of three lines occurs at the bottom of Col. XXVII, separating the two volumes.'

[1] C. H. Roberts 1963 not only confirms this last objection, but observes also that, if there were rolls and they had been rolled up in opposite directions, in one of them not only the order but the parts themselves would have been back to front, and the mistake would have been quickly rectified.

[2] See a discussion of this problem in Blackman 1948, Ch. II.

One other ingenious attempt has been made to find an individual to whom to attribute the formation of the Pauline collection. This is E. J. Goodspeed's theory (see p. 259, above) about Ephesians. Noting the close relation between Ephesians and Colossians, and, at the same time, the very remarkable differences, and convinced that Ephesians was not Pauline, Goodspeed reached the conclusion that it must be the work of a student and admirer of the Pauline Epistles, who was particularly familiar with Colossians, but knew and echoed all the others also. Who might such an individual be, and what led him to know the whole Pauline *corpus?* Might it not have been the reading of the Acts that led this person to go round the Pauline centres looking for the letters? It is well known that the Acts shows practically no trace of a knowledge of the Pauline Epistles; whereas Ephesians (assuming its non-Pauline authorship) is the first writing to reflect them all, and thereafter they are often echoed. Moreover, a fashion for issuing collections of Epistles seems to have set in— witness the seven letters of the Apocalypse and the seven letters of Ignatius (note that the Pauline *corpus* can itself be seen as addressed to seven churches *plus* one—Rome, Corinth, Galatia, Philippi, Colossae, Thessalonica, Laodicea, [Philemon], *plus* Ephesus). Of Goodspeed's theory that Philemon was 'Laodiceans' we need not here speak. What concerns us at the moment is that, on his showing, Ephesians is, as it were, the covering letter to the collection. Instead of writing an introduction in his own name, as a modern editor would, this disciple and admirer writes a glowing recapitulation of the apostle's message, modestly concealing his own identity by the then familiar technique of writing as from the apostle himself. And who was he? If an identification were to be hazarded, Goodspeed (supported here by J. Knox 1959) would suggest Onesimus. Who would be more intimate with Colossians (and Philemon) than the slave whose future depended so completely on the success of these letters? And who is so naturally associated with Ephesus as Onesimus who (according to Ignatius' letter to Ephesus) was in later years Bishop of that Church? There are many minor difficulties in the way of this skilful solution of the Ephesians problem (for which the reader must be referred to works of introduction and exegesis); but one major problem is the position of Ephesians in lists of the Epistles. Is there any evidence that Ephesians occurred at the beginning or end of the first collection of Paul's epistles, as Goodspeed's theory seems to require? A. C. Sundberg (1973, 37) points out that Origen, *Contra Cels*. III. xx, alludes to Ephesians, Colossians, Thessalonians, Philippians, and Romans, in that order. But this hint, whatever it may be worth, seems to stand alone, and it is not evident that Origen is here referring to any settled order: he is simply citing epistles which illustrate Paul's doctrine of wisdom. This, and Knox's conjecture about the original order of Marcion's and of the Muratorian lists, are hardly substantial enough (see above, pp. 260 f.) to give us much confidence. To G. Zuntz's critique of the theory we shall come shortly (see p. 265 below).

If we abandon the idea that the collecting of the Pauline letters was the work of an individual, such as Onesimus or Marcion, we are left with the time-honoured alternative— the slow, anonymous process of accretion, the snowball theory. We have to suppose, that is, that the intercourse between one Pauline centre and another gradually led to the exchange of copies of letters, until, at any given centre, there came to be not only the letter or letters originally sent to it, but also copies of certain others, collected from other Pauline Churches. Thus in each centre there would come to be little nests of letters, and gradually these would move into wider circulation and would be augmented, until the full number, as we know it, was reached. Then all that remained to be done was the making of a careful 'edition' of the whole *corpus*.[1]

Such a theory ignores Acts as a precipitant; it also depends a good deal on the assumption of a live interest in Paul between his death and the decisive acceptance of his letters; and there is no evidence that Paul dominated the Christian world of those days as he has (for the most part) dominated it since the inclusion of his letters in scripture. Papias (to cite

[1] See Mitton 1955.

a famous example), although the friend of Polycarp, shows no evidence of the use of the Pauline writings.[1] Yet, even so, it is hard to believe that the churches of Paul's own founding did not treasure his memory (cf. I Clement xlvii. 1 with its 'Take up the epistle of the blessed Paul the Apostle', implying that the Corinthians had treasured one letter at any rate);[2] and that would be enough to start the process of gradual accretion. Communications were good between different centres, and a process of exchanging and transcribing is not difficult to imagine. Moreover, as against Goodspeed's theory, it must be remembered that Acts makes no mention whatsoever of Paul's letter-writing activities, in spite of its mention of other epistles (see Acts xv. 23-29, xviii. 27, xxiii. 25-30, xxviii. 21).[3] At best, then, Acts can only have provided the incentive in the sense that it recounted Paul's activity as a founder of various local churches. But the churches in question did not need Acts to tell them that.

Thus, although one-man theories are attractive, they are highly speculative, and the anonymous, gradual evolution is not by any means ruled out. If one other individual name were to be suggested, however, might it not be that of Luke himself? It has just been pointed out that the Acts would not provide a reader with any knowledge of the Pauline Epistles; but what if it was after the writing of the Acts, and after Paul's death, that Luke himself—who must have known about the letters although he had not written about them— began to revisit the Pauline centres which he had described, and to look for the letters there? No one knew better than he the fact that they were written. It is entirely in keeping with his historian's temperament to collect them.[4] And the

[1] See, e.g. Westcott 1875, 77 f. (attributing the silence to Papias' Judaistic sympathies). It must be remembered, however, that Papias' work only survives in scattered fragments, and the silence is not therefore specially significant.

[2] See Kennedy 1900.

[3] J. Knox 1966 suggests that the writer deliberately refrained from mentioning the Pauline epistles because they had been so widely used in the interests of heretics.

[4] H. Chadwick reminds me that Eusebius collected the letters of Origen, *H.E.* VI. xxxvi. 2.

considerable link, in respect of vocabulary, contents, and outlook, between the Pastoral Epistles and Luke–Acts lends some plausibility to the suggestion that Luke was the collector, editor, and augmenter of the Pauline *corpus*. Whether the Pastorals were in existence by the time of Marcion or not is still a matter of dispute.[1]

On the nature of the archetype of the Pauline *corpus* there is a valuable discussion in G. Zuntz's Schweich Lectures for 1946 (1953). A careful criticism of Goodspeed's hypothesis leads him to the conclusion (276 f.) that 'Whoever wrote Ephesians, it was not the editor of the *corpus*....' He then points out that 'faithfulness, completeness, and non-interference with the available material' are the characteristics of 'the traditions of editorship in antiquity generally'. As instances, he adduces the editing of Thucydides, Lucretius, and the *Aeneid*; of the private diaries of the Emperor Marcus; of Plotinus' essays, with special reference to interesting information about methods in the 'life' of Porphyry, Plotinus' editor. He thinks, therefore, of the arising of many faults in the Pauline Epistles, individually and (perhaps) in earlier collections, in the fifty years between the autographs and the formation of the *corpus*—a period during which he believes there was some use and circulation—*ergo* copying—of the Epistles; and then he thinks of a *corpus* produced about A.D. 100, which, in the scholarly Alexandrine tradition (and perhaps at Alexandria) aimed at the qualities already mentioned, and thus (e.g.) produced an *Ephesians* with a blank in i. 1 and with ἐν Ἐφέσῳ in the margin.[2] Thus there came to be a splendid *variorum* archetype, from which we may derive many of the later variants.

However and whenever the Pauline *corpus* emerged, at any rate we have Marcion's date as one landmark; and not many

---

[1] If Luke wrote them (see Excursus II below), then conceivably he omitted them from his original Pauline corpus for precisely that reason (though Quinn 1974, 385, holds that letters to individuals fall into a separate category). Boismard (1961–62) goes so far as to speculate on the possibility of Luke's having had a hand also in the redaction of the Fourth Gospel.

[2] Note, however, the conjecture by Santer 1968–69.

THE BIRTH OF THE NEW TESTAMENT

decades later, in about A.D. 180, we can listen (J. Stevenson
1957, No. 22) to the martyrs of Scilli or Scillium (in
Numidia, in *Africa proconsularis*) being interrogated by the
proconsul about the books in their possession: 'What is there
in your *capsa* [book box]?' and replying *Libri et epistulae Pauli
viri iusti* (i.e. probably the Gospels, and the Epistles of Paul
...). If we could date II Peter with any certainty, it might
prove (iii. 16) to contain the earliest reference to Paul as
scripture. But who can say when it was written?

What, now, may be said of a Johannine *corpus*? Extremely
little, it must be confessed.[1] One clear fact, however, is that
there is a close connexion between the Fourth Gospel and the
Johannine Epistles (whether or not they are actually by the
same hand).[2] Both these groups, though anonymous, are
associated by tradition with the name of John and with
Ephesus. The Apocalypse, itself claiming to be written by
one named John and also associated by tradition with
Ephesus, is still held by some modern scholars to be by the
same hand as some or all of the other Johannines: but despite
certain contacts in vocabulary and thought, its style, and,
still more, its theological outlook, are very different. However,
that may be, it is perhaps more useful to think in terms
not so much of a Johannine *corpus* as of an Ephesian
tradition, and to speculate cautiously about the courses
along which diverse streams of tradition flowed to that
centre. T. W. Manson revived, in a modified form,[3] Sanday's interesting suggestion that there was 'an anticipatory
stage of Johannean teaching, localized somewhere in Syria,
before the apostle reached his final home in Ephesus'.
Manson proposed Antioch as a centre of 'Johannine' tradi-

---

[1] But see the careful investigations by Smalley 1968, 1970, 1970–71.
C. H. Roberts wrote (1963) 'some tentative support for a "Johannine
corpus" may be found in the Antinoe St John'.

[2] See Katz 1957 for an ingenious bid for the inclusion of II, III John in
the Muratorian Canon, by suggesting that *duas* (*leg. duae*) *in catholica habentur*
represents an original Greek such as δύο σὺν καθολικῇ, *two in addition to the
Catholic* (*Epistle*). This seems to me to be in principle convincing; but I do
not see why the original should not have had πρὸς καθολικήν—even more
natural Greek for *in addition to*, and more easily translated *in*.

[3] See Manson 'Fourth Gospel' (1962), with Sanday 1905, 199.

tions *en route* to Ephesus. He did not discuss the relation of the Epistle to the Ephesians to the Johannine traditions; but it is well known that, whereas this Epistle (as has been already observed) does not fit beyond doubt into the typically Pauline mould, it does present certain affinities with Revelation (e.g., the Church as the Bride of Christ, and as founded upon the apostles and prophets). There is not here, as a matter of fact, any necessary contradiction to the Pauline phrases about Christ as the one foundation; but may not Ephesians represent the flowing together and fusing of Pauline and other types of thought, and may not Ephesus (possibly with Antioch as a kind of halfway basin or reservoir) be the centre of confluence—especially if much of the Johannine tradition really does go right back to Palestinian sources (see p. 134)? Possibly it is worthwhile to throw into the discussion the fact that Matthew is the only Gospel that speaks of the Church and its (apostolic) foundation, and that there is something to be said for an Antiochene connexion for this Gospel.[1] The letters of Ignatius of Antioch seem to contain nothing that can demonstrate any knowledge of the Fourth Gospel or of Ephesians. But it is not Ignatius' manner to *cite*, and he may still allude. In these conjectures, however, we are on a quaking bog of uncertainty. Notions of ecclesiastical authority might seem to provide a more fruitful clue to classification: Matthew, Ephesians, the Fourth Gospel, and the Johannine Epistles are all very vigorously concerned with authority; but again it is impossible to group them together in an undifferentiated way, for, in a sense, the Fourth Gospel is remarkably non-ecclesiastical in its treatment of authority (as indeed throughout). Non-apocalyptic eschatology is, to some extent, common to Ephesians and the Fourth Gospel; but this applies less clearly to the Johannine Epistles—still less to the Apocalypse; and there is non-apocalyptic eschatology in Rom. viii. also.

In short, we know pitifully little about the cross currents of

[1] For discussions of Matthew's provenance, see, e.g., Manson 'Matthew' (1962), 68 ff.; Kilpatrick 1946; Stendahl 1954; Nepper-Christensen 1958; Trilling 1964; Blair 1960; Hummel 1963; Hill 1972; H. B. Green 1975.

Christian teaching and apologetic at Ephesus or elsewhere that led to the ultimate recognition of those Johannine writings by the whole Church. What we do know is that St John's Gospel was the latest of the four to gain this status and that it was opposed by a group, seemingly of ultra-conservatives, whom Epiphanius jocosely dubbed the 'Alogi'[1] (a double-entendre for 'irrational' and 'rejecting the Logos'); likewise that the Apocalypse was roughly handled by those who were opposed to millenarianism, of which it alone, within the New Testament, is the spokesman.[2] Conversely, it is a familiar fact that certain other writings associated with the name of John never gained wide recognition at all; while writings widely read at one time for edification, such as the Apostolic Fathers, were ultimately excluded. The necessity for decision on authoritative books as against the false or the unauthoritative, was imposed by heresy from within and attack from without. Perhaps a fruitful line of advance may lie (cf. Chapters I and VIII) in the direction of freshly investigating the purposes of some of the New Testament writings. II Peter and Jude are manifestly attacks on perversions of Christianity, perversions which had arisen, at least in part, through the kind of misappropriation of Pauline doctrines which Paul himself attacks (e.g. in Rom. vi). The Pastoral Epistles are also concerned in part with correcting perversions of Pauline teaching, and it is notoriously possible that James may (though it is far from certain that Paul is presupposed) have something of the sort in view in Chapter ii. The Johannine Epistles, attacking a docetic type of misinterpretation of Christ, may similarly be viewed as a corrective to perversions of the teaching in the Fourth Gospel.[3] And in addition to insidious dangers from

[1] *Haer.* li. 3 ἐπεὶ οὖν τὸν λόγον οὐ δέχονται τὸν παρὰ Ἰωάννου κεκηρυγμένον, Ἄλογοι κληθήσονται. (etc.)

[2] For anti-millenarianism, see Euseb. *H.E.* III xxviii; VII. xxv; and (e.g.) Beckwith 1919, 340 ff. The 'Alogi' opposed the Johannine writings because they seemed to offer a handle to the charismatic anarchy of the Montanists. See also Sundberg 1973, 34.

[3] Cf. J. A. T. Robinson, 'Destination ... of the Johannine Epistles' (1962) and 1976, 254 ff.

within, necessitating a clear recognition of what was sound in Christian writing, there were attacks of opponents from without. In controversy with these, authoritative references were needed; while in times of persecution, it might be of vital importance (as we have seen at Scilli) to define the sacred Christian manuscripts. The story of the fluctuations on the fringe of the canon—on one side the ultimately excluded, on the other the doubtfuls ultimately included (II Peter and Jude, II and III John, Hebrews, etc.)—is told in all books of introduction, and need not be repeated here, any more than the final settling down of the present canon, in Athanasius' 39th Paschal letter of A.D. 367[1] containing the first datable list identical with what ultimately remained the canon. The purpose of this chapter has been not to retell the whole story but rather to throw into relief—so far as is possible in a realm too remote to focus clearly—some of the motives and principles, theological and disciplinary, behind the long process. All the time, moreover, it is viewed, so far as possible, as a human process. That it is also the tale of a divine overruling of the gropings and mistakes of men is here assumed without further discussion.

[1] H. Chadwick (in a letter, 15 Feb. 80) suggests that it may well be this letter which led to the cache of the Nag Hammadi gnostic library that was probably in use at the nearby Pachomian monastery (which is in sight of the spot where it was found). See his review of E. Pagels, *The Gnostic Gospels*, in the *Times Literary Supplement*, 21 Mar. '80 (p. 309).

CHAPTER XI

POSTSCRIPT

THROUGHOUT this book the general standpoint of 'form criticism' has been adopted, namely, that it is to the circumstances and needs of the worshipping, working, suffering community that one must look if one is to explain the genesis of Christian literature. Probably at no stage within the New Testament period did a writer put pen to paper without the incentive of a pressing need. Seldom was the writing consciously adorned; never was adornment an end in itself. Accordingly different aspects of the community's life have been successively considered, with a view to illustrating how various types of Christian literature grew up in response to these circumstances and needs and can only be adequately understood against this setting.

But if the standpoint of 'form criticism' has been thus adopted, a good many of the assumptions that frequently go with it have been discarded or qualified. A caveat has been entered against too lightly assuming that we have the very words of liturgy in certain passages which are frequently so interpreted. It has been urged that the probabilities favour a more fluid interchange of forms, such that snatches of prayer and hymnody flow in and out of the texture of pastoral exhortation, and liturgical phrases at the close of an Epistle do not necessarily imply that it is being formally linked as a homily to the eucharist. Again, the immense importance and prominence of Old Testament scripture in Christian thinking and reasoning, while it explains and accounts for much in the New Testament, must not, it has been argued, lead to the conclusion that whole sections of Christian narrative were created by the Old Testament or by a Jewish midrashic technique. Neither should the essentially theological, apologetic, and edificatory intention of Christian writing lead to the assumption that the early Church took little or no interest in the actual circumstances of the Jesus of history. In particular, it is here maintained that the Gospels, as documents of Christian apologetic (direct or indirect), are very considerably concerned to reconstruct the story of 'how it all began'.

In the chapter on persecution, the view is taken that the greater part of the 'persecution' sections of the New Testament may be explained by postulating primarily Jewish antagonism, without invoking the Roman arm. In the treatment of the edificatory passages, stress is laid upon the relativity of Christian ethics, and the comparative individualism which, of necessity, was imposed upon them by the circumstances of the Christian communities. The last two chapters stress the wide variety of outlook and the often deplorable vagueness that must have obtained in the underworld of the congregations scattered over the empire, over against the substantial agreement on certain basic convictions that characterized their leaders and was ultimately reflected in the canon, despite its complicated history and seemingly haphazard development. Devotion to the person of Jesus Christ—as was said at the outset—is the clue to this phenomenon.

Hundreds of problems remain. Too little is still known about the Jewish background of the life of Jesus and of the primitive Church; the peculiarities of the Christian uses of Scripture still present unsolved riddles; the varying social conditions of the different centres of Christendom are still largely in the shades of obscurity; the story of the canon bristles with unsolved—perhaps insoluble—problems.

But perhaps two conclusions of major importance arising from this study may now be underlined. One is the primacy of the divine initiative; the other is the urgent need today to clarify the basis of ethical decisions for Christians.

With regard to the first, a too cursory glance at the chapter headings of this book might lead to the conclusion that the early Church was engaged in an intensely self-regarding struggle—explaining itself, defending itself, edifying itself, unifying itself, authenticating itself. But that would be a false impression. It was by deliberate intention that these chapters were prefaced by one on the Church at worship; and it is in fact in a steadily Godward attitude that the Church undertook all its other activities—and still does, whenever it is really being its true self. Explanation, defence, edification, unification, authentication—none of these is Christian unless undertaken under the compulsion of the Spirit of God and for his glory; and it would be quite contrary to the intentions of this study if the growing self-consciousness of the Church here traced—from the earliest assumption that it was nothing other than 'Israel', to the latest awareness of itself as a *tertium genus* with its own scriptures (though this does not become explicit until after the New Testament period)—were seen as anything but the corollary of a growing understanding of God and his purposes in Jesus Christ.

With regard to the second matter much needs to be said, though it cannot be said here. Perhaps nothing is more urgently needed than a concerted effort to hammer out the basis of ethics for Christians now. But that requires joint action by experts in very many different fields, and is quite beyond the competence of a mere New Testament student as such. Indeed, one of the most important lessons of this book is that the guidance of the Spirit of God was granted to Christians in the form not of a code of behaviour nor of any written deposit of direction, but of insight communicated by God through Jesus Christ. It was granted *ad hoc* to Christians as they met together, confronting the immediate problems, with the gospel events behind them, the Holy Spirit among them, and the will to find out the action required of the People of God in the near future. If the pages of the Pauline Epistles are searched, they reveal various lines along which the apostle sought guidance: through 'direct' revelation—in vision or audition; through the words and example of Christ; through the Jewish scriptures read in the light of Christ; through community custom; even through 'natural law'. But it is tolerably clear that the most characteristic Christian way of guidance was in the kind of setting indicated in I Cor. xiv, where the Christians assemble, each with a psalm or a teaching or a revelation or a burst of ecstasy: *and the*

congregation exercises discernment. That is how Christian ethical
decisions were reached: informed discussion, prophetic insight, ecstatic fire—all in the context of the worshipping, and
also discriminating, assembly, with the good news in Jesus
Christ behind them, the Spirit among them, and before them
the expectation of being led forward into the will of God.[1]
And if there is one lesson of outstanding importance to be
gleaned from all this, it is that only along similar lines,
translated into terms of our present circumstances, can we
hope for an informed ethic for Christians of the present day.
It will probably be different in different areas of the world:
each Christian Church has its peculiar problems and oppor-
tunities and its unique conditions. And it will always be
based, not on a rigid code of ethics but on the guidance of the
Spirit in the light of the unchanging Gospel and of contemporary conditions carefully studied by experts. One of the
contributions to this will be hard, scientific, statistical data,
brought to the Christian group by those who are specialists
in various realms of study. Only in the light of this will
guidance of the Spirit be realistically apprehended. Efficient,
intelligent historical reconstruction of the past is another
necessary contribution: the very writing of the Gospels bears
witness to the Christian awareness of the importance of
understanding and constantly recalling the origin of the
Christian *kerygma*. Only by such means as these can an
applied ethic that Christians can appropriate be hoped for.
Unless the Church expects the living voice of the Paraclete in
such a context, to lead it forward into all truth, it will look in
vain for specific guidance. Christian ethical practice in the
past may, and must, be carefully studied. But in the last
analysis we shall only know what Christian conduct today
should be by letting the Holy Spirit direct the message—by
trusting to contemporary guidance. It was only so that the
Church progressed and met its problems in those early years.
If this adds up to 'situation ethics', so be it. The critics of
situation ethics seem sometimes to forget that all particular
decisions, even when taken by the most resolute anti-
situationalists, and upon the firmest foundation of principle,

[1] Cf. Cullmann 1962, 228, 1967, 328 ff.

are bound to be situational. Perhaps equally they forget that it is with particular decisions that situation ethics are concerned. Situationalism may indeed be justly criticized by a Christian if its principle of love is divorced from the definitive implementation of love in Jesus Christ and made vague and nebulous; but even with a full grasp on incarnation, no Christian can escape the difficulty of *ad hoc*, particular decisions.[1] In the last analysis, it is questionable, indeed, whether a Christian ethical system, as such, can exist. Christianity is concerned with the transformation, in Christ, of personal relations. The code which provides a framework or scaffolding within which this operates must, strictly speaking, be a borrowed one, for Christianity, as such, does not offer a distinctive *code* or *system* of conduct. Often the dictates of Christian relations will cause conflict with the existing framework, whether of law or of moral codes, whencesoever derived (in the ancient world it was Jewish or Roman or that of some local sub-culture or government). In that case—so the New Testament seems to imply—the Christian must not use violence to break down the opposition. He may have to break the law, but if so he will accept, and not evade or combat, the penalty. It will be 'passive resistance'. But he has no alternative *code* to offer.[2] That, at least, is the direction in which the New Testament seems to point. And it is mentioned here as one of the conclusions arising from this study of circumstances, causes, and motives behind the writing of the New Testament. But it is not something which can be adequately followed through without more space and vastly more expertise.

Many other matters have come up in the course of this inquiry, all of them in some measure important for this always necessary study of Christian beginnings. About some of them suggestions have been made which are, perhaps,

[1] A presentation of situation ethics in an extreme form may be found in Fletcher 1966. There are four lectures on the question by J. A. T. Robinson 1964. Among criticisms of the position, note P. Ramsey 1965 and Burtchaell 1973. There is a discussion of some of the issues in Cullmann 1967, 328 ff.; and studies in the application of Pauline teaching to the present day in P. Richardson 1979; Furnish 1979.

[2] See Moule, 'Decisions' (1966).

POSTSCRIPT

unusual. It will be for others to assess their value. The estimate of the purpose of the Gospels, the guesses about the character of Matthew and Hebrews, the attitude to the liturgical factor, and the speculations about the relation of Luke the physician to the canon of scripture: these may or may not be well advised. But the problems they represent are ones with which the student of the New Testament must constantly wrestle; and his reading of the New Testament situation will, in its turn, be one of the contributions which it is his ministry to bring to the congregation of Christian people to which he belongs, as they try, in the light of all the available data, to place themselves under the guidance of the Spirit.

It is hoped that this study, even if indirectly, may be a contribution to the further study of contemporary ethics, as well as helping the reader to enter imaginatively into the circumstances in which the New Testament was brought to birth.

TRANSLATION GREEK AND ORIGINAL GREEK IN MATTHEW

IT is worth while to ask whether too little attention has not been paid to the word ἡρμήνευσεν in the much-discussed words of Papias quoted by Euseb. *H.E.* III. xxxix. 16. Considerable thought has been devoted to the meaning of 'Εβραΐδι διαλέκτῳ (in the light of H. Birkeland and his critics and of others' researches, see p. 243 n. 3); and τὰ λόγια is a phrase round which hundreds of pages have been written.[1] But are not the implications of ἡρμήνευσεν worthy of closer consideration?

Behm, in his article on this word-group in *T.D.N.T.* ii. 661 ff., distinguishes three main senses—(a) explain, interpret; (b) express; (c) translate. All three are Classical—indeed, all three can be exemplified from Plato alone, not to mention other writers; and, although only (a) and (c) are found in the New Testament ((a) only in Lk. xxiv. 27 (διερμ., D ἐρμ.), (c) only in Jn i. 38 (*v.l.*), 42, ix. 7 (ἐρμ.), I Cor. xii. 30, xiv. 5, 13, 27 (διερμ.), Heb. vii. 2 (ἐρμ.), (b) not at all), there seems to be no particular reason why the word in Eusebius should not mean whichever is the most appropriate to its context.

Clearly the second sense ('express') is here inapplicable; but there is at least some option, linguistically speaking, between 'interpret' and 'translate', and it is, I think, just conceivable (in the abstract) that τὰ λόγια might mean a collection of parables and parabolic sayings which were differently *interpreted* by different hearers, just as the sayings in *The Gospel of Thomas* are being variously interpreted today. In that case Matt. xiii would contain specimens of the process in question. However, I suppose all will agree that the preceding sentence, with its reference to the language of the original, virtually clinches the third sense—translation.

What follows? Surely a much firmer rejection of the theory that τὰ λόγια means Old Testament *testimonia* than is to be obtained from an investigation merely of the meaning of λόγιον. For, had

[1] See Manson 'Matthew' (1962); *T.D.N.T.* iv. 137 ff.

Old Testament *testimonia* been intended by τὰ λόγια, in the first place, 'Εβραΐδι διαλέκτῳ is not a completely rational way of expressing 'in their [original] Hebrew' and secondly it is difficult to imagine why it is described as *necessary* for them to be translated by each reader, 'as best he could' (ὡς ἦν δυνατὸς ἕκαστος). It is perfectly true that it is precisely Matthew's *testimonia* that are notoriously not septuagintal; but the fact that Old Testament *testimonia* were individually rendered into Greek still does not justify the phrase ὡς ἦν δυνατὸς ἕκαστος which implies some *necessity* for private translation. There were already well-established Greek versions of the Old Testament available—especially, of course, that of the LXX: why should each reader be compelled to use his own make-shift? The translation clause points, as it seems to me, almost conclusively to τὰ λόγια being some original and hitherto unknown composition. In other words, this clause points strongly to the theory that the writing in question was some such document as we associate with Q, though it certainly does not tie it down to being a collection of nothing but sayings.[1]

If, then, Papias' tradition really does point to variant translations, is there any trace left of these? It has often been observed that a comparison of Matthew and Luke suggests that, in some cases, they represent different translations of the same sources (see a useful list, based partly on Wellhausen, in Barrett 1942-3). But is it not possible that, actually within Matthew itself, variant versions of a single source have left their trace? In v. 22, not only may μωρέ be a gloss on ῥακά, but συνέδριον and κρίσις may be alternative translations (see my note, 1969-70); xii. 31 f. is possibly a conflation of the Marcan and Lucan versions of a saying, of which the Marcan may be nearst to the original; in xvi. 22, ἵλεως and οὐ μὴ ἔσται are *alternative* renderings of *ḥālîlāh* (see Katz 1960); in xxiii. 8, 10 ῥαββεί and καθηγητής are transliteration and translation respectively; in xxvii. 6 f., both 'treasury', *'ôṣār* and 'potter', *yôṣēr* are represented (cf. Zech xi. 13, ℭ 𝕾 and M.T. respectively).[2]

At any rate, it is clear that the Evangelist was, in many respects, a conservator, conflating, combining, sometimes duplicating. Is it possible to say, further, that the Semitisms in his Gospel are survivals from his sources, while he himself naturally wrote purer Greek?

[1] For warnings against hasty identification of 'Matthew's *logia*' with Q, see Bacon 1930, xii, and J. A. Robinson 1902. For a discrediting of Jerome's 'authentic Hebrew', see Nepper-Christensen 1958, Ch. II.

[2] See a slightly fuller treatment of this question of the 'anthological' tendency of Matthew in my paper, 'Matthew' (1964).

THE BIRTH OF THE NEW TESTAMENT

(i) It is noticeable that at least some passages which are obviously editorial contain fairly clear Semitisms. In the first place, there are the five famous 'link-passages' or 'connecting panels', vii. 28, xi. 1, xiii. 53, xix. 1, xxvi. 1. Here, if anywhere, we may be reasonably confident that we see the hand of the editor himself. And each of these begins with the characteristically Semitic καὶ ἐγένετο ὅτι. ... Then, again, many a section begins with a vague and strictly illogical use of ἐκεῖνος such as: ἐν ἐκείνῳ τῷ καιρῷ (xi. 25, xii. 1, xiv. 1) or ἐν ἐκείνῃ τῇ ὥρᾳ (xviii. 1) or ἐν τῇ ἡμέρᾳ ἐκείνῃ (xiii. 1)—all of them apparently meaning little more than 'on *one* occasion' or '*one* day'; and I suspect that this, too, is Semitic rather than native Greek,[1] cf. Gen. xxi. 22, Josh. v. 2 (*bā'eth hahî*) and Gen. xxxix. 11, I Sam. iii. 2 where *kᵉhayyôm hazzeh* and *bayyôm hahû'* are interpreted (e.g. by Brown, Driver and Briggs, *Lexicon s.v. yôm*) as meaning 'on this particular day (when the incident occurred)'. Further, the use of εἷς = τις (which is generally regarded as Semitic) occurs in certain passages where it is simpler to assume that it is Matthew's own introduction than that it came from a source. Thus: εἷς γραμματεύς (viii. 19), ἄρχων εἷς (ix. 18), μία παιδίσκη (xxvi. 69) are instances where the parallel passages are without this idiom; προσήχθη εἷς αὐτῷ ὀφειλέτης (xviii. 24) is in a passage peculiar to Matthew, and may or may not have been in his source; only εἷς προσελθὼν αὐτῷ (xix. 16) is paralleled (Mk x. 17). On the other hand, the εἷς ἐκ τοῦ ὄχλου of Mk ix. 17 becomes simply ἄνθρωπος in Matt. xvii. 14, which is a warning against too light an assumption that the construction is systematically introduced by the evangelist. However, enough has perhaps been adduced to suggest that the editor himself did use Semitisms.

(ii) Were these Semitisms, then, spontaneous and natural to this writer, or did he deliberately introduce them? That the latter is the more likely is suggested by two phenomena:

(a) There are passages where we find quite accomplished Greek, free from Semitisms. On the whole, the *Aktionsart* of the verbs is correct throughout Matthew. But the most striking instance of good Greek is, perhaps, xvii. 24-27, the *pericope* about the coin in the fish's mouth. Here there is a comparatively elaborate use of participles, a wide range of vocabulary, and a liveliness almost like Luke's at his most free and individual (e.g. in the latter chapters of Acts). One may note especially the phrase (xvii. 25) καὶ ἐλθόντα εἰς τὴν οἰκίαν προέφθασεν αὐτὸν ὁ Ἰησοῦς (for this competent handling

---

[1] That it is common in Luke is not necessarily any disproof of this. See, e.g. Black, 1967, 106 f.

of participles, cf. ix. 27, xxvi. 71). A reasonably stylish passage of this sort might, of course, come straight from a source and not represent the author's own style; but on the whole the balance of probability, if we allow that Semitic sources lie behind the Gospel tradition at all, is against attributing to a source features which are linguistically the opposite of Semitic. It must be admitted, however, that even here there is (v. 26) what Classical Greek would less easily tolerate—an ostensible genitive absolute which turns out to be, after all, not absolute; and throughout this Gospel there are, side by side, correct genitives absolute and this incorrect type (the latter even in so clearly editorial a passage as viii. 1).

(b) Secondly, there is the introduction into otherwise apparently pure Greek of such Semitic phrases as ἰδού. In the story of the magi (ii) almost impeccable Greek is given a slightly Semitic flavour by this means (as also, perhaps, by ἐχάρησαν χαρὰν μεγάλην σφόδρα v. 10); and in the narrative of the baptism Matthew seems (iii. 16) to rephrase Mark (i. 10) in such a way as deliberately to introduce this interjection.

On the whole, this adds up to a balance of evidence in favour of the editor's own Semitisms being deliberate and artificial.

(iii) There are, of course, fairly clear signs of the extensive use of sources which already contained Semitic idiom. Very much has been written on the Aramaic behind the Sermon on the Mount and many other passages. Let it merely be remarked here, by way of one illustration, that the use of ἄνθρωπος in apposition with a noun, which is likely to be a Semitism, is, though peculiar to Matthew, yet invariably in parables (ἐχθρὸς ἄνθρωπος, xiii. 28, ἄνθρωπος ἔμπορος, xiii. 45 (v. l.); ἄνθρωπος οἰκοδεσπότης, xiii. 52, xx. 1, xxi. 33, ἄνθρωπος βασιλεύς, xviii 23, xxii. 2); and the likelihood, therefore, is that the idiom came by tradition with the parable. This is only one phenomenon out of a wealth of evidence that Matthew simply took over much that already had a Semitic cast.[1]

(iv) Among other features of the language of this Gospel may be mentioned the following miscellaneous items: ὅτι *recitativum* is comparatively rare; τοῦ c. infin. of purpose is sparingly used (iii. 13, xi. 1, xiii. 3, xxi. 32); the Marcan εὐθύς is sparingly used, and εὐθέως is much commoner; δεῦτε is frequent, and not only in borrowings from Mark. There are several Latin words: μίλιον,

[1] N. Turner 1963, 38, cites Matt. xxv. 26 (ὁ κύριος αὐτοῦ εἶπεν αὐτῷ) as 'extreme' semitism, and, *ib.* 341, refers to Matthew's frequent semiticizing τότε.

κῆνσος, κουστωδία, perhaps συμβούλιον λαβεῖν (xxvii. 1, 7 ? = *consilium capere*). There is a wide and rather remarkable vocabulary (in what follows * denotes a passage paralleled in Mark or Luke or both; † denotes special to Matthew): There is a large number of verbs in -ζω, some of them unusual, e.g.: εὐνουχίζω, xix. 12,† ἅπ. λεγ. in N.T.; καταποντίζω, xiv. 30,† xviii. 6,* not elsewhere in N.T.; πυρράζω, xvi. 2,† (*si vera l.*), ἅπ. λεγ. in N.T.; σεληνιάζω, iv. 24,* xvii. 15,*, not elsewhere in N.T. Other noteworthy words include: τὸν δεῖνα, xxvi. 18,* ἅπ. λεγ. in N.T.; διασαφεῖν, xiii. 36,† xviii. 31,† not elsewhere in N.T.; θαυμάσιον, xxi. 15,† ἅπ. λεγ. in N.T.; παλιγγενεσία, xix. 28,* elsewhere in N.T. only Tit. iii. 5; πέλαγος, xviii. 6,* in N.T. elsewhere only Acts xxvii. 5; συντέλεια, xiii. 39,† 40,† 49,† xxiv. 3,* xxviii. 20,† elsewhere in N.T. only Heb. ix. 26; τὰ ὕδατα *pl.*, viii. 32,* xiv. 28 f.† elsewhere in N.T. only Jn iii. 23 and Revelation *passim*. It speaks strongly for these words belonging to the evangelist's own vocabulary that they are spread over both his peculiar material and passages which have parallels in the other Gospels, which do not, however, use the words in question.[1]

Thus, as a preliminary estimate, one might say that the editor was an educated person commanding sound Greek with a considerable vocabulary; but he derived many Semitisms, and perhaps some Latin, from his sources; and he also had some feeling for Semitic 'atmosphere', occasionally introducing a Semitism on his own account, though less histrionically than Luke. So far as it goes, this conclusion fits well enough with my suggestions about the provenance of the Gospel.

[1] N. Turner 1963, 330 f., calls attention to the frequent use of μὲν ... δέ in Matthew. See further Jeremias 1959.

LUKE AND THE PASTORAL EPISTLES

MY Manson Memorial Lecture (1965) renders unnecessary the reprinting of the original excursus on this subject. But the following references and notes may be added to the lecture.

(i) In the lecture, I declared my inability to accept either the Pauline authorship of the Pastorals (at any rate *in toto*) or P. N. Harrison's theory. I felt it incumbent on me, therefore, to offer some alternative, and I suggested to myself Lucan authorship (in which I found I had been anticipated) as a rather desperate remedy. In preparing the lecture, I found that the arguments in favour of this idea were surprisingly weighty; but I could not declare myself totally convinced, especially in view of Christological and 'traditionalist' pointers in the direction of a later date. I was, and still am, unable to come down with conviction on the side of the Lucan theory, and it is not accurate to describe me (as I am sometimes described) as a convinced supporter of it. But I remain attracted by it and impressed by the work of others such as Strobel, Quinn, and Wilson.

(ii) See, now, Strobel 1969; Quinn 1974, 1975, 1978, 1980, and forthcoming; Lestapis 1976; Feuillet 1978; S. G. Wilson 1979. Quinn suggests that the Pastorals, originally short communications from Paul in which Luke collaborated, were subsequently re-edited and expanded by Luke, as a third volume to the Gospel and the Acts. Wilson develops and modifies previous proposals, making the Pastorals Lucan but post-Pauline.

(iii) (1) Add to significant words the following:
(a) Kilpatrick 1950-51 notes that νομοδιδάσκαλος (Lk. v. 17, Acts v. 34, I Tim. i. 7) failed to establish itself in New Testament terminology (p. 57); and, *in re* νομικός, notes that it occurs in our printed texts at Matt. xxii. 35, Lk. vii. 30, x. 25, xi. 45, 46, 52, xiv. 3, Tit. iii. 9, 13; but argues that it may not be the original reading in Matt. xxii. 35, whereas in Lk. xi. 53 there is a case for reading νομικός instead of γραμματεύς. (I

owe the application of these observations to the present question to D. R. Catchpole in a letter, 12 May 1965.)

(b) παρακολουθεῖν, apart from Mk. xvi. 17, is exclusive to Luke and the Pastorals: Lk. i. 3, I Tim. iv. 6, II Tim. iii. 10.

(c) ἐπιφαίνειν, Lk. i. 79, Acts xxvii. 20, Tit. ii. 11, iii. 4; ἐπιφάνεια, II Thess. ii. 8, but otherwise only I Tim. vi. 14, II Tim. i. 10, iv. 1, 8, Tit. ii. 13; ἐπιφανής, Acts ii. 20. (Cf. Daniélou 1966, 27.)

(2) Add to significant phrases or collocations:

(a) teaching and heralding or evangelizing—Acts v. 42, I Tim. ii. 7, II Tim. i. 11 (perhaps only a slender parallel).

(b) the 'equipped' disciple—Lk. vi. 40 (κατηρτισμένος), II Tim. iii. 17 (ἐξηρτισμένος).

(iv) Against the theory, note the following:

(a) 'Priscilla' is Luke's form of the name, 'Prisca' is Paul's; and 'Prisca', not 'Priscilla' occurs in II Tim. iv. 19. (See Lake 1927, 327, n. 2. I owe the reference to G. P. Richardson in a letter.)

(b) The chances are that, in any case, the similarities between Luke–Acts and the Pastorals may be due not to the authors' being identical but to both authors' belonging (more than other New Testament writers) to a particular Hellenistic culture. Note, especially, W. D. Davies' remarks about the nuances of συνείδησις, in 'Conscience' (1962) and in 1964, 379.

(c) Note also Ehrhardt's interpretation of the Muratorian Canon's phrase about Paul's taking Luke with him *quasi ut iuris studiosum* as meaning that Luke was to Paul as the legal expert was to the Roman provincial governor, and Ehrhardt's observation that such an expert might issue documents *in his own name:* Ehrhardt 1964, 11 ff., referred to by Bruce 'Paul' (1974), 15.

(v) I regret that I misinterpreted the late J. Jeremias in my lecture (1965), 438 (top).

ΠΙΣΤΟΣ Ο ΛΟΓΟΣ

[To the original form of this excursus, reprinted below, add the following references and notes:

See Swete 1917; Duncan 1923; Bover 1928; Knight 1968. Knight's is the fullest investigation known to me so far. After carefully examining the textual and contextual evidence for the sayings to which reference is made with the formula, he reaches the conclusion that the sayings referred to are: I Tim. i. 15, iii. 1, iv. 8, II Tim. ii. 11-13, Tit. iii. 4-7. He cites Theodore of Mopsuestia *ad* I Tim. i. 15: '*fidele verbum.* simile est dictum quod in euangelio est expressum: *amen, amen dico vobis'.* He cites Field 1899, 203 (cf. Moulton and Milligan 1930, *s. ἀποδοχή*), on *ἀποδοχῆς ἄξιος* as a formula. He cites Nauck 1950 for Hebrew analogies to the phrase. He observes: 'The briefer and more objective sayings (I Tim. 1:15; I Tim. 4:8) would seem to have a "non-liturgical" outward look, whereas the longer and "we-type" sayings (Titus 3: 4-7; II Tim. 2: 11-13) would seem to have a more inward and "liturgical" perspective. The latter have within them the human response (the "we") . . .' (p. 143). He concludes, against my original excursus (as below), that *πιστός, not ἀνθρώπινος*, is to be read in I Tim. iii. 1. (In I Tim. i. 15, *ἀνθρώπινος* is, in any case, poorly attested.) But when all is said and done, it remains very difficult to explain what the *πιστός*-formula could mean in I Tim. iii. 1 and iv. 8. A. E. Harvey, in letters (1966, 1967), points out that *ἐπισκοπή* occurs in no known document except in the specific sense of 'the office of *ἐπίσκοπος*'. He thinks, therefore, that the saying in I Tim. iii. 1 may reflect an attack on episcopacy. See Harvey 1970, 666.]

πιστὸς ὁ λόγος is a phrase common to all three Pastoral Epistles (I Tim. i. 15, iii. 1, iv. 9, II Tim. ii. 11, Tit. iii. 8; cf. the closely similar . . . *ἀντεχόμενον τοῦ κατὰ τὴν διδαχὴν πιστοῦ λόγου* in Tit. i. 9) and confined to them, though Rev. xix. 9, xxi. 5, xxii. 6 has the analogous *οὗτοι οἱ λόγοι πιστοὶ καὶ ἀληθινοί (εἰσιν).*

In I Tim. iii. 1 both the connexion and the reading are uncertain. Starting to read at ii. 15 we have . . . *σωθήσεται δὲ διὰ τῆς*

τεκνογονίας . . . πιστὸς [v.l. ἀνθρώπινος D* it Ambst.] ὁ λόγος· εἴ τις
ἐπισκοπῆς ὀρέγεται, καλοῦ ἔργου ἐπιθυμεῖ. Is the 'word' in question
that which precedes or that which follows? If it is that which
follows, then πιστός seems to make nonsense (that *volo episcopari* is a
good wish can scarcely be described as a *trustworthy* aphorism!),
and we are bound to read ἀνθρώπινος—'they say . . .', or 'it is a
human, i.e. common, saying . . .' But may it be that the phrase was
intended to refer back to the promise about childbirth, and that it
was only a mistaken effort to relate it to what followed that led to
the desperate expedient of altering πιστός to ἀνθρώπινος? Hardly;
for it would be a very violent and arbitrary alteration; and, besides,
ἀνθρώπινος is a v. l. also at I Tim. i. 15 (r, Ambst., Aug.), where no
such motive could be operative; and the suggestion in Westcott
and Hort 1881, Introduction, 132 that it is there probably transferred from iii. 1 seems unlikely. But even if we are driven to accept
ἀνθρώπινος in I Tim. i. 15 also, it is in any case there reinforced by
a phrase almost equivalent to πιστός, namely πάσης ἀποδοχῆς
ἄξιος.

Thus on any showing we have this latter phrase and at least
three firm occurrences of πιστὸς ὁ λόγος besides, and the related
phrase in Tit. i. 9, all seeming to point to a certain selective
consciousness, as though here maxims (they are mostly soterio-
logical) were being designated as 'sound' and worthy of inclusion,
as it were, in a canon of Christian aphorisms. Contrast the λόγος of
II Thess. ii. 2, which is emphatically not accepted.

There seems to be no cogent reason for treating the phrase as a
reader's comment (C. H. Turner 1926, 21): the γάρ in II Tim. ii.
11 hardly carries this weight; it seems to imply rather the author's
own knowledge that 'some collection of Christian maxims analogous to the λόγοι τοῦ κυρίου Ἰησοῦ, Acts 20[35], and the Oxyrhynchus Sayings' was in process of formation. See Lock 1924, on Tit.
iii. 8.

THE PRIORITY OF MARK
By G. M. Styler

I

In the hundred years or more up to the middle of this century it had come to be accepted that Mark was the oldest of the three Synoptic Gospels, and was the principal source used by Matthew and Luke. It was common to refer to this belief as 'the one assured result' of synoptic criticism.

It was also generally agreed that Matthew and Luke shared a second source of material, denoted by the symbol 'Q'. Many held that there was a single document, and that it could be reconstructed to some extent. Others postulated a number of documents or traditions, known to Matthew and Luke, sometimes in language closely similar, at other times less so. For the purpose of re-examining the priority of Mark, the unity of Q is irrelevant. But the validity of the Q-hypothesis in some form[1] is not wholly irrelevant, as will be seen.

The priority of Mark and the existence of Q have been, and still are, widely accepted, and are conveniently denoted by the title 'the two-document hypothesis'. The classic statement and defence for English readers was made by B. H. Streeter (1930).[2]

The main arguments deemed to establish the priority of Mark are well-known, and may be summarized briefly.

(i) The bulk of Mark is contained in Matthew, and most of it is in Luke; there is very little that is not contained in one or the other.

(ii) The Marcan material usually occurs in the same order in all

---

[1] A good *prima facie* case can be made for postulating *both* a clear-cut single document, reflected in passages which occur in Matthew and Luke in closely similar wording and in almost the same relative order *and* a variety of common material and traditions, whether written or oral, reflected in passages where there is significant divergence in respect of wording or order.

[2] He gave the labels 'M' and 'L' to the material peculiar to Matthew and Luke or (more precisely) to the sources which he postulated.

three gospels. There are some variations in order;[1] but it is hardly ever possible to find a sequence of any substantial length where Matthew and Luke 'agree' with one another against Mark in respect of order.

(iii) The same relationship holds good for most of the wording: Mark's wording is frequently shared with one or both of the other two; only exceptionally[2] are Matthew and Luke found to have more than a few significant words in common unless Mark has them also.

(iv) A comparison of the wording of the gospels in parallel passages frequently invites the judgment that it is Mark's wording which is the oldest. His language is the least polished, and so the natural presumption is that the others have made improvements. His statements about Jesus and the apostles sometimes appear to show less 'reverence', and so once again there is a natural presumption that the others have made modifications in order to reduce the danger of causing shock or misunderstanding.[3] Sometimes Mark is obscure, and the parallels, especially those of Matthew, look like attempts[4] to offer the reader something more edifying.

[1] In about the first third of Mark and Matthew there are striking variations in the order of much of their common material; from Mk vi. 1 onwards they are always closely in step. Nearly all of the material which Mark and Luke have in common occurs in the same order throughout; but Luke has a number of sections which are only roughly parallel with Mark, and these usually come in a totally different place.

[2] This generalization does not apply to an important group of passages, in which (according to Streeter) there is an overlap between Mark and Q; such passages will often be found in Luke in a different context from that of Matthew and Mark. But there are also a large number of exceptions in passages which occur in the same order in all three gospels; these are often referred to as 'minor agreements' (*sc.* between Matthew and Luke). Some may be coincidental; and others may be due to textual corruptions or assimilations. Even so, enough remain to cast doubt upon the simpler versions of the two-document hypothesis, and the title 'minor agreements' could be misleading. Cf. further p. 300, with n. 4, p. 301, with n. 5.

[3] E.g. Mk iv. 38, vi. 5-6, x. 17-18.

[4] E.g. Mk viii. 14-21 (Matt. xvi. 5-12), and especially Mk iv. 10-12 (Matt. xiii. 10-15). In the latter passages it is possible that the differences can be explained as the result of variant translations of an Aramaic particle. Alternatively it is often argued that Matthew is searching for a tolerable sense from Mark's seemingly intolerable version. For Mark's obscure 'all things are [done] in parables', Matthew has 'I speak in parables'. This I believe to be a misunderstanding of the true meaning.

(v) Mark has a greater wealth of circumstantial detail[1] than the others, especially Matthew. This is commonly accepted as a sign that he stands closer to the original tradition.

(vi) Matthew sometimes has extra material in passages parallel with Mark. Judgments may vary on the status of such passages, e.g. the famous *Tu es Petrus* passage, Peter's walking on the water, and a number of short paragraphs in the Passion Narrative. But the common judgment has been that, in relation to the oldest tradition, these are secondary additions by Matthew rather than omissions on the part of Mark.

Opposition to the two document hypothesis has revived and increased in the second half of this century. The first attack to receive wide attention was delivered by Bishop B. C. Butler in 1951. In his book *The Originality of St Matthew* he attacked both the Q-hypothesis and the priority of Mark. He argued in a detailed study in favour of the view, which goes back to St Augustine, that Mark was dependent on Matthew, and Luke on both of his predecessors. A further attack on Q was made by Dr A. M. Farrer 1955. Soon afterwards Professor W. R. Farmer, in his book *The Synoptic Problem* (1964), made a vigorous and often convincing attack on much of the logic of the Marcan advocates, and argued in favour of his hypothesis, largely based on that of Griesbach 1789–90, 1794, that Matthew was the oldest gospel, that Luke drew on Matthew, and that Mark was the latest of the three and drew on both of his predecessors. Others have followed along these rediscovered paths. It is perhaps fair to say that their conclusions have not won general acceptance, but their attacks on the old assurances have been effective in creating a sense of uncertainty. Most scholars have continued to work from the postulate of Marcan priority, and to find the results coherent and satisfactory, but think it necessary to enter a warning that the postulate stands under challenge. In this excursus that challenge will be taken up. First, however, we must mention an even more surprising challenge.

Neither Butler nor Farmer challenged the accepted view that

---

[1] Including Aramaic words. It is easy to believe that where Matthew's account is briefer, this is due to deliberate abbreviation; the reverse hypothesis—that Mark is expanding—is not at all plausible. Mark's extra words are seldom mere wordiness; they usually express what looks like an authentic part of the narrative. His stories normally develop naturally, whereas in the more compressed parallel versions we often encounter something illogical or abrupt (Cf. Sections II and IV of this Excursus).

there is a close literary relationship between the three Synoptic Gospels. Scholars in earlier times, as late indeed as Westcott, had appealed to *oral* tradition as a sufficient explanation of the similarities in content and language. But there is such a close similarity at many points, in arrangement and order as well as in wording, in narrative as well as in reported speech and dialogue, that the ascription of all this to anything but a literary relationship, direct or indirect, is very hard to credit. Not that all scholars believed that *every* similarity and overlap must be the result of direct copying of one gospel by another, or common use of the same written source. There is no difficulty in supposing that Jesus' sayings were variously remembered and reported, or that he himself repeated his teaching, often in similar form. Behind our canonical gospels there may well be a complex plurality of sources, both oral and written. If so, not every similarity need indicate direct literary connexion, nor must every divergency (within paragraphs largely similar) be explained as due to deliberate rewriting by a later evangelist.

Professor J. M. Rist (1978) has pushed these possibilities to the extreme, and has boldly argued that Matthew and Mark were written in complete independence of one another:[1] they draw on many parallel and overlapping traditions, and these traditions had in places assumed and retained a fairly solid shape and order. He rejects firmly and briefly the theories which would make Mark dependent on Matthew, and devotes the bulk of his space to an attack on the converse view that Matthew depends on Mark.

Rist examines many passages in some detail, and emphasizes the differences between Matthew and Mark as they occur, both in order and in wording. He urges that it is often difficult to provide adequate explanations if these divergences are due to deliberate alteration. His work has certainly strengthened the case for a plurality of sources and traditions. It remains to be seen how widely his arguments will carry conviction. He concedes that in many passages the verbal similarity is close, the variations are easy to account for, and therefore the theory that Matthew is here using Mark is perfectly possible; but he passes over them somewhat rapidly. It needs to be reasserted that these passages are striking and considerable, and in particular that the similarities are *not* confined to reported speech, but extend to the language (including verbal *minutiae*) and the structure of the narratives. The present

[1] This book does not contest the usual view that Luke knew and used Mark.

writer finds it impossible to accept 'oral traditions', or even 'oral tradition', as an adequate explanation for every one of these close literary similarities. Rist does not rule out 'written materials'. But if Matthew and Mark are independent, these must have included something firmer and more elaborate than he appears to envisage. Some details will be given later in support of this contention.

It is salutary, however, to be reminded, and reminded so forcefully, of the possibility of a plurality of sources. Scholars naturally would prefer[1] a simple solution to a more complicated one; but if the simple ones are unable to explain all the phenomena satisfactorily, then more complicated solutions cannot be ruled out.

The present excursus will concentrate on drawing attention to passages which point to the priority of Mark,—especially in relation to Matthew, since it is on that side that it has been strongly challenged. The relation to Luke will be looked at more briefly. If it is accepted that there must be direct dependence, this comparison should help to establish its direction. But since the belief in direct dependence is now challenged, I shall also point to indications, as they occur, that Matthew is familiar not only with the substance and wording of the Marcan version but also with its structure, and (at least occasionally) with its characteristic language. Some examples may prove no more than that Matthew is familiar with material which is more fully and logically presented by Mark; some require that he must be familiar with a narrative that has the structure of Mark's account, and a few suggest that it is with Mark's own idiosyncratic language that Matthew is wrestling. But before attempting this, I shall offer some comments on the standard arguments that I have already summarized and on the criteria employed in attempting to determine relative priority.

The standard arguments have been attacked along two main lines. First, it has been shown that the arguments from formal relationships are inconclusive. Argument (i), (the formal comparison of the contents of the gospels), proves nothing at all if it is presented as baldly as in my summary, or even if full statistics are supplied. Such statistics *fit* Marcan priority perfectly well; but they

---

[1] There is no logical reason for doing so. The principle that 'entities should not be multiplied *praeter necessitatem*' ('Ockham's razor') expresses a natural preference for economy, but leaves the door open. Rist has a charming reference to a parody of this principle, 'the law of the drunkard's search': if you have lost something in an otherwise dark lane, the best place to look is under the one lamp.

fit other hypotheses also. If, however, the argument is transferred from statistics to a comparison of the actual contents of the gospels, and especially to the absence from Mark of much important material, then an important argument[1] for Marcan priority is forthcoming.

Arguments (ii) and (iii) (from comparative order and wording) certainly demonstrate that in some sense Mark stands in the centre or provides a link between Matthew and Luke, and no doubt they serve to rule out a number of theories. But there are still several possibilities left open: Mark may be the common source of the other two, the hook from which both of them hang; or it may be the link in the middle;[2] or it may be a pendant hanging from the other two.[3] Earlier scholars were undoubtedly guilty of a logical fallacy insofar as they supposed that the formal relationships sufficed to prove Marcan priority. But it should be noticed that some of their modern opponents are in danger of a similar fallacy, if they fall into the trap of supposing that by demonstrating a flaw in the logic of Marcan priorists they have *ipso facto* disproved Marcan priority.[4]

The well-known formal arguments, therefore, do not give us logical proof. If they are to have any validity in the current debate, the texts must be compared in detail and their content assessed before any claim can be made. But when this is done, the arguments cease to be formal or 'objective', and, like the remaining arguments, involve judgments about probabilities. To avoid misunderstanding I should add that arguments from order remain important; but they have to be *argued*, and not just asserted.

The second line of attack is, in fact, on judgments about relative priority. Such judgments are described as 'subjective',[5] or are

[1] Mark has no infancy narrative, and no account of any post-resurrection appearance. He gives very little of the detailed ethical teaching which Matthew supplies in abundance. Most strikingly, he has no parallel to Matthew's Sermon on the Mount. If he wrote with knowledge of Matthew, these omissions are extremely hard to explain; attempts to explain them are usually more ingenious than convincing. The omissions are less surprising (*pace* Butler) if Mark was the first to compose a full-scale gospel, and did not find reason to include these elements, even though in substance they were in the tradition.

[2] As for Butler, in the succession of Augustine.

[3] As for Farmer, following Griesbach and others.

[4] Cf. Rist's reference to a 'syndrome' on p. 1. His remark has some wit, but poor logic.

[5] In the end, the scholar must not be deterred by this pejorative description; he *has* to exercise his judgment.

dismissed as resting upon uncertain criteria. Mark's roughness of style and expression may be a fact about *him*, rather than a sign that his material is primitive; even his vividness and wealth of detail may reflect his liveliness as a story-teller and not the direct testimony of an eye-witness. Further, if Matthew (or Luke) seems to have a characteristic viewpoint or interest which is absent from Mark, it is dangerous to assume that Mark's apparently neutral version really is so, or that neutrality would guarantee priority. Besides, there are at least a few passages where, if a phrase is to be given the label 'secondary', it is Mark's phrase[1] which deserves it, rather than a parallel phrase in Matthew or Luke. There are passages, especially in Matthew, which invite the judgment that they are 'secondary' because they reflect a more 'advanced' christology or ecclesiology. But against this it is argued that such judgments are precarious, and any chronological inference is unwarranted; the evidence of the Pauline epistles proves the secure establishment of theologically 'advanced' views well before the earliest suggested date for the gospels; and in any case a later writing may seem theologically more primitive than an older one. In the midst of uncertainty about both the chronological development of theology and also the dates and order of the gospels, we have ample room for circular argument.[2]

The criteria usually applied are various.[3] If they are classified in the hope of achieving greater objectivity, it is found that some of them seem to cancel out. As we have seen, Mark's wealth of circumstantial detail is a *prima facie* indication of priority. But on

[1] E.g. vii. 27 ('Let the children be fed first'); ix. 41 ('because you belong to [the] Christ').

[2] Advocates of Marcan priority are sometimes accused of prejudice against miracles and anything more than the most rudimentary christology. It would be easy to make counter-accusations of bias against the other side. But in any case it is surely clear that Mark, no less than the others, is a firm witness to the miracles of Jesus and to a definite christology. What I believe we find in 'later' gospels is a tendency to be more explicit or emphatic, and to avoid misunderstandings. Such a development seems to me to be a likely one, whereas the reverse would be unlikely. It is true that the Pauline epistles show that the essentials of christology were held and proclaimed well before our gospels were written. But that does not necessarily imply that the traditions about Jesus——implicitly christological, I believe—already carried the christology as explicitly as we find it in e.g. the Fourth Gospel.

[3] For fuller discussion, see Burton 1904, Farmer 1964, Ch. VI, Palmer 1968, 121–6.

the other hand it is often held that later tradition likes to *amplify*.[1] Again, it is usually supposed that the 'harder' version of a saying is likely to be prior to a version which could well be a simplification. But on the other hand there are passages that contain contradictions or awkwardnesses, which can most easily be explained as the result of an editor's carelessness. Again, knowledge of Jewish customs and the inclusion of Semitic words and constructions can be evaluated in various ways.[2] With such a wide choice of criteria available, some of them contradictory, the critic is open to the charge of selecting the criterion that will yield the result he wants. But it would be wrong, in my opinion, to set up a few criteria that are unikely to conflict, and apply them blindly; it is part of the function of *judgment* to decide in each case which of the criteria are applicable.[3]

The critic's task is all the harder because we do not know the precise aims and methods of each evangelist. If we did, we should be better placed to say whether Matthew has probably done *this* or Mark has done *that*. My own argument in what follows makes Matthew capable of a measure of pedantry, and also of errors and illogicalities in some of his sequences.[4] Likewise with Luke: for one

[1] Marcan priorists would assign the naming of disciples by Luke or Matthew to this tendency; cf. e.g. Lk. xxii. 8. For an attempt to identify the most likely trends in the course of transmission, see E. P. Sanders 1969. Form-criticism has often worked from the postulate that a story is more likely to be primitive if it conforms with the skeleton ideal pattern than if it contains 'later' amplifications.

[2] Prof. J. W. Bowker (1973, 38–42 and especially 51) has an interesting reconstruction of the history of 'Pharisees' and their relationship, as a group, to that of 'Scribes'. The position in the period covered by the gospels was, he claims, a transitional one, and it is accurately reflected in Mark, but in Matthew and Luke is often blurred. He argues that Mark's accuracy is a reflexion of the actual circumstances, and not the result of conscious historical study. If he is right, there is an important argument here for Marcan priority.

[3] On a recent occasion, when challenged to state my criteria for assessing priority, I could only make the feeble-sounding reply 'We must use our judgment in every case'. But I stand by it. We must, of course, try out all the possible criteria, and must not prefer one *just because* it yields the result we want.

[4] Rist agrees that Matthew has 'botched' the narrative sequence at a number of points, and argues that he would scarcely have done so if his source had been free from such blemishes. My argument will be that he has done so through using his source without primary regard for dramatic

scholar, he will be a subtle and original thinker; for another, a careless editor.

II

I turn now to an examination of some key passages, and to the line of argument which in my judgment puts the substantial priority of Mark beyond doubt. My contention is that in these passages there is an inherent flaw in Matthew's version which can only, or best, be explained by the hypothesis that he is following a source somewhat quickly, and that source is either Mark or an identical equivalent. In each case there is some word or phrase which in Mark is perfectly natural, but which is awkward or alien in Matthew's context. In short, he betrays knowledge of what we have in Mark.

Example A, the death of the Baptist (Matt. xiv. 3-12; Mk vi. 17-29). Mark's account is fuller throughout, and in particular he explains Herod's attitude to John carefully: he respected him, but was perplexed; and the determination to kill him lay with Herodias. The story then follows coherently, and shows how she got her way in spite of the king's reluctance. Matthew's introduction is briefer: Herod wanted to kill John, but was deterred by fear of the populace. He then relates substantially the same story, but it hardly helps to explain why Herod was able to put aside his fear of the populace.

There are two features in Matthew's version which (I claim) undoubtedly betray knowledge of Mark. First, there are the tell-tale words (xiv. 9) 'and the King[1] was *sorry*'. These words are an integral part of Mark's story; in Matthew they are quite alien, and are a plain contradiction of his own introductory statement that Herod *wanted* to kill John. The judgment must be that Matthew has oversimplified his introduction, and now betrays knowledge of the more complicated account of the position that we have in Mark, and of Mark's words at this point.[2] What Mark

and historical sequence. This is understandable if his main concern was to give the *gospel* faithfully and fully, rather than the full factual details.

[1] At xiv. 1 Matthew has more correctly called Herod 'the tetrarch'. Here he lapses into using the less accurate title 'King'. This may be, but need not be, due to the influence of Mark.

[2] Attempts are made to evade this inference, but all that I have seen strike me as special pleading: e.g. Matthew means that Herod was 'upset' at being forced into acting in a hurry.

gives us is surely the 'authentic'[1] version of this story as a unit.

The second tell-tale feature is that in both Mark and Matthew this story is introduced as a 'retrospect' or 'flashback' to explain Herod's remark that Jesus was John risen from the dead; after telling it, Mark correctly resumes his main narrative with a jump, but Matthew builds a smooth transition: John's disciples inform Jesus; 'and when Jesus heard [it] ...' etc. (xiv. 12-13). In doing so, Matthew has made another blunder: he has overlooked the fact that the story began as a 'flashback'. He has, as it were, buttoned his jacket to his waistcoat.[2]

There is a further point to notice: Matthew jumps lightly into the flashback from the brief statement that John has been raised from the dead, whereas Mark's fuller statement, 'this is John whom I *beheaded*, raised from the dead', provides the jumping-off ground for the account of how Herod came to behead him. Matthew's abbreviation presupposes Mark's logic, but obscures it.

Example B, the rich man and Jesus (Matt. xix. 16-17; Mk x. 17-18).

In Mark the man asks, 'Good Teacher, what must I do to inherit eternal life?', and Jesus replies, 'Why do you call me good? No one is good but God alone.' In Matthew he asks, 'Teacher, what good *deed* must I do ...?', and Jesus replies, 'Why do you ask me about what is good?' Up to this point Matthew's version is at least internally consistent;[3] what is at issue is goodness of *deeds* (neuter).

---

[1] By 'authentic' I do not mean that it must be historically accurate. Josephus' version may be more historical, and Matthew's introduction likewise. But at the critical point Matthew betrays knowledge of Mark's version and falls into a contradiction.

[2] In an unpublished paper that I have been allowed to see this argument is contested. The author suggests that in xiv. 13, where Matthew resumes his narrative, he means 'When Jesus heard [what Herod said]' *sc.* in xiv. 2. With all respect, I affirm that ἀκούσας can only refer to what Jesus was told in the immediately preceding words.

The author also attacks Mark for resuming after a digression with καί, whereas Matthew, with better style, uses δέ. But no-one who is familiar with Mark will be surprised; cf. Mark's use of καί in v. 9 and v. 43, in each case after a digression (admittedly brief) introduced by γάρ. Many such examples can be found of καί; few of δέ.

[3] It is distinctly feeble. Attention has often been drawn to this passage. It is usually held—and in my judgment correctly—that Matthew has modified Mark because he found it christologically disturbing. The fact that Luke (xviii. 18-19) did not find it so is (*pace* Farmer) of little force. Nor am I impressed by the appeal to second-century Fathers, or to scribal

But now comes a logical flaw, and Matthew is surely once again betraying his knowledge of Mark's version. For in Mark the issue raised by Jesus is the goodness of *persons*; and Matthew shows knowledge of this when he makes Jesus continue (xix. 17b) with the words 'One [masculine] there is who is good'. It would be claiming too much to call this a logical contradiction. But it is certainly a surprising transition which Matthew does nothing to make clear.[1] The only natural explanation is that he has retained a vestige of what we have in Mark.

Example C, the question about David's son (Matt. xxii. 41-45; Mk xii. 35-37a).

In Mark, and also in Matthew apart from his introduction, the question is whether the Christ can be David's *son*, when the Psalm shows that he is David's *lord*. But Matthew's introductory question, 'whose son is he?', obviously has in mind a different antithesis: Christ is not son of *David*, but of God. Again, there is a flaw in Matthew's logic. Here again also, as in Example B, Matthew shows an 'advanced' christological interest, although he doesn't develop it. But it is his awkward logic that I am concerned to stress.

Example D, the disciples' private question (Matt. xxiv. 3; Mk xiii. 3).

In the previous verses Jesus has been talking about the Temple to his disciples (Matthew) or to one of them (Mark). Then, on the Mount of Olives, he is questioned further in private by his disciples

copyists. For it is Matthew who more than once shows signs of scrupulosity and pedantry. The closest parallel to what I judge him to be doing here is Matt. ix. 3 (cf. Mk ii. 7). Other examples of pedantry are the two animals in the Triumphal Entry, and his explanatory comment that the five thousand men who were fed excluded women and children.

[1] Opponents of Marcan priority have tried to do so, with varying (and, in my judgment, incomplete) success. The author of the paper referred to *supra* argues that the good one ($\varepsilon\tilde{\iota}\varsigma$, masculine), is the law, being masculine in Greek. (For details, see Cope 1976, 114.) This seems to me quite impossible; the word does not occur in the context, nor indeed anywhere in the whole chapter. Rather more credible is the suggestion made by Rist: Jesus' quotation to the rich man should be understood as 'why do you ask *me* about what is good?', and as implying the question 'Since only God is good in the full sense, are you prepared to grant *me* the divine power to legislate?' I find this ingenious, but not convincing: the logic is still far from obvious in itself, and the wording of the Greek does nothing to help. There is no indication in the Greek that the pronoun 'me' is meant to be emphatic.

(Matthew), or by Peter, James, and John (Mark). The phrase 'in private' has an obvious force in Mark; in Matthew it has much less force[1]—Jesus is talking to exactly the same group as he was in the previous two verses. Once again it seems likely that Matthew has unthinkingly retained a phrase from Mark.

Example E, Pilate's offer to release a prisoner (Matt. xxvii. 15-18; Mk xv. 6-10).

Mark's sequence is comparatively clear and intelligible:[2] he mentions (a) the custom of releasing a prisoner on the people's request; (b) the existence of Barabbas and the circumstances of his arrest; (c) Pilate's offer to release 'the King of the Jews', meaning Jesus;[3] and (d) his awareness that Jesus had been handed over to him out of envy on the part of the Jewish leaders.[4] The logic seems to be that Pilate expected the release of Jesus to please the people, because he took it that Jesus was popular with them, and, perhaps for that very reason, was the object of their leaders' envy and hatred. Mark goes on to relate that the chief priests urged the 'crowd' to ask for the release of Barabbas instead.

But Matthew blurs the picture badly. At point (c) in the sequence he makes Pilate offer a choice between Jesus and Barabbas; nevertheless he continues with (d), 'he knew that it was out of envy that they had delivered him up'. It is very hard to find any clear logic[5] in Matthew's sequence. Once again, the inference is that Matthew has retained, without quite assimilating, some words that had a good logic in Mark.

---

[1] Jesus is now on the Mount of Olives, and no longer near the Temple, and in that sense the conversation is now 'private'. But the order of the words in the Greek attaches the 'privacy' to the questioners, not to the setting of the scene.

[2] 'Intelligible'; whether it is factual is a separate question. It is to be noticed that Mark does not make Pilate explicitly offer a choice between Jesus and Barabbas. (This element in Brandon's (1967) criticisms of the gospel accounts of the Passion applies to Matthew, not to Mark.)

[3] This is made clear by the next verse, and the similar title in xv. 12.

[4] Mk xv. 10. Most mss. read 'the chief priests had delivered him up'. B, with fair support, omits the subject of the verb. If, with *N.E.B.*, we take the latter reading as correct (*pace* most editors), we may have an instance of Mark's impersonal use of the plural, as in ii. 18. He cannot mean that the *populace* had been responsible for Jesus' arrest.

[5] Matthew, if taken literally, appears to ascribe the envy and the arrest of Jesus to the populace. If so, his logic is very obscure. The easiest explanation is that he has followed Mark without thinking. This applies equally whichever reading we adopt in Mk xv. 10.

Example F, the question about fasting (Matt. ix. 14; Mk ii. 18). Mark reads: 'John's disciples and the Pharisees were fasting; and they' (i.e. 'people', *R.S.V.*) 'came and said to him, "Why do John's disciples and the disciples of the Pharisees fast, but your disciples do not fast?"' Matthew has a more compact beginning: 'The disciples of John came to him, saying, "Why do we and the Pharisees fast, but your disciples do not fast?"' Marcan priorists will have no hesitation in asserting that Matthew has made a tidy but unjustified abbreviation of Mark, making some of the contrasted group into the speakers; and that he was misled into doing so because he failed to understand Mark's idiomatic use of the third person plural ('they . . . said') to denote certain unspecified persons.

No doubt more is necessary to prove a thesis than the citing of a few favourable pieces of evidence. There are, of course, many other parallels between Mark and Matthew which fit well with the thesis of Marcan priority. The selection that I have made, however, appears to me not just to invite or fit Marcan priority but actually to demand it.

Suppose first that Matthew is prior, and that the material or traditions that he employs are in part accessible to Mark also. Then *Matthew* could have imposed his own extra christological interest on (C), the Son of David pericope; he might perhaps have created his revised version of (B), the question about goodness, as far as xix. 17*a*; he might even have created his contradictory or conflated account of (A), the death of John the Baptist, to the extent of remembering just in time that in the 'rash oath' story the King was trapped against his will and 'was sorry'. But I do not see how, without a literary source which had the firm logical structure that we have in Mark, he could have half-created and then 'botched' the flashback structure of (A), or the sequence in (E) (Pilate's offer to release a prisoner); and it seems highly unlikely that he would have 'retained' the phrase 'one alone is good' in (B), or hit on the phrase 'privately' in (D), or produced the awkward introduction to the question about fasting, (F). Conversely what about Mark? With Matthew before him, and also some independent knowledge of the traditions, which may have been derived from Peter, he might indeed have corrected the matters of substance in (A), (B), and (C). But could he have reconstructed the logical structure of (A), or sequence of (E)? Would he, by accident or design, have given a logical force to the phrase 'privately' in (D)? Or is it likely that he would have been able to create a sequence so logical and so characteristic at (F)? In my judgment, while all these arguments are strong, passages (A) and (E) are decisive.

Suppose next that Matthew is prior to Mark, but that Matthew has access to a *literary* source, or an oral tradition in Greek so firmly structured as to be equivalent to a literary source, and that this source is also accessible to Mark. This hypothesis meets most of the points raised in the key passages. But unless this postulated source is virtually a proto-Mark and even has Mark's stylistic traits—in which case the hypothesis that Mark knows Matthew becomes otiose—it fails to account for (F), the passage where Matthew seems to have misunderstood Mark's actual phrase. The same considerations also suffice to rule out the hypothesis that Matthew and Mark are independent of one another, unless a proto-Mark source is also postulated.

III

Butler presents his case for the originality of Matthew very carefully, with detailed arguments to which it is not possible to do justice in a limited space. He concedes that Mark's wealth of detail comes from an authentic early tradition, and ascribes[1] it, in accordance with the second-century evidence of Papias, to Peter himself. The literary connexion with Matthew he explains by taking up a daring suggestion: that Peter himself had access to a copy of Matthew, and consulted it to refresh his memory while speaking to Mark. A less fantastic speculation would be that Mark drew on Matthew as his main literary source, and amplified it from his memory of what Peter had said. But no such suggestion will meet the arguments I have put forward unless it is conceded that Matthew himself was using, and sometimes misusing, a literary document which is at the vital points indistinguishable from our Mark.

Butler's chief lines of argument are as follows. (1) He effectively exposes as inconclusive the purely formal arguments for Marcan priority. (2) He attacks the Q-hypothesis as unnecessary, and claims that in nearly every passage the text postulated for Q must be almost exactly what in fact we have in Matthew. (3) If Q is abandoned, then a comparison of Mark with Matthew in those sections where Streeter argued that Mark and Q overlap compels

---

[1] But note that Mark writes with equal vividness whether Peter was present at the events or not.

us to admit that Mark betrays knowledge[1] of Matthew's text. The best example comes in John the Baptist's proclamation. Mark breaks off abruptly at a point where Matthew[2] continues coherently and smoothly. The judgment is almost inescapable that Mark has abbreviated the fuller version which we have in Matthew, and so must be acquainted with it. Rather less convincing are passages where Mark refers to Jesus' teaching, or to parables (in the plural), and goes on to give at most one example, whereas Matthew gives more. Certainly Mark here betrays knowledge of more than he relates, and certainly Matthew relates more of what he knows than Mark; but it is gratuitous to suppose that Mark's knowledge must be derived from Matthew. (4) Matthew's parallels to Mark often have a greater polish, in wording and structure. If Butler is right—but this will often be contested—they have a superior inner coherence, even where Matthew has extra matter. Even if it is conceded that Matthew's version is 'superior', it may be held that Butler defeats himself; the better his defence of Matthew, the harder it becomes to see[3] why Mark should have altered something 'smooth' into something less smooth.

It can now be seen that the Q-hypothesis, in whatever form, helps to counter some important objections to Marcan priority. But far less than a Q-hypothesis will suffice. The objections stem from the presence in Matthew of material which is fuller, and may be judged more 'original', than Mark's equivalent. All that is necessary in reply is to postulate the existence of a non-Marcan source or sources, used extensively by Matthew and less so by Mark. There is no *prima facie* improbability in such a hypothesis, even if 'Q' is dismissed. If, on the other hand, 'Q', in whatever form, is judged to be probable, then *ipso facto* the non-Marcan source that we postulate becomes probable also. The case for Q depends, of course, on a comparison of Matthew with Luke, and that is, in principle, a separate problem. What needs to be said at this point is that the priority of Mark does not either stand or fall with the validity of Q. But Q helps. For if it is valid, then the priority of Mark is sheltered from the force of one wind, to which it is otherwise exposed.

[1] This is the proto-type of the argument that I have developed in reverse. It was from Butler that I learned to see how strong such an argument is. The reader must judge which side in the debate uses it more effectively.

[2] Luke continues likewise, in words which are identical with Matthew's except for one or two stylistic variations.

[3] But see my reference to conflicting criteria *supra*, and my recognition of the need to judge every case on its merits.

The case for Q, and its main use, is that it offers the most satisfactory explanation of the major agreements between Matthew and Luke. These are to be found (i) in sections absent from Mark, and (ii) in sections which, though present in Mark, are given by Luke in substantially different words from Mark and (usually) put in a context of his own.[1] Besides these two groups there are (iii) numerous agreements between Matthew and Luke against Mark even in sections belonging to 'the triple tradition'.[2] These have been called 'the minor agreements', although they are of more than minor importance, and have always been a big stumbling-block for advocates of the two-document hypothesis. They do not directly call in question the priority of Mark; but they make it difficult, if not impossible, to be content with the two-document hypothesis in its simplest form. Not all of them are equally embarrassing: many are stylistic improvements[3] which it is not difficult to suppose two later writers might have hit on independently; and some can be set aside by an appeal to textual variants and the likelihood of assimilation by copyists. But too many remain to be ascribed to coincidence, especially if omissions and variations in word-order are taken into account as well as verbal identities.[4]

[1] The Beelzebub controversy (Lk. xi. 17-23), and the parable of the mustard seed (Lk. xiii. 18-19), are in a different position from that assigned by Matthew or Mark. Similarly Luke's mission charge to the Seventy (Lk. x. 1-16), which has words in common with Matthew's charge to the Twelve, is in a position of its own. It is true that the proclamation of the Baptist and the Temptation narrative occur in the same order in all three gospels; but the position of these was presumably more firmly determined.

[2] 'The triple tradition' denotes passages which are clearly similar in all three gospels.

[3] Where Mark has historic presents, Matthew and Luke (or one of them) often have aorists instead, or have the sentence in a different form. Frequently there are 'minor agreements' in such passages. Similarly with καί (of which Mark is fond) and δέ.

[4] One agreement that cannot be lightly dismissed is the disciples' reply to Jesus' command to feed the Five Thousand. In Mark they ask 'Do you mean we should go and buy food?' But in Matthew and Luke they reply 'We have only five loaves and two fishes'. (The Greek words for 'we have only' are different). In effect, both writers are forcing the story forward too fast, in contrast with the more natural development in Mark. That Matthew should do so is not at all surprising: cf. ix. 18, where the father immediately on arrival asks Jesus to restore his daughter to life, and xix. 19, where the inclusion of love of one's neighbour in Jesus' summary of the

EXCURSUS IV

To ascribe these minor agreements to 'Q' would be a desperate expedient.[1] Critics of the two-document hypothesis even challenge the propriety of invoking Q to account for the major agreements in group (ii). The group (ii) agreements are much more extensive than the ones in group (iii), but is this a legitimate reason for treating them separately? If it stood alone, perhaps[2] it would not be. But it is supported by the fact that a number of the sections are given by Luke in a different order from that of Matthew and Mark.[3]

Q, then, offers no safe support as a way of accounting for the minor agreements. Other possible explanations include not only 'pluralist' theories of lost narratives, but also theories of varying recensions of Mark, either an 'Ur-Markus' (i.e. an edition used by Matthew and Luke older than the one that has come down to us), or Deutero–Markus[4] (i.e. a later recension than ours). But the *obvious* alternative explanation of the minor agreements is to suppose that Luke was acquainted with Matthew (or *vice versa*); and once that possibility is conceded, must it not appear to be the most likely explanation for the major agreements also?[5]

commandments is premature, anticipating the later development of the argument. But that Luke should have exactly the same structural flaw in the Five Thousand demands an explanation. Luke (unlike Matthew) includes the suggestion of going to buy food, appending it by a slightly awkward join. I cannot deny that *for this verse* the easiest explanation is that Luke is conflating Mark and Matthew.

[1] The statement in the text must stand, if 'Q' denotes the source or sources for the *major* agreements. But there is no real objection to a pluralist hypothesis, by which there may have been many parallel traditions, even written or fixed accounts, underlying the gospel narratives.

[2] In groups (i) and (ii) Luke shares a little over 45% of his words with Matthew, in group (iii) a little over 36%. (The figures are averages for the whole; as between individual sections there is considerable variation.) The proportion of words which Luke shares with Matthew against Mark is over 25% in group (ii), but only just over 5% in group (iii). The difference is striking, and can hardly be dismissed. (These figures are taken from, or based on, figures given by de Solages 1959, pp. 1034, 7, 9–40.)

[3] See p. 300 n. 1 *supra*.

[4] The main virtue of a Deutero–Markus theory is that it can account when necessary for stylistic improvements by Matthew and Luke and for neutral changes which they share. But it does not account satisfactorily for some striking phrases in Mark which have a 'secondary' appearance, and which are absent from Matthew and Luke.

[5] The present writer has no new solution of the minor agreements to offer. It is possible that there is no single explanation for them all. Besides

Nevertheless—and this is the root of the case for Q—there are serious objections to the belief that Luke knew and made extensive use of Matthew (or *vice versa*). Until recently these objections were generally agreed to be decisive, and although this judgment is now widely challenged they still retain great force and cannot be lightly dismissed. The two leading arguments are: (a) First, Luke's ordering of the Q-material is inexplicable if he drew it from Matthew; unlike the Marcan material, which he gives in almost exactly the Marcan order (and indeed—though with a larger number of exceptions—in much the same order as Matthew), he gives the Q-material in an order that is not easily related to Matthew's. (b) Secondly, if his version of Q-passages is compared with Matthew's, and a judgment on 'priority' is made, it will sometimes be Matthew's version and sometimes Luke's that appears more 'original'. If so, this fact makes it difficult to believe that either of the two is the source of the other.[1] (c) A third objection may be added, of some force: Matthew and Luke diverge

those mentioned in the text there is the possibility of *partial* (and spasmodic) use of Matthew by Luke. But although the possibility of various explanations must be kept open—unless, of course, full and direct dependence of Luke on Matthew or vice versa is conceded—, the common line of explanation should not be lightly abandoned; for it remains true that a large number of the minor agreements can be seen as stylistic improvements, or reactions against certain features of Marcan style. Neirynck 1974 has collected and set out the data in a way that makes it possible to subject this point of view to examination. He has classified the phenomena under more than thirty headings, corresponding to features of Mark's style (καί for δέ, historic presents, etc.); in addition to listing the passages where there is a 'minor agreement' against Mark, he lists also those where only one of the others deviates from the Marcan usage, and also the 'exceptional' cases (not always infrequent) where it is Matthew (or Luke) and not Mark who has the 'Marcan' feature. The reader is thereby put in a position to hazard a judgment whether the proportion of agreements is too high to be ascribed to chance. For example, there are about fifty instances of καί in Mark where Matthew and Luke both have δέ; slightly more where Matthew has δέ and Luke either agrees with Mark's καί or has no equivalent; and much the same number of cases where it is Luke who has δέ and Matthew has either καί or no equivalent. There are also a few contrary examples, where it is Mark who has δέ.

[1] Luke gives the more historically 'probable' setting of the parable of the Lost Sheep (Lk. xv. 1-2; Matt. xviii. 14), and the more probable identification of those who will express surprise when they are disowned (Lk. xiii. 26 f.; Matt. vii. 22f.). Luke's obscure saying about cleaning the outside of cups etc. can hardly be derived from Matthew's straightforward

strikingly, indeed show no traces of mutual knowledge at all, in the Infancy narratives and in the post-resurrection appearances—two substantial narrative sections to which Mark has no parallel.[1]

The two main arguments, which had long seemed to settle the issue, have come under attack, not least from some scholars who accept Marcan priority.[2] (a) Luke's ordering of his material may seem erratic; but reasons can be suggested for the rearrangements that he has made. (b) His wording, though it may sometimes seem more 'original' than Matthew's, can often be explained as a recension reflecting his particular interests and outlook. Opinions will vary on the persuasiveness of such arguments. It should be noticed that, where the second argument is concerned, there could be an element of truth on both sides: it is not *a priori* impossible that Luke should sometimes be giving us an edited version of material drawn from Matthew, and at others be giving an independent (and possibly more 'original') version of something contained in Matthew.[3]

Nevertheless, the case for Q remains strong; there are key passages with phenomena that are hard to explain satisfactorily on the hypothesis that Luke is using Matthew,—with or without knowledge of Mark. The most cogent one is the Beelzebub controversy.[4] In this section there is little close identity of wording

version; nor is the reverse likely (Lk. xi. 39-41; Matt. xxiii. 25 f.). Most scholars 'prefer' Luke's text of the first beatitude.

[1] Farmer 1964, 221, argues differently. He claims that Matthew and Luke share the same ground-plan and structure. If they have enlarged Mark's gospel independently, is it not a surprising coincidence that both of them have enlarged it in the same way—by supplying these narratives at the beginning and end, as well as amplifying the teaching throughout? But in doing all this they may both be following the outline of the primitive Kerygma, which included a reference to Jesus' Davidic descent and post-resurrection appearances.

[2] Farrer 1955, and Goulder 1977–78, also *id.* 1974. In some of his examples he makes the strong point that features or words in Luke's version not only agree with Matthew but echo or reflect something in Matthew that is *distinctive* of him.

[3] Note that even *full* dependence of Luke on Matthew is compatible with the priority of Mark.

[4] Matt. xii. 25-37; Mk iii. 23-30; Lk. xi. 17-23. For a fuller analysis and discussion see Downing 1964–65; to the present writer his arguments are convincing. Similar points can be made in respect of other passages where it can be claimed that Mark and Q overlap: e.g. the parable of the mustard seed. It is in the Beelzebub controversy that the phenomena are most obvious.

common to all three synoptists, and even less that unites Luke and Mark against Matthew; but there are close parallels in some verses between Matthew and Luke and in other verses between Matthew and Mark. This is easily explained if Matthew is conflating what he found in Mark with what he found in Q,[1] and if Luke is following Q faithfully. But if Matthew is the source of one or both of the others, it is extremely difficult to create a plausible sequence of events. If Luke came last, knowing both Mark and Matthew, his procedure here must have been quite extraordinary: he must have carefully *subtracted* from Matthew almost all that was common to Matthew and Mark and retained *verbatim* much of what was left. Exactly the same argument can be used against Griesbach and his followers: if it was Mark who came last, knowing both of the others, he must have *subtracted* Luke from Matthew before using the remainder as his source. Such a procedure would not be difficult to carry out. But to produce a plausible explanation for doing anything so apparently crazy is very difficult indeed.

IV

It is now time to look more carefully at the case for Marcan priority over *Luke*. This has been less widely and vigorously challenged than Mark's priority over Matthew, largely because there are fewer divergences between Mark and Luke in respect of order,[2] and some kind of literary relationship is therefore beyond serious doubt. A few arguments and examples will be given in support of the view that this relationship is dependence by Luke on Mark. Some preliminary points, however, must be made first.

Luke's superior literary polish makes it natural to suppose that he follows Mark in time rather than *vice versa*. So too does his explicit acknowledgment that he is writing in succession to 'many' predecessors[3] (i. 1). Further, there are many passages where it is

[1] Or, of course, if Matthew knew both Mark and *Luke* and was conflating them. The hypothesis that Matthew knew Luke has certain attractions: besides accounting satisfactorily for the facts here mentioned, it avoids objection (a) *supra*. But it is vulnerable to objections (b) and (c). It has had a few advocates but not won wide support.

[2] Excluding, of course, the 'remote' parallels, where wording and content are significantly different; and excluding also the Passion narratives, which raise special problems.

[3] Farmer 1964, 221 f., argues for the suggestion that Luke is referring only to one gospel, *sc.* Matthew, and the 'many' of whom he speaks are those who have contributed to its creation. I do not find this the natural meaning of the Greek.

easy to believe that Luke's version is 'secondary', and indeed many where it is hard to believe otherwise. The most elaborate is the scene in the synagogue at Nazareth (iv. 16-30). Luke retains the themes that are prominent in Mk vi. 1-6.[1] But some of them are worked in rather artificially; and, in the *logion* 'a prophet has no honour in his own πατρίς', the ambiguity of πατρίς ('home-district' or 'home-country') is used as a pivot for Luke's transition to his big theme of the Gentile mission. How far Luke is conflating separate sources and how far he is re-working them is a notorious problem; but that his final version is 'secondary' can hardly be denied. The same is true of many smaller touches: e.g. his sensitive reference in xxii. 47 to Judas' kiss of betrayal, which he hints at rather than states, using an infinitive of purpose, and not making a plain statement in the indicative; his inclusion of 'scourging' in the third prediction of the Passion,[2] which is inconsistent with his omission of an actual scourging in the Passion narrative itself; his reference to 'tiles' in the roof through which the paralytic was let down to be healed by Jesus; and his paraphrase of 'The Power' (i.e. the Almighty) as 'the power of God' in xxii. 69.

Luke, then, is secondary. Most of these examples seem to presuppose a structured narrative, and Mark would satisfy the conditions well; Matthew less well. Up to this point, however, it must be conceded that an older or intermediate source could satisfy them too. Such a source could perhaps be in Hebrew.[3] There are, however, a few passages which lead on to a stronger confidence that Luke's source is *Mark*, rather than some related narrative.

Example A, Jairus' daughter (esp. Lk. viii. 51, cf. Mk v. 37, 40). In Mark, when Jesus follows Jairus to his house he does not allow anyone to accompany him except his three closest disciples; and after they have entered and found a scene of confusion, Jesus says the child is asleep, not dead. When 'they' laugh at him, he turns out 'all' of those present, and goes into where the girl is, taking

---

[1] Cf. also Matt. xiii. 53-8. But Matthew tones down the reference to the absence—or comparative absence—of miracles. Lk. iv. 23 echoes the more downright statement of Mark rather than the muted one in Matthew.

[2] Lk. xviii. 33; cf. Mk x. 34 and Matt. xx. 19. Mark has six of the seven verbs used by Luke, Matthew has three. 'Scourging' is in all of them.

[3] The ambiguity of πατρίς, a Greek word, is important, as we have seen. Would any Hebrew word explain equally well what Luke has done? For the likelihood of a principal source in Hebrew cf. *infra* pp. 312 ff.

with him only her father and mother and the three disciples. In Luke there is only one reference to a limitation of numbers: on reaching the house Jesus allows no-one to enter with him except the three disciples and the child's father and mother. It will be seen that Luke's account is marred by at least two infelicities and one palpable blunder. To suggest that Jesus 'allowed' the father to enter his own house is at least awkward. So too is the impression given that those who ridicule Jesus are this inner group. But the mention of the *mother* among those allowed to *enter the house* is a sheer blunder; she was, of course, at home all the time, not with the father on his mission to Jesus. Luke must surely be guilty of carelessness here; he has compressed Mark's two plausible limitations into one that is very implausible. It should be stressed that there is no limitation of numbers in Matthew. I find it almost impossible to believe that *Mark* could here have mended Luke's torn narrative. If Luke is following not Mark, but a common source, then Mark has reproduced it far more faithfully.

Example B, the scribes' commendation of Jesus (Lk. xx. 39; cf. Mk xii. 28, 32).

After Jesus' reply to the Sadducees' question about resurrection, Luke records a comment of approval ('well spoken, Master!'), ascribing it to 'some of the scribes'. He has not previously mentioned 'scribes' in this section, nor in the preceding one. When mentioned earlier (xx. 19), they were clearly hostile to Jesus, looking for a chance to arrest him. Perhaps Luke means their comment here to be one of wry admiration: Jesus has avoided every trap, and has not been caught out.

But the natural force of the words is genuine approval—and that is inconsistent with the last mention of the scribes. The easiest explanation is that Luke has incorporated a phrase from the section which in Mark follows immediately, to which Luke has no direct parallel: the story of *one* of the scribes, who had listened with approval to Jesus' reply to the Sadducees, and went on to approve warmly of what Jesus said about the 'first' commandment. Luke could easily have picked up the phrase out of Mk xii (either 28 or 32);[1] but it is awkward as it stands, and some such explanation seems necessary.

Example C, the injunction to secrecy (Lk. ix. 21; Mk viii. 30).

After Peter's confession of him as Messiah, Jesus (in Mark) 'strictly commanded' them to tell no-one about him. Mark's verb ($\epsilon\pi\iota\tau\iota\mu\hat{\alpha}\nu$) regularly means 'rebuke', and this is one of three

---

[1] Matthew's parallel has not got either of these.

passages where he uses it to mean '(strictly) command', along with a dependent clause giving the content of the command. It is a rare usage, apparently characteristic of Mark; Matthew has it in two of his parallels, Luke in just one of them.[1] In the present passage, both Matthew and Luke have different verbs to denote 'command'. But Luke surely betrays knowledge of Mark, since he adds Mark's verb as a participle: 'he *rebuked* them and charged them not to ...'

These three examples, taken together, suffice to make at least a good *prima facie* case for Luke's dependence on *Mark* rather than on a common source. The first, Jairus' daughter, shows that Luke is secondary to a narrative which has fuller details—just like Mark; the second, that Luke is secondary to a gospel with the sequence of paragraphs that we have in Mark; and the third, that Luke is secondary to a source which is fond of ἐπιτιμᾶν ἵνα ... —and Mark seems to be that. Perhaps the case I have made is not overwhelming; it seems to me less strong than the case for Mark's priority to Matthew. Certainly it falls a long way short of indicating that Mark is Luke's *only* source, even for the triple-tradition material. He may well have an alternative source or sources; and one of them might be known also to Mark. There is at least one passage which calls for this possibility to be taken seriously: Mk vi. 9, and Lk. ix. 3, part of Jesus' charge to the Twelve. Mark has been using indirect speech (ἵνα with the subjunctive), and Luke direct sppech (the imperative). But at the same point in their sequence both switch to an alternative construction[2]—an accusative and infinitive. Such a switch is idiomatic Greek, although both evangelists handle it awkwardly: Mark especially, since he gives only an accusative participle, and fails to complete the construction with the expected infinitive; whereas Luke interpolates an infinitive, before returning to this series of imperatives. Luke does not have any actual word in the accusative—the subject of the infinitive is left unexpressed. This

[1] All three gospels have it in the story of Bartimaeus: Matt. xx. 31; Mk x. 48; Lk. xviii. 39. Mark and Matthew both have it on another occasion: Matt. xii. 16; Mk iii. 12. Luke also combines the verb (as a participle) with a different main verb in a further passage: iv. 41 'and he rebuked them and did not permit them to speak ...'. But Mark's direct parallel to this (i. 34) has not got the verb at all; it does come in iii. 12—a similar account of healings.

[2] Not quite for the same injunctions. Mark uses the accusative participle for 'wear sandals', and then moves to direct speech for 'do not put on two coats'; Luke uses the infinitive 'and not to have two coats each'.

complex phenomenon is not explained satisfactorily by direct
dependence of either Luke on Mark or *vice versa*; but it becomes
intelligible if we postulate common use of a source which at this
point contained both an accusative participle and an infinitive.

Once again, the evidence is slight. But it is even slimmer for the
hypothesis that Mark might be directly dependent on Luke.[1]
Advocates of absolute Lukan priority (i.e. over both the others)
have not been numerous, but there have been some. R. L.
Lindsey[2] has published a translation of Mark into Hebrew, and in
a fascinating introduction has described the stages by which he
moved from the two-document hypothesis towards his later position. He holds that there were two major sources behind our
gospels: a primitive narrative in Hebrew, and Q. Luke draws on
both of them; Mark draws on the former of them and on Luke, and
possibly on Q; while Matthew draws on the two original sources
and on Mark. Lindsey underlines, and describes admirably, an
element of great importance in the synoptic phenomena: that in
respect of the so-called Q-material there is often an extremely high
degree of verbal correspondence between Matthew and Luke, but
only a low degree of correspondence of order; whereas in respect of
'triple-tradition' material there is a high degree of correspondence
of order, but a varying degree, often quite a low one, of verbal
similarity. Since this contrast is somehow connected with the
presence (or absence) of Mark, he calls it 'the Marcan cross-
factor'. An hypothesis, to be satisfactory, must give an adequate
explanation of this. The present writer has found his statement and
analysis most helpful, and has sympathy with a number of points
in his reconstruction.

Lindsey goes on to argue (i) that many of the verbal similarities
between Mark and Luke reflect independent translation of a
common Hebrew original, although some are to be ascribed to use
of Luke by Mark; (ii) that Mark has introduced Hellenisms in his
translation, and that these are wholly absent from Luke and in part
retained by Matthew; (iii) hence that Luke is prior to Mark, and
Mark to Matthew; (iv) that this is confirmed by the numerous

---

[1] A passage likely to be used by anyone wanting to maintain the priority
of Luke (over Matthew as well as Mark) is xxii. 64. Luke is the only
evangelist to tell us that Jesus was *both* (a) veiled or blindfolded *and* (b)
challenged to say who struck him; Matthew omits (a) and Mark omits (b).
But it is not immediately obvious that either of them is abbreviating Luke.
Cf. also note 1 on p. 312.

[2] In recent times there has also been W. Lockton, to whose work
Lindsey refers.

points of contact and similarity between Mark and *Acts*, which are absent from Luke; (v) that the close verbal similarities between Luke and Matthew reflect common use of Q;[1] and (vi) that the minor agreements of Luke and Matthew occur whenever their translation of the primitive narrative is more faithful than Mark's.

Lindsey's concrete examples, in my opinion, fall short of proving his case. Nor am I persuaded that independent translation from a common Hebrew source is an adequate explanation of the bulk of the verbal similarities. To this we must return in the concluding section of this excursus.

V

In recent years, since the publication of Farmer's book, the hypothesis associated particularly with the name of Griesbach has attracted wide interest and regained a certain amount of support. During much of the nineteenth century it was the dominant view, until it was gradually supplanted by the two-document hypothesis. According to the Griesbach–Farmer hypothesis Mark was the latest of the three synoptists, and drew on both Matthew and Luke. When they gave events in the same sequence, Mark did not disturb it; when they diverged from one another, his procedure was to follow the order of sometimes one, sometimes the other, usually staying with one of the two for a considerable time, though making some use of the other also. Only rarely did he desert both of them, and only rarely introduce material that was not in either. His language tends to be closer to that of the source whose order he is following when there has been a divergence.[2]

Anyone brought up at the feet of Streeter will be surprised to discover that the principal, and strongest, argument in favour of Griesbach is the argument from order. Mark's order, as we have already seen, almost always tallies with that of one, if not both, of

[1] I presume that he takes Q to be in Greek.

[2] Farmer (following e.g. Bleek) claims that this is a recognizable trend, but no more. If it is established that there is such a trend it must be noticed that it is no embarrassment to Marcan priorists: it could well be due to a tendency on the part of (e.g.) Matthew to depart further than usual from Mark's text when he abandons Mark's order. Marcan priorists would indeed be embarrassed if it were shown that (e.g.) the language of Mark and Luke were regularly closer in those passages where Matthew has a deviant order than in those passages where all three have the same sequence. I have examined de Solages' figures for passages in both classes, and cannot detect any trend in this 'embarrassing' direction.

the other two; and we have said that this fact is compatible with Marcan priority but does not of itself require it. Griesbachians contest even this moderate statement, and argue that if both Matthew and Luke were drawing on Mark, usually following his sequence, but sometimes changing the order and sometimes making omissions, then, since *ex hypothesi* they are acting independently, they ought, according to statistical probability, to coincide, at least occasionally, in making an alteration at the same time. But this happens so rarely as to cast serious doubt on this hypothesis. When one 'alters' or 'omits', the other so regularly 'supports' Mark as to defy any reasonable random expectation.[1] On the Griesbach hypothesis, however, the phenomena of *order* are easy to explain: Mark often reproduces the order of Matthew and Luke when they are in agreement, and follows the order of one of them when they are *not*.

The second argument in favour of Griesbach is that it can explain the 'minor agreements' of Matthew and Luke against Mark very simply: they are no more than words or phrases which for some reason Mark has chosen to omit, alter, or amplify, even though they were in both his main sources.

So far, the Griesbach case seems excellent. But no further. Even the argument from order turns sour on closer examination. Mark's procedure, on this hypothesis, seems incredible. There are many paragraphs in Matthew and Luke which in language are very close indeed—passages which in the two-document hypothesis are labelled 'Q'—but which come in different places; why did Mark omit them? The difference in order is an insufficient explanation, since

[1] Any reduction to statistics will be rough, since the identification of separate paragraphs may be arbitrary. On a count based on the table of contents in Huck-Lietzmann's synopsis from Mk i. 16 to vi. 44, the figures are as follows: out of 32 paragraphs in Mark, Matthew has 21 in the Marcan order, omits 4, and has 7 in a different order; Luke omits 1, moves 1, and has remote parallels to 3 or 4—and *all* of these belong to Matthew's 21 paragraphs which are in Marcan order, and none to his 7 (or 11). If their procedure is random, I reckon that the chances against this result are about 10:1. *But* there is one paragraph in this section (the parable of the seed growing secretly) which *both* Matthew and Luke omit, as well as many individual sentences. Further, the assumption that Matthew and Luke are making alterations *at random* is unwarranted. If it is conceded that Matthew has altered the order of seven miracle stories in order to form a compact group—so that this is seen as *one* deliberate act, and not seven *random* ones—the statistics cease to be alarming to supporters of the two-document hypothesis.

he has included a number of passages which Matthew has in a different order, where the language of Matthew and Luke is less close. Most striking of all is his omission of much of the preaching of John the Baptist and the details of the temptations of Jesus, which *do* come in the same order. Not only is Mark's method of selection from Matthew and from Luke strange on the Griesbach hypothesis, so too is Luke's method of copying from Matthew.[1]

When we turn to a detailed examination of parallels, the attraction of the Griesbach hypothesis dwindles even further. It is possible to produce passages where Mark *might* have composed his version by conflation from Matthew and Luke, harder to find ones where this can be shown to be *probable*, and harder still to argue in any particular case that he *must* have done so. This argument can be stated even more strongly: in the Beelzebub controversy passage it is beyond belief that Mark did create his version by joint reference to Matthew and Luke; his method would have to have been subtraction, not conflation—cf. *supra* p. 304. In contrast we must set the examples we have examined earlier, which (I argued) indicate not merely that Matthew and Luke *might* have been following Mark but that they well-nigh *must* have been doing so.[2]

Finally, it is virtually impossible, on the Griesbach hypothesis, to explain why Mark was ever written at all. Ingenious attempts have been made, and no doubt more will be attempted.

The revival of support for the Griesbach hypothesis has focused attention on the importance of seeing which of the gospels at any point occupies the middle position. In general, it is Mark who does

[1] These objections are clearly and strongly expressed by J. C. O'Neill 1974–75. They are also made by Lindsey and characterized by him as neglect of 'the Marcan cross-factor'. 'Even if we grant that Luke has decided for some unexplained reason to treat part of his material from Matthew as worthy of careful word-copying yet almost never to be put where Matthew puts it and to treat another great part of Matthew as if the order is usually good but the wording mainly unacceptable, we have to imagine Mark managing to record *only* those portions in Matthew and Luke which are verbally distant. By what streak of genius did Mark succeed in avoiding all those word-by-word parallels of the Double Tradition?' (pp. 23 f.). The point is valid, even if there is some exaggeration.

[2] In my examination of parallels between Mark and Luke my concern was to find passages which *compelled* the conclusion that Luke was using Mark. Many of the parallels, I admitted, might be explained by common use of a lost source. But there are hardly any which point naturally to Marcan dependence on Luke.

so—especially in respect of the sequence of paragraphs, but also to a large extent in respect of wording. We have already seen that no automatic conclusion can be drawn from these facts: he may be the common source, he may be chronologically the middle link, or he may be the latest in time, drawing on both of his predecessors. But it is not always Mark who stands in the middle. We have seen that in certain passages, of which the Beelzebub controversy is the most striking, it is Matthew who does so. The hypotheses which would make him the common source here are very difficult to credit; the only hypothesis which makes the procedure of all the evangelists seem sensible is that Matthew is here conflating two versions.

Brief passages can also be found where it is Luke who apparently occupies the middle position; one or two examples have been noticed already. In Lk. ix. 13 the disciples, as in Matthew, interpret Jesus' command to feed the multitude as meaning that they should do so out of their available resources; but they then go on to ask, as in Mark, whether he means that they should go and buy food. This certainly looks like conflation. On the other hand, in xxii. 64, Luke is the only evangelist who mentions *both* the veiling (or blindfolding) of Jesus *and* the challenge to name the man who has struck him; and this looks as though Luke had a fuller understanding of the event, and therefore access to a better source, than either of the others.[1] A simple solution remains elusive, and formal arguments are once again seen to be inconclusive. Judgment has to be exercised in each case, and also in deciding which of the sometimes conflicting judgments are to carry the most weight.

VI

We must now look in more detail at the possibility of a common Hebrew source for the synoptics. Dr J. C. O'Neill (1974–75), though reaching some conclusions very different from Lindsey's, starts from the same basic phenomenon—what Lindsey calls 'the Marcan cross-factor'. First, he stresses the contrast between the almost identical wording which we sometimes encounter in 'Q' passages, and the noticeably lower degree of similarity in the triple tradition. A close literary relationship is implied by the former; for the latter he argues that independent translation from a source in Hebrew (or Aramaic) is a preferable explanation. In any case, the phenomena are so different as to require different explanations.

---

[1] But the challenge put to Jesus to name the striker may be secondary. Mark's simple 'prophesy!' may carry the sense 'do something to vindicate your high claim to speak in God's name as a prophet', and if so this may well represent the original tradition. See Bowker 1973, 50, n. 2.

Secondly, he stresses a similar contrast in respect of order. For much of their narratives the Gospels are in the same sequence. This very fact makes the differences in respect of order that we find between Matthew and Mark down to Mk vi. 1 hard to explain: why should one of them, presumably Matthew, adopt *two* different policies in different parts of his Gospel? O'Neill offers the suggestion that the original source contained only those paragraphs which follow in a common sequence in all three gospels; that a separate collection[1] was made containing the paragraphs that interrupt this sequence; and that the two collections were woven together—but independently, and with different results: in one case, resulting in the order that we have in Matthew, and in the other case in the order that is reproduced in both Mark and Luke.

That a Hebrew or Aramaic original lies behind many of the gospel-*sayings* is hardly to be denied.[2] There is also much to be said for a plurality of sources; indeed, we are forced to look in that direction if no simpler hypothesis proves satisfactory. Dr O'Neill's arguments and suggestions deserve a warm welcome.

But as they stand it is difficult to accept them.[3] His two main postulates are far from obvious. In respect of order, it is clear that some explanation is needed to account for Matthew's variations. But the one usually offered—that Matthew has concentrated many of the miracles into one continuous narrative section—is, to say the least, not absurd. It is seldom doubted that Matthew has played a big rôle in the composition of the great sermon, by collecting material and fitting it together; why, then, may he not have acted similarly in the arrangement of an important part of his narrative? If so, then nearly all the variations in order are accounted for.

In respect of wording, it is certainly surprising that the proportion of identical words varies so strikingly. But it is doubtful whether independent translation is a helpful explanation. In the first place, the differences are frequently a matter of *substance*, not

[1] Or 'collections' etc. My summary has oversimplified O'Neill's reconstruction, which allows for rather more stages.

[2] One needs only to think of Dalman 1902, Black 1967, and Jeremias 1971, among many others.

[3] His hypothesis consists of two separate parts. From the phenomena of wording he argues for a Hebrew original, and from the phenomena of order for successive and divergent stages in compilation. In order to link the two lines of argument and confirm his hypothesis, he points to a linguistic feature (Luke's rendering of the phrase 'one of [a class]'), and claims that there are different translation policies, which reflect the stages he postulates. His case, until strengthened, is flimsy.

just wording: compare, e.g., the accounts of the death of the Baptist discussed above. And if a writer can make changes of substance he can as easily make changes in wording. Many of Matthew's variations consist in the absence of some Marcan phrase;[1] if he is barred from omitting it as a redactor, why does it help to suppose he might have omitted it as a translator?

Secondly, the wording, though not identical, is often so close that independent translation seems wildly improbable; the coincidences would be far too numerous. O'Neill appeals to the fact that we seldom find an *identical* sequence in all *three* Gospels of more than eight words; but we do find some *almost* identical sequences, between *two* evangelists, of many more words than that.[2]

Finally, there are some verbal identities or parallels where the Greek phrase or construction is so striking that it can hardly be the result of coincidental translation from Hebrew. It is worthwhile to look at a few examples in detail.

Example A, Mk i. 24; Lk. iv. 34. Mark and Luke have many identical words here in sequence; of special significance are the words 'I know thee who thou art'. The construction is idiomatic Greek, whereas a direct Hebrew equivalent looks artificial.[3]

Example B, Mk viii. 2; Matt. xv. 32*b*. The degree of verbal identity is high here also. But the selected verse has two remarkable phrases. First, 'Already three days they have been with me'. 'Three days' is in the nominative, a construction very hard to justify in Greek.[4] It does indeed stand reasonably close to an idiomatic Hebrew construction if only the word 'and' is inserted, but it would be a startling coincidence if two independent translators both omitted the connecting 'and', and were content to

---

[1] Small, but substantial, 'omissions' are common in Matthew, and can be found in both of O'Neill's postulated main collections: cf. Mk x. 38b and 39b, 49b, and 50; also Mk ii. 20.

[2] E.g. Mk i. 23f.; Lk. iv. 33f.: Mark has 31 words, Luke has 30; 25 are identical. Mk viii. 34f.; Matt. xvi. 24f.: Mark and Matthew have a common sequence of 35 identical words. Of course, there are always variant readings in the mss.

[3] Hebrew often brings forward the subject of a 'that'-clause and makes it the direct object of the governing verb. But I have failed to discover a parallel instance in the case of an indirect *question*.

[4] Some parallels have been found in papyri. It is possible to take προσμένουσιν and ἔχουσιν as dative plurals of participles, and I can just bring myself to believe that *Matthew* may have taken them so. I do not believe that Mark did.

produce such ungrammatical Greek. Secondly, the phrase 'and have nothing to eat' is characteristically Greek (lit. 'have not what they may eat'), with no obvious Hebrew equivalent to account for it.[1]

Example C, Mk viii. 28; Lk. ix. 19. (Cf. Matt. xvi. 14.) Greek has two ways of expressing an indirect statement: by the accusative and infinitive, or by a 'that-clause' with a finite verb. In this passage, both constructions are used by Mark and Luke, in a condensed way. Mark may be literally translated: 'Whom do men say me to be?—They told him that (men say you to be) John the Baptist, and others (to be) Elijah, and others that (you are) one of the prophets'. That is to say, Mark uses the accusative and infinitive construction, without actually repeating the infinitive, as far as 'Elijah', putting the predicates, John and Elijah, into the accusative; then, for the last limb, he moves to the construction that uses a conjunction ('that'), and without expressing the verb, correctly puts the predicate ('one of . . .') into the nominative. Luke has exactly the same pattern as Mark: accusatives for John and Elijah, and a 'that-clause' at the end.[2] There could be nothing in a Hebrew original to prompt this change of construction at all. The fact that both Mark and Luke make exactly the same change at exactly the same point is a clear demonstration of literary relationship inside the *Greek* period of writing.

The verse is not quite as strong a proof of Greek literary contact between *Matthew* and Mark, but very nearly so. Matthew stays with the accusative construction to the end of the verse; but the fact that he uses it in the same condensed way as Mark, i.e. without repeating the infinitive, is itself a clear pointer.

Example D, Mk xv. 14; Matt. xxvii. 23; Lk. xxiii. 22. In Mark, Pilate has offered to release Jesus, and when the crowd ask for Barabbas instead, has asked what he should do to Jesus; their answer, 'Crucify him', clearly surprises him, and he asks, or rather exclaims, 'Why, what evil has he done?' The word 'why' exactly represents the Greek word 'for', which is used idiomatically as an elliptic way of expressing a variety of attitudes, e.g. assent, or dissent, or, as here, surprise.[3] Exactly the same words are spoken

---

[1] Hebrew has no straightforward verb corresponding to ἔχω.

[2] Luke supplies a new verb: 'that a prophet, one of the ancient ones, has risen up'.

[3] Sophocles *Antigone* ll. 730–770 contains many examples of this idiom; on my count, six of them express surprise.

at this point by Pilate according to Matthew and Luke.[1] Hebrew has no exact equivalent; the literary contact is undoubtedly inside the Greek tradition.

This example provides a suitable end for the present study. Not only does it point strongly to Greek literary contact, it reinforces confidence in the priority of Mark. The logical sequence in Mark is excellent: Pilate has made an attempt to avoid sentencing Jesus to death; the attempt has failed, and Pilate's surprise when the crowd call for Jesus' crucifixion is well expressed in his question. The logic is inferior in Matthew, and still worse in Luke. Matthew has made Pilate offer the crowd a choice between Jesus and Barabbas; he must therefore have been prepared to sentence either of them, whichever they rejected. In Luke we should note that Pilate has already heard the charges listed against Jesus; and also that he has already twice pronounced Jesus innocent. Luke now states that Pilate did so for the third time. But he uses Mark's phrase—which denotes surprise and perplexity, rather than assurance of Jesus' innocence—and reinforces it with his own 'I have not found him guilty of any capital offence'. Both Matthew and Luke betray (in my judgment) knowledge of Mark. The conclusion of this excursus must be that the possibility of a plurality of sources behind the synoptic gospels remains open; but that the dependence of Matthew and Luke on Mark, or on a source which is often indistinguishable from Mark, is proved beyond reasonable doubt.[2]

---

[1] Luke adds a subject ('this man') to the verb.

[2] Rist (1978, 95 f.) draws attention to what he regards as one of the strongest arguments for Marcan priority—the facts relating to the text of Old Testament citations and allusions, investigated in detail by R. H. Gundry (1975). The situation is complex: the formal citations in Mark, and in the synoptic parallels, are nearly always close to the text of the LXX; so too are a small number of the formal citations in Matthew. But the informal allusions, in all the Gospels, are a baffling mixture of approximations, now to the Hebrew, now to Aramaic Targums, and now to the LXX or other Greek renderings. The same is true of most of the formal citations peculiar to Matthew. Gundry's view is that Mark himself was thoroughly Hellenized, and conformed to the LXX all the Old Testament passages that he recognized; and that Matthew's agreement at these points reveals his partial dependence on Mark. But the Gospel-material in general, he holds, comes from men, or from someone, who could and did think freely in all three languages.

INDEX OF SUBJECTS

INDEX OF SUBJECTS

318

INDEX OF SUBJECTS

319

INDEX OF SUBJECTS

INDEX OF SUBJECTS

INDEX OF SUBJECTS

INDEX OF SUBJECTS

INDEX OF SUBJECTS

INDEX OF SUBJECTS

INDEX OF SUBJECTS

327

INDEX OF BIBLICAL AND OTHER
REFERENCES
OLD TESTAMENT

INDEX OF BIBLICAL AND OTHER REFERENCES

INDEX OF BIBLICAL AND OTHER REFERENCES

INDEX OF BIBLICAL AND OTHER REFERENCES

INDEX OF BIBLICAL AND OTHER REFERENCES

INDEX OF BIBLICAL AND OTHER REFERENCES

INDEX OF BIBLICAL AND OTHER REFERENCES

INDEX OF BIBLICAL AND OTHER REFERENCES

INDEX OF BIBLICAL AND OTHER REFERENCES

354

INDEX OF MODERN AUTHORS
AND
DETAILS OF PUBLICATIONS
MENTIONED IN NOTES

N.B.: This is NOT a select (still less a complete) list of recommended works. It is purely to supply details of publications mentioned in the book mainly by author's name and date alone. By adding the few modern names not associated with publications in the book, it is possible to combine this with the index of names.
Where there is an English translation, the date of the original is not given.
So far as possible, only the latest edition of a work is listed.
Sub-titles are not, in most cases, given.

INDEX OF MODERN AUTHORS

INDEX OF MODERN AUTHORS

INDEX OF MODERN AUTHORS

INDEX OF MODERN AUTHORS

INDEX OF MODERN AUTHORS

INDEX OF MODERN AUTHORS

INDEX OF MODERN AUTHORS

INDEX OF MODERN AUTHORS

INDEX OF MODERN AUTHORS

INDEX OF MODERN AUTHORS

INDEX OF MODERN AUTHORS

INDEX OF MODERN AUTHORS

INDEX OF MODERN AUTHORS

INDEX OF MODERN AUTHORS

INDEX OF MODERN AUTHORS

INDEX OF MODERN AUTHORS

INDEX OF MODERN AUTHORS

INDEX OF MODERN AUTHORS

INDEX OF MODERN AUTHORS

INDEX OF MODERN AUTHORS

Nägeli, T. 1905, *Der Wortschatz des Apostels Paulus* (Göttingen: V. und R.) . . . . 212 n. 1

Nairne, A. 1922, *The Epistle to the Hebrews* (Cambridge: U.P.) . . . . 39 n. 3

Nauck, W. 1950, 'Die Herkunft des Verfassers der Pastoralbriefe' (unpublished dissertation, Göttingen) . . . 283

Neill, S. C. 1976, *Jesus through Many Eyes: Introduction to the Theology of the New Testament* (London: Lutterworth) . 131 n. 1

Neirynck, F. 1974, *The Minor Agreements of Matthew and Luke against Mark* (Leuven: U.P.) . . . . 301 n. 5 (on p. 302)
 1978, 'The Symbol Q (= Quelle)', *Analecta Lovaniensia Biblica et Orientalia*, Ser. V, Fasc. 31 (Leuven: Universiteitsbibliotheek), 119 ff. . . . . 105 n. 2

Nepper-Christensen, P. 1958, *Das Matthäusevangelium: ein judenchristliches Evangelium?* (Aarhus: Universitetsforlaget) . . . . 93 n. 2, n. 3, 126 n. 1, 243 n. 3, 244 n. 1, 267 n 277 n. 1

Neusner, J. 1970, *A Life of R. Yohanan b. Zakkai* (Leiden: Brill, 2nd ed.) . . . . 173 n. 3

Nock, A. D. 1928, 'Notes on Ruler Cult, I–IV', *Journal of the Hellenic Society* 48, 21 ff. . . . . 166 n. 1
 1928, 'Religious Development from Vespasian to Trajan', *Theology* 16, 152 ff. . . . . 166 n. 1
 1955, Review of E. R. Goodenough's *Jewish Symbols . . .*, *Gnomon* 27, 558 ff. . . . . 21 n. 5
 1960, 'The Apocryphal Gospels', *J.T.S.*, n.s., 11, 63 ff. . 12 n. 1, 118 n. 2, 160 n.
 1964, 'Gnosticism', *H.T.R.* 57, 255 ff. . . . . ix n. 2, n. 4, 147 n. 4

O'Neill, J. C. 1970, *The Theology of Acts* (London: S.P.C.K., 2nd ed.) . . . . 7, 133 n. 1, 174 n. 2
 1974–5, 'The Synoptic Problem', *N.T.S.* 21, 273 ff. . . 5, 311 n. 1, 312, 313, 313 n. 1, 314, 314 n. 1

Orchard, B. and **R. W. Longstaff,** edd. 1978, *J. J. Griesbach: Synoptic and Text-Critical Studies 1776–1976* (Cambridge: U.P.) . . . . 5 n. 1

Osborn, E. F. 1973, *Justin Martyr* (Tübingen: Mohr) . . 167 n. 1, 254 n. 2, 257 r

Palgrave, F. T. 143

Palmer (of Tübingen) . . . . 41 n. 1

Pamer, H. 1968, *The Logic of Gospel Criticism* (London: Macmillan) . . . . 291 n. 3

Pardee, D. 1978–9, 'An Overview of Ancient Hebrew Epistolography', *J.B.L.* 97, 321 ff. . . . . 15 n. 2

Pauly-Wissowa 1894– , *Real-Encyclopädie der classischen Altertumswissenschaft* (Stuttgart: Metzler) . . . . 167 n. 1

Perrin, N. 1974, *The New Testament: an Introduction* (New York/ Chicago/San Francisco: Harcourt Brace Jovanovich) . 1 n. 1, 198 n. 1

Pesch, R. und **R. Schnackenburg,** Hrsgg. 1975, *Jesus und der Menschensohn* (für A. Vögtle) (Freiburg/Basel/Wien: Herder) . . . . 129 n. 2

Pickett, J. W. 1933, *Christian Mass Movements in India* (New York/Nashville: Abingdon) 179, 180

Piper, J. 1979, *Love your Enemies: Jesus' Love Command in the*

INDEX OF MODERN AUTHORS

INDEX OF MODERN AUTHORS

372

INDEX OF MODERN AUTHORS

INDEX OF MODERN AUTHORS

INDEX OF MODERN AUTHORS

INDEX OF MODERN AUTHORS

INDEX OF MODERN AUTHORS

INDEX OF MODERN AUTHORS

INDEX OF MODERN AUTHORS

INDEX OF MODERN AUTHORS